with contemporary contexts, reflecting the profound influence of the great epics on his writing.

Amar's interests encompass philosophy, psychology, religion, and the concept of human existence in relation to space and time. He views science and religion as complementary, stating, "A non-scientific person cannot be truly religious, and a non-religious person will never know beyond the known sciences."

Currently residing in Noida with his wife Meeta and their two children, Ananya and Aaryaveer, Amar B. Singh continues to inspire readers with his insightful and thought-provoking works.

NEPAL – FROM WAR TO PEACE

Legacies of the Past and Hopes for the Future

NEPAL – FROM WAR TO PEACE
Legacies of the Past and Hopes for the Future

Bishnu Raj Upreti, PhD

ADROIT

Published by
ADROIT PUBLISHERS
4675/21, Ganpati Bhawan, Ansari Road,
Daryaganj, New Delhi-110 002
Phones : 011-23266030

Distributors
AKHIL BOOK DISTRIBUTORS
e-mail: akhilbooks@yahoo.com
akhilbooks@hotmail.com

ISBN 978-81-87392-88-0

Printed in India on behalf of M/s Adroit Publishers
by Arpit Printographers • E-mail: arpitprinto@yahoo.com

This book is dedicated to:
The Nepalese people, who are working hard to transform this country from war to peace, democracy and stability.

Contents

List of Tables 9

List of Maps, Figures and Boxes 11

Abbreviations and Acronyms 13

Acknowledgment 17

Chapter 1
An Overview of the Trajectory of Nepal from War to Peace 21

Chapter 2
Land Conflict, Power and Politics 100

Chapter 3
Armed Conflict, Displacement and Environmental Stresses 130

Chapter 4
Hydro-conflict and Politics in Nepal: Links Beyond the Border 151

Chapter 5
Public Legitimacy of Post-conflict Constitution Making in Nepal 175

Chapter 6
Armed Conflict and Tourism in Nepal : Some Reflections 191

Chapter 7
Reorienting the Development Sector in the Post-conflict Situation in Nepal 203

Chapter 8
Legacies and Consequences of the Armed Conflict in Nepal 234

Chapter 9
Women's Role in Nepal's Peace Process 318

Chapter 10
Security Systems Restructuring in Nepal 341

Chapter 11
War-to-peace Transition in Nepal 376

References 437

List of Tables

Table 1.1: World Bank Institute Governance Index for Nepal (1996-2006) 30
Table 1.2 : Causes of the armed conflict in Nepal 44
Table 2.1 : Provision of Land Ceiling made by Land Act 121
Table 2.2 : Ceiling proposed by Badal Commission 122
Table 2.3 : Distributions of Operational Land-holdings by Size, Classes and Territorial Zones (1961) 123
Table 2.4 : Land Distribution Situation in Nepal 125
Table 2.5 : Size and Area of Holdings 126
Table 5.1 : Constitutional Life and Public Legitimacy Continuum for Durable Peace 181
Table 6.1 : Tourist Arrival Trends During Armed Conflict in Nepal 195
Table 7.1 : Summary of Potential Sources of Social Tension and Violent Conflict 206
Table 7.2 : Examples of conflict indicators 215
Table 8.1 : Number of Incidences and Attack in the Natural Resources Sectors 236
Table 8.2 : An overview of attacks in the forestry related infrasturcutres in the districts by CPN (M) during the time of armed conflict 245
Table 8.3 : Damage of forest offices by district 245
Table 8.4 : Wildlife casualities 1996-2006 256
Table 8.5 : Park-related Physical InfraStructure Damaged during the Period of Armed Conflict 261
Table 8.6 : Damage caused in NTNC and ACAP areas 266

Table 8.7 : An Overview of focus of conflict assessment 295
Table 8.8 : Women and Children Killed by the State and CPN (M) during the Time of Armed Conflict 300
Table 8.9 : Number of People Killed by the State and the CPN (M) 301
Table 8.10 : Disappearance of People by the State and the CPN (M) 302
Table 8.11 : Number of Households and Food Sufficiency Situation 309
Table 8.12 : Damages of Physical Infrastructure during the Armed Conflict 312
Table 9.1 : Composition of the Negotiation Team and Facilitators in Nepal's Peace Process 329
Table 9.2 : Party-wise Gender Composition of Members of Constituent Assembly 334
Table 9.3 : FTTP Party-wise Candidates Constituent Assembly 336

List of Maps, Figures and Boxes

Tourist Map of Nepal showing major tourist destinations 192

Figure 9.1 : Women's Qualitative and Informed Participation in Possible Peace Structures 328

Figure 10.1 : Major components of security system restructuring 351

Box 8.1 : Main Features of Pro-Poor and Social Inclusion Strategy of LFP 252

Box 8.2 : Dysfunctional grass root sorganizations in ACAP 264

Box 8.3 : Erosion of Social Capital 305

Box 11.1 : Uniqueness of Nepal's Peace Process 383

Abbreviations and Acronyms

ACAP	Annapurna Conservation Area Project
ADB	Asian Development Bank
AI	Amnesty International
BBC	British Broadcasting Corporation
B-BNP	Makalu-Barun National Park
BNP	Bardiya National Park
BoG	Basic Operating Guidelines
BRCCCM	Berghof Research Centre for Constructive Conflict Management
BRM	Basic Risk Management
CA	Conflict Assessment
CAE	Constituent Assembly Election
CBO	Community-Based Organisations
CCOMPOSA	Coordination Committee for Maoist Parties and Organisations in South Asia
CDO	Chief District Officer
CF	Community Forestry
CFUG	Community Forest Users' Group
CIA	Conflict Impact Assessment
CITES	Convention on International Trade in Endengered Species of Wild Flora and Fauna
CNP	Chitwan National Park
CPA	Comprehensive Peace Agreement
CPN (M)	Communist Party of Nepal (Maoist)
CPR	Common Property Resources
CRA	Conflict Risk Assessment
CTEVT	Council of Technical Education and Vocational Training

DAP	District Administration Office
DDC	District Development Committee
DFID	Department for International Development of UK
DFO	District Forest Office
DHR	Dhorpatan Hunting Reserve
DNPWC	Department of National Parks and Wildlife Conservation
DNPWCA	Department of National Parks and Wildlife Conservation Act
DoF	Department of Forests
FECOFUN	Federation of Community Forest User Groups of Nepal
FMIS	Farmers' Managed Irrigation Systems
FNCCI	Federation of Nepalese Chamber of Commerce and Industries
FUG	Forest User Groups
GIS	Geographical Information System
GoN	Government of Nepal
GSI	Gender and Social Inclusion
HAN	Hotels Association of Nepal
HRW	Human Rights Watch
IC	Interim Constitution
ICC	International Criminal Court
ICG	International Crisis Group
ICIMOD	International Centre for Integrated Mountain Development
IDD	Inter-Agency International Displacement Division of UN
IDP	Internally Displaced Person
IED	Improvised Explosive Devices
IEDs	Improvised Explosive Devices
IGA	Income-Generating Activity
IIMI	International Irrigation Management Institute
ILP	Interim Legislative Parliament
IMC	Irrigation Management Centre
IMF	International Monetary Fund
INGO	International Non Governmental Organisation
INSEC	Informal Sector Service Centre
ISDP	Integrated Security and Development Programme
ISSP	Irrigation Sector Support Project

IUCN	International Union of Conservation of Nature
JTMM	Janatantrik Terai Mukti Morcha
JTMM	Janatantrik Terai Mukti Morcha
KCA	Kanchanjungha Conservation Area
KMC	Kathmandu Metropolitian Corporation
KMTBC	King Mahendra Trust for Nature Conservation.
KNP	Khaptad National Park
KTWR	Koshi Tappu Wildlife Reserve
LFP	Livelihoods and Forestry Programme
LNP	Langtang National Park
LPC	Local Peace Committee
LSI	Livelihoods and Social Inclusion
LTTE	Liberation Tiger of Terai Elem
MCA	Manaslu Conservation Area
MoFSC	Ministry of Forest and Soil Conservation
MoPR	Ministry of Peace and Reconstruction
NA	Nepal Army
NARMSAP	Natural Resources Management Sector Assistance Programme
NCP (D)	Nepali Congress Party (Democratic)
NCP	Nepali Congress Party
NEFEN	Nepal Federation of Indigenous Nationalities
NGO	Non-Governmental Organisations
NHRC	National Human Rights Commission
NPM	National Programme Manager
NRM	Natural Resource Management
NTFP	Non-Timber Forest Products
NTNC	National Trust for Nature Conservation
OCHA	Office for the Coordination of Humanaterian Affairs of UN
OCHA	Office for the Coordination of Humanitarian Affairs
OECD	Organisation for Economic Co-operation and Development
P&E	Poor and Excluded
PCIA	Peace and Conflict Impact Assessment
PCP	Participatory Conservation Programme
PLA	People's Liberation Army
PPSIS	Pro- poor and Social Inclusion Strategy
PR	Property Rights
PSC	Project Steering Committee

QIA	Quick Impact Activities
R& R	Reconciliation and Reintegration
R& SPR	Reconciliation and Social and Political Reintegration
RIM	Revolutionary Internationalist Movement
RM	Risk Management
RMO	Risk Management Office
RNA	Royal Nepal Army
SAARC	South Asian Association for Regional Cooperation
SAGA	Social and Geographical Audit
SDC	Swiss Agency for Development and Cooperation
SNP	Shivapuri National Park
SoE	State of Emergency
SPA	Seven-Party Alliance
SPNP	Shey-Phoksundo National Park
SWR	Suklaphata Wildlife Reserve
TAL	Terai Arc Landscape
TDACPO	Terrorist and Detructive Activities Control and Punishment Ordinance
ToR	Terms of Reference
TRC	Truth and Reconciliation Commission
UAIS	Upper Andherikhola Irrigation Project
UC	Unity Centre
UNDP	United Nations Development Programme
UNEP	United Nations Environmental Programme
UNHCR	United Nations High Commissioner for Refugees
UNICEF	United Nations Children Fund
UNIDIR	United Nations Institute for Disarmament Research
UNIFEM	United Nations Development Fund for Women
UNMIN	United Nations Mission in Nepal
UNPKF	United Nations Peace-Keeping Force
UPC	United People's Council
UPF	United People's Front
USAID	United States Agency for International Development
UXO	Un-Exploded Ordinance
VDC	Village Development Committee
WB	World Bank
WTO	World Trade Organisation
WWF	World Wildlife Fund
WWG	Wildlife Watch Group

Acknowledgment

I would like to extend my sincere gratitude to all the informants who have provided valuable information and openly shared their perspectives and opinions. This book would not have materialised without their support. I would also like to thank the politicians, journalists, and academics who gave me constructive comments and suggestions during the course of writing this book.

I am thankful to NCCR North-South, Political Divison-IV of Federal Department for Foreign Affiars of Swiss Government, Intercooperation, Ministry of Peace and Reconstruction, WWF Nepal, UNDP Nepal, Livelihoods and Forestry Programme, Care Nepal, Department for International Development of British Government, Asian Development Bank, Danish International Development Agency, World Food Programme for the responsibility they gave me to analyse Nepal's conflict and develop assessment documents and or background papers from which I have greatly benefited and developed a part of the contents of the book.

My special thanks to Dr Ghana Gurung, Dr. Sabita Thapa; Mr Ramu Subedi, Mr Vijaya Shrestha, Ms Bimala Poudel Rai, Mr Vinod Chapagain, Mr Peter Neil, Mr Nahakul K.C; Dr. Madhav Karki, Dr. Siddartha Bajryacharya, Mr. Narayan Belbase, Dr. Keshav Kanel, Dr. Krishna C. Poudel, Mr Khum Raj Punjali, Mr Tikaram Adhikari, Dr. Tirtha Bahadur Shrestha, Dr. Udaya Raj Sharma, Mr. Prakash Shrestha, Mr. Ukesh Raj Bhuju, Mr. Bashanta Raj Misra, Mr. Yuba Raj Regmi, Mr. Vijaya

Singh, Mr Shiva Raj Bhatta, Dr. Judy Oglethorpe, Mangal Man Shakya, Mr Janak Raj Joshi, Mr Shyam Sundar Sharma, Mr Sandesh Hamal, Mr Govenda Gyawali and Dr Krishna Pahari for their valuable inputs and suggestions. I would like to extend my warm thanks to Sulava Piya for her hard work in reading the manuscript and pointing out typological errors.

I extend my sincere gratitude to Professor Dr Ulrike Muller-Boeker of Zurich University/NCCR North South and Mr Markus Heiniger, Special Peace Building Advisor of Political Divison Four of Federal Department of Foreign Affairs of the Swiss Government for their encouragement, creating a flexible environment for writing the book. I would also like to thank Dr Bharat Pokahrel, Head of Intercooperation Nepal, Professor Kailash Nath Pyakuryal, Chair of the Consertiuom of Land Research and Policy Dialogue (COLARP), Dr Sagar Sharma, Head of Human and Natural Resources Studies Centre of Kathmandu University for their encouragement, comments and feedback in various stages of preparing this book. Special thanks to Sulava Piya for her painstrainking work in going through the manuscript. I would like to thank our PhD students Anita Bhattarai-Ghimire (conflict and displacement), Purna Bahadur Nepali (land, social exclusion and conflict) and Pranil Kumar Upadhaya (conflict, tourism and peace) and masters' students who have helped me during the time of preparing this book.

I would like to express my sincere thanks to all other persons whose names are not possible to mention but who were generous to give time for discussion and valuable information. I would like to thank them for their encouragement and suggestions, support, sharing and arranging the necessary documents, meetings and field visits.

I thank Mr D. K. Sharma of Akhil Distributors and Adroit Publishers for his instant willingness to publish my book.

I am indebted to my wife Ms Yamuna Ghale Upreti, Senior Programme Officer of Swiss Agency for Development and Cooperation Nepal Country Office for her intellectual inputs and other suppors. Cooperation of our children Asmita and Ayush during the writing of the book and their compromise for the time they deserve from their father is highly admired.

I take sole responsibility for any shortcomings and weaknesses of this book but I share the merits with all those who hailed me to bring out this book in this form. I request readers to give me constructive comments and suggestions.

Kathmandu **Bishnu Raj Upreti**

Chapter 1

An Overview of the Trajectory of Nepal from War to Peace

1.1 INTRODUCTION

Nepal is moving from war to peace[1] with enormous changes in the super structures of the country. The centuries-old feudal system of monarchy has peacefully ended, in which the then King Gyanendra played an important role. In fact, his behaviour and actions provided suitable conditions required to go for a broader republican form of political change. The country faced a decade-long armed insurgency, conflict, insecurity and instability and is moving towards peace, democracy and development. The hopes, aspirations and expectations of the Nepalese people are emerging from the political changes that occurred in this decade. People's empowerment is massively expanded and they are assertive enough to ask for their rights.

The main objective of this book is to reflect on what happened between the period 1996 and 2008 and to analyse why it happened as it did. As a researcher, teacher and practitioner of conflict transformation and peace building and actively engaged in Nepal's political change process, I have amply reflected my observations, perspectives and assessment in this book.

The contents and issues discussed in this book cover matters ranging from power, politics, land, biodiversity, natural resources, environment, displacement, reconciliation, rehabilitation, development, hydro-politics and conflict, national security policy and restructuring of security sector to role of women in peace process, causes and consequences of the conflict and ingredients of peace and democracy.

Nepal, previously recognised as a peaceful country, faced severe violent conflict for ten years, which took a toll of more than 13,300 lives, and billions of rupees worth of damage to properties and infrastructure. This not only created fear, mistrust, insecurity, civil strife and social, political and developmental instability but also created tremendous opportunities for fundamental political transformation in Nepal.

The Nepalese polity for several years became incapable and ineffective to deal with armed conflict that led to chaos and anarchy. The situation further became complicated after the royal takeover from October 4, 2002. Consequently, the bi-polar conflict turned into a tripartite conflict of the king, the parliamentary parties and the CPN (M).

Poverty and inequality, social and political exclusion, gender disparity, caste or ethnic-based discrimination, corruption and malgovernance provided fertile ground for the expansion of the conflict. The usual causes for the conflict have been much documented. However, not enough explanations have been made on the paradoxical aspect why the conflict triggered immediately after the restoration of a multiparty democracy. In many countries, even with existence of worse indicators in root causes of conflict, armed conflict of this scale has not been observed. Furthermore, given the established religious and cultural tolerance of the diverse Nepali society, it would not support violence, even as a last resort.

The Maoist insurgency has been interpreted from different perspectives. From the conflict perspective, it is a violent form of frustration of people. From the security perspective, it is a threat to society. From a political perspective, it is an ideologically-based political power struggle to control the state. From a sociological perspective, it is a violent form of social change and transformation evolved to dismantle the centuries-old poverty, discrimination and injustice. However, from all perspectives it is an opportunity to dismantle feudalism and socio-economic transformation and political conflict in Nepal.

1.2 FOUNDATIONS OF THE ARMED CONFLICT

First, I would argue that the Maoist insurgency was not the sole product of the failure of newly restored multiparty democracy[2] in 1990. It was the cumulative effect of more than 345 years of exploitation. The post-1990 governance failure gave space to escalate this conflict because of (a) its inability to fulfil people's expectations and malgovernance, and (b) the freedom it offered.

The 1990 Constitution of Nepal had opened windows of opportunities to entertain the rights of Nepalese citizens. From the 1990 popular movement, Nepalese people came from a closed hierarchical society to an open society. This 1990 movement also raised unrealistically high expectations of the people where the political parties in the early 1990s irrationally fuelled these expectations to win the popular vote. At the same time, the state failed to address their concerns and meet their expectations. A plausible explanation of the emergence of the Maoist conflict in particular time was the growing awareness and empowerment of the Nepalese people during the initial years of multiparty democracy. People become more aware about poverty, inequality, discrimination, corruption and lack of employment opportunities. They were empowered to raise their voices against injustice, poverty and social exclusion. Therefore, paradoxically the current crisis was not only the syndromes of system failure but also an indicator of social awareness and people's empowerment.

The multiparty democracy gave ample opportunities for different categories of people to organise, to form an organisation to fight for their rights that had tremendously helped to empower people. The NGO sector strongly emerged after 1990 and advocacy became one of the crucial components of many NGOs. Several identity-based organisations emerged to protect their rights or fight to secure the rights they deserve from the state. Likewise, several INGOs came to help Nepal and some of them were explicitly focusing on empowerment of the marginalised group of people.

Core issues in the Nepalese conflict remained both complex and controversial. It is well known that poverty is both the cause and consequence of conflict, but the precise determinations in each specific case are opaque. At the root of conflict lie complex factors: the imbalance of political, socio-economic and cultural opportunities among different identity groups; the lack of democratic legitimacy and effective governance; the absence of a vibrant civil society; and the absence of effective mechanisms for non-violent conflict management of group interests.

Often social tension and violent conflict build upon the complicated structural forms of political, social, economic, geographical discriminations and ideological ground. When the existing governing system of the state fails to address the socio-economic and political inequalities which are often protected or ignored by the state, potential for social tension and violet conflict is high.

While analysing the political source of violent conflict, it is necessary to understand how the political structures and processes are developed in the history of a country. The centralized, feudalistic, power-biased governing system and political control of the state by certain groups for a long time (privatisation of politics) provided fertile ground for social tension and violent conflict (Upreti, 2006a). For example, one of the main causes of social tension and armed conflict in Nepal for the past 10 years was Nepal's governing system (e.g. the people were kept at the level of subjects by the Rana oligarchic system and the continuity of the same governing practices in different forms even after subsequent political changes of 1951, 1962 and 1990).

Since conflicts transform political, economic and social realities, the factors that sustain conflicts are not necessarily those that originally caused them. Analysing the dynamics of conflict requires understanding multidimensional nature of causes resulting from unequal patterns of power distribution (socially determined power as well as state power). Major causes of the conflict have been discussed in the following sections:

1.2.1 Socio-Economic Foundations

Social exclusion, acute inequalities, absolute poverty, lack of access to resources and failure of political structures to address these issues made the Nepalese society extremely vulnerable to conflict and mass movements like the CPN (M)' 'people's war'. Deep-rooted social cleavages in terms of caste, ethnicity, gender and regional, cultural, linguistic and religious forms of discrimination provided fertile ground to escalate the conflict. The CPN (M) successfully capitalised the wide frustration of people towards poor performance of political structure and process, highly unsatisfactory democratic transition of the 1990 regarding the transformation of the state, politics and the society. Dominance of certain groups (e.g. Brahmin, Chhetri and Newar and lately emerged neo-elite group[3] from within the excluded groups) in all social, political and economic sectors promoted feeling of injustice and revenge among exploited people. They strongly believe that they have been excluded from opportunities and resources. The CPN (M) tactically utilised this feeling. The rebels organised people in their support not only on the social concerns but also on the ethnic and geographical identity (Sharma, 2003).

Centralisation and regional imbalance, skewed distribution of state resources and power, access and control of natural and other productive resources by elites and neo-elites, dominating influences of religiously and culturally biased traditional Hindu values and culture, discrimination against women, minorities, and dalits that fuelled feeling of injustice, frustration and contributed to escalate the armed conflict.

The performance of privatisation was extremely poor; market price of basic needs goods was sharply hiked, which means ineffective market regulation.

The state has failed to reduce poverty, control exploitation of the disadvantaged communities by those in power. It also became unsuccessful to generate employment opportunities to large mass of unemployed people. Semi-educated, left-out and unemployed frustrated youths become a source of the CPN (M)'s insurgency in Nepal (Upreti, 2004b). Corruption and irregularities increased and became an integral part of the political process (Thapa, 2002).

Centralism and social exclusion could be intentional and

unintentional. But intentional exclusion is more common and serious. Intentional social exclusion is a deliberate action of certain powerful elite[4] to fulfil their vested interests (to maintain prevailing economic and social structures upon which their existence is largely based) (Upreti, 2002b). They overtly or covertly develop or use filtering mechanisms, (such as higher fees for services, literacy and numeric skills requirement to access certain facilities, rigid regulations, etc.) that limit many people to access resources and services, and exercise power. Overt social exclusion includes inheritance of traditional exclusionary social practices[5], myth, belief systems (e.g. caste-based hierarchy, untouchability, restriction on marriage, religion and occupation, etc.). The structural basis of Hindu society is principally shaped by a notion of exclusion and goes beyond the general social division of society. It promotes centralised exclusionary practices in individuals' lives, their food habits, marriage, religious belief, education and day-to-day activities. It maintains rigid hierarchy. These blatantly exploitative social structures and practices are not eradicated by any political systems and still have tremendous influence in Nepalese society. Polygamy[6], discriminations against girls and women, untouchability, sexual harassment and exploitation, inhumane treatment to women by blaming them as witch-craft were contributing to emerge and expand conflict in Nepal.

The CPN (M) became successful in attracting women to their arm force. Almost 40 per cent of the guerrillas were women (Upreti, 2006a). They were actively leading platoons, companies and battalions. Many women participated in the insurgency because of feeling of injustice and discrimination. Majority of the women guerrillas were from poor, peasant, illiterate and janajati women. Sobha Gautam and her colleagues report that, *"poor peasant women, and women from the oppressed nationalities have been the most active in joining the 'people's war'. Nearly 70 percent women in the 'people's war' are from the Tibeto-Burman and Dalit communities, e.g., Magars, Tamangs, Kamis and Gurungs"* (Gautam et Al., 2003:102). Perhaps, majority of the women's participating in the insurgency was not because of ideology, but because of the pragmatic need of liberation from inequality and discrimination (Mackinlay and Upreti, 2003). Gender discrimination in Nepal could not fundamentally change even after the 1990s' political change. Traditionally and religiously sanctified exclusionary practices were dominant in cultural, social, economic and political spheres of society.

The ethnic dimension was very strong in the armed conflict. There are wider sources of differences between ethnic groups[7] and caste groups on language (Nepali v/s ethnic language), religious practices, legal and judicial system, recognition of indigenous arrangement, issues of representation, citizenship and entertaining state's privileges, etc. (Upreri, 2004a; Sharma, 2003). The Maoist insurgency brought the ethnic movement to a turning point as it awakened ethnic groups to seek their rights and articulate their demands. Though the ethnic movement had appeared earlier, it strongly emerged especially during the 1990s' popular movement. However, the 1990s' political change failed to properly address the aspirations of ethnic population. When CPN (M) started a people's war, this also divided the ethnic movement into two lines, i.e. pro-Maoist and non-Maoist lines (Sharma, 2003). Basically the Pro-Maoist ethnic movement focused on rights to self-determination whereas the non-Maoist ethnic movement focused on guaranteed autonomy with a federal system. However, this distinction gradually faded and more radicalisation strenghthened in the later stage. The focus shifted to radical ethnic identity. The ethnic federalism with right to self-determination cum anti-caste radicalism is an example.

If social and economic structures and their governing practices are promoting and providing protection to elite-biased, power-centred discriminatory social practices, potential for social tension and violent conflict is high. If we look the socio-economic source of the armed conflict in Nepal, social evils and perversions such as un-touchability, injustice, oppression, discriminations against race, religion, gender, caste, and the inability of the state to abolish such evils, rather directly or indirectly encouraging them were the main sources. When there is great disappointment and rebellious sentiment developed in the suppressed people, social tension is inevitable.

Rampant poverty and widespread unemployment provide fertile ground for social tension and violent conflict in any society. The experiences of violent conflict in Congo, Rwanda, Chechnya, Mindanao (the Philippines), Guatemala, Columbia, Mozambique, Angola and Nepal show that poverty, injustice, oppression and discrimination are fundamental contributing factors (Bhattarai, 2003; Aditya, et al., 2006; Gersony, 2003; Howel et al., 2005; Hutt, 2004; Karki and Seddon, 2003; Kumar, 2004; Misra, 2004; Thapa, and Sijapati, 2003).

In Nepal, social harmony and tolerance were abused by ruling elites to strengthen their power base. Freedom of expression, people's right to participate in the political process and social change, diversity in terms of language, culture, religion, race and ethnicity were selectively interpreted and abused for the benefit of ruling elites. The systematic denial and exclusion of Janajaties, Dalit, Madeshi people, women, disabled community and minorities by the state in ensuring rights and access to decision making was precisely the reason for social tension and violent conflict for the last 11 years.

1.2.2 Political foundations

The armed conflict was the cumulative outcome of the failure of the political systems, which goes back to the Rana regime and beyond. People were frustrated with these regimes and looking for a change. As a consequence, people widely supported the democratic movement of the 1990s and multiparty democracy was restored. General public had great expectations from this change. However, the post-1990 polity failed to govern the country based on the democratic ideals and the constitutional provisions detailed in the Constitution of Nepal 1990. That made the general public very frustrated and unhappy (Upreti, 2003b, Hogger, 2001). This frustration became a mighty ground for the CPN (M) to undertake armed rebellion. The explicit aim of CPN (M) was to control state power to implement their agenda. There were distinctly different political perceptions of CPN (M), the government and other political parties on the legitimate authority and representation. The CPN (M) were saying that they were seeking *agragami chhalang* (progressive political change), which required total restructuring of the state.

The United People's Front, a political wing of the CPN (Mashal) led by Babu Ram Bhattarai decided to participate in the parliamentary election of 12 May 1991 (Nickson, 2003). The UPF won 9 seats in the Parliament with 5 per cent of the total votes. Their aim was to expose monarchy and the parliamentary system. They raised several concerns. However, the then government did not respond properly and took a very autocratic approach towards UPF's concerns. On the 4th of February 1996, a frustrated UPF submitted a 40-point demands agenda to the Deuba government, which had set a deadline of two weeks and if the government would not respond then the UPF would wage a 'people's war'. Unfortunately, the Deuba government did not take the demand seriously. Consequently, the UPF started rebellion on 13th February 1996, 3 days before the given deadline, attacking police post at Holeri (Rolpa) and Thbiskot (Rukum). This time too, the government took it very lightly. The then home minister said, *"I am confident that we will be able to bring the present activities under control within four five days"* (Sharma, 2003: 371).

It was widely recognised that Nepali political parties failed to govern the country. They failed to reform governing system, they failed to reduce poverty reduction. Instead, power struggle within and between the political parties added to the conflict. Major parties either in the form of a coalition government or majority government or minority government, ruled the country during the past 17 years but none of them were able to demonstrate governing ability according to the principles of democracy. Very unwanted practices like Pajero culture, corruption, politicising bureaucracy, buying to form government, pension culture, floor crossing, etc. have been observed regulary that made general public frustrated and discredited the political parties but also helped to escalate conflict.

TABLE 1.1: World Bank Institute Governance Index for Nepal (1996-2006)

Years	*Dimensions of Governance (in %)*					
	Voice and accountability	*Political stability*	*Government effectiveness*	*Regulatory quality*	*Rule of Law*	*Control of Corruption*
1996	50.2	25.0	48.3	23.4	51.4	44.7
1998	44.2	23.6	37.4	24.4	52.4	43.2
2000	44.7	14.4	39.3	27.3	45.2	40.3
2002	22.6	6.7	36.5	30.7	41.0	46.1
2003	23.6	5.3	32.2	32.7	36.7	51.0
2004	17.8	2.9	22.3	24.4	33.9	34.5
2005	13.9	1.4	15.6	26.3	24.8	28.6
2006	13.0	1.9	19	28.8	29.0	25.2
South Asia Average (2006)	25.5	26.8	37.7	37.0	39.3	33.9

Source: Narayan Manandhar, the Kathmandu Post 19 July 2007.

Table 1.1 shows that the governing situation of Nepal has deteriorated since the armed conflict, which started in 1996. All the six governance indices used to measure the various dimensions of governance indicate the worsening trend over time in Nepal.

In the past, political parties had fully politicised civil administration. Even the police force was abused for political gains of the ruling party. Political parties and the government did not work sincerely to restructure the malfunctioned civil administration to make it factually competent to devise and implement reform agenda and exercise inclusive democratic practices. The bureaucracy was absurdly used to fulfil vested political and party interests, which were often contradictory to the will of the general public (Upreti, 2004a). These weaknesses helped conflict to emerge and expand.

The conflict turned into a new mode from 23 November 2001. The Prime Minister's unilateral ceasefire and the call for peace talks in July and the CPN (M)'s positive response resulted in three rounds of peace talks. However, on 23rd November 2001 the CPN(M) suddenly and unilaterally called off the negotiation. They proclaimed a national peopl's government and started violent attacks in different parts of the country (e.g. Dang, Syanja and Solukhumbu). On 26 November, the king declared a State of Emergency (SoE) under the provision of the Article 115 of the then constitution. In the SoE constitutional rights of Nepalese people such as freedom of opinion and expression, freedom to assemble peacefully, freedom to move throughout the Kingdom and reside in any part thereof, freedom of any profession, or occupation; freedom of press and publication rights; rights against preventive detention; right to information; right to property; right to privacy and right to constitutional remedy were all suspended, except the right to file habeas corpus. The King, on the recommendation of the Cabinet, also issued the Terrorist and Destructive Activities Control and Punishment Ordinance. At the same time, the government had declared CPN (M), its sister organisations; and any organisations and individuals supporting them as terrorists. Then the army came into the battlefield and intense fights between the rebels and the army continued, with serious casualties. Human rights violations against the Hague Convention became common. The parliament had approved the SoE for the second term with the support of the CPN-UML. The parliament had passed and the King approved the Terrorist Control Ordinance, which became an act for another two years. When the CPN (M) ran away, unilaterally breaking the ceasefire in 2001 November, the then Prime Minister became too rigid and was not ready to initiate a dialogue. The Prime Minister was determined to crack down on the CPN (M) through military means with the help of some power-ful foreign countries. He visited the USA, UK and European countries, including Belgium and pleaded with them for support to crash the insurgents. The severe disputes between the ruling party and the government on the issue of the SoE had also clearly indicated his intention to control the CPN (M) by military intervention. The ruling NC party and other political parties were not in favour of the extension of the SoE but Prime Minster Deuba called the parliamentary session at "short notice" to extend the SoE for another three months. The intra- and inter-party dispute between the parliamentary parties diverted the attention of the nation from the armed conflict. It was not a priority of the political parties as they were busy in their own conflict. Time and again, military thinking had dominated both the government and the CPN (M), which ultimately sidelined political thinking to solve conflict through negotiation and dialogues and promoted militarisation of society.

Legitimacy of the governments formed after October 4, 2002 was seriously questioned. After the October 4 event, major political parties were excluded from the governance process, which further created conflict between the King and his government and the parliamentary parties.

It was not an irresolvable conflict, as it was not an ethnic cleansing, religious conflict or separatist movement. This was a political conflict for the social transformation and political change that had escalated and expanded on the ground of governance failure.

In summary, inter- and intra-party tension and conflict in all major political parties (Nepali Congress, Nepal Communist Party United Marxist and Leninist, Rastrya Prajatantra Party and other smaller parties), vested political interests of political parities and influential leaders to allocate development resources to their constituencies, alleged engagement of some of the powerful ministers and political leaders in the corruption and criminalization of politics were some of the visible political sources contributing to the escalation of conflict in Nepal.

1.2.3 Ideological Foundations

There was an ideological dimension in this conflict. The CPN (M) were following Mao's ideology and strategy. The CPN (M) perceived that the deep-rooted oppression coupled with the feudalistic mode of production relations and unequal power structures and the capitalistic democratic system are the problems and communism is the solution. They even developed their own ideological framework from the 2001 February second convention, called "Prachanda Path". On the contrary, the government, the parliamentary parties and the other small parties believed in capitalist multi-party democracy and constitutional monarchy. These two seemingly opposite ideologies were leading to ideological conflict between warring parties. In the past, the subsequent governments had treated CPN (M) as heinous, criminal and directed towards damaging the norms and values of the democratic system of governance, which law and order can counter. The ruling and the main opposition parties were either confused or unwilling to realise the ideological dimension of the Maoist insurgency.

The CPN (M) claim that new theoretical orientation, i.e. *Prachandapath,* is needed to address new challenges of the 21st century, which was not possible to address by the classical proletariat revolution. It was claimed that the Prachandapath allows going beyond the classical communism and envisioned a model of revolution combining a Chinese strategy of protracted people 's war (entering from villages to town and cities) and Russian strategy of armed insurrection (Sharma, 2003). There was direct ideological influence of the RIM in the Maoist movement in Nepal (Thapa, 2003).

1.2.4 Psychological Foundations

The individual and collective political psyche has so far preferred to ignore the reality rather than to accept the challenges that are threatening Nepali democracy. A powerful defence mechanism, used by politicians and power centres alike, is denial.[8] They deny the seriousness of the current situation, and are afraid to admit that their prevailing attitudes and practices are inappropriate and causing problems. They feel even more obstinately defensive when Nepali people confront them with evidence of their actions and the need for change. In Nepal, denial is rooted in the individual and institutional level in political parties, government departments, and other power centres. Overcoming this magnitude of denial in democratic reform should not be underestimated. It requires replacing the ideas, values, greed, and orthodoxy that underlie formidable complex obstacles with a new set of shaping ideas and values. If this paradigm shift were accepted as inevitable, the armed conflict would be a great opportunity for the fundamental reform of Nepali society.

There was also a growing feeling of injustice and revenge,

as the innocent people are increasingly becoming victims of conflict. Many people who were neglected by the state are now supporting the rebellion on the hope that their life will be better in the CPN (M)'s rule.

Ideology is often observed as a source of tension, be it religious, political, ethnic or otherwise. More than 25 armed insurgencies in different parts of the world in the past 5 decades are erupted because of the communist (Communist philosophy and revolutionary ideology of Karl Marx, Frederic Angles, V.I. Lenin, Joseph Stalin the Mao) and capitalist ideology. Religious extremism has created many social tensions and violent conflicts (e.g. conflict in Mindanao, Northern Ireland, Hindu Muslim fight in India).

Often ideologically guided insurgency of one area is influenced by the success or failure in other area (e.g.,Nepal's armed insurgency was very much influenced by the armed revolt of Peruvian CPN (M) in the South American Country, Peru). The Nepalese CPN (M) seems to have taken the Peruvian Maoist revolt as a successful model, (Nixon, 2003). While summarising the ideological aspect of the Nepal's armed conflict the following issues aooear:

- Radical ideological orientation and utopian thinking of mainly CPN (M) and some other political actors,
- Conceptual unclearity, ideological confusion and operational contradictions within mainstream political parties,
- Ideological back-up to CPN (M) by similar groups of other parts of the world
- Ideological divergence and dislike among the parliamentary political forces.

1.2.5 Spatial Foundations

Geographical disparity, especially between the Mid-Western and Far Western Regions and remote areas, where there is widespread poverty, disparity in resource distribution, structural inequality, injustice and discrimination, has heavily fuelled the CPN (M) conflict. Hence, the Maoist insurgency first started from Mid-Western Region (Rolpa, Rukum, Salyan and

Jajarkot). Since then their influence has been spread across the country and they were present virtually in all 75 districts, from rural to urban and hills to Terai areas (Philippson, 2002).

Nepalese geographical terrains are composed of numerous mountains, hills, gorges, valleys, churiyas, dense forests, caves and remote areas, which were extensively used by rebels in their insurgency. Lack of good networks of transport and communication also favoured rebels to launch their rebellions and hindered security forces. The open border (1808 km) between India and Nepal gave CPN (M) easy access to transport arms and ammunitions as well as to run political activities in India.

The geographical expansion and growth of the CPN (M) were sharp and ubiquitous mainly because of two reasons. First, they effectively and successfully utilised media, opinion leaders, frustrated masses (e.g. ex-bounded labourers, unemployed youths) and poor, marginalised and underprivileged groups. They also created fear of terror that help them to expand their activities. Second, there was complete failure of the government to govern according to the democratic ideals. The government had also failed to recognise the gravity of the problem associated with geographical areas. The government was extremely weak in early warning and early response measures. Furthermore, the rebels were able to give the impression to the general public that they truly represent the interests, needs and aspirations of poor rural population who have been excluded from the economic, political and social opportunities mainly because of staying in geographically remote and backward areas.

The security situation in remote areas was weak from the beginning because the presence of security forces in these areas was either light or police posts had closed or combined with few areas of heavy presence of the CPN (M). People of most of the geographically remote areas are almost under the Maoist rule. The Integrated Development Programme (November 2000 to March 2001) in Rolpa, Rukum, Salyan, Kalikot and Jajarkot, and Integrated Security and Development Programme (ISDP) in the CPN (M) stronghold districts (since May 2001) were not effective. Presence of security forces was concentrated mainly in district headquarters and town areas. Both the rebels and the government had continued to expand their geographical influence and duel rule existed in geographically remote areas.

Geographical discrimination and isolation is observed as a source of social tension and violence in most of war-torn countries (OECD/DAC, 2002; OECD, 2001; Nyheim et al., 2001; Nagel, 2006; Leonhardt, 2000; Aditya et al., 2006). Regional discrimination by the state is one of the min structural sources of conflict. The Karnali zone is one of the several examples of how state is geographically discriminating against people living in remote areas. Often the states do not pay proper attention towards investment of resources for the development of infrastructures in geographically remote and isolated areas. This is clearly demonstrated in the case of Nepal, as the government has concentrated its resources in easy and accessible areas and the city centre where elites live. Boluchistan of Pakistan is another example. Due to such discriminations, the people dwelling in the remote regions remained deprived of the advantages of contemporary development as if they were second-class citizens. These geographical discriminations caused serious frustration to the inhabitants of the remote areas. The recent violent tension in the Terai region is one of the manifestations of such geographical isolation. The Madheshi people of the Terai region were discriminated against, neglected and denied their identity for centuries. People from remote rural areas of Nepal such as Rapti and Karnali zones felt geographically excluded, which became a prominent source of conflict.

1.2.6 External foundations

The CPN (M) was a member of Revolutionary Internationalist Movement (RIM). RIM was formed in 1984 in London where CPN (Mashal) was one of the 19 signatories to establish RIM from the second international conference of the hardliner Maoist parties from around the world. At present,RIM has recognised and supported only the CPN (M). So there was direct ideological influence of the RIM in the Maoist movement in Nepal (Thapa, 2003). It is also reported that the CPN (M) has relations with the People's War Group and Maoist Communist Centre of India (Jwala, 2002:146-147) and CCOMPOSA. Another ideological dimension of Maoist insurgency was similarities with the insurgency of the Peruvian Communist party-Sinning Path. Critiques say that source of inspiration of the Nepalese insurgency is the Peruvian people's war waged by the Sinning Path. The CPN (M) has also official relations with RCP (USA). The CPN (M) obtained ideological support from other members of RIM (Roy, 2008).

After 11 September 2001, international security interests in Nepal began to grow. High-level government's officials and military visits from the USA, India and the UK and their direct response to the current conflict clearly indicated such interests. The strong reactions of the US Ambassador[9] to the CPN (M) and listing them in the second category of the terrorist list by the USA were examples of hardline stance of the USA towards the CPN (M). USA placed Nepal in the list of top six countries to support for the 'war against terrorism' and provided military assistance in security intelligence, training and millions of financial supports to strengthen the Nepal army. Despite the serious opposition in the Parliament and difference in the cabinet, the Belgian government sold weapons to Nepal. Thus Belgium was also associated with Nepalese conflict. Selling arms was one of the major international interests in the Nepalese conflict.

India was another major influencing force in the current conflict. Its attitude towards the CPN (M), its level of support to the government, its influence on the political decisions of the Nepalese political parties and its perceived security concerns determine the degree of Indian influence in the conflict. Before September 11, CPN (M) had easy access to India, strong ties with Indian Naxalites and other ultra leftists, obtained training and supports like weapons from there, used Indian territories for meetings, organisation and publications. But after September 11, India was publicly supporting the Nepalese government, declaring CPN (M) as 'terrorist', searching Indian territory for Maoist cadres and arms caches, reinforcing border security (deploying troops) and sealing of borders and providing military equipment and helicopter support to crack down the rebels. But many analysts say that India was not really willing to help resolve this conflict in Nepal. Though India was an unwelcome player in Nepalese politics, its role was most influential in Nepal's politics. India was a crucial player in assisting political parties to reach the 12-point understanding between the CPN (M) and the Seven-Parties' Alliance (SPA) to fight against the direct rule of the then king.

Before the end of the monarchy, China was not a major player in Nepalese conflict. Contrary to many speculations, China did not support the CPN (M) and expressed dissatisfaction at the use of the name of Mao in this violent conflict. However, China changed its position after the end of monarchy and engaged more directly in Nepal's affairs. Role of international powerful actors in dealing with Nepal's armed conflict was often criticised in Nepal.

The following points are especially important:

- Vested multiple interests of powerful countries and particularly neighbouring countries,
- Changing global security paradigm and subsequent responses (e.g. war against terrorism and consequent violence around the world),
- Mismatch between international priority/interests and local community/states.

1.2.7 Catalytic Foundations

Conflict within the CPN (Mashal) mounted on the issue of participation in the parliamentary election of 1991. The faction, led by Babu Ram Bhattarai, separated to participate in the election under the banner of UPF, a political wing of Unity Centre. The Unity Centre won 9 seats in the parliament and became 3rd largest party. UPF had also stood in the local election. However, the ruling party took a very repressive approach to wipe out UPF from its stronghold areas by using ex-panchas and local administration and police force. They brutally suppressed the members and supporters of UPF. Because of such repressions, ordinary people did not feel any change from the widely acknowledged political change of 1990.

The excessive and unlawful act of police under *Operation Romeo* has terrorised the local people. The parliamentary Investigation Committee had also highlighted this event. The following statement also highlights this event in a more concrete way, *"Between 1990 and 1996, successive regimes in Kathmandu, starting with that of strongly anti-communist Girija Koirala, pursued a conscious policy of trying to undermine and ultimately dismantle the considerable electoral clout of the CPN (M) in Rukum, Rolpa, Salyan and Jajarkot - a region with strong left support since 1950s. ...Mobilising not only party cadre, but local and regional civil administration and the police force as available and the necessary, the Girija government started a trend of committing and compromising state resources to undermine opposition parties to win local and national election. ...If free and fair elections are to be regarded as forming the most inviolable aspects of democracy, then the trend initiated by the Nepali Congress government under Koirala in the Maoist hinterland and beyond can be taken as the beginning of a series of egregious and systematic violence of democracy from within the state in post-1990 period* (Pahari, 2003:7). Karki and Seddon (2003) had also made similar observations in this regard. This event implanted deep frustration within UC and ultimately they organised to fight the government-sponsored aggression (Jwala, 2002). Within UC a debate on 'new direction' led to its breakdown into Unity Centre (Maoist) and Unity Centre. Both the breakaway factions applied in the Election Commission for legitimacy and recognition. However, the Election Commission only recognised the minority breakaway faction led by Nirmal Lama and majority led by Prachanda was barred from participating in the election. This case gave no room for them to engage in the parliamentary practices and ultimately gave way to the CPN (M) to start a rebellion. If this faction had also been allowed to participate in the parliamentary election the scenario might have been different. There would be strong opinion within the CPN (M) to continue parliamentary struggle, which could delay or stop to the start of the armed rebellion. Even critiques like Prakash Jwala (ex-MP of UML) argue that assassination of central member of the CPN (M) Ram Vrikshya Yadav in Dahnusha in 1994 by the NCP's government administration forced CPN (M) to take up arms (Jwala, 2002).

Triggering factors appear in a specific time and manifested within a specific context or circumstance. Triggers and catalysts influence the rate, duration or intensity of conflict. Triggers or catalysts activate various channels in conflict. In this conflict, the trigger for the armed rebellion by the CPN (M) was the chosen time for their actions. They started the rebellion at the time of much frustration of people with the performance of political parties and the successive governments. The impoverished situation of mass population, intra- and inter-party conflicts and power struggle, failure of NC and CPN-UML party to address root causes, change in power relations, widespread corruption were responsible for triggering the conflict.

The massacre in the Royal Palace, expansion of Indian Maoists in different states of India and their relations with Nepalese CPN (M), open border with India and transportation of small arms and ammunitions, events of September 11 and subsequent 'war against terrorism', failure of negotiation and unilateral break-up of peace talks by Maoists and attack on security bases, sole aim of main opposition party to go to power, courts' decision to release some arrested suspected CPN (M), dual role of the main opposition party, sympathy of small leftist parties toward the CPN (M), brutal killing and arbitrary arrests and hijacking of people and the SoE were the main catalysts or triggers of the conflict. The announcement of the government to award millions of rupees to those who brought the Maoist leaders dead or alive, red corner notice and labelling CPN (M) as terrorists, had further triggered the conflict.

The explicit or implicit long-term target of the CPN (M) seemed to establish a republican socialist political system in Nepal. They believed that such a political change is the only solution for all cultural, social, political and economic problems of Nepal. Basically the CPN (M) wanted to achieve this target through the approach adopted by the Mao in China, i.e. control villages and steadily encircle core cities and carry out guerrilla war in cities. On the contrary, the target of the government was either to eliminate the CPN (M) or bring them to the current multiparty political system. However, it was difficult to identify the hidden target of the main actors in the conflict. Financial gains might be the obvious hidden target among many indirect players of conflict.

The CPN (M) became successful in utilising the dichotomised group identities such as oppressed-oppressor, ruler-ruled, poor-rich, landlord-landless, patriot-non patriot to establish political, social, cultural, and economic cleavages. These dichotomies fuelled the already developed feeling of injustice and frustrations of the Nepalese people. The CPN (M) got widespread sympathy for their objectives and demands, if not their approaches to achieve these (Seddon and Hussien, 2002).

When the CPN (M) concentrated their activities in city centres and particularly in Kathmandu after the second ceasefire break, the Kathmandu-based elite became more sensitive towards the conflict. Though the scale of attacks after the break of first ceasefire was bigger, they were in rural districts and Kathmandu elites were less concerned but now that had changed.

In the early years (1996-1999) of the insurgency, neither the government nor the donor community in Nepal gave enough attention to democratic development (transparent, bottom-up, accountable, equitable and participatory). Donors started to rethink only when their development programmes and projects were affected by the conflict. Reconciling development and security became a major challenge after the 2001 State of Emergency and then donors started to rethink critically and assess their project activities. Consequently, some donors (e.g. DFID, SDC) changed their approaches, procedures, and practices to translate the 'do-no-harm' principle into practice. However, Seddon and Hussein (2002) argue that it is difficult for donors to follow basic tenets of humanitarian aid and 'do-no-harm' principles. Images of neutrality and biases of donor funded development projects and programmes and hidden political agenda of the donors became icons of debate and criteria of acceptance of the projects by the rebels in the conflict-sensitive areas. The immediate security concerns to the continuation of projects became a major threat.

Rampant poverty, structural inequality, political oppression, social discrimination against certain groups (e.g. Kamaya, women, Dalit), failure of the public administration, widespread corruption and continuous failure of the successive governments to address these structural problems were the root causes of the armed conflict in Nepal. The Maoist insurgency was only the manifestation of these problems. Feudal legacy, political instability, dependency syndromes, lack of transparency and the social exclusion were further contributing to fuelling the conflict.

The people of Nepal had lost trust in the political change of 1990 because of broken promises and failed delivery. They harbour a deep mistrust toward the government and political parties because of their poor performance and their many failures. This book argues that many of the challenges faced by the young democracy in Nepal were the products of the inherent social exclusion, the lack of public engagement in governance practices and failure to recognise pluralism in Nepali society. The principle of inclusiveness must be exercised by civil society, political actors and other segments of the nation. The chapter concludes that a culture of tolerance, respect for diversity, inclusiveness, and reconciliation must be incorporated into governance principles and practices. The root causes of conflict such as social exclusion, centralism, unequal access to resources, and marginalisation of ethnic minorities, gender discrimination and religious biases need to be addressed properly to create lasting peace in Nepal. It is essential for all political and social actors to change their perceptions, shed stereotypes and promote tolerance and the principle of inclusiveness. In essence, the armed conflict provided great opportunities for broader political change and social transformation in Nepal. It is extremely essential to combine 'an agenda for peace' and 'an agenda for development' to make 'an agenda for human security'.

To summarise:

- Suddenly emerging situation (e.g., 1st June 2001 Royal massacre in Nepal),

- Failure of political leaderships (e.g., the then prime ministers were not able to deal on the issue of constituent assembly, which was the prime demand of the CPN (M)),
- Psychological factors- revenge and retaliations,
- Ambition of some politicians, military and social leaders to consolidate the power and rule,
- Irresponsibility factor,
- Culture of denial, as politicians, military and the CPN (M) were not able to acknowledge their weaknesses and therefore failed to search for negotiated options.

1.2.8 Legal foundations

Potential for social tension and violent conflict remains high when the constitution and laws provide special treatment to certain classes, religions and castes and discriminate against other castes, races and religions. For example, constitutional and legal provisions during the Rana era and the Panchayat regime (e.g., Civil Code) were not only discriminatory but also directly and or indirectly promoted to homogenise the cultural, religious, ethic and language diversities under the framework of 'single language' and 'single dress'. Actions such as declaring the nation a 'Hindu Kingdom' in the constitution, searching and arresting Christians, looking down upon Muslims, showing indifference to Buddhists, etc. were usual, during the Panchayat era. Restriction on the freedom of expression was imposed by the laws. Even after the introduction of the multiparty system in 1990, many legal provisions of the Panchayat constitution and laws relating to religion (declaring Hindu Kingdom), citizenship, women's rights, etc. were given a place in the Constitution of the Kingdom of Nepal, 1990 and in other laws.

If the state is not willing to show its commitments in international protocols and conventions related to human rights and humanitarian assistance, child rights and women's rights, ethnic rights, etc. and violates them, potential for civil unrest and social tension exist.

1.2.9 Summary of the various sources, foundations and roots of conflict

Table 1.2 presents a summary of the main social, economic, political, geographical and legal causes of the armed conflict and crisis in Nepal (Aditya et al., 2006; Upreti, 2004b, 2006a and 2004d; Karki and Seddon, 2003; Thapa and Sijapati, 2003; Pandey, 1999 and 2001; Thapa, 2002; Hutt, 2004; Upreti, 2007a, 2005a, 2002b; 2002c, 2004c, 2006c, 2005b):

TABLE 1.2 : Causes of the armed conflict in Nepal

S.N.	*Causes*	*Elaboration of causes*
1.	Structural (socio-economic) causes	Rampant poverty and widespread unemployment, Injustice, inequalities and discrimination based on class, caste, gender, ethnicity and geography, Centralized, power-biased and corrupt governing system, Denial of access to and control over of production resources and basic services to poor and marginalized sections of society, Constitutional failure
2.	Ideological causes	Radical ideological orientation of the CPN (M) leaders, Conceptual unclearity, ideological confusion and operational contradictions within parliamentary political parties, Ideological back-up to Nepalese CPN (M) by Revolutionary Internationalist Movement (RIM), Coordination Committee of Maoists Parties and Organizations in South Asia (CCOMPOSA) and other radical communist groups, Ideological divergence and dislike of powerful western governments to the expansion of CPN (M)
3.	Geographical	Geographical isolation Ignorance and marginalization of remote and inaccessible areas

	Concentration of resources in city centres and accessible areas
4. International causes	Growing interests of powerful nations (political, economic: natural resources-water; historical legacy; religious; strategic and military), particularly multiple interests of India and USA in Nepal, 11 September 2001 terrorist attack in USA and consequent changes in global security paradigm and responses, Various interests of influential external actors (World Bank, Asian Development Bank, International Monetary Fund, others), Changing international responses after 1st February 2005 Royal coup
5. Environmental causes	Demographic stress on environmental resources Irrational exploitation of natural resources Denial of access of poor and marginalised people to natural resources Skewed distribution of land resources Inequity and exploitation of people whose livelihood is based on natural resources by the powerful elites
6. Governance deficiency	Politicisation of bureaucracy and security Institutionalised culture of denial and inaction Vested interests (both political and personal) of powerful actors Rampant corruption and glaring mal-governance Favouritism and nepotism (*afnomanchhe*) Strategy of palace and political parties to use the armed insurgency as a means to gain and consolidate power Development mismatch and failure
7. Triggers and catalysts	1st June 2001 Royal massacre, Failure of political leaderships King's direct involvement in politics (since 4 October 2002) Psychological factors-revenge and retaliations

8.	First February 2005 royal takeover	Unrealistic ambition of the then King Gyanendra to control politics and society, Monopoly and abuse of power and authority Distortion of rules and laws and wrong interpretation of democracy Regulation or control of civic liberty, Restrictions on socio-economic, political, cultural, religious freedom and rights Denial or misinterpretation of multi-linguality, multi-ethnicity, multi-cultural and religious identities Creation of unconstitutional control mechanisms such as Royal Commission on Corruption Control, appointment of zonal administrators, etc. Creation of fear, threat and insecurity to those who do not support the coup Resistance to change and reform in the name of national unity,

Sources: Compiled from different sources

The above Table 1.2 highlights the different causes of the armed conflict in Nepal.

In another way, I summarise the sources or foundations of the armed conflict as follows:

- Exclusionary state structures that prevent access of powerless and marginalised sections of society to the state's political decisions,
- Non-transparent state operation system,
- Corruption and malfunctioning of state's governing apparatus,
- Systematic denial and violence of rule of laws and human rights by the state,
- Political decisions favouring certain political and interest groups,
- Dysfunctional security system,
- Denial of access to and control over of production resources and basic services to poor and marginalized sections of society,
- Development mismatch and failure.

1.3 THE FORMER KING GYNENDRA: EPICENTRE OF THE POLITICAL CHANGE IN NEPAL

Actions and behaviour of the then king Gyanendra and his coteries betrayed parliamentary parties and international communities who were firmly committed to multi-party democracy and constitutional monarchy before the takeover of 1st February 2005. The King's 1st February proclamation to the nation seriously charged the leadership of political parties and blamed them for political crisis and insecurity. His actions helped to bring the Seven-Party-Alliance (SPA) and CPN (M) together and international community distanced from him and supported the popular people's movement of April 2006.

The 1st February 2005 takeover was a serious blow to the political parties, as the king blamed them for the corruption, insecurity, and violence and weakening of the national unity and sovereignty. Main leaders of the political parties were detained or arrested and jailed for several months. Distance between the king and the political parties widened. Consequently, they gradually realised that the King's move was not to control terrorism but to weaken political parties and multiparty democracy. Hence they united to fight against the King's takeover. Seven major parliamentary political parties joined together to restore the suspended democracy. They agreed to a six-point programme that contained restoration of House of Representatives as an entry point and the election of constituent assembly as an exit point for resolution of the armed conflict. As protest, the seven political parties declared to boycott the municipal election of February 2005. They prepared different protest programmes. Likewise, they tried to get international support. Senior leaders of main political parties such as Girija Prasad Koirala (NCP), Bam Dev Gautam (CPN-UML), Gopal Man Shrestha (NCP-D) visited India and discussed Nepal's political crisis with Indian senior political leaders and the government. The seven political parties and the CPN (M) collaborated to restore democracy in Nepal. Consequently, *Janaandolon* II started to restore democracy.

1.3.1 *Janaandolon* II of April 2006 against the king

The aims of Nepal's *Janaandolon* II of April 2006 were to topple the king's rule, to resolve the heightened armed conflict and achieve lasting peace and democracy in Nepal. It was realized that these aims would be possible only by changing the competitive and adversarial relationships between the seven-party alliances (SPA) and the CPN (M)[10] into one of partnership approach.

The *Janaandolon* II in Nepal was a non-violent struggle by the people to end the autocratic rule of the King and restore peace by ending the armed conflict and transforming the country with a viable democratic political system. A Non-violent initiative for social change required a fundamentally different approach (Ackermann and Duvall, 2005), which was clearly demonstrated in *Janandolan* II. Non-violent action theory (BRCCCM, 2003) provides a strong analytical framework to understand the civic movement of Nepal. In the area of conflict transformation and peace building, the conceptual framework of non-violent action put forth by Sharp (1973), Ghandi (1938 and 1950), King (1963) and other peace theorists and leaders provides a new dimension. Proponents of non-violent theories of conflict transformation highlight the importance played by the people's convictions and ideologies, and their commitments to achieve their goals through a peaceful means. In the understanding of this theory, conflict is a non-violent struggle for bringing about social justice and change. The notion of non-violent actions for social change brings out tensions and contradictions that already exist in society, but which remain denied and covered up (McCarthy and Sharp, 1997).

The *Janaandolon* II was basically the result of the king's action and behaviour. Repression, gross violence of human rights, blatant abuses of state power and resources, abuse of authority, and tense relations with the international community marked the king's direct rule. If the king had not repressed the political parties, perhaps they would not have needed to align with CPN (M) to jointly fight against his regressive regime. The 12-point understanding between the SPA and CPN (M) was the outcome of the suppression by the king. Three of the 12-

point understanding actually paved the path for the April movement:

1. Today, democracy, peace, prosperity, social advancement and a free and sovereign Nepal is the main desire of all Nepalese. We completely agree that autocratic monarchy is the main hurdle in (realizing) this. It is our clear view that without establishing full democracy by ending autocratic monarchy, there is no possibility of peace, progress and prosperity in the country. Therefore, an understanding has been reached to establish full democracy by ending autocratic monarchy by exerting all forces against it, thereby creating a nationwide storm of democratic protests.
2. The seven agitating parties are fully committed to the fact that only by establishing full democracy through the restoration of Parliament with the force of agitation, forming an all-party government with complete authority, holding elections to a constituent assembly through dialogue and understanding with the CPN (M), can the existing conflict in the country be resolved and sovereignty and state power completely transferred to the people. It is the view and commitment of the CPN (M) that the above-mentioned goal can be achieved by holding a national political conference of the agitating democratic forces and through its decision, forming an interim government to hold a constituent assembly election. An understanding has been reached between the seven agitating parties and the CPN (M) to continue the dialogue on this procedural work-list and find a common understanding. It has been agreed that the power of people's movement is the only alternative to achieve this.
3. Today, the country demands the establishment of permanent peace along with a positive solution to the armed conflict. Therefore, we are committed to ending autocratic monarchy and the existing armed conflict

> and establishing permanent peace in the country through constituent assembly elections and a forward-looking political outlet. The CPN (M) expresses its commitment to move along the new peaceful political stream through this process. In this very context, an understanding has been reached to keep the armed CPN (M) force and the royal army under the supervision of the United Nations or any other reliable international supervision during the holding of the constituent assembly elections. It is also agreed that the result of the free and fair elections would be accepted by both the parties (SPA and the CPN-M). We expect reliable international mediation even during the dialogue process.

The SPA had protested against the king's rule right from the beginning, but the Nepalese people had lost faith in these parties because of their poor performance in the past and therefore had not meaningfully participated in the earlier protest programmes (Upreti, 2006a). Once the SPA reached the 12-point understanding with the CPN (M) and publicly acknowledged their past mistakes and promised not to commit the same mistakes again (points 6 and 7), the situation changed. The CPN (M) made a similar promise to work together to resolve 10 years of armed conflict establish peace and to work toward restoring full democracy in the country. Once this was done, people in massive strength came out on the streets and challenged the royal regime. The *Janaandolon* II was precisely the outcome of it.

The non-violent action theory adopted by Mahatma Gandhi (1938 and 1950) and Martin Luther King (1963) stresses the need for peaceful protests against the adversary and for a search for moral defeat of the resisting force (Mitchell, 1981). A conflict transformation strategy embedded in non-violent action theory begins with a three-fold understanding of the mass movement to transform the conflict, i.e. (a) conflict as an element of society, (b) conflict as a catalyst for social change, and (c) conflict as a form of reflection of people's power to establish social justice. Hence, a non-violent mass movement provides a basis to understand conflict as a means of social change, political reform and internalization of the fundamentals of democracy. The impact of a non-violent people's movement in different parts of the world have demonstrated that a non-violent civil movement has a more powerful impact than that of violent approaches (Aditya et al.; 2006). The instances of the 1905 Russian popular uprising, the popular non-violent struggle led by Mohandas Karam Chand Gandhi for the independence of India, the civil rights movement of the USA led by Martin Luther King, the non-violent struggle of the Chilean people against Augusto Pinochet in 1983; the overthrow of Ferdinand Marcos, the president of the Philippines, by people's power in 1986; The Rose Revolution of Georgia (2003), the Orange Revolution of Ukraine (2004); Kyrgyzstan's popular 'Tulip' Revolution[11] (2005), People's movement of Lebanon (2005), and the People's movement of Nepal (April 2006) (Pyakuryal et al., 2008) have all proved the importance of non-violent movements against the unpopular and despotic governments.[12] However, the success of a non-violent movement very much depends upon the strategy used to forge the unity of the people, follow non-violent methods, press for issues of importance, and display ability to organize people's agency (Ackerman and Kruegler, 1994).

Galtung (1996; 2000a and 2000b) argues that once they emerge, conflicts pass through a series of transformational processes, i.e. articulation or dis-articulation, conscientization or de-conscientisation, complexification or simplification, polarization or depolarization, escalation or de-escalation. Incompatibilities between conflicting parties can be overcome by transcending the contradiction, or through compromise, or by deepening or widening the conflict structure, and by associating or dissociating the actors (ibid). All these transformational processes were clearly observed in the 10 years of the armed insurgency in Nepal as explicitly reflected in the 12-point understanding they reached. Galtung (1996), Krippendorf (1973), Shell (2003) and Curle (1971) emphasize the ever-growing global asymmetric relationships as the structural source of conflict around the world. Asymmetric relationships can be transformed through a shift from unbalanced to balanced relationships, and a process of conscientisation, confrontation, negotiation and development (BRCCCM, 2003). The post-1st February 2005 relationship between the SPA and the CPN (M) was transformed from an asymmetric to a cooperative relationship, which was reflected in the 12-point understanding. The improved relation between the SPA and the CPN (M) has been ultimately successful in ending the rule of monarchy and suspending the King's power in a move to ultimately overthrow the monarchical system and replace it with the Federal Democratic Republican system for Nepal.

Nepal has changed from the centuries-old feudal, top-down, autocratic and exclusionary monarchical regime triggered by the non-violent April movement of 2006. An understanding was reached between the SPA and the CPN (M) of the conditions that developed across the nation following the start of the CPN (M) 'People's War. The intense power struggle between the political parties and the palace reached its peak when the King resumed all the executive power on 1st February 2005 by a coup; the parliament was dissolved, and the elected prime minister overthrown. This action of the king motivated the major political parties to come together and form an alliance (popularly known as the Seven Party Alliance[13]) to protest against the King's action. They also decided to collaborate with the CPN (M) to revolt against the King, which the CPN (M) had been proposing to do for the past two years. That strategy brought together the two major forces of the country fighting against the king. As a consequence, they reached a 12-point understanding, which ultimately paved the path to launch the mass agitation of April.

The *Janaandolon* II of 6- 24 April 2006 proved that people's power can defeat the autocratic, feudal regime that the 10-year armed conflict was unable to. This section of the chapter highlights the reasons for success of the non-violent movement. Women, marginalized groups, ethnic communities, disabled, youth, children, students, housewives, labourers, peasants, workers, street-vendors, business people, retailers, peace and human rights activists, journalists, lawyers, scholars and researchers, poets, writers, school teachers, university professors, doctors, nurses, shoe makers, tailors, government employees, technicians, artists, film actors and actresses, in short, people from every walk of life participated in the non-violent *Janaandolon* II. This section also sheds light on a similar nature of wider and inclusive participation by the people in this movement. During the King's time (15 months) of direct rule, the state was very coercive. The high-handedness of the government during April 2006 was excessive and autocratic.

Once people organize for resistance movements, it is very hard for autocratic rulers to politically survive through suppression. In Nepal, despite the rigorous efforts and attempts by the king to justify his takeover, domestic protest mounted, but the international community remained unconvinced by it. In his attempt to convince the Nepalese people and the international community the monarch reiterated the 'grand failure of the political parties' to contain violence, to restore peace, control corruption and to improve the deteriorating economic situation of the country. In all his speeches, public comments, and media interviews, the king vehemently expressed his dismay with political parties as, "*Nepal's bitter experiences over the past few years tend to show that democracy and progress contradict one another. Multiparty democracy was discredited by focusing solely on power politics. Parliament witnessed many aberrations in the name of retaining and ousting governments. Not a single House of Representative was allowed to complete its tenure. Continuous confusion and disorder resulted in the obstruction of the democratic process.*[14] He further said, addressing the Nation at the time of the royal takeover on February one, '*...today we have once again reached a juncture, where in keeping with popular aspirations, a historic decision must be taken to defend multiparty democracy by restoring peace for the nation and people. Even when bloodshed, violence and devastation have pushed the country on the brink of destruction, those engaged in politics in the name of country and people continue to shut their eyes to their welfare. Tussle for power, abuse of authority on gaining power and unhealthy competition in fulfilling personal and communal interests at the expense of the nation* *and citizenry contributed further to deterioration in the situation. ...It is now time to bring to an end the ongoing act of terrorist violence and pledge, in earnest, to fulfil the people's aspirations with the restoration of peace and security in the country.... As it is our responsibility to preserve our nationalism, national unity and sovereignty as well as to maintain peace and security in the country and ensure that the state of the nation does not deteriorate any further, we have, by virtue of the State Authority as exercised by us and in keeping with the spirit of the Constitution of the Kingdom of Nepal 1990, taking into consideration Article 27 (3) of the constitution, dissolved effective from today, the current Council of Ministers to fulfil the people's desire for the restoration of peace and security and to activate soon the democratic dispensation*[15]'.

Time and again, the king highlighted the role of the Shah Dynasty in the nation building of Nepal, referring to the unification process initiated by King Prithvi Narayan Shah. Like his forefathers, he wanted to be at the centre-stage of Nepal's politics, which was opposed by the SPA and the CPN (M). The King had miscalculated the people's desire for peace and his own ability to deliver it. Ordinary people were tired of the continuing violence, but monarchy itself was the root cause of the structural conflict because of its feudalistic, exclusionary and regressive nature. The ordinary people's expressed desire for peace was misunderstood by the king who was only keen to strengthen his direct rule in the name of 'fighting against terrorism'. Hence, without declaring a ceasefire, he, invited the CPN (M) for peace talks, ignoring the other political parties. He was over-reliant on the security forces and in using coercive strategy than political negotiation. But his strategy and tactics to get support for his regime from the international community in the name of 'war against terrorism' and military-reliant coercive approach failed.

1.3.2 People's Power in 6-24 April 2006

The SPA called a nationwide general strike (*Nepal bandh*) for 4 days (6-9 April). In response, hundreds of thousands of people came on to the streets across the country. On 5th April, CPN (M) declared a ceasefire in support of the general strike. In spite of the SPA's promise of a peaceful the general strike, the royal government was claiming that the CPN (M) would infiltrate the general strike to make it violent and the government would take necessary measures to protect the people's life and property. The government asked the SPA to call off the general strike and threatened to suppress it with the use of force. Despite the threat from the government and Nepal army (which led to the formation of a unified command of police, armed police, military and intelligence), the SPA decided to go ahead with their plans of agitation and protest (Pyakuryal et al., 2008).

On the first day of the general strike on 6th April, protesters organized mass rallies all over the country. In some areas, protestors dismantled the statues of the Shah Kings. This protest was expanded in the following days. Even before the start of *Janaandolon* II, the royal government mobilized unified command to prevent people from coming on to the streets. Political leaders and activists were arrested from their residence or at the first encounter in the demonstration. People organized demonstrations in different parts of the town and district headquarters all over the country. The King's government took all sorts of repressive measures and indulged in excessive baton charges and gun fire. On the first day of the general strike, CPN (M) fiercely attacked the unified command in Sarlahi district and the defeat severely demoralized the security forces. Consequently, the security forces vented their anger against peaceful demonstrators in different parts of the country. Mass demonstrations in the streets of Kathmandu and other parts of the country were expanding rapidly, irrespective of gunfire and other repressive measures employed by the autocratic government. On the evening of 7th April, the government imposed a night curfew, extending it to day-and-night curfew on 8th and 9th April with a 'shoot at sight' order. However, people defied the curfew and came out on to the streets en masse. By April 9, almost 90 per cent of the political leaders who had actively led in the protest, and more than 70 per cent of local civil society members, human rights activists and journalists supporting the protest were arrested and jailed.

The nationwide general strike (6-9 April) called by the

protesters got expanded for an indefinite period and people form all walks of life came out on the streets to protest against the brutal regime of the King in greater numbers. Civil disobedience across the country paralyzed the nation. The King's government and its home minister with a proven track record of anti-democratic convictions totally failed to keep law and order in the country even after full mobilization of the unified command and mobilization of all state resources and power. Government employees from law courts, ministries and departments, from corporations and companies all joined the civil disobedience and in the protest. Civil servants, banking sector and state-owned public sector employees joined in the protests. Even tourists and foreign citizens joined in the protests held in Kathmandu and Pokhara. Solidarity for the democratic movement was evident on a massive scale. Even in remote rural districts, more people gathered every day[16] and the number of people coming on to the streets of Kathmandu reached 2 million in strength. The then 'Royal Nepal Army[17]' used helicopters for surveillance over peaceful demonstrations in different parts of the country and directed the ground troops to suppress them. Ground forces opened fire at the demonstrators in different parts of Kathmandu under the orders of the army officers in the surveillance helicopters. The then Home Minister himself was working at the Army headquarters for coordinating with the Army Chief and the Valley Command Forces to suppress the movement. The government justified its suppression by saying that it found infiltration by CPN (M) cadres in the demonstrations. So, during the 19 days of peaceful protests, 25 people got killed, with more than 5,500 people wounded that created a horror all over the country. The government massively mobilized 'vigilantes', criminals, and royalist youths to suppress the pro-democracy movement. The Home Minister spent millions of rupees weekly for this purpose.[18] But this measure did not work.

When the *Janaandolon* II rapidly spread, the king invited SPA to talk with him. In his message to the nation on the occasion of New Year's Day on 14th April, he said, '...*Democracy demands restraint and consensus as all forms of extremisms are incompatible with democracy. While facing the challenges confronting the nation democracy also emphasizes acceptance of the pre-eminence of the collective wisdom in charting a future course'*.[19] However, the SPA 'Movement Coordination Committee' said that the king's message was 'meaningless' and 'contains nothing'. It stated, *'The king has used the trump card of dialogue at a time when he is completely isolated at the national and international level. The idea of the dialogue is a ploy by the royal regime to create confusion among the people and the international community'*. The King failed to weaken the resolve of the people's movement in the name of dialogue. The interesting contradiction is that, during the 14 months of his direct rule, the king consistently denied requests from political parties, the civil society and the international community to open dialogues with the political parties and to reach a negotiated settlement with them.

When the king failed to convince SPA to come up to talk, he attempted to use the international community (particularly India and the USA were in favour of the constitutional monarchy), to help him out. The international community in general and these two countries in particular pressurized the SPA to accept the king's offer. Dr. Karan Singh,[20] who was a relative of the Nepalese royal family, came as a special envoy of the Indian Prime Minister, Dr. Manamohan Singh, to mediate with the SPA. On 19 April, Dr. Karan Singh met the SPA leaders and discussed the package he brought from the Indian government. His formula prescribed negotiation between the king and the SPA, ensuring constitutional monarchy, and handing over of the executive power by the king to the SPA. The King accepted this package of negotiation. Accordingly, on the night of 21 April, he addressed the nation and said, "*We, through this proclamation, affirm the executive power of the Kingdom of Nepal, which was in our safekeeping, from this day, shall, be returned to the people and be exercised in accordance with Article 35 of the 1990's constitution.*[21] . However, people in the streets were in no mood to compromise unless the king accepted all the demands of the protesters (full acceptance of the 12-point understanding, and election to a constituent assembly).

After this offer from the king, India expressed its hope that the king and political parties would reconcile and move ahead. At the same time, Envoys of USA, France, Sweden, UK, Germany and Finland went to the residence of SPA senior leader, Girija Prasad Koirala, on 22 April to pressurize SPA leaders to accept the offer of the king. People opposed their action vehemently.[22] However, once the protesters knew that the foreign diplomats are exerting pressure on SPA leaders to compromise with the king, a huge mass of demonstrators reached the residence of Girija Prasad Koirala where foreign envoys and SPA leaders were having a meeting. They chanted slogans against the king's offer and warned the SPA leaders not to surrender to the pressures by the foreigners and to keep the movement going on. In the end, the SPA leaders rejected the King's offer as well as the suggestions made by a group of foreign diplomats. The movement continued with strength and received wider support. By 23rd April, more than half the of country's population had come out on to the streets protesting against the king's rule and demanding the election for a constituent assembly. The street demand now shifted suddenly in favour of a republican state and punishment to the king.

Mass demonstrations turned into violent confrontations in different parts of the country. The royal regime brutally tried to suppress the masses by mobilizing the army. This was not acceptable to the people, who opposed the repression by coming out on to the streets in millions. The Army failed to control the mass uprising and the SPA leaders were encouraged with the people's support. They threatened to form a parallel government (which CPN (M) leaders had been suggesting to them from the time of signing of the 12-point agreement), if the royal regime was not willing to surrender. Public pressure was mounting against the King tremendously.

Finally, the army succumbed in front of people's power, since they could not control millions of demonstrators rallying on the streets. The army feared the possibility that the teeming millions of protesters could storm the royal palace if the mass demonstrations continued further in the coming days. As the army was the sole base of the king's 1st February coup, and since the royal force was already demoralized, the king had no option but to submit to the wishes of the people. Then a tactical package of negotiations was offered from the Royal palace and from the international power centres to the SPA leaders. This package had two conditions to be fulfilled by the SPA leaders, which they accepted just before the king's address of 24 April. The first condition was to keep the constitutional monarchy and the second, not to interfere with the army. A negotiation between the SPA and the Royal palace reached on the midnight of 24th April 2006. In a televised speech, the King said,' *Realizing the people's movement and seven party alliance's roadmap we have revived the House of Representatives which would help resolve the national problems, including violence...'*.[23] The CPN (Maoists) and some critical analysts were not happy with the negotiated settlement accepted by the SPA. They argued that the people's movement would have definitely overthrown the monarchy with the peaceful street protest continuing for two more days, if the SPA had not accepted the negotiation. It was also suspected that SPA leaders had assured the king about the continuity of the monarchy in the country upon which the king accepted the roadmap of the SPA. At the same time, the CPN (M) too was unable to continue the movement alone without further support from the SPA.

1.3.3 Political Alliance for *Janaandolon* II

The major political parties such as the Nepali Congress (splinters were reunited in November 2007), the Communist Party of Nepal (United Marxist-Leninist) and to some extent other members of the SPA and the CPN (M) had had a deep adversarial relationship, attempting to politically finish each other. The SPA parties were in the government previously and using the state power to suppress the CPN (M) rebels fighting against the state and also the ruling parties. Despite the vehement request by peace activists, civil society leaders and intellectuals to opt for a non-violent approach to conflict transformation, for 8 years parliamentary political parties had continuously ignored this request and were using force to defeat the CPN (M). Political parties never realized the need for state restructuring and transformation of a stratified vertical social structure and a skewed economic and political relation (Upreti, 2006a; 2006b). All major political parties showed a power-hungry attitude and behaviour of status quo. They were not only intensely engaged in their own internal power struggle, but also continuously bargaining with the King for power. Hence, they never made serious efforts to end the violent conflict with a negotiated settlement. Instead, they used the CPN (M) armed conflict as a pretext to retain their own power. Political parties realized their mistakes and erosion of public trust in them when the king arrested and jailed them, and imposed his autocratic rule on 1st February 2005.

On the other side, CPN (M) leaders were concentrating on strengthening their army power and weakening the political parties, instead of meaningfully engaging them to change the feudalistic political order. They let the palace and other regressive forces erode the popularity of the political parties and vice versa. However, their magic expansion and success in managing a 'people's war' was able to bring 80 per cent of the country under their control, though they were not able to capture the state. Therefore, the armed conflict reached a situation of strategic stalemate. The CPN (M) defeated the Nepal Army in many individual armed fights, but it was not able to defeat the state on their own. Hence, they sought to defeat the king and his army in a concerted arrangement. For that, they not only changed their strategy but they also ideologically shifted their aims of a totalitarian government and a centrally controlled political system and opted for a more competitive multi-party political system.

Therefore, the decision of CPN (M) and the SPA was based on the 'necessity and compulsion' of circumstances created by the king. It was the king and his autocratic government, which were primarily responsible for bringing these two opposing forces together and for reaching the 12-point understanding which laid the foundations for the *Janaandolon* II. In the modern history of Nepal, significant political changes have taken place in the last two years: the April 2006 popular uprising being the most important one. The *Janaandolon* II also brought the ten years of armed conflict to the final stage of negotiated settlement.

1.3.4 CPN (M) and *Jananadolon* II

After serious discussions, the CPN (M) and the SPA leaders reached an agreement in New Delhi on 19 March 2006 and agreed to coordinate their plan for a nationwide general strike during 6-9 April[24]. CPN (M) not only declared a unilateral ceasefire on 3rd April 2006 and called halt to all offensive operations by it in the district headquarters and in the Kathmandu valley, but also lifted the indefinite transportation blockade they had imposed on Kathmandu in the previous weeks.[25] These steps were necessary for making the people's movement successful.

Once the SPA and the CPN (M) agreed to hold the constituent assembly elections, restructure the state, and to decide the fate of the monarchy by the constituent assembly meeting, public support for the movement suddenly increased and the masses came out on to the streets. CPN (M) leader Prachanda issued several statements against the royal takeover and expressed his commitment to support the political parties to restore democracy. Senior CPN (M) leaders and SPA leaders visited New Delhi to discuss the modalities of collaboration to fight against the royal takeover. They discussed the issue with various Indian politicians. In October, SPA gave a mandate to Madhav Nepal and Girija Prasad Koirala to hold talks with the CPN (M). After a series of discussions and meetings,[26] they agreed to a 12-point understanding. The CPN (M) declared a unilateral ceasefire for three months on September 3rd, 2006, and promised that it was a step forward with the political parties in political collaboration. This ceasefire was a very strategic choice of the CPN (M) because:

- They gave the message across the world that they wanted peace and an end to political conflict,
- They made the King's position difficult in winning international support on the mere ground of controlling terrorism. The king had planned to attend the UN General Assembly where he could strongly put his case to justify the royal takeover as a step to combat terrorism. When the CPN (M) declared a

ceasefire, the king faced an awkward situation. He had to justify his takeover in the UN as a move for peace in Nepal but if his government would not reciprocate the ceasefire, how could his steps (royal takeover) be justified? This raised serious questions about the intention of the king. Obviously, his intention was not to restore peace and he therefore did not reciprocate the ceasefire. All this led him to cancel his plan to address the UN General Assembly in September 2005.

- CPN (M) also gathered more sympathy from the Nepalese people and the international community because of their unilateral ceasefire.
- Pressure mounted on the king's government both domestically and internationally for reciprocating the ceasefire.,
- In between, the CPN (M) could organize political programmes, train their cadres and fighters, and accomplish organizational activities, such as meetings and conventions, training and orientations, expansion of public relations, etc.

During the king's direct rule, CPN (M) made strategic moves, demonstrating to the Nepalese people and the international community that their side was genuinely committed to peace, willing to collaborate with political parties, and accepted multi-party democracy, and respect for the rule of law and human rights. But they kept on pressurizing the army and the King. In collaboration with the SPA, they foiled all bids for local election, which the King intended to launch to show his commitment to democracy. The CPN (M) had earlier declared a national strike in the first week of April, but later withdrew it to make the 5-day protest organized by the SPA successful. Further, the CPN (M) sent laarge number of people from rural areas to the cities and town centre to hold mass rallies and protests; they publicly supported the general strike and mobilized their forces to make the protest successful. Thus the CPN (M) contributed substantially and procedurally to make the *Janaandolon* II successful. Ten years of CPN (M) armed conflict and the 12-point understanding laid the foundation for the success of the *Janaandolon* II.

1.3.5 Seven-Party Alliance and *Jananadolon* II

The SPA was the leading force of the *Janaandolon* II. As mentioned earlier, the credibility of the political parties had been eroded, and people were frustrated with them for their failure to bring about peace, and give them good governance. Soon after the royal takeover, however, people realized the importance of the role of political parties. The king's rule failed to address the expectations of the people in establishing peace, controlling corruption, and in stopping abuses of state power and resources by the government personnel. Instead, corruption increased manifold, insecurity reached a peak in the history of Nepal, resources and power of the state were blatantly abused by government official and ministers .The King's poor performance helped political parties to gradually regain the confidence of the people.

The role of SPA during the nineteen days of *Janaandolon* II was quite noteworthy, in which primarily the youth leaders of political parties played an important role in making a success of the movement. The SPA initiated the movement and later a spontaneous participation of the mass followed. SPA leaders publicly acknowledged this fact by saying that the *'movement from now onward is in people's hand'*.[27] Local coordinator of the Mass Movement Coordination Committee in Kathmandu said, *'even if the seven parties accept the king's offer, we are in no way going to compromise...the people will choose their leader'*. Most SPA leaders were not that active in the people's movement, but they showed their political maturity by not surrendering to the wishes of the King.

The Royal takeover was a serious blow to the political parties. The main leaders of the political parties were detained, arrested or jailed. The SPA leaders viewed these moves by the king as a strategy to weaken the resolve of the political parties. This motivated the political parties even more to unite to fight against the King's takeover and reinstate democracy in the country. They signed a six-point programme that called for the restoration of the House of Representatives as an entry point and the elections to the constituent assembly as an exit point for resolving the ongoing conflict. Some political parties even changed their position on the constitutional monarchy, opting for a republican political set-up.

The SPA had boycotted the municipal election arranged held by the royal government in February 2006. They tried to get more international support to their cause. Leaders of the main political parties[28] visited India and discussed Nepal's political crisis with the Indian government, the Indian political leaders as well as CPN (M) leaders. On 16 November 2005, CPN-UML leaders Madhav Kumar Nepal and Khadga Prasad Oli suddenly flew to New Delhi, only 5 days after their return from India. The Indian Ambassador met Madhav K. Nepal the same day before departing for New Delhi. Girija Prasad Koirala too was in New Delhi for a week. The Indian Ambassador also flew to New Delhi on the same day. CPN (M) leaders were already in New Delhi. The CPN (M) and the SPA leaders held several rounds of talks and Indian politicians helped in coordinating these meetings. As a result, the historic 12-point agreement comes into being.

The Delhi meeting and consultation of SPA prepared a roadmap[29] called 'the declaration for a united effort to resolve the national crisis', making the following provisions:

1. Take up the democratic road and not the one leading to extremism,
2. Today's need is to do away with the King's autocratic rule,
3. Reinstatement of the parliament for a people's representative government,
4. Some important points mentioned to resolve the national crisis were:
   a. The government shall be responsible to the parliament,
   b. Conflict management and reinstatement of peace,
   c. Commitment toward the future progressive programmes,,
   d. Constitution shall adhere to the norms and values of liberal multiparty democracy ,
   e. Progressive political movements to be based on the constitution of 1990,
   f. Plans to hold national elections.

This roadmap of the SPA laid the basis for reaching the 12-point understanding between the CPN (M) and the SPA later.

The SPA formed a Joint People's Movement Central Coordination Committee to organize and coordinate the people's movement and passed a resolution on 13th March to organize a 'Let's Go to Kathmandu' campaign to affect the 6-9 April national strike successful.[30] Youths, students and trade union wings of SPA played a crucial role in making the non-violent people's movement successful.

1.4.6 Civil Society and *Jananadolon* II

Immediately after the royal takeover, the civil society became active in organizing rallies, debates, discussions that provided a strong support to the SPA cause to fight against the cessation of democracy. Initiatives taken by the civil society to promote the people's movement for democracy encouraged the political parties gain confidence and win back the lost trust with the people. The civil society for the first time defied the curfew with a march from the Teaching Hospital, one of the coordination centres for the mass protest, and came out on the street despite the 'shoot-at-sight' order.

Human rights groups and professional organizations such as the associations of journalists, lawyers, medical practitioners, actors, engineers; students unions, university teachers and labourers; writers and poets, guild, artists, and private sector media houses all got active in protest of the royal takeover. Specialized associations such as the Federation of Community Forestry Users in Nepal, Nepal Poultry Entrepreneurs' Forum, Nepal Hotel Workers' Association, Nepal Chartered Accountant Association, Airline Operators Association, Forest Technicians Association, National Dalit Rights Forum, Indigenous Peoples Peace Commission, the Sociological and Anthropological Society of Nepal, Maithili Federation, Loktantrik Newa Struggle Committee, and National Disabled Federation also backed the people's movement. Civil society initiative was also supported by international organizations and networks, such as The UN High Commission on Human Rights, the Amnesty International, The International Commission of Jurists, The

Human Rights Watch, The International Federation of Journalists, Reporters without Borders, The World Association of Newspapers, The World Editors' Forum,[31] etc. The Civil society mobilized hundreds of thousands of people not only in the Kathmandu Valley, but also in small cities, towns, urban areas and villages across the country. In terms of keeping anti-regression movement going in the face of a heavy handed suppression, human rights groups, lawyers and journalists all played a crucial role.[32]

The contribution of the civil society to successfully accomplish the people's movement was acknowledged and appreciated by political leaders. This was reflected in the formation of a 5-member Peace Talks Observation Team (to which 5 prominent leaders of the civil society were selected) and a 31-member National Code of Conduct Monitoring Committee by the negotiation team composed of CPN (M) and the government on 15th June 2006. On top of it, CPN (M) proposed to allot 33 per cent seats to the civil society in their nomination to the interim parliament.[33] Sadly, however, the prestige accorded to many of the civil society leaders by nominating them to positions of responsibility has been eroded, making them a baseless and opportunistic group of people having no roots among the grass roots.

1.4.7 Nepali People in the *Jananadolon* II

The expectations of the Nepalese people had risen quite high because of the regime change from an autocratic system to one of a multiparty parliamentary democratic system in 1990, with commitments of political leaders to readdress the people's sufferings. But these assurances were systematically denied them not only by the previous regime, but also by the political parties who came riding the waves of political change. They completely ignored their commitment made to the Nepalese people during the time of the 1990s' movement. Hence, people were frustrated and alienated by them. The King used this frustration of the people to play against political parties, and staged his coup. He made a promise to fulfil major expectations of the Nepalese people, restore peace and security, control corruption, maintain law and order, achieve national unity and prevent the nation from further deterioration. However, his actions and behaviour in the 15 months of royal rule proved to be just the opposite of his public reiterations. The king did not make any attempt to resolve the CPN (M) armed conflict. Rather, he used the opportunity as a means to hold on to power. Nepalese people soon came to realize that the king's direct rule was even more harmful to people and the country. Therefore, they lent their full weight to the *Janaandolon* II. One uppermost concern of the April mass movement was restoration of peace in the country. Women, disabled persons, children, elderly, farmers, street vendors, and even rickshaw pullers actively took part in the peaceful mass protest. It was estimated that more than 16 million people came out on the streets across the country.

1.4.8 The King's Government in the *Jananadolon* II

The king was in no mood to compromise with the SPA during the early days of the movement. He was neither interested in listening to the SPA and CPN (M) nor ready to listen to the international community and the civil society. Rather, he made unsuccessful attempts repeatedly to convince the international community to help him fight terrorism in Nepal. This becomes clear from his address to the SAARC Summit at Dhaka on 12 November 2005. He said, *"It is ironical to note that the global war on terrorism is not matched by global action against it. The global war on terrorism has failed to reach every nook and corner of the world, especially in weak and vulnerable countries, as if they do not deserve justice and protection from terrorism. It is this double standard and selective approach that is assuming a dangerous character rather than terrorism itself. We cannot make a distinction between good and bad terrorism; terrorism is terrorism. In our region, the Declaration of the 11th SAARC Summit held in Kathmandu categorically stated that "terrorism, in all its forms and manifestations, is a challenge to all states and to all of humanity, and cannot be justified on ideological, political, religious or any other ground". We agreed that "terrorism violates the fundamental values of the United Nations and the SAARC Charter and constitutes one of the most serious threats to international peace and security in the Twenty-first century". Nepal has ratified the SAARC Convention on Suppression of Terrorism and its Additional Protocol with the belief that these instruments provide an effective tool to counter terrorism in the region. We call upon the SAARC member states to forge a strong partnership to eliminate terrorism from the region as well as spearhead a coordinated and earnest action against it"*. His heavily worded statement was a clear message to the international community that he was fighting terrorists and the SAARC countries should not criticize for his war on 'terrorism'. His statement in the SAARC Summit was in essence a response to the demand made by the international community to hand over power to political parties.

Interestingly, the King had nominated his cabinet members who were notorious figures in the autocratic panchayat regime (this time also, all political parties remained banned) with a track record of crime, human rights violation, rape, corruption, hooliganism and default on bank loan behind them.[34] None of them had democratic credentials and a commitment to multi-party democracy. Therefore, all their efforts were concentrated on reviving all but the old autocratic panchayat regime. Hence, under the direct guidance of the king, the cabinet members made systematic efforts to dismantle all the democratic institutions one by one, evolved during the 12-13 years of multi-party political rule earlier. The king's government had issued more than 6 dozens of ordinances to strengthen the King's autocratic rule.

The ministers in the autocratic government of the king made every effort to get the political parties to surrender themselves before with the king. They treated progressive democratic forces as supporters of the CPN (M). The actions and behaviour of the ministers and of the king's coterie thus widened the gap between the progressive political forces and the palace that contributed to materialize the *Janaandolon* II.

As the king took a very regressive path, he was unable to find enough capable people to accomplish the important state tasks such as those of ambassadors, ministers, planners, analysts and strategists, security and political advisors. He did not trust capable and honest people who had earlier served in the autocratic panchayat regime. He had to fully rely on incapable persons with regressive attitudes. Their main role during the 15 months of autocratic rule was to widen the gap further between the palace and the political activists, suppress human rights activists, journalists and political parties, and to wipe out the CPN (M) cadres. These acted as some contributing factors to unite people for the *Janaandolon* II.

The King similarly made unsuccessful attempts to use religion in strengthening his power. He had mobilized radical extremists and the orthodox Hindu clerics, and had hired people working under the banners of Hindu religion to oppose progressive political forces, which only back fired.

The hard-line royalists moves helped to widen the gap between the king and the political parties and that contributed to the birth of the idea of republicanism. A former Chief of the army staff, who was said to be one of the close advisors to the King, had publicly asked the government to declare political parties as anti-nationalists force. The then Vice-Chairman of the Cabinet, Dr Tulsi Giri clearly said that monarchy and democracy in Nepal cannot go together and therefore Nepalese people should either choose monarchy or democracy (Upreti, 2006a). In a television interview he further said that sovereignty cannot originate from two sources, it should only be with the king, not with the people, judging from past experiences. It is unlikely that he could speak on such a fundamental issue without the consent of the king.[35] This meant that the King was not ready to give up power yet and was not interested in holding talks with the political parties. It is because of these factors that Nepal's politics is headed toward a republican system.

The CPN (M) demand for a republican system is gradually progressing. The CPN-UML has decided to go in for a republican political system. Similarly, the Nepali Congress, another big party and a past supporter of the idea of constitutional monarchy, has changed its stance by removing the provision of a constitutional monarchy from its party constitution. Other leftist political parties had been already in favour of a republican system. Youths, intellectuals, and the civil society members are increasingly aligned to the republican idea. In this way, influential forces in Nepal, which had defended the constitutional monarchy earlier, are now asking for a republican political set-up. Thus, the 1st February move by the king paved the way for the termination of the life of the monarchy in Nepal.

The security forces were also abused grossly in suppressing the *Janaandolon* II. The movement was suppressed by the Unified Command under the leadership of the then Chief of the then Royal Nepal Army, who was leading the fight against CPN (M) insurgency. The army had created a special valley command to suppress the people's movement in the Kathmandu Valley. Similarly, a core team composed of the Army Chief, the Home Minister and the palace representative was made responsible for the mobilization of this security forces and in foiling the people's movement. The army and the armed police used force excessively. The army used air patrolling by flying helicopters over rallies and demonstrations to create fear. Tanks and army vehicles were moving on the streets of Kathmandu Valley and in areas of mass rallies. When security forces unleashed brutal suppression against the people, national and international media had vehemently criticized the security forces. Nepalese people came out even in greater numbers than ever to protest the use of force. Twenty-five demonstrators were killed. Many of them were deliberately shot to death. Security forces shot at the demonstrators on the orders of their higher authorities (core team and valley command) .So they did not bother to take any precautionary measures. The use of excessive force thus became counter-productive in effect and millions of people came out on to the streets to oppose the brutalization even more in number.

Security forces on the ground were also facing other serious dilemma. On one side, their own family members ('wives of security personnel', 'family members of the security forces') not only came out in protest on the streets and participated in mass demonstrations, they also issued statements asking their husbands and sons to stop shooting at the rally. On the other side, their seniors in command were ordering them to shoot.

1.4.9 International Communities and *Jananadolon* II

The role of the international community during the royal regime had been largely favourable and supportive of the people's resistance movement since most of the international members were not happy with the takeover of 1st February 2005. However, their role in the eyes of Nepalese people seemed suddenly suspicious as envoys of the USA, France, Sweden, the UK, Germany and Finland rushed to the residence of SPA senior leader Girija Prasad Koirala (where SPA leaders were having a special meeting) and wanted to exert pressure on the SPA to accept the king's offer of 21st April 2006. However, this offer amounted to nothing less than legitimizing the king's rule and accepting him as the custodian of the constitution and the protector of the national interests and institutionalizing monarchy in the future also. Hence, hundreds of thousands of protestors reached the venue of the meeting and warned the SPA leaders not to make any compromises and keep the people's movement going.

On the other side, Finish Charge de Affairs Mr Pauli Mustonen[36] (who was also the local chair of EU at that time), said, *'Many EU countries have welcomed the king's proclamation of 21 April and the EU is monitoring the situation'*. Similarly, the then British Ambassador Keith Bloomfield said *'it could be a basis to move ahead but parties do not accept it.*[37] *.The* EU issued a statement saying that the royal proclamation is an opportunity for parties to move ahead. Similar supports to the king were coming from China, Canada, and the UN welcoming the Royal proclamation. But, the SPA leaders in the end took the side of the Nepalese people and did not listen to what the foreign diplomats had to say. India changed its position at once and its foreign secretary Shyam Sharan said the next day (22nd April 2006) that the king's address of 21st April was not sufficient to solve the ongoing political problem.

Some of the international non-governmental organizations had also expressed their solidarity with the demonstrators. The Alliance of INGO even came on to the streets to express their solidarity and to protest against the human rights violation during the *Janaandolon* II. Many senior Nepalese staff working in the INGOs and donor organizations got actively involved in the *Janaandolon* II in their individual capacity.

There was thus a good synergy from concerted efforts of the local and global civil society organizations in making the people's movement a success. The critical position of influential global organizations against the king and support for people's struggle almost paralyzed the royal government. A few days before the surrender by the king, The Amnesty International, The Human Rights Watch and The International Commission of Jurists called for a travel ban on the king, the army officers and his senior advisors and aides for travelling in foreign countries, which placed the king in an extremely difficult situation. In a meeting organized by the Swiss government in Geneva, these three international organizations also suggested freezing the assets kept in foreign countries of any person(s) associated with the royal regime.[38] The same meeting also discussed 'targeted' and 'smart sanction' against the king and his aides. When the king's brutality against peaceful demonstrators was escalated from the 6th of April 2006, bilateral countries and inter-governmental organizations became even more vocal in opposing the suppression.

Since the morning of 24th April 2006, a series of meetings was held by the key international players (Ambassadors of USA, India, Norway and few other diplomats), representatives of the Palace and the leaders of CPN (UML) with the NC. The main agenda of these meetings was how to peacefully end the movement. The Palace, through the diplomats offered to negotiate with the leaders and expressed its willingness to accept the roadmap of the SPA. Diplomats conveyed this missive of the King to the leaders of the political parties, and in response, a positive message was conveyed back by the political parties to the Principal Secretary of the King, Mr Pashupati Bhakta Maharjan. Next, the Principal Secretary of the Palace visited Girija Prasad Koirala and Madhav Nepal individually and informed the willingness of the king to accept the SPA roadmap. Restoration of the Parliament was the main demand of the Nepali Congress, therefore it at once agreed to the King's offer. Likewise, UML leaders were also convinced by the King's willingness to accept the SPA roadmap. Finally, a few selected leaders of NC, UML, and the Principal Secretary of the King (and some diplomats working behind the scene) drafted the text to be read by the king in the evening. The king's speech was broadcasted on Nepal Television. In this way, the 19-day peaceful[39] movement was ended. If this movement had been extended for another one or two days, the king would have been overthrown. However, the priority of SPA seemed to be to force the king to accept SPA roadmap, instead of ending the monarchy. Therefore, the negotiation that followed between the SPA leaders and Palace was a logical sequel despite the vehement opposition to it from the CPN (M) who wanted to use the movement to end the monarchy immediately from this country. It is also widely speculated that an understanding between the political leaders of the NC and the representative of the king was reached to keep the constitutional monarchy in some form once the king agreed to the SPA roadmap. This became obvious from the fact that the restored Parliament reduced the role of the king but continued to recognize its existence .The government allocated a huge amount of the country's budget to pay allowance to the King and his immediate family members. Many analysts and people close to the Prime Minister indicate that the frequent expression of Prime Minister G.P Koirala about the need for a 'ceremonial king' or 'baby king' was a reflection of this hidden understanding between the SPA and the King. However, the situation emerged in such a way that no one could save the monarchy.

1.4.10 *Jananadolon* II and Downfall of the Royal Dynasty

The 10 years of republican campaign led by the CPN (M) on the one side, and the behaviour of the reigning king, his son and his close allies on the other contributed to the end of the royal dynasty. After the royal takeover of 1st February 2005, major parties supporting constitutional monarchy such as the CPN (UML) have decided to opt for a republican political system, and the Nepali Congress, the other big party of the SPA, too has deleted the clause of the constitutional monarchy from its party constitution. The youth, ethnic communities, *dalit* communities, intellectuals, scholars, journalists, and young politicians have all been overwhelmingly demanding for a republican political set-up in the country. Even those who used to support the king and the active monarchy in the past had changed their positions. Those who wanted to retain monarchy in this country mainstreamed in the wave of republicanism in Nepal. The Constituent Assembly finally ended the centuries-old monarchy of Nepal.[40]

Based on the experiences of a 19-day-long people's peaceful resistance movement, I argue that the conventional concept of civil society needs to be redefined, based on the potential of civil movement in changing the political system and shaping the future of the nation-state. From the experiences of Nepal, it can be concluded that the non-violent resistance movement has great prospects of settling conflict and building peace.

As explained in the theory of conflict transformation through non-violence (Wehr et al., 1994; Clark 2000), the *Jananadolon* II of Nepal has succeeded in transforming an autocratic and feudal regime. Non-violent resistance movements can transform conflict by detaching it from the use of force or coercion and through exercise of tolerance by harnessing conciliation, through promotion of co-operation and through use of other peaceful alternatives. The major actors of the *Jananadolon* II demonstrated possession of these characteristics while fighting the army, state power and resources in a peaceful manner. Nepal's experience highlights that *Jananadolon* II takes origin from below and contributed to the downfall of dictators and autocrats.

The Nepalese experience of *Jananadolon* II has confirmed that the success of resistance depends upon certain complementary elements. These were: a unity of purpose; a broad-based, non-violent and disciplined home-grown movement participated by all concerned stakeholders, organizations, the media, support from national and international organization, and through use of a host of other tactics, such as strikes, demonstrations, boycotts, street speeches and street drama. Therefore, 'people's power is a form of consciousness', and is 'about restoring the invisible institution of morality' (Ackerman and Duvall, 2005:42) in the process of transformation of a state.

Summary of the characteristics of the *Jananadolon* II of April 2006:

- It often remained non-violent in nature.
- It first started as people were suppressed with violence by the repressive regime.
- It was of a relatively shorter duration, lasting just 19 days, but the results were radical and the output obvious.
- It emerged from an unique combination of frustration, alienation and a hope for the future.
- It had put faith in mass action and mass movement, motivating maximum people for participation in the resistance.
- It resulted in a regime change and the same happened in this instance as well.
- Convictions and ideologies, values and commitments of people were the basis of resistance.
- It focused on the peaceful protest against the adversary, resulting in a moral defeat of the resisting force.
- It opened space for a radical socio-political transformation.;
- The repressive action and behaviour of the rulers provided necessary conditions for its success.

1.5 POST-*JANAANDOLAN* II: THE PATH TO THE REPUBLIC

The successful *Janaandolan* II created a conducive environment for signing of the Comprehensive Peace Agreement (CPA) that opened the path to the republic. The government and the CPN (M) jointly (with identical letters) invited the United Nations Mission in Nepal (UNMIN)[41] to assist in Nepal's peace process. This step gave the external legitimacy and created a favourable environment internationally. Agreement on Management of Arms and Armies between the CPN (M) and the government was another milestone of the peace process. Promulgation of the Interim Constitution constitutionalised several provisions of the CPA and finally provided a legal framework for the implementation of the CPA. The Interim Legislative Parliament became instrumental in legalising and institutionalising the elements of the peace process. The Interim Government was formed including former rebels. UNMIN completed the verification process[42] of the 'people's liberation army' (PLA) by a Joint Monitoring Coordinating Committee[43] composed of the representative of the Nepal army, PLA and UNMIN. This was a technically fundamental step in strengthening the peace process. The Nepal army and PLA demonstrated their full commitment to peace process and fully cooperated in the process as per the provisions stated in the Agreement on Management of Arms and Armies. Further, the interim government reached agreements with Madeshis, Janajaties and other concerned stakeholders on various issues which had emerged one time as severe threats to peace process. Similarly, the government and the Election Commission successfully completed the highly awaited and frequently postponed election of the Constituent Assembly (CA), where CPN (M) emerged as the largest party. On 28th May 2008, the first meeting of the CA declared Nepal a 'Democratic Republic'. The suspended king accepted the decision of the CA and moved from the Narayanhiti Palace to a building provided by the government and lived there as an ordinary citizen.

1.6 POST-CPA PROGRESS

The high-level committee of the seniormost leaders of eight political parties (now seven parties after the merger of two factions of Nepal Congress Party) is so far the supreme decision-making body to deal with the political process and the country is operating on the decision of this committee. All agreements and understandings are the product of this supreme mechanism.

By the proclamation of the House of Representatives in May 2006, the power of the king was stripped, he was removed from his position of Supreme Commander of the Army and the Prime

Minister was assigned the position of head of state and Nepal was declared a secular nation. The HoR proclamation regarding the executive issues of Nepal stated, "*(2.1) All the executive rights of Nepal as a state shall rest on the Council of Ministers; 'His Majesty's Government' shall be termed 'Government of Nepal' from now onwards. (2.2) Persons who are not the members of the House of Representatives can also be nominated in the Council of Ministers; (2.3) The Council of Ministers shall be responsible towards the House of Representatives. The Council of Ministersand the ministers collectively and for the works of their ministries shall be personally responsible towards the House of Representatives. The administration, army, police and all the executive organs shall be under the purview of the government that is responsible towards the House of Representatives. (2.4) The allocation and transaction of business of the government shall be presented at the House of Representatives after its passage from the council of ministers*". Similarly, regarding the army, it wrote, "*(3.1) The name "Royal Nepal Army" shall be changed to "Nepalese Army", (3.2) The Existing provision regarding the National Security Council has been repealed. There shall be a National Security Council under the chairmanship of the Prime Minister in order to control, use and mobilize the Nepalese Army, (3.3) Chief of the Army Staff of the Nepalese Army shall be appointed by the Council of Ministers, (3.4) The existing arrangement of Supreme Commander of the Army has been revoked*". On the issue of royal palace, the proclamation stated, "*(5.1) The right to make laws, amend and nullify regarding the succession to throne shall rest on the House of Representatives; (5.2) Expenditure and facilities for His Majesty the King shall be as per the decision of the House of Representatives, (5.3) The private property and income of His Majesty the King shall be taxed as per the law; (5.4) Acts performed by His Majesty the King are questionable in the House of Representatives or in court; (5.5) Existing Royal Palace Service shall be made part of the civil service; (5.6) The security arrangement for the Royal Palace shall be as per the arrangement made by the Council of Ministers*". These were fundamental arrangements towards paving path to republican system.

The Ministry of Peace and Reconstruction (MoPR) was created to deal with the policy, strategy and programmes related to conflict transformation and promotion of lasting peace in the country. A Consultation Committee on Peace and Rehabilitation was formed under the convenorship of Minister of Peace and Reconstruction representing a wide spectrum of society to advise MoPR on policy, strategy and programmes. The MoPR has also established an Advisory Committee to get technical advice in the peace process, and a High-Level Monitoring Committee (representing senior leaders of civil society). However, effectiveness of these committees is yet to be observed.

The 5622nd Meeting of the Security Council had established UNMIN by unanimously adopting the resolution 1740 (23rd January 2007) as per the request of the Government of Nepal and the CPN (M). Its mandate is to monitor the ceasefire and assist in the election of a Constituent Assembly, monitoring the management of arms and armed personnel of both sides through a Joint Monitoring Coordinating Committee.[44]

A joint committee represented by Nepal Army, PLA and UNMIN under the convenership of the UNMIN security expert is working for the management of cantonments and verification process. Similarly, a technical committee is formed to deal with landmines-related issues and problems.

Government of Nepal has started to establish the Local Peace Committee (LPC), which has the task of promoting peace and reconciliation at the district level. Therefore, LPC is potentially a crucial arrangement to help local people to overcome difference, to find collective solutions and to make sure that local people work together to build a new future. LPC is an important mechanism to implement the CPA in the district. If implemented properly, LPC will greatly contribute in achieving reconciliation and social and political reintegration. However, effectiveness of LPC entirely depends upon the process. If it is not imposed from top, well represented by local actors and allowed to work independently without interference and support from political parties and civil society, it wiill work.

The MoPR has also drafted the bill for Truth and Reconciliation Commission and invited comments from civil society, human rights communities and legal experts. However, for a long time this urgent bill is not moving ahead. It is a crucially important and appropriate time for the establishment of TRC.

Similarly, the government also formed a committee on the issue of disappearance but not much progress has been made so far. The Ministry has also conducted a series of talks with Nepal Federation of Indigenous Nationalities (NEFEN), Chure Bhabar Ekata Samaj, Madeshi Janaadhikar Forum and reached to some agreements. However, these organisations are asking for the sincere implementation of the agreed issues by the government. The MoPR has also developed a Policy for IDPs and now a 'Co-existence Settlement Programme' for IDPs is started[45] but the effectiveness is yet to be seen.

The government, with the help of different donor agencies, has also established a Peace Trust Fund to deal with the peace-related issues such as addressing issues of IDPs and conflict victims, rehabilitation and reconstruction. However, the effectiveness of this fund is yet to be realised. A similar fund has been established by UNDP to help the peace process.

International human rights provisions reflected in the CPA and provisions of the Interim Constitution such as killings, kidnappings, abductions, etc. are so far not fully respected. According to the NHCR, the human rights violations are continued even after the signing of CPA and insecurity is mounting across the country.

The 28th of May 2008 was an important day in the history of Nepal because the newly elected Constituent Assembly as per the provision of the Interim Constitution in its very first seating declared Nepal a Federal Democratic Republic by abolishing the centuries-old institution of monarchy and King Gyanendera became the last, 13th king. In the voting for the decision, 560 CA members from the total of 564 members were present in the meeting. Only 4 royalist CA members had voted against the motion. The Constituent Assembly gave 15 days' time for the newly abolished king to leave the palace. As a result, he left the palace on 11th June, with issuing a statement. It reads:

"Dear Nepalese brothers and sisters,

This country which came into being 240 years back as a garden of four castes and thirty-six sub castes as imagined and established by our ancestor His Majesty, the Great King Prithvi Narayan Shah, is going through a period of very serious and sensitive upheaval. It is well known that the Nepalese Monarchy which has always been activised for people's prosperity and progress has always been working together and cooperating with the happiness and woes of Nepali people. Burning examples of that are unification, preservation of nationalism, democratisation and modernisation through the united effort of the king and national integrity as equivalent to the value of our lives. Our committed energised feelings towards these values and standards have remained constant from the past and are equally strong in the present and will remain so in the future.

I would like to inform everybody concerned that when seven years back because of an unnatural, unexpected and tragic incident while shouldering the responsibility of the Head of the State according to the national heritage and ages of old monarchical traditions, I had no other interests except considerations for the sovereignty, independence, national pride, territorial integrity, peace and the institutional development of democracy, and overall progress of all the citizens. In the then Hindu kingdom of Nepal, the birthplace of Buddha the efforts started, with the best of intention trying to ensure the peace and prosperity in the country were not successful over time, which I have already accepted earlier. The chain of events and ensuing results are obvious to everybody like an open book.

I would like to express, with God as my witness, certain things which I couldn't express earlier because of my official responsibilities but which was troubling my inner heart all the time, through you dear journalist friends to my Nepalese brothers and sisters and the international community. May be we should call it destiny that when I was innocent child, I had neither any wish nor desire nor any possibility of having a distinct role except the compulsion to have to quietly accept the crown. Likewise, for the second time when an unimaginable and horrifying event took place on the night of Jestha 19th, 2058, I could not express through word my internal pain when I was compelled and tied up by the chains of tradition and duty without being even able to shed tears over the mortal remains of those respected and beloved family members and lighten the burden of pain at the gruesome destruction of my close relatives. Even at that time some people blamed and accused me and my family with great indiscretion and cruelty but we had no alternative but to tolerate that too, nor were there people who spoke on our behalf. Being prejudiced against me and my family members the efforts which were continuously started through different means by taking advantage of those circumstances and events, have been very painful to us and are still so. Other members of the Royal Family who were wounded but survived the incident in the Royal Palace are still alive. They are also witness to it. The bullet fragments which couldn't be taken out for technical reasons are still in the body of my wife who was also wounded and survived. The detailed facts had also come out from the medical doctors involved in their treatment. The high level Royal Investigation Commission had already made public the detailed report about the incident. When all the Nepalese people and the Royal Family were overwhelmed with grief, at that time, to level accusations and blame in this way seems to be a strategy to damage the goodwill of the Nepalese people towards the institution of Monarchy and to spread ill will, which was also not compatible with human suffering.

Likewise, I have also heard false rumours about allegations that I have property abroad. All my property is in Nepal. I have no movable or immovable property in foreign lands. The property which had been bequeathed to me from my ancestors, according to Nepalese laws is also not in my name and I have institutionalised it maintaining that property and have only conserved it. During the last seven years neither have I added any property nor have I taken any action by which the traditional property has been reduced. I have not also usurped the right to property of any member of the Royal Family. I believe that I would also have rights to maintain private property according to the prevalent laws of Nepal.

Respecting Constitutional Assembly elections and the decision taken by the constituent assembly meeting on Jestha 15th, I am cooperating in every way towards the successful implementation of that decision. I have also not thought of leaving the country. I would like to live in my own Motherland and contribute in whatever way possible to greater good of the country and peace in this land. I believe that there will be support for this from all sectors.

I pledge to be completely dedicated to the independence and territorial integrity of the nation of Nepal which was formed and has remained independent and sovereign because of the blood, sweat and sacrifice of the great ancestors of us Nepalese, wherever and whatever circumstances I may be in. I love the independence of this nation. My feelings and sentiments are that of sanctity, indivisibility and original values of this independent nation should always be preserved. My heartfelt good wishes are for the overall welfare of the self-respecting common Nepalese people.

Today, on this date, I have handed over the Crown and Sceptre used by the Kings of Shah dynasty and which has remained as heirloom in this dynasty to the Government of Nepal for safekeeping and protection for ages to come.

Finally, on behalf of my family members and myself, I would like to express my sorrow, if anybody has been inadvertently hurt by actions of my own or of the members of my family while I was working as head of State for the welfare of Nepal and the Nepalese. I would like to express gratitude to all citizens, constitutional organs, judicial sector, security organisations, civil servants, teachers, professors, students, farmers, labourers, industrialists, businessmen, intellectual youths, religious organisations, journalists, civil society, personnel working in the Royal Palace service and all others from different walks of life and all the other associated Nepalese inside and outside Nepal who extended their cooperation to me. I would also like to thank the friendly neighbouring countries who have always wished well for Nepal, the international community and representative of diplomatic corps. I would also like to thank the members of the Committees for Security and management recently deputed by the government of Nepal. I would like to thank the government of Nepal for all the help and cooperation extended to me. I also hope that like now, I would keep on getting the same level of necessary cooperation from the Government of Nepal in the future too.

May Lord Pashupatinath bless us all. Jaya Nepal.[46] "

This statement made great efforts to justify his political actions and showed several emotional and psychological dimensions as a human being.

While examining the efforts made by the state in the peace process, it is clearly observed they are not enough and much more can be done with the existing level of resources. Competencies are not accomplished mainly because of the divergences, differences and multiple interests at the political level. One of the main weaknesses at the political level is the lack of commitment to fulfil the written or unwritten promises made. The major gap exists at the political level especially in what has been said and what has been done. Hence, though some important initiatives have started at state level, they are not enough to make the peace process successful. Ensuring transitional security and transitional justice on one side and the sincere implementation of the agreements and understandings made in the past are crucial factors for making peace process successful, which is largely lacking at present.

1.7 A BRIEF CHRONOLOGY[47] FROM WAR TO PEACE 1996

- February 13: the CPN (M) began armed conflict to abolish monarchy and establish People's Republic.
- CPN (M) carried out minor attacks on police posts in the mid-western region.
- A soft-drink bottling factory owned by a multi-national company was attacked and a portion of the building torched in Kathmandu.
- A liquor factory blown up in Gorkha district.
- Office of the Small Farmer's Development Programme of the state-owned Agricultural Development Bank in Chyangli VDC Gorkah was attacked.
- A landlord's house was raided at night cash and other properties worth 1.3 million rupees seized, and loan documents worth several million rupees reportedly destroyed in Kavre district.
- One police outpost each raided in Rolpa, Rukum and Sindhuli districts. The store of the outpost at Holeri in

Rolpa seized. Athbiskot-Rari in Rukum was also raided. The Sindhuligadi police post in Sindhuli was attacked.

1997

- Power struggle within ruling Nepali Congress resulted in loss of no-confidence motion by the then Prime Minister Sher Bahadur Deuba resulted into political instability.

1998

- April: Prime Minister Girija Prasad Koirala calls for talks, but CPN (M) turn down the offer.

2000

- GP Koirala returns in power as 9th prime minister in 10 years.

2001

- January: The government formed the Armed Police Force (APF) to fight against the insurgents.
- June 1: Royal massacre - 9 members, including King Birendra, Queen Aishwarya, Crown Prince Dipendra and other close relatives were killed.
- June 4: Prince Gyanendra became King.
- July 27: Prime Minister GP Koirala replaced by Sher Bahadur Deuba.
- August 3: The first round of peace talks started.
- November 23: Peace talk failed and the CPN (M) end a four-month old truce with government and started coordinated attacks on army[48] and police posts in 42 districts.
- November 25: CPN (M) attacked army barrack in Salleri, Solukhumbu.
- November 26: State of emergency declared. King Gyanendra ordered army to crush the CPN (M).

2002

- January 18:US Secretary Colin Powel visited Nepal and committed military assistance
- February 17: CPN (M) raided Mangalsen, Accham where 123 people were killed.

- May 7: PM Deuba met US President.
- May: Parliament dissolved, political confrontation mounted on extending the state of emergency. Sher Bahadur Deuba renewed emergency.
- The United States Congress approved US$12 million to train Nepal Army and officers and supply 5,000 M-16 rifles.
- May 11: Army released the photographs of Maoist leaders Pushpa Kamal Dahal 'Prachanda', Dr Baburam Bhattarai, Hishila Yami, Ram Bahadur Thapa 'Badal', in western Nepal.
- May 22: Prime Minister Deuba dissolved parliament to thwart parliamentary opposition to the state of emergency and announces fresh elections.
- May 27: 100 PLAs of CPN (M) killed in Khara village of Rukum.
- July 11: Media reports disclosed that Belgian arms manufacturer FN Herstal is given contract to provide 5,500 M249 'Minimi' rifles to the Nepal army.
- August 12: Interpol issued red corner notice to CPN (M) leaders.
- October 4: King Gyanendra deposess Prime Minister Deuba and the Council of Ministers, assumes executive power, and cancels the elections to the dissolved House of Representatives, which had been scheduled for November 11.
- October 11: King Gyanendra appoints Lokendra Bahadur Chand as new Prime Minister.

2003

- January: Rebels, government declare ceasefire.
- May: PM Lokendra Bahadur Chand resigns.
- June: Surya Bahadur Thapa appointed.
- August: CPN (M) pull out from the peace talks with government and seven-month long ceasefire ended.
- January: The United States military officials conducted a joint drill with the Nepal army.
- January: CPN (M) gun down Armed Police Force Inspector General Krishna Mohan Shrestha, his wife

Nudup and his bodyguard when they were on their morning walk near Jawalakhel, Lalitpur.

- January 29: A second ceasefire announced and peace talks begin.
- May 13: Government and the CPN (M) signed ceasefire code of conduct.
- August 17: RNA killed 19 rebels and civilians in Doramba, Ramechhap district, when the talk process was on.
- August 24: The CPN (M) threatened to withdraw the ceasefire if the government fails to agree on the demand for a Constituent Assembly within 48 hours.
- August 26: Maoist ultimatum expired.
- August 27: The rebels called for a daylong strike to denounce the army attacks on their cadre in Doramba. The rebels unilaterally withdrew ceasefire. Prachanda issued a statement: *"Since the old regime has put an end to the forward-looking solution to all existing problems through the ceasefire and peace talks, we herein declare that the rationale behind the ceasefire and peace process has ended."*
- September 27: Twelve CPN (M) fighters died in a gun battle with security forces at Chhita Pokhara in Khotang district. The CPN (M) killed two policemen in the Jaljale-Gaighat area. The rebels bomb Road Department and the Nepal Electricity Authority and a telecommunications tower.
- October 13: At least 37 people died when an estimated 1,000 CPN (M) cadres storm a police training centre in Bhaluwang.
- November 19: Four CPN (M) supporters were caught at the Chinese Khasa border point on charges of smuggling weapons from Tibet into Nepal.

2004

- May: Prime Minister Surya Bahadur Thapa resigned from street protests by opposition groups.
- June: King Gyanendra reappointed Sher Bahadur Deuba as prime minister.

- February 5: Security forces raid Bhimad village in Makwanpur district and 14 suspected Maoist activists and two civilians and summarily execute them.
- February 10: India handed over two central committee members of CPN (M) Matrika Yadav and Suresh Alemagar to the Nepal government, who were arrested in Lucknow, India.
- February 15: Ganesh Chilwal, leader of Maoist Victims Association, shot dead in his Kathmandu office by two suspected Maoits.
- February 15: Security forces encountered with CPN (M) fighters in the jungle of Kalikot district where 1,000 fighters were undergoing training.
- February 17: A private helicopter carrying troops to Kalikot was hit by Maoist fire but returns safely to Kathmandu.
- February 18: 65 were reportedly killed in the area, though the casualty remained sketchy. Lawmaker Khem Narayan Faujdar, a member of the parliament dissolved by King Gyanendra in 2002, shot dead by two suspected CPN (M) cadres in Nawalparasi district.
- April 4: CPN (M) attacked a police post in western Nepal, killing at least nine policemen at around 9 p.m. 35 police were reported missing with 9 dead and 7 wounded. 8 to 9 rebels were reported dead. The fighting lasted for two to three hours.
- April 5: A three-day national strike was called by the CPN (M) but it was opposed by an alliance of five political parties that were protesting against the monarchy in the capital. Prachanda then calls for a joint movement.
- August 16: CPN (M) carried out blast at the main gate of Soaltee Hotel for defying their call to close down the hotel.
- September 10: A bomb went off at the United States Information Service office in Kathmandu. No casualties.
- September 13: U.S. Peace Corps suspended operations and non-essential U.S. Embassy personnel were evacuated.

- December 15: Twenty security personnel died when the rebels raid Arghakhanchi district headquarters, Sandhikarkha.
- December 16: Sixteen CPN (M) fighters died in clashes with security forces in Dailekh district.
- December 23: CPN (M) announced blockade in Kathmandu.

2005

- January 8: CPN (M) detained and later release 300 passengers from six buses for defying their blockade of Kathmandu.
- January 10: Prime Minister Deuba announced increase in defence spending to fight the CPN (M) unless they come forward for talks with the government.
- February 1: King Gyanendra sacks Prime Minister Deuba, dissolves parliament and enforces curb on independent media, arrests senior political leaders, journalists, trade unionists, human rights activists and civil society leaders, cuts telephone and internet connections and resumes direct power, citing the need to defeat CPN (M).
- April 13: Sixty CPN (M) cadres died during clashes in an attack on a security patrol at Dalphing in Rukum district.
- April 19: Twenty-two insurgents and three soldiers died in clashes at Rankot and Ramja in Rolpa District.
- 30 April: King lifted the state of emergency.
- May 15: At least 50 CPN (M) cadres and two soldiers died during a clash at Jarayatar in the Sindhuli District.
- June 6: More than 38 civilians killed and over 70 injured after a packed passenger bus runs over a rebel ambush in Bandermude in Chitwan district.
- June 7: Fourteen security personnel, one civilian and six CPN (M) cadres died in a clash when hundreds of heavily armed CPN (M) fighters attack a security patrol at Masuriya jungle in Kailali District.
- June 25: Twelve soldiers and six insurgents die during a

Maoist attack on an army patrolling team at Khandaha in Arghakhanchi district.

- July 3: Twelve insurgents died and two police personnel sustained injuries in a Maoist attack in Diktel, headquarters of the Khotang District.
- August 7: The RNA recovers at least 40 bodies of its soldiers killed in a Maoist raid on the Pili base camp in Kalikot District. The Maoists also conceded the death of 26 cadres in the clash.
- August 9: Maoist rebels killed 40 security men in an attack in mid-western Nepal.
- September 3: The CPN (M) declared a three-month unilateral ceasefire in an attempt to forge ties with opposition political parties.
- November 19: After negotiations, the Maoist rebels agreed to work with opposition politicians as a common front against King Gyanendra's direct rule. A 12-point agreement is signed between the seven-party alliance and CPN (M) in New Delhi.
- 21 November: CPN (M) and Seven-Party Alliance reached a 12-point understanding to fight against the king and to restore democracy.

2006

- 24 April: King Gyanendra reinstated the dissolved parliament
- GP Koirala is appointed prime minister.
- CPN (M) called a three-month ceasefire.
- May: Parliament votes unanimously to curtail the king's political powers.
- The government and CPN (M) began peace talks.
- January 2: Rebels end four-month unilateral ceasefire, saying that the government had violated the ceasefire with numerous attacks.
- February 8: The royal government conducted municipal elections amidst widespread boycott.
- April 5: General strike begins along with CPN (M) blockades while they promised not to instigate violence.

- April 6, 7: Protesters clash with police, hundreds arrested, dozens injured.
- April 8: A curfew was imposed in Kathmandu from 10 p.m. to 9 a.m. The government led by King Gyanendra issued clamps shoot-on-site curfew in Kathmandu and several places around the country.
- April 9: General strike nears end. The government extended curfew. Three protesters died during two days of unrest, as thousands of demonstrators' defied curfews.
- April: 24: King relinquished power in the wake of a massive people's movement and reinstates House of Representatives.
- April 27: Maoist insurgents, responding to a demand by the newly named Prime Minister Girija Prasad Koirala announce a unilateral three-month truce.
- April 30: Koirala sworn in as prime minister. He invited CPN (M) for talks.
- 16 June: Talk between Prachanda and PM Koirala and SPA leaders to agree on power sharing arrangement in the interim government.
- June 16: Prachanda arrives in Kathmandu and starts talks with Koirala and leaders of seven parties. The SPA and the CPN (M) sign an 8-point agreement. On the same day, Prachanda makes his first public appearance after 10 years.
- July 4: Government and the CPN (M) invite the United Nations for management of arms and troops.
- Nov 8: Top leaders of the seven parties and Prachanda sign a landmark deal on arms management and political issues like constituent assembly, interim government and interim parliament.
- Nov 21: Prime Minister Koirala on behalf of the seven-party government and Prachanda sign a historic peace agreement that that ended 10 years of armed conflict.

2007

- January : CPN (M) joined the parliament
  - Violent protests started in Terai.

- March: Interim constitution amended and CPN (M) joined interim government.
- May: Elections for a constituent assembly pushed back to November.
- September: Three bombs blasted Kathmandu.
  - CPN (M) quit interim government, demanding a fully proportional election and declaration of Nepal as a republic
  - Postponement of November's constituent assembly elections.
  - December: Parliament approved abolition of monarchy.

2008

- January: Terai unrest mounted.
- Jan 11: Constituent Assembly election date announced for April 10, 2008.
- 10 April: Constituent Assembly Election. CPN (M) emerged as the largest political force.
- May 28: The Constituent Assembly declared Nepal a Federal Democratic Republic with high majority 560 out of 564 members present in the assemblynand olby 4 royalist members voted against it.
- June 11: Ex-king Gyanendra Shah left the Narayanhiti Royal Palace and now it is changed to a new palace museum.
- June: Maoist ministers resign from the cabinet to press PM Koirala to open the way for forming new government.
- July: Ram Baran Yadav elected by CA as the first president of Nepal.
- August: Prachanda elected as PM and formed new government.
- PM Prachanda visits China on the Olympic closing ceremony.
- September: PM Prachanda Visits India.
- September 20: PM Prachanda Visits USA to attend the UN General Assembly.

1.6 ARRANGEMENT AND CONTENTS OF THE CHAPTERS

This book is arranged in eleven chapters. The first chapter introduces the context, the contents and overview with some elaboration on the process how and why conflict started and how it was solved. The *Janaandolon* II and its contribution to the political change of Nepal and post-*Janaandolon* II are discussed.

Chapter 2 of the book discusses the land conflict, land politics and its relations with power. Citing several global examples and evidences, this chapter argues that land is one of the main sources of conflict and power. This chapter concludes that addressing root causes of conflict requires addressing land-based exploitation and skewed distribution of land resource.

Chapter 3 establishes relationships between armed conflict, displacement and environmental stresses. Based on the in-depth case study in an urban setting of displacement this chapter demonstrates that internally displaced persons (IDPs) not only faced tremendous challenges and difficulties in their livelihoods but also suffered from environmental health and sanitation related problems in their settlements mainly because of the illegal status of these settlements. They were not able to get electricity, drinking water and other basic services from the formal state structures such as electricity authority, drinking water supply offices of the government.

Chapter 4 gives an insight into the changing political context and its relations with hydro-conflict in Nepal. This chapter has analysed the South Asian water stress and consequent conflict. The role of India in shaping and reshaping the hydro-politics is discussed. This chapter has highlighted that new foreign policy and international relations, public engagement, bureaucratic reorientation, equity and social justice, and human security perspectives and constructive engagement with international power are needed for Nepal to benefit from the huge water resource existed in the country.

Chapter 5 presents the socio-psychological dimensions of constitution making in the post-conflict situation. It examines various dimensions of public legitimacy of the constitution making and brings elements of public engagement in the constitution-making process to increase the horizontal public legitimacy of the new constitution.

Chapter 6 examines the relationships between armed conflict and the tourism sector and its potential for peace building. As tourism is one of the main contributors of national economy and the bridge between Nepalese society and international community, its potential for peace building is realised as crucially important, particularly addressing the root causes of conflict through generating employment for rural and urban poverty alleviation. This chapter has documented the coping strategies adapted by the tourism sector during the time of the active armed conflict. It has also analysed the strengths, weakness, opportunities and threats in the tourism sector to address root causes of the conflict and contribute to building peace.

Chapter 7 examines the relationship between conflict and development. This chapter argues that the great potential of the development sector to address the structural causes of the conflict was not utilised in the past ten decades. This chapter highlights that Nepal's planned development has largely failed to attend its objectives and therefore provided a breeding ground for violent conflict and instability. This chapter stresses that reorientation of the development sector is a precondition for meeting the challenges of the post-conflict situation. By examining the causes and impacts of the armed conflict, this chapter has offered a conceptual framework for reorienting development through a conflict-s-ensitive development approach.

Chapter 8 discusses the legacies of the ten years of armed conflict and its consequences in various sectors. It examines the impacts of armed conflict on environment and natural resources, development, society, politics.

Chapter 9 critically examines the role of women in Nepal's peace process. Bringing the global experiences of contribution of women in the peace process, this chapter highlights the needs, complications, potentials and challenges for women in peace process. This chapter concludes that women have great potential for making the peace process successful but the powerful actors are not much interested in realising this and therefore not provided much space for women in the peace structures. Nevertheless, the current composition of the CA is cited in the chapter as one of the most praiseworthy involvements of women in the decision-making super structure.

Chapter 10 discusses the importance, need, conceptual framework and principles for the security sector restructuring in Nepal after ending the ten years of the armed conflict. This chapter argues that changing military laws, or dealing with a single security agency or integrating PLA into state security structures is not restructuring of the security sector. It has to start with the redefining and refining of the national security policy vis-à-vis international relations with a national consensus and then restructuring of all security providing structures in accordance with the principles of parliamentary oversights and civilian control. This chapter has also offered the steps, procedures and identified the major areas of restructuring.

Chapter 11 summarises the whole book and envisions what should be done in future to make the war-to-peace transition successful in Nepal. It has identified fundamental elements of transition and procedures to make the transformation complete, stable and democratic.

End Notes

1. Peace is a state of well being that that is characterised by trust, compassion and justice. In this state people can be encouraged to explore as well as celebrate diversity and search for good in each other without the concern for personal pain and sacrifice (Troste, 1992 in Sandy and Perkins, 2002). Peace is not merely the absence of war but the [presence of justice, of law, of order-in short of government, once said Albert Einstein.
2. It involves rights of citizens to determine their forms of government on the basis of popular will, which involves representation, accountability participation and equity.
3. Neo-elites are those people emerged from within the excluded groups who are benefiting most from advocating for the excluded groups, such as Dalit, ethnic groups, women, etc. From this chance

a power is shifted from more classical power centres to new power centres and tis is becoming a phenomenon.

4. Intentional social exclusion also occurs within ethnic minorities. We have repeatedly observed that elite from within ethnic groups are exploiting weak and poor members of their own ethnic community.
5. The caste system is one of the most influential forms of social exclusion, as it is very rigid and fixed at birth (based on traditional hierarchical four-fold layers of society, i.e., Brahmin, Chhitri, Vaishya and Sudra).
6. Polyandry exists only in a negligible scale in some remote parts of Nepal
7. Ethnic groups are those non-Aryan Mangoloids who do not fall into traditional Hindu *Verna* system (Brahman, Kshatrya, vaishaya and Sudra).
8. See Gore (1992: 232-237) for details of use of denial by politicians. Al Gore, former Vice President of the USA, vividly explains the notion of denial in terms of 'dysfunctional civilisation' in the global context. He argues that denial by politicians is destroying the natural world.
9. He said, *'the Maoists are terrorists, under the guise of Maoism or the so called people's war, they are fundamentally the same as terrorists elsewhere, be they members of the Shining Path, Abu Sayaf, the Khmer Rouge, or Al Qaeda'. The Kathmandu Post*, 26 February 2002.
10. The details of the Maoists' insurgency are covered in books of the author entitled (a) 'The Price of Neglect: From Resource Conflict to Maoists Insurgencyin the Himalayan Kingdom. Kathmandu: Bhrikuti Academic Publications (Upreti, 2004a) and(b) Armed Conflict and Peace Process in Nepal The Maoists Insurgency, Past Negotiation and Opportunities for Conflict Transformation New Delhi: Adroit Publishers (Upreti, 2006a).
11. The Tulip Revolution refers to the overthrow of President Askar Akayev and his government in the Central Asian republic of Kyrgyzstan in March 2005. The revolution sought the end of rule by Akayev and by his family and associates, who in popular opinion had become increasingly corrupt and authoritarian. In the early stages, this revolution was referred as "Pink", "Lemon", "Silk", "Daffodil", or "Sandpaper" Revolution by the media. But the term "Tulip Revolution", was nomenclated by Akayev himself when he was forced to resign from the post of president in a speech warning that no such Color Revolution should happen in Kyrgyzstan.

12. See The Economist.Com, Bloodless Regime Change (2006) for details.
13. The Alliance is composed of The Nepal Communist Party United Marxist-Leninist (CPN-UML), The Nepali Congress Party (NCP), The Nepali Congress Party (Democratic) (NCP-D), The Nepal Sadbhawana Party (Anandidevi), The Nepal Peasants and Workers Party, United leftist Front and Samyukta Janamorcha.
14. The King's address to the nation at the time of the Royal takeover on 1st February 2005. It was the morning of 1st February (10:50 a.m.), security officials under the command of army were deployed in all strategic places such as the media houses and party offices. Security forces were sent to arrest or detain political leaders and human rights activists. Telephone lines were cut and the king's address to the nation lasted more than 34 minutes. The Prime Minister and ministers were detained in their own offices and residences (Upreti, 2006a). There was a meeting of the king held with the security forces (The military, police and the armed police force in the evening of 31 January. The king met the Prime Minister on the same day but the prime minister was not aware of the plan. Later, Mr Deuba acknowledged that when he met the king he felt that something could happen but he did not suspect that the king would take such a big step.
15. See *The Kathmandu Post* of 2 February 2005 for the full text of the speech by the King.
16. *The Kathmandu Post,* April 24, 2006.
17. After the successful April revolution, the name of the Royal Nepal Army was changed to Nepal Army by the revived Parliament.
18. The government appointed after the April movement formed a high level commission under the chairpersonship of ex-judge of the supreme court Mr Krishna Jung Rayamajhi (Popularly known as the Rayamajhi Commission) to investigate the atrocities caused by the King's government to suppress the 19 days of *Janandolon*. This commission came to the conclusion that the whole team of the king's government was responsible for killing 25 people and wounding more than 45,500 people with the misuse of millions of rupees from the treasury.
19. *The Himlayan Times*, 14 April 2006.
20. Foreign Secretary Mr Shyam Sharan (who was Indian Ambassador to Nepal earlier) and Mr Pankaj Sharan (Joint Secretary of Indian External Affairs) also accompanied him and Mr Shayam Sharan had also talked with the Royal Nepal Army at that time.
21. Article 35 of the 1990's constitution states that the executive power

shall, pursuant to this Constitution and other laws, be vested in His Majesty under this constitution shall be exercise upon the recommendation and advice, and with the consent of the council of ministers, except as otherwise expressly stated that it may be exercised exclusively by Him Majesty or at his discretion or on the recommendation of any institution or official. Such recommendation, advice and consent shall be submitted through the Prime Minister.

22. See "Open questions to European Diplomats" from Bishnu Raj Upreti on 23 April 2006 at web page http://www.europe-solidaire.org/spip.php?article1975 for details about the public opposition to their pressure to SPA leaders. The main questions asked were: 1. How many times the king has used its commitment on multiparty- democracy and respect of human rights during his direct autocratic rule and did he ever translate this rhetoric into practice? Why should Nepalese people believe rhetoric this time? 2. Do you truly believe that the attitude, intention and behaviour of the king are committed to democracy and establishing people's sovereignty? 3. Political history and culture of your country revels that there is respect of people supremacy and will. Should you not respect this principle in the case of Nepal? 4. Do you want political leaders not to respect the aspiration of people protesting in street? 5. How do you see possibility of resolving the deepening crisis by just accepting the prime minister offered by the king? Did this arrangement in the past produce any result? 6. Are you in support of the king's manipulation or with Nepalese people struggling to establish people's true sovereignty?]
23. *The Kathmandu Post*, 25 April 2006.
24. *Kantipur Daily*, 20 March 2006.
25. *Kantipur Daily*, 4 April 2006.
26. See *Nepal Weekly*, Vol. 6, No. 15, 20 November, 2005 for details on the talks between the Maoistss and the political parties.
27. *The Himalayan Times*, 22 April 2006.
28. For example, Girija Prasad Koirala (NCP), Bam Dev Gautam (CPN-UML), Gopal Man Shrestha (NCP-D) visited India to finalise the 12-point understanding.
29. A Joint Declaration for a United Effort to Resolve the national Crisis, signed by the leaders of 7 parties and issued on 8 May 2005 (25 Baisak, 2062).
30. *Kantipur Daily*, 14 March 2006.
31. All of them issued strong statements, wrote to the king to stop

attack on people, and condemned gross violation of human rights and some of them even threatened.

32. Human rights activists were the first to break the no-go zone declared by the royal government, journalists and lawyers were in the street continuously to protest the king's regime at the time when political parties were not able to come on to the street.
33. This was reflected in the suggestions given by the CPN (M) to the Interim Constitution Drafting Committee.
34. His vice-chairperson and other two of the powerful members of the cabinet were defaulters of the banks' loan, one senior minister was charged as attempt rapist of hospital nurse, many of his cabinet ministers were declared as guilty of suppressing 1990's peoples movement by the Mallik Commission, two of the cabinet members were charged by the court as guilty of corruption.
35. For example, Dr Mohamad Mohasin, Communication Minister in the *Deuba* government, said to be a representative of the king, repeatedly indicated in late 2004 and early 2005 the forthcoming 1st February event. Keshar Jung Rayamajhi had publicly asked the King to take over. It happened after a few weeks of these statements.
36. Mr. Mustonen died in a helicopter crash in Taplejung on 23 September 2006 with other 23 persons, including State Minister of Forest and Soil Conservation, Director Generals of Forest and Wildlife Departments, Dr Harka Gurung, Head of WWF Nepal Dr Chandra Gurung, and others.
37. *The Himalayan Times*, 23 April 2006.
38. *Kantipur Daily*, 19 April 2006.
39. Though the repressive government killed 25 people and wounded more than 5,500 people in 19 days, the protesters were peaceful in this resistance.
40. The Interim Constitution has made provision of deciding the fate of the monarchy by simple majority decision of the first meeting of the constituent assembly and finally in the last week of August 2008 the institute of monarchy was formally abolished.
41. The 5622nd Meeting of Security Council had established UNMIN by unanimously adopting the resolution 1740 (23 January 2007) as per the request of the Government of Nepal and the CPN (M).
42. A total of 19,604 people have been qualified from the UNMIN verification process.
43. For details about the Joint Monitoring Committee, see the decision (SC/8942) of 5622nd Meeting (PM) of the Security Council of UN.

44. See the decision (SC/8942) of 5622nd Meeting (PM) of the Security Council of UN for details.
45. MoPR work-related information was obtained through informal talks with the senior officials of the ministry.
46. www.nepalnews.com
47. Compiled from www.nepalnews.com, BBC webpage and other many documents.
48. CPN (M) took 12 truck loads of arms and ammunitions from the army barrack of Dang including Israel made Galil ARM 5.56 mm rifles, 81 mm mortars, shoulder-propelled grenade launchers, self-loading rifles, light machine guns, AK 47s, 5.56 rifles, wireless sets and tons of ammunitions (Roy, 2008). The CPN (M) commanders estimated that they could fight for 4 years with these arms and ammunitions.

Chapter 2

Land Conflict, Power and Politics

2.1 THE CONTEXT

Global experiences show that the mounting inquiry brought by the capitalist production relations in agriculture and its effects on agrarian structure provide fertile ground for emergence of conflict (Ali, 2000, Aliston et al., 2000; Andre and Platteau, 1998; Upreti, 2004a and 2004b). The issue of ownership of land has remained at the centre of socio-political contention since before the emergence of modern state. Once the state took control over the land used traditionally by the indigenous communities, the conflict over this resource started. Hence, a historical analysis is needed. The historical dimension of any country provides a vivid lens to examine the relationship of power, land ownership and conflict (Wolf, 1969; Upreti et al., 2008).

According to Alston, Libecap and Mueller (2000:171), land-related violent conflict is "personal injury or death and/or physical property damage in a land dispute". However, it is too narrow an interpretation to cover the dynamics of land-related conflicts. It is also not always easy to analyze land-related violent conflict in isolation as it is immediately linked with other social and political issues and goes beyond mere land conflict. Hence, understanding of land conflict requires a holistic understanding of the context, its contents and the temporal aspects of a society and the international dynamics.

According to OECD (2001:87), violent conflict appears in four stages or categories:

(*i*) Situations of submerged tensions;
(*ii*) Situations of rising tensions;
(*iii*) Eruption phases of open confrontation and violent conflict;
(*iv*) Fragile transitional and post-conflict situations.

This is a general categorization and can be applied to any conflict. Hence, this categorisation can be used to examine the relationship between land ownership and violent conflict. In every stage or category, power relation plays a crucial role and therefore power is intricately linked with conflict.

Inequality is a logical product of skewed power relations of society, as unequal power distribution produces inequality. Jean-Louis Arcand and Nicolas Pons-Vignon (2003:6) have outlined the following four claims concerning the link between inequality and conflict:

- A linear relationship between the degree of inequality and the likelihood of conflict (Russett, 1964, Nafziger and Auvinen, 2002, Muller and Seligson, 1987). In other words, the more unequal a society, higher the likelihood of the outbreak of conflict. Inequality is directly related with the power structure of a society. The cases of Nepal, India, Pakistan and many other developing countries in general and conflict-ridden countries in particular are evidence of this relation.
- A quadratic relationship, where the likelihood of conflict reaches a peak at an intermediate level of inequality. Some authors have found the curve to be U-shaped (Hirschman, 1981; Nafziger and Auvinen, 2002), indicating that there is some threshold level of inequality for which the likelihood of conflict is minimized.
- Rising inequality would be conducive to conflict until a "peak" level is reached. Beyond this level, possibly because of stronger state repressive capacities, the rise in inequality is associated with *declining* risk of conflict.
- No firm patterns of relationship between inequality and conflict exist (Collier, 2000). As power dynamics frequently change in a society, it is not possible to have a firm and stable pattern of such relationship between inequality and conflict.

Several evidences have demonstrated that land can be one of the major sources of conflicts, be it in the Philippines, Brazilian Amazon, Nepal, Guatemala or Ivory Cost, when extremely unequal agrarian relations prevailing in a society are not addressed by the state (Elbadawi and Sambanis, 2000; Ali, 2000, Aliston et al., 2000; Andre and Platteau, 1998; Upreti, 2004b; Platteau, 1996). The link between land issues and violent conflict is mainly related with the land policies and social structure and relations of a particular nation shaped by national and local power relations. When land policies, institutional arrangements and legal provisions are built to address the structural causes of the unequal and skewed distribution of land resources, it could prevent, halt or reduce violent conflict. However, it is not easy as land issues are directly linked with prestige, social status, power, and economic incentives (Ghimire, 1992; Pandey, 1999; Upreti, 2004a; Fitzpatrick, 2002).

Conflict often occurs over land, when two or more parties possess competing claims over its control and use, and no agreement can be reached between the parties to determine which claim has precedence (Upreti, 2001; 2004a). At the structural level, often such claims originate from the differential power sources, reflected in the unequal power relations and dominated by influential people of various power centres. Ownership and control are therefore the central issues in land conflict. In this regard, at the operational level, conflict over land resources is often linked with the absence of efficient and accepted institutional and administrative arrangements to regulate the ownership, control, and use of land.

Land policies, institutional arrangements and legal provisions alone do not necessarily resolve conflict and sustain peace in societies that are going through transition or countries suffering from wars. Land issues should be one of the core subjects of political negotiation in war-torn and armed conflict-ridden countries. The cases of East Timor, Afghanistan and even Nepal show that dealing with land issues in peace agreements is one of the best ways of addressing land-related disputes and contributing to peace. It has been observed in different war-torn countries that when donors impose conditionality in their support for the post-conflict development and reconstruction, the outcome in terms of resolving land conflict and sustaining peace is often problematic; as land is the most complex power issue.

This chapter discusses the relationship between the state and the land, and also examines the concepts of property and land ownership. It further discusses the impacts of exclusion and class issues associated with land, and analyses the social structure and power relation in the contexts of social transformation and agrarian change in Nepal.

2.2 STATE, POWER AND LAND

A state is a self-governing political entity with internationally recognised territories, which has its citizens and operates independently in terms of international relations, economic organisation and social engineering (Upreti et al., 2008). Hence, any state exercises its power over its citizens and the citizens run the state through their representatives. State acquires the rights to deal with the welfare concerns of its citizens.

Power is a form of constraint or enabler of human actions. Italian political philosopher Niccolò Machiavelli (1469-1527) and French philosopher Michel Foucault (1926-1984) were the pioneers of power debate. They viewed power as a complex strategic situation in a given social setting. Later, Anthony Giddens also contributed significantly to the power discourse, especially on the enabling concept of power (Tarnow, 2000; Dowding, 1996; French and Raven, 1959). Power often contains two elements, i.e. physical power (which involves coercion-force or threat of force) and political power. Hence, power may be simplistically defined as unilateral real or perceived ability or potential to bring about change in a society through actions and counter actions (Clastres, 1974).

Power manifests in a relation structure and has to be compared with another actor or group of actors. It is not possible to refer that one particular social actor is more powerful without comparing or specifying another actor or group of actors in a given social setting. Hence, it is reflected in certain relationship such as subordination and super-ordination, strong and weak or influential or less influential. One of the characteristics of power is its operational reciprocity, i.e. to control action and behaviour of one actor, another actor has to have exercise, measures of control, influence or force. Power operates both in relational and reciprocal levels, which is called balance of power in the sociological term and power exercise in political term. Often in the sociological perspective, power is also seen as unilateral strength (Tarnow, 2000; Dowding, 1996).

In the structuralist social theory, power is interpreted as a process embedded in a social structure (Upreti et al., 2008). In a society, power could be gained through delegated authority by certain democratic process (for example by election); obtained through personal charisma or ascribed charisma (e.g. acting on perceived or assumed abilities without proven evidences); or by expertise (e.g. ability, skills, knowledge), or by persuasion (direct or indirect), or by use of money and resources (monetary influence, control of ownership), or by use of force (violence, military might, coercions), or by religious influence, etc. J.K. Galbraith[1] has grouped power (Clastres, 1974; Tarnow, 2000; Dowding, 1996; French and Raven, 1959) as:

- based on force,
- compensatory (by use of various resources),
- conditioned (as a result of persuasion),
- individual personality influence,
- use of property, and
- organizational power.

Social power is the ability of an actor to change the incentive structures of other actors, in order to bring about outcomes. Hence, according to the social power perspective, social interactions amongst various actors develop their ability to exert power over others (by a powerful actor to a weak actor). Following the Marxist tradition, the Italian sociologist Antonio Gramsci elaborated upon the role of cultural hegemony in ideology as a means of power. In the literature of feminism, power is linked with patriarchy, as often power concentrates on masculinity. Feminists use terms like 'power-over' (influence on other people) and 'power-to' (ability to perform). In the feminist perspective, power is a product of constructed societal norms related to gender, race, sex, class, and other forms of social division (Dowding, 1996; French and Raven, 1959).

Michel Foucault argues that power is reflected everywhere in human activity. Foucault's analysis of power is based on the notion of technologies of power, i.e. it is a complex bundle of power technologies developed over time. In his perspective, power is actions and counter actions among the members of a society. He very much focuses on the knowledge as power. Foucault feels that belief systems are a form of power, as many people have particular views linked with the belief system; which he calls common knowledge or hegemony. Particular belief systems define authority and thus give power (Tarnow, 2000; French and Raven, 1959).

Inappropriate and irrational use of power often polarizes society and divides into groups. Those who are relatively homogeneous in term of wealth, social status, positions and authorities and recognitions, cluster into one block with similar socio-political interest and often work to maintain these interests. Whereas those who are financially weak, socially marginalized and politically excluded form bigger clusters of left-outs but are weak in pursuing their collective interests and forming interest-based alliances, mainly because of lack of knowledge, resource, and information. Such a polarization provides fertile ground for emergence and escalation of conflict (Clastres, 1974; French and Raven, 1959). Armed conflict in Nepal can be seen in this framework.

Inequality between various social groups is one of the major causes of conflict in agrarian societies (Upreti et al., 2008). As discussed above, land is often a source of inequality in feudal and traditional societies. Relationship between inequality and conflict is based on the relative privileges and frustrations of competing groups within society. This has been observed in the seventeenth and eighteenth centuries in Europe and in the nineteenth and twentieth centuries in Asia and Africa. The armed conflict in Nepal is also the manifestation of centuries-old inequalities.

It is also frequently reported that donor's aid policy for developing countries is also one of the prime causes of conflict. Their aids are often directed to maintaining status quo and strengthening existing power relation and dictating to certain vested interests (Bigombe et al., 2000). For example, the structural adjustment programme of World Bank had increased tensions between different economic groups (e.g. rich and poor) leading to conflict in a fragile situation in Rwanda (Story, 1999), Sierra Leone and Liberia (Cramer and Weeks, 2000). Interference by donors (particularly by the former colonial power on the redistribution of land to poor black people in Zimbabwe) in the 1980s had given rise to serious conflict related to land reform in the 1980s (HRW, 2002). The conditions set in the funds provided to the Zimbabwean government for the purchase of land made the task of land distribution almost impossible because the full market price had to be paid for the purchase of land to the willing sellers. This condition was favourable only for redistribution of poor quality land in higher prices. The land distribution was shaped by vested interests of white land owners of British origin and multinational companies engaged in the Rhodesian plantation sector (HRW, ibid). In Pakistan, the World Bank initiated land tax. The rigid market-based approach to potential land reform (e.g.land bank as component of land reform) advocated by the international financial agencies creates more problems. Various conditions posed by international financial institutions have created enormous land related problems and social tensions in different parts of the world. For example, abolition of subsidy on non-profitable food depots, which were mainly operating in the remote areas, was a condition attached by the Asian Development Bank to provide the loan assistance for Agricultural Perspective Plan, not only created starvation in the remote areas but also implanted serious tension in the area and contributed to escalating the armed conflict in Nepal. European and North American countries are providing subsidies to their farmers but imposing conditions on their assistance to developing countries to remove similar subsidies in agriculture. Such a double standard of developed countries is also becoming a source of conflict in developing countries.

There are several cases of land being the major source of bloody conflict and regional instability. The origin and expansion of the Mindanao conflict of South Philippine and the case of Palestine and Israel conflicts are two of many glaring examples of land-based tensions in the world.

In Nepal, land is one of the historical means of feudalism and source of revenue for the feudal state (Upreti et al., 2008). Historically, land was considered as the property of the state [state landlordism] and this land was called "*Raikar*" (Regmi, 1976). Mahesh Chandra Regmi argues that there were mainly two types of land tenure system in Nepal, i.e. *Raikar* and *Kipat*. All other tenured forms of land were derived from Raikar (Regmi, 1976; 1978). The meaning of *Raikar* land has changed since 1951, from crown-land, to land owned by individuals. *Raikar*-land ownership denotes an ultimate state ownership over those lands, which were actually cultivated by individuals as direct tenants of the state.

The state had the right to alienate land through sale, mortgage or bequest. Using this right of alienation, the rulers granted cultivated or uncultivated state-owned lands to their loyalists in different forms such as *Jagir, Birta, Rakam, Sera and Rajya* and charitable or religious organizations in the form of *Guthi* (Regmi, 1963; 1976). The granting of land to individuals and institutions was used deliberately, not only for paying them for their services but also for ensuring their loyalty and promoting social and religious activities. Hence, the land tenure system that has historically existed in Nepal is still a prime source of inequality, social exclusion and power-biased social relations.

In Nepal, land was historically granted to a noble as a reward for a service rendered to the state (Upreti et al., 2008). There were several forms of such granted land. Some of them are given below;

Birta: One form of land grant was *Birta*. The land granted under the *Birta* arrangement had no time limits and it could be rented out or inherited until confiscated or recalled by the state. *Birta* owners usually had full rights to possess, occupy, sell, lease, subdivide and bequeath their lands. Most *Birta* lands were not taxable. It has become the foundation of the modern, private land-property arrangement and source of land-based exploitation in Nepal.

Jagir: Another form was *Jagir*. The *Jagir* land holding was more conditional and subtle and often granted to government servants rather than to members of the ruling elite. A *Jagir* assessment was usually an assignment of the income from *Raikar* lands in lieu of a salary and it could not be assigned or sold. *Jagir* rights lapsed together with the cease of employment, or at the discretion of the government. The *Birta* and *Jagir* forms were abolished in 1959, with the enacting of the *Birta* Abolition Act and converted to *Raikar* land (New Era, 1988; 28-31).

Sera: Sera was another form of land tenure system explicitly used by the royal palace to meet the food-grain and other land-related requirements. This land tenure system clearly indicates the total control of land resources by the palace, which was used for their own interests.

Rakam: Rakam was yet another form of land tenure where cultivators had to compulsorily provide unpaid labourers to the government as carpenters, masons, and postmen. *Rajya* was a modified form of land tenure granted as the princely state award for members and relatives of Royal families. This land-granting practice was common, up until the Rana regime. Rulers granted large portions of lands to soldiers as Jagir to keep them under their control. The Rana rulers confined the land-grant practices to their relatives and key officials.

Guthi: There was another form, called *Guthi. Guthi* is an arrangement of an endowment made by philanthropist with religious or philanthropic motives. It is for the performance of any regular or ceremonial religious function or festival of any monastery or deity or construction, maintenance, or operation of temples, religious rest-houses, roadside shelters, wells, tanks, ponds, waterspouts, and arrangements for supply of drinking water, roads, bathing *Ghats*, bridges, and shelters under tree, medicals, hospitals, dispensaries, libraries, schools, and the likes. The Guthi land-tenure system also included the endowment of private lands (obtained from the state) by individual landlords for religious purposes.

Kipat: Kipat was an ancient type of communal land tenure system, where particular ethnic groups were granted land by their king, in recognition of traditional communal tenure. The head of the state had the authority to grant individuals the right to cultivate certain areas and collect forest products from other areas (Regmi, 1978). In the *Kipat* arrangement, individual ethnic group derive kipat-land rights, located in a particular area (Regmi, 1963). Regmi (1972:27) states that *"individuals who cultivated land in their capacity as a member of a Kipat-owing ethnic group owed allegiance primarily to the community, not to the state"*. Almost one-third of agricultural and forest land of the nation was granted to private individuals by 1950, and the remaining belonged to the Ranas themselves (Regmi, 1978). Local functionaries, all favourites of the Ranas, implemented the land-grant policy in the villages and were able to assure most benefit for themselves. They obtained large portions of land from the state through *Jagir* and *Birta* grants and rented these lands to peasant farmers under tenancy arrangements. In this way, local functionaries turned into landlords. Peasant farmers had to pay half of their crop yields as the rent to the local landlords (Upreti, 2004d).

All these land grant systems practised by rulers had strengthened centralised and hierarchical society and promoted exclusion and consequently, social conflict. As the land grant system advanced, landlords introduced the *Kut* (contract) system to ensure their rent, where only those tenants who were able to pay high rents could get a contract. Irrespective of the performance of their crops, even if the crops failed, farmers had to pay the rent as *Kut*. Eventually, these peasant farmers effectively turned into slave labourers of the *Jagir* and *Birta* holders (Regmi, 1978). This is an example of structural and deliberate way of creating unequal society and implanting social conflict.

If we look at the history of indigenous communities, they often did not have the system of property ownership in the form of land as an individual private property. Land was their common property and used by their members, depending upon their needs. This traditional resource use system was disrupted once the land grants system was introduced by the ruling elites. Then gradually, tension between the indigenous communal land tenure system operated by the indigenous communities and the state-control land tenure system administered by the state emerged, and later became perennial source of social conflict (Upreti and Adhikari, 2006).

The evolution of land administration system shows that the state, by initiating modern land control system, has created further tension in the society. When the indigenous community started to raise their concerns, the state started to resist. Territorial rights of the indigenous people over their ancestral land were not recognized for a long time. However, in recent years, indigenous rights-centred movement has taken momentum and international environment has become favourable, particularly since the ILO Convention 169, which exerted heavy pressure on the government to recognize indigenous land rights and their management systems. Nevertheless, policy confusion still exists in Nepal, because of the conceptual un-clarity that has remained with the decision makers/rulers as a remnant of the centuries-old feudal mindset.

Over time, the poor and the marginalized people are becoming landless and lack access to other resources, which has placed them in the situation of deprivation trap (Upreti and Adhikari, 2006). Not only have they lost their traditional land rights, they also do not get a decent means of livelihood. Furthermore, force of globalization and privatization has further marginalized them (Bhandari, 2003). The skewed domestic power structure and external influences (aid conditionality, interference, etc.), have greatly contributed to creating and strengthening deprivation trap.

2.3 CONFLICT ON OWNERSHIP AND ACCESS TO LAND

Often, land-ownership arrangements in many South Asian countries are unequal and promote landlordism. In the case of Nepal, landlordism has prevented economic development of the poor and the marginalized farmers because they are systematically excluded from the state benefit systems.

Landlords exploit poor farmers by renting their lands and by getting unpaid labour and demanding various payments (Koseli, Mukheuli, etc.), apart from getting agricultural rents from their tenants. Ownership rights of most of the valuable lands are possessed by local elites and are close to power centres. A study conducted in 2000 by the Socioeconomic and Ethno-Political Research and Training Consultancy (P) Limited for ICIMOD concludes that 'Land policies in Nepal were, in general, found to have a negative impact on the majority of the population and to cause land degradation. It is a mutually reinforcing process in which degradation has aggravated poverty and poverty has further exacerbated degradation. Land ownership and tenure entitlements are unfavourable from both equity and efficiency perspectives' (ICIMOD, 2000).

Access of the poor people to land resource is an unresolved perennial issue in Nepal. Various high-level commissions, task forces and working committees have been formed by the government in the past four decades to address this issue, with no visible results. Government laws, policies and regulations are not able to ensure access of poor people to land and land-based resources. The existing power relations have a heavy influence on exercising these policy and regulations in favour of elites and the landlords. The poor and the marginalized groups are mostly concerned with:

- Access to and ownership of land and land-based productive resources,
- Equity in benefit sharing, including safeguard of customary rights on these resources,
- Meaningful participation in decision making, and
- Access to information and justice.

In Nepal, ownership of land resource translates into wealth, power, social prestige and security of livelihood of many people. However, low-caste people, particularly the *Dalits* within the caste system and ethnic groups are usually marginalized and land ownership is a major issue for them. For example, 80 per cent of the population of indigenous group is 'marginal cultivators' (with less than 0.40 hectare) or small cultivators (having 0.40-0.80 hectare). Because of this low level of land ownership, they tend to experience enormous food insecurity. A large number of these people rely on wage labour with no land of their own for farming. Being landless, the vast majority of these groups of people have no access to resources related to land ownership. Only some 2.8 per cent of the *Tharu,* 0.32 per cent of the *Tamang,* 0.76 per cent of the *Rai,* and 0.63 per cent of the *Magar* communities, respectively, have self-operated land of more than 10 acres (UNDP, 2004: 63).

A large proportion of people do not have access to non-farm employment opportunities as they lack land ownership, which is essential to secure funds for investment. Accordingly, they work as agricultural labourers or lease land for their livelihoods. Often *Kamaiya*[2] (bonded labour), *Kamalari* (female domestic worker), *Kamara/Kamari* (servants), *Gothala* (cowherds), *Khetala* (farmhand), *Haruwa* (ploughmen), *Charuwa* (herders) and *Bhariya* (porters) were facing this situation. Their access to land and other natural resources provides a basis for safe livelihood. However, access of the poor and the disadvantaged people to land resources depends upon conducive policy, favourable legislations, responsive institutions and effective translation of policy and legislations into practices (Upreti, 2004a, 2006a), which is badly lacking in Nepal.

Nepali indigenous people had a special relationship with land resources and their identity was determined by such basic relationships (Caplan, 1990). With the territorial unification of Nepal, indigenous people lost their traditional rights to land, land-based resources and their territories (Gurung, 2005). The traditionally communally-owned land of these people, especially of the *Tamang, Dunuwar, Sunuwar, Majhi, Chepang, Hayu, Sherpa, Kumal, Lepcha, Rai,* etc. was known as kipat. *Kipat* thus means the land communally owned and collectively used. The *Kipat* land was confiscated along with the unification of the country (particularly after Land Reform Act of 1964) and was distributed to other people (Caplan, 2000). Moreover, state resources like land were distributed to indigenous people because the political power was vested in other groups.

The marginalized and poor people had been generally living at the periphery of the power centre, but were charged high taxes (Regmi, 1972). Those who could not pay the taxes had to forsake the land. The indigenous people also fled their places because of this reason, and new settlers occupied their ancient lands. These people had no concept of land measurement, and in fact did not like the idea of measuring the land as they considered land as their 'mother'. But when the land was measured, they had to divide the communally-owned lands on an individual basis. Those who did not claim the communally-owned lands as private property were deprived of the rights.

The natural economy of indigenous people historically meant that they had no concept of the modern ownership of property, capital formation, transaction and the interest or profit in the investment (Upreti & Adhikari, 2006). Knowledge of the national language and basic literacy and mathematical skills were other problems faced by them. Lack of competent skills gave opportunities to the elites, the recent immigrants and the people having access to power to exploit them. The study of Lionel Caplan on Hindu-indigenous relations in East Nepal in the late 1960s shows the dynamics of how indigenous people lost in this economic-political relationship (Caplan, 2000).

Unequal social relations are strengthened by the process of Hinduization (Gaige, 1975; Bista et. al. 1982). Though the term has specific meaning, it generally explains the homogenisation of social, cultural, religious, economic and political diversities (Upreti and Adhikari, 2006). People were forced to accept or imitate the Hindu religion, one language (Nepali) and one culture of the ruling class as the survival strategy that seriously undermined the diversity. Hinduization has also distinctly polarized the ethnic groups themselves. Families from ethnic groups or some ethnic groups as a whole ascended to higher or respectable caste or class (Bista, 1991), which also created division among the ethnic groups. The National Hindu Code (Muluki Ain) in 1854 expedited the process of Hindualization and degraded the status of indigenous people and converted them to *namasinya* (nonslaveable) and *masinya* (slaveable), *Matwali* or alcohol drinker. This continued even after the overthrow of the exploitative Rana oligarchy in 1950. The constitution of 1962 declared Nepal as a Hindu state and Nepali as a national language, which emphasised homogenization of language, dress, and local practices and severely undermined the religious and linguistic diversities. The uniformity imposed by the state has also ruined the traditional practices in resource management.

The establishment of various protected areas (like national parks, conservation areas, hunting reserves and the likes) is generally on the private lands of the Nepalese people. Because of this, a large number of people have been displaced from their lands. These people have also been deprived of their traditional rights to use these resources (Gurung, 2005). The traditional skills and knowledge of people have also come under attack of large industries. A study of Upreti and Adhikari (2006) demonstrates that, increased use of factory products such as umbrellas, modern hats and plastic baskets have replaced traditional products of indigenous communities like reed straw, bamboo hats, baskets, and mats in different parts of Nepal. Livelihood of poor and marginalized people is mainly based on the access to and ownership of land and land-based resources. Access of local people to food, water, fuel wood, fodder, timber, medicinal herbs, fruits, mushrooms, bamboo shoots and such other products ensures their livelihoods. But if their access in these resources is altered, they suffer from livelihood insecurity. The landless and poor people constantly face this problem in Nepal.

2.4 PROPERTY RIGHTS AND LAND CONFLICT

Access to and control of land resource is greatly influenced by property relations. Property Rights (PR) is therefore a central issue in land conflict. Property can be considered as the rights and obligations of individuals or groups to use the resource base (Ostrom, 1990). Property rights are complex because resource tenure often involves bundles of rights, including user's rights, rights to exclude others, rights to manage and the rights to sell (Schlager and Ostrom, 1992). Theoretically, people can acquire rights over land and land-based resources, either by using their historical association or by citing riparian rights or interpreting legislated laws in their favour (Steins, 1999; Bromley, 1992).

Benda-Beckmann (1999:2) points out, "*Natural resource property rights serve to legitimate control over the means of production, whether production is for market or for subsistence. They can be an important material basis for the social continuity of groups. They usually have political functions for states and non-state social organization, and tend to be a source of individual power and prestige. Natural resource property often also has considerable cultural religious meaning [...]. Given this political, economic and ideological importance, legal property regulations and rights therefore constitute crucial social resources in people's strategies, negotiations and struggle over natural resources.*" Hence, it is important to analyze the context (e.g. the presence or absence of rules about the uses of land and land-based resources, market forces, political dimensions, power dynamics, alternatives to exploitation of common resources, ways of monitoring and controlling the behaviour of others) to understand the characteristics of conflicts in land resource.

It is essential to look at the social nature of property and property institutions to understand PR. As McCay and Acheson (1987) explained, PR deals with sanctioned behavioural relationships between people that arise from the existence of things and pertain to their use. Property rights are closely embedded in the historical and social contexts, and their meaning can vary from community to community and culture to culture (Benda-Beckmann, 1999). To answer the question on how PR claims affect land-related conflicts, it is essential to explore the use-pattern and the relationship between power and access to land and land-based resources.

Land resource traditionally used for one particular purpose, for example, grazing is now allocated to other purposes such as the construction of a particular project. Therefore the rights over land resource are also changing to meet these needs of the people. Changes have occurred either by state-induced forces, for example, by forest-related acts, water-related acts, mines and minerals-related acts, protection areas related acts and similar regulatory provisions, incentives given by the state, or by market forces), or by local practices. These changes are affecting the existing access patterns and ownership rights, and ultimately inducing conflict. A concrete example is the government-induced land measurement and registration programme, which has given rise to several conflicts in the community (Upreti, 2001).

Land resources are often interchangeably used with and commonly understood as common property resources[3] and common property is often confused with open access (*res nullius*). This misnomer originated from the human ecologist Garrett Hardin's "tragedy of the commons".[4] The concept of 'tragedy of the commons' had heavily influenced the policy formulations during the 1970s and 1980s that prioritized private or state control over resources and leads to contradictions and conflicts between resource users and the state (controllers). Hardin (1968) argues that the source of problems is common property, which poses an irreconcilable contradiction between individual and common interests. The notion "common" created confusion, because Hardin fails to distinguish between common property management and open access (Steins, 1999; McCay and Acheson 1987; Benda-Beckmann, 1999; Richards, 1997). Critics argue that Hardin's generalisation is too simplistic, because all natural resources used by villagers do not have open access, but are used under special arrangement.

Common property is controlled and managed by groups of resource users, with correlated duties, rights, rules and obligations that help to collectively regulate individual use (Ostrom, 1990; Schlager and Ostrom, 1992). This occurs in a variety of cultural, institutional and ecological settings, and with different kinds of land and land-based resources. In most cases, these land and land-based resources have been defined by different interest groups in different ways, according to geographical, physical and cultural criteria (Steins, 1999) and this leads to unavoidable conflict. Before the emergence of contemporary nation states, people lived with the availability of plenty of land and land-based resources and therefore there was no competition and conflict on land. All decisions related to access, distribution, control and management were framed within cultural, social and institutional mechanisms. The legacy of such a specific interface between natural resources and people still exists. However, over time, governments and several other interest groups have directly intervened to regulate land and land-based resources. People who were using these local land and land-based resources want to continue these arrangements, but there are mounting economic pressures. All these contradictions lead to conflict.

In agrarian and traditional societies, access to and control over land resource is not only determined by formal policies, legal instruments and state programme of the states, but also conditioned by local power relations, historical social structures, customary laws, bundles of traditional property rights, and value systems which Franz von Benda-Beckmann calls 'legal pluralism' (Benda-Beckmann, 1999). Hence, the concept of property rights embedded in legal pluralism better explains relationship of power, land rights and land ownership, and conflict.

Land conflict is largely about access to, control over, and profit from the land and land-based resources. Access and control are greatly influenced by power in the frame of PR. Hence, PR is therefore a central issue in land conflict. Property can be considered as the rights and obligations of individuals or groups to use the land resource base. Property rights are complex because resource tenure often involves bundles of rights, including users' rights, rights to exclude others, rights to manage and the rights to sell (Schlager and Ostrom, 1992). Theoretically, people can acquire rights over natural resources either by using their historical association or by citing riparian rights or interpreting legislated laws in their favour (Bromley, 1992).

The social nature of property and property institutions that largely deal with sanctioned behavioural relationships between people and land resources in a specific social setting determines property rights and patterns of their ownership and use. It is therefore closely embedded in the historical social context and can vary from community to community (Benda-Beckmann, 1999).

2.5 LAND AS A SOURCE OF POWER, PRESTIGE AND IDENTITY

Several researchers (Grossman, 1991, Thapa, 2002; Upreti, 2006a) found that rent seeking is one of the main sources of conflict. However, Collier (2000) and Collier and Hoeffler (2001; 2002) argue that rent seeking does not spur rebellion; it is the very condition for its survival.

Land is the primary means of production for the livelihood of majority of people of agrarian societies. Historical examination reveals that most of the powerful, rich and successful people of today (in economy, education, politics and bureaucracy) are mostly from the background of landlords. Hence, historically, people acquiring more land are in higher social power structure and status. Large numbers of policies and plans are not able to secure rights of marginalised communities and socially excluded and poor people.

For a long time, it was very difficult to obtain citizenship by those people who had no land ownership certificate. This provision has largely changed after the popular people's movement of 6-24 April 2006. But it is impossible for a citizen to buy land without the citizenship certificate. Obtaining most of the state-sponsored benefits requires a citizenship certificate. Such a vicious cycle is excluding poor ethnic groups from opportunities provided by the state, and is also threatening their identity in society. Hence, class issue is crucially important in studying land-related issues.

Land-based exploitation is socialised as social prestige in traditional society in many parts of Nepal and India (Upreti et al., 2008). Those who have several hectares of land rented to tenants, left uncultivated, or cultivated through *Haruwas and Charuwas* are socially recognised and respected. Marrying girls in a family with several *Haruwas and Charuwas* is still the preferred option in several parts of the country.

2.6 LAND AS A PERENNIAL SOURCE OF CONFLICT

Different studies, assessments and experiences around the world have demonstrated that land is a perennial source for social, ethnic and political conflict. The work of Ali (2000) has documented the political economy of African conflict, whereas Alston and its team (2000) examined the relationship between land reform policy and violent conflict in Brazil and concluded that land reform policies are often the sources of violent conflict. Andre and Platteau (1998) have documented the population pressure over land resources and its relationship with the civil war in Rwanda.

Conflict over the distribution of land ownership is quite a common feature of rural societies. Skewed land distribution and inequality is often the result of historical land appropriation. The Brazilian state of Amazon (Pará) and Rwanda have demonstrated that conflict is the inevitable result of the combination of inequality in the distribution of land ownership, competing claims to land, and underlying ethnic or social tensions. Land conflict in the Brazilian Amazon was because the landlords have title to their lands through statutory law, whereas squatters have the rights to land through expropriation (according to constitutional provision). Arcand and Chauvelt (2002) argue that, in a civil war situation, rent-seeking behaviour is a prevalent character that ultimately fuels conflict. The work of Bigombe, Collier and Sambanis (2000) on policies for building post-conflict peace in war torn societies, analysis of Binswanger *et. al.*, (1995) in relation of power, distortions, revolt and reform of land resources, and the study of Brockett (1992) on political violence in Central America demonstrate that land is one of the major sources of conflict.

Cramer and Weeks (2000) have examined the relationship between conflict and agriculture in the developing countries. Similarly, Fitzpatrick (2002) examines *land policy in post-conflict in East-Timor* where-as Herbst (2000) shows the close relationship between economic incentives, natural resources, and conflict in Africa. The documentation of Human Right Watch (2002) on Fast Track Land Reform in Zimbabwe; and increase of violent conflict between herders and farmers in

Africa (Hussein et. al. 1999) are other examples of land as a centre of concern in conflict contexts.

Jean-Louis Arcand and Nicolas Pons-Vignon (2003) have established that land is not only a source of violence and conflict but it can also be a means of resolving violent conflict and securing sustained peace. Skewed land distribution creates inequalities and inequalities fuel violence (Nafziger and Auvinen, 2002). Unequal distribution of land also creates spatial disparities and ultimately contributes to the escalation of civil unrests (Murdoch and Sandler, 2002). Stewarf (2000) argues that tackling horizontal inequalities is an effective way of preventing crisis. The work of Russett (1964) also concludes that politicising land tenure and consequent inequality contributes to insurgency. Some scholars such as Skaperdas (1992) and Theotocatos and Zetter (2003) have examined the situation of cooperation or conflict from the power-based property rights and role of property rights in peace building. Daniel Buckles (1999) has also demonstrated the relationship between natural resources and conflict and the potential of natural resource is peace building. A study of Willy (2003) in Afghanistan shows that restoring tenure security and land rights is effective in managing crisis. Similarly, Zimmermann and Hubner-Schmid (2000) have extensively documented land tenure issues in Bosnia and Herzegovina.

Land is a source of political manipulation and social exploitation in Nepal. Numerous studies have demonstrated that land is a core of social, economic and political relations. Bhandari (2003); Bhattarai and Pokharel (2004); Caplan, (2000); Chapagain et al., (1998); CSRC (2003, 2004 and 2005); Seddon and Adhikari (2005); Ghimire (1992); Pokharel (2005), Pradhan et. al. (2000); Regmi (1963, 1976 and 1978) and Upreti (2000a&b, 2001, 2002a, 2004a, 2004b, 2004c, 2004d); Yadav (2005), Chapagain (1999 and 2001), Mathew and Upreti (2005), Upreti, Sharam and Basent (2008) and Upreti and Ghale (2002) have extensively analysed various dimensions of land issues and their relationship with social conflict and tensions including armed insurgency in Nepal.

Land reform has been a strong political slogan of all political forces since 1951 in Nepal. In 1961, King Mahendra started land reform as a means of legitimising his autocratic partyless panchayat political system. He had banned the multi-party political system and had required a popular programme to divert the attention of the people of Nepal and the international community. Further, land reform was a popular programme in many parts of world, especially in South East and East Asia. Hence, King Mahendra started this programme envisioning as a strong means to consolidate his power and gain popularity. Thereafter, almost all the political forces followed his strategy to gain popularity instead of using land reform as an important means of social transformation and economic development. None of the leftist, the rightist, or the centrist political forces took land reform as their agenda.

With constant pressure from civil society, a few progressive political leaders and the CPN (M), in 2001, the government[5] decided to reduce land ceiling defined by the Land Act 1964. The reduction was 61 per cent in Tarai, 22 per cent in the hills and 48 per cent in Kathmandu. However, this revised provision was not implemented because of the severe resistance from within the influential leaders of the ruling and opposition parties, who were themselves landlord and blossomed from the land-based exploitation. Table 2.1 shows the revised land ceiling in 2001:

TABLE 2.1: Provision of Land Ceiling made by Land Act

S. No.	*Category of areas*	*Ceiling provision*	*Additional areas provided for housing*	*Revised ceiling by Deuba govenrn-ment in 2001*
1.	All hills/ mountain areas	80 Ropani (4.07 ha)	16 Ropani (0.8 ha)	70 + 5 rop (3.75 ha)
2.	Kathmandu Valley	50 Ropani (2.54 ha)	8 Ropani (0.4 ha)	25+ 5 rop (1.5 ha)
3.	Tarai and inner Tarai	25 Bighas (16.93 ha)	3 Bighas (2.30 ha)	10+ 5 bigha (7.43 ha)

Source: Badal Commission Report, 1996.

Some efforts, such as tokenism, made by the state to provide access of the poor and the marginalised people to land resources, have yet to demonstrate their relevance. One of the initiatives from the government was providing degraded land to the poor people through Leasehold Forestry Programme. However, such provisions are seriously criticized. The study of Mathew and Upreti (2005) revealed thatdenying access and ownership of poor on land and land-based natural resources poses uncertainties, confusions, conflicts, and creates livelihood insecurities.

Another most frequently referred to initiative of the government is the formation of a high commission in 1995 to recommend the government on how to address the land reform programme. Table 2.2 demonstrates the ceiling proposed by the Badal Commission:

TABLE 2.2: Ceiling proposed by Badal Commission

S. No.	*Area*	*Ceiling (ha)*
1.	Tarai and Innar Tarai	3 ha
2.	Middle Hill Area	2 ha
3.	Himalayan Area	4 ha
4.	Kathmandu Valley	1 ha
5.	Urban Area	
	5.1 Municipal area of Kathmandu, Lalitpur and Bhaktpur	*0.5 ha*
	5.2 Other municipalities, district headquarters and developing urban areas	*1 ha*

Source: Badal Commission Report, 1996.

If these recommendations on land ceiling were translated into operation, they might have increased access of marginalised communities to land resources. The Badal Commission identified problems related to land and suggested very useful integrated measures for the overall land reform in Nepal. However, none of the governments operating since then took any initiative to implement the recommendations of this commission.

Land distribution and gross disparities in land ownership are one of the major sources of feeling of injustice and conflict

TABLE 2.3: Distributions of Operational Land-holdings by Size, Classes and Territorial Zones (1961)

Territorial Zones		*Size and classes of land-holdings (ha)*								
		Landless	*<0.40*	*0.40-1.0*	*1.0-2.0*	*2.0-4.0*	*4.0-10*	*>10*	*>100*	*Total*
Mountain	Area	N.A.	N.A.	N.A.	N.A.	N.A.	N.A.	N.A.	N.A.	N.A.
	HH	N.A.	N.A.	N.A.	N.A.	N.A.	N.A.	N.A.	N.A.	N.A.
Hill	Area		27.87	38.83	21.02	8.46	3.35	0.48		100
	HH	0.28	63.11	27.91	6.98	1.44	0.27	0.01		100
Eastern	Area		23.34	37.00	24.41	10.63	4.12	0.5		100
	HH	0.15	58.57	29.71	9.11	2.06	0.38	0.02		100
Central	Area		30.5	39.88	19.4	7.43	2.7	0.08		100
	HH	0.28	65.22	27.06	6.08	1.18	0.2	0.003		100
Western	Area		31.36	40.26	17.88	6.45	3.02	1.03		100
	HH	0.46	66	26.78	5.5	1.02	0.23	0.02		100
Kathmandu Valley	Area		25.24	48.78	19.9	5.1	0.9			100
	HH	0.23	55.05	36.73	6.94	0.92	0.08			100
Inner Terai	Area		5.17	12.02	13.37	25.17	24.86	19.41	0.56	100
	House-hold	2.57	35.44	27.56	13.72	12.76	6.28	1.68	0.007	100

(Contd....)

Territorial Zones		*Landless*	*<0.40*	*0.40-1.0*	*1.0-2.0*	*2.0-4.0*	*4.0-10*	*>10*	*>100*	*Total*
			Size and classes of land-holdings (ha)							
Eastern	Area		10.86	16.82	14.27	25.72	20.56	11.77		100
	HH	0.34	51.39	25.54	9.63	9	3.4	0.71		100
Central	Area		4.98	15.35	14.34	27.11	20.92	17.31		100
	HH	0.5	30.17	34.55	14.75	12.97	5.18	1.34		100
Western	Area		0.8	3.61	11.33	22.11	33.66	28.46	1.77	100
	HH	13.09	10.52	14.17	20.6	21	15.8	4.79	0.04	100
Terai	Area		1.51	5.17	13.52	24.67	30.28	24.5	1.65	100
	HH	3.57	17.83	20.1	21.82	21.15	12.19	3.13	0.02	100
Eastern	Area		1.98	6.14	13.87	27.29	31.46	19.37	0.81	100
	HH	3.59	20.39	19.94	20.69	21.26	11.75	2.39	0.01	100
Central	Area		0.9	5.54	15.33	22.35	25.69	30.19	0.58	100
	HH	5.04	10.61	20.59	27.5	21.18	10.95	4.12	0.02	100
Western	Area		0.28	3.52	7.41	13.15	30.03	45.61	7.931	100
	HH	2.62	6.08	20.87	21.49	19.91	19.97	9.05	0.14	100
Nepal	Area		8.81	15.22	15.37	20.31	22.67	17.67	1.13	100
	HH	1.43	47.97	25.92	11.72	7.84	4.1	1.02	0.007	100

Source: CBS, 1961; Bhattarai, (2003): (Table 2.21, p-125).
Note: N.A= Not Available; HH =Household.

(Upreti, 2002a). The Nepal Human Development Report 2004 shows that 5 per cent rich people hold 37 per cent of total arable land and 47 per cent poor people hold only 15 per cent (UNDP, 2004).

When there is a greater control on natural resources by a small section of society and another large section has to depend on a limited amount of available resource, there is always competition. When some people gain more and others suffer, a feeling of injustice develops. The land ownership pattern presented in Table 2.4 below clearly demonstrates that the unequal distribution of land and land-based resources not only threatened the livelihoods of people but also excluded them from access to other resources and implanted a feeling of injustice. The insurgents tactfully capitalized on this feeling and gained sympathy of the exploited people. The state was simply not able or was unwilling to address the concerns of the poor and marginalized people (Upreti, 2004a and 2004c).

TABLE 2.4: Land Distribution Situation in Nepal

S. No.	*Category of People*	*% of Total Population*
1.	Landless	24.44
2.	Semi-landless (owing less than 0.20 acre or 0.08 ha)	6.98
3.	Marginal cultivators (owing 0.21 to 1 acre or 0.084 to 0.4046 ha)	27.59
4.	Small cultivators (1.01 to 2 acres or 0.4087 to 0.809 ha)	20.15
5.	Semi-medium (2.01 to 4 acres or 0.809 to 1.618 ha)	13.42
6.	Medium cultivators (4 to 10 acres or 1.659 to 4.05 ha)	6.25
7.	Large cultivators (more than 10.01 acre or 4.06 ha)	1.17

Source: Table 11, UNDP (2004: 176).

It is astonishing to observe that nearly a quarter of the total population of the country based in subsistence agriculture is landless (Table 2.4). Further, one million agricultural workers have no ownership of land, 450 thousands of tenants are not registered and consequently not able to claim the tenancy rights.

Table 2.5 provides comparative information on the size of land holdings.

TABLE 2.5 : Size and Area of Holdings

S. No.	Size of Holding (Hectare)	In Per cent Household 1962	1972*	Area Owned 1962	1972*
1.	Less than 0.51	56.1	52.9	13.9	21.1
2.	0.51 to 2.03	30.7	37.4	32.3	32.7
3.	2.03 to 5.09	9.5	6.9	31.1	30.2
4.	5.09 to 10.17	2.6	1.6	1.9	1.7
5.	10.17 to 20.35	0.8	1.1	11.2	9.9
6.	20.35 to 50.87	0.2	0.1	6.6	3.6
7.	50.87 and above	0.1		3	0.8
	Total	100	100	100	100

Source: Ministry of Food and Agriculture, Agricultural Statistics of Nepal, 1972, P.8 and CBS, National Census of Agriculture, 1961-62 and 1971-72.

In Nepal, approximately 300,000 *Hali* (who base their livelihood by ploughing land of other people) do not have land ownership. According to HDR 2004, 15 per cent of hill and 44 per cent of Tarai *Dalits* are landless and they have no access to land water and forest and are dependent on landlords and rich people for their daily subsistence. These inequalities are manifested in conflict. Small holders are marginalised and rapidly transformed into landless people (Shrestha, 1997). Most of them are socially excluded and disadvantaged groups and *Dalits*.

From the foregoing discussion it is clear that, land is one of the most contested natural resources in Nepal. This has also been documented by the court cases of Nepal. Majority of disputes[6] in the courts of Nepal are directly or indirectly related to land. Land- related disputes in every court of Nepal occupy more than 60 per cent (Bhattarai and Pokharel, 2004).

Commenting on the complications in obtaining justice from the courts on land conflicts, one lawyer of the District Court claimed that the provisions relating to appeals further worsened the matter. He further said, "*Even as a small claim where the appeal court does not confirm the decision of the district court, the losing party can file a second appeal to the Supreme Court..*[7] *The misery of the winning party does not end here. Even after she wins the case the enforcement again takes years due to frustratingly cumbersome procedures. These procedures are again full of legal loopholes, which oftentimes give scope for supplementary disputes. In the absence of an initiative to create a less disputative legal order by suitable legal reforms, by helping people to settle disputes through conciliations and mediations at the local level and also by smoothening the court procedures for effective and speedy dispute resolution, the land disputes in Nepal will continue to burden the people and the courts"* (Bhattarai and Pokharel, 2004: 64-65). This quotation is self-explanatory and illustrates the level of complexity of land conflicts dealt with by the court proceedings.

2.7 CONCLUSIONS

Land in Nepal is not only the means of livelihood for many people but also a stable source of power and prestige and consequently the basis of exploitation of poor and marginalized people. Exclusion and discrimination are some of the major constraints in achieving equitable land titles and access to natural resources for the poor and marginalised people (Upreti et al., 2008). Even though marginalised communities and disadvantaged groups are protecting and promoting biodiversity, their contributions are rarely recognised in policies. The land titles are denied to some of the disadvantaged groups because of lack of their access to power centres. Consequently, they are excluded from various land-based benefits provided by the state (e.g. agricultural loan, inputs).

For centuries, most of the policies and legislations of Nepal were not sensitive to social inequalities (based on the social structure concepts of caste, ethnicity, clan and class) and derived from the patronage politics. Some of the policy and legislations were also restricting the basic rights of indigenous peoples to have access to resources, which they have been using since the past many years to derive livelihoods and support traditional occupations. Most of these policies and regulations assumed communities as static and relatively homogenous entities to be regulated by a central governing system. However, after the 2006 people's movement, the situation has significantly changed and the concerns of the *Dalits*, the marginalized and the excluded groups are getting heard.

There are two major problems in assuring benefits to the poor and the marginalised people from land and related natural resource. First, polices and legislations are not sensitive enough to the concerns of the poor and the marginalised people. Second, the existing policies and laws are not sincerely translated into practices and manipulated in interests of elites and landlords. Further, lack of democratic and inclusive resource governance practices, weak institutional responses and effects of rapid globalisation are posing enormous threats on natural resources (Gore, 1992).

The disharmony and contradictions within and between land resources-related laws and policies have great ramifications in Nepal and are causing negative consequences to the poor and the marginalised people. The tendency of maintaining supremacy of each law or policy related to particular natural resource (land or forest or water) and lack of integrated approach is adding other complications. Several contradictions have been observed in the absence of a coordinated approach at the central level among the concerned ministries (Water Resources, Agriculture and Cooperative, Land Reforms, Forest and Soil Conservation, etc.).

Tensions between peasants and large landowners on the issue of land ownership are often linked with historical context. If land distribution is focused on large-scale programme to socially excluded groups as in Mozambique and Vietnam, the land ownership issue can indeed be addressed.

Informed debates on land can contribute to seeking answers and solutions to the land problems discussed in this chapter. It is essential to move from moral bankruptcy, deterrent actions and pollutant mindset to address land conflict and contribute to peace and stability in society. We need a change in our collective thinking, behaviour, action and response. If we do not change, we may face inescapable consequences, and as a result get in return what the former US Vice-President and a noted environmentalist Al Gore calls dysfunctional civilization and destruction of natural world (Gore, 1992).

If land is intended to be used as a means of conflict

resolution and peace building, then the land distribution system has to foster economic efficiency, environmental sustainability, long-term stability and equity, and social justice. This system should ensure clear property rights. The political context and the people's movement of 2006 have provided great opportunity to address the centuries-old land-based inequalities, discriminations and manipulations. State restructuring and federalization of the country could provide great opportunity if the political actors are committed.

End Notes

1. Work of J.K. Galbraith explains in detail about the power relation in his work 'An Anatomy of Power'.
2. The Deuba government abolished the Kamaya system seven years ago and the Maoist-led government abolished the haruwa system in September 2008.
3. Common property resources may not necessarily be all natural resources and vice versa. But community members may treat many natural resources as common property resources because of their mode of appropriation and management.
4. The thesis 'The Tragedy of the Commons' (Hardin, 1968) emphasises that 'when CPR are used by an increasing number of people, often for different purposes, and agreement governing resource use are absent, collective use may lead to over exploitation, degradation and eventual ruin of the resource, which is attributed to the users' incentive to maximise their own utility,' (Steins, 1999:3).
5. The Deuba government redefined the land ceiling through the 2001 budget speech.
6. They are related to boundary conflict, claims over or partition of family property, gifts, lease, claim of tenancy rights, access and use of common land and pastures, community forestry, right of succession, etc.
7. Nepal contains a three-tiered court system, with the District Court at the bottom, Appellate Court to hear the first appeal, and the Supreme Court as the highest court.

Chapter 3

Armed Conflict, Displacement and Environmental Stresses

3.1 THE CONTEXT

A decade-long armed conflict has brought enormous impacts on people, society and environment. The ongoing armed conflict has severely altered the existing socially constructed relations between environment and human beings. The armed conflict has not only altered the inter- and intra-household relations but also their environmental functions associated with conventional roles and responsibilities.

The main objective of this chapter is to examine the impacts of the armed conflict on environmental sanitation and public health of IDP in Nepal. This chapter focuses on the analyses of:

(a) environmental causes of armed conflict, such as pressure on environmental resources, unequal and power-based pattern of use and control of these resources, and weak environmental governance practices, and

(b) the impacts of armed insurgency on environmental sanitation and health issues of IDP of urban areas of Kathmandu valley.

There is a problem of definition of IDPS. Diferent people define IDPs differently. HOwver in this chapter the UNHCR definition is used becase of it is relatively wider and covers different aspects of IDPs. The UNHCR defines IDPs as the uprooted people from their community as a result of persecution, armed conflict or violence. They are forced to abandon their homes and leave their usual place of residence but remain within the borders of their own country'[1] (UNHCR, 1997). IDPs are therefore among the most vulnerable victims of the armed conflict and often they constitute largest at-risk population. Armed conflict induced displacement is often linked with violence, human rights abuses (such as arbitrary killing, rape, torture, kidnapping, etc.) and psychological oppressions. In the armed conflict, IDPs are mostly elderly, women, children and disabled people. They are often traumatized and fearing for their lives and therefore forced to leave their homes and communities to seek refuge in perceived to be more secure areas.[2]

The case study was conducted in slum areas where clusters of IDPs settlements are located in the banks of Bagmati and Manohara Rivers of Kathmadnu Valley. They were self-organized settlements, without any external support. The government and Kathmandu Metropolitan Corporation (KMC) termed these settlements as illegal and therefore did not provide any supports. The IDPs in the settlements (approximately 500 huts and 3500 people) were mainly coming from the form western, central and eastern Nepal. First, some of the IDPs came in 2002 and built small huts. In 2003, a large number of IDPs arrived and settled there. As they were illegally settling in the slums, they had no formal access to electricity, drinking water and other services provided by the KMC. Hence, they were using these services illegally.

The methods used in the study were ethnography (a process of close observation and interpretation of behaviour and function of people and organizations through intimate participation in a community), focus group discussion, observation, in-depth interviews, triangulation and review of secondary literature. The analysis is made from the sociological perspective. In the observation method, the situation of IDPs: living conditions, physical facilities and livelihood bases were the main focus. Semi-structured interviews with individual IDPs, key-informant interviews with selected individuals (representatives of Maoist Victims Association; local social and political leaders and IDP activists, state victims). Secondary source of information was collected from reports and publications of Global IDP Project, Geneva Conventions, UNDP, UNICEF, UNCHR, OCHA, Red Cross Society, Government of Nepal and NGOs. Triangulation was made to confirm the findings.

3.2 ARMED CONFLICT AND DISPLACEMENT

Conflict-induced displacement in Nepal is still a major concern. The phenomenon of mass displacement has significantly increased, together with the increased intensity of the armed conflict.[3] A report of the Inter-Agency Internal Displacement Division (IDD) Mission to Nepal (11-22 April 2005)[4] had concluded that '*Nepal faces a very serious political, security and humanitarian situation in which preventive measures are urgently required to prevent further deterioration.*' It further states, '*While the full magnitude of population displacement is unknown, best reliable estimates suggest that up to 200,000*[5] *Nepalese may have been internally displaced by the conflict, with perhaps 2 million or more moving to India in recent years*' (IDD, 2005).

It is still very hard to find the clear and authentic data on IDPs in Nepal. The situation of silent IDPS is even unclear. The official estimate of the government is 6000-7000 IDPs[6] which was revised after signing of the CPA and now it is said to be 44,861 in July 2008.[7] However, human rights activists and advocacy groups estimate the number of IDPs is 400000-600,000. Nevertheless, the international community says that Nepal was not willing for humanitarian intervention to address conflict-induced displacement. Based on experiences of other countries, they argued that IDPs are managing themselves. Often IDPs were illegally settling around the East-West Highway and other roadsides; diffusing in urban areas and big cities like Kathmandu, Nepalgunj, Biratnagar, which were perceived to be relatively safe locations with more livelihood opportunities. Many IDPs diffused with host communities and stayed with their relatives. It was often said that if humanitarian assistance is provided, influx of IDPs would further increase.[8] However, since 2004 only the United Nations Office for the Coordination of Humanitarian Affairs (OCHA) and some I/NGOs had initiated minor activities supporting IDPs in different parts of Nepal (Aditya et al., 2006; Khatiwoda, 2004).

Clusters of settlements of IDP can be observed in many urban centres of Nepal, such as Surkhet, Nepalgunj, Dang, and Kathmandu Valley (Upreti and Ghimire, 2008; Adhikari, 2006). Hundreds of thousands of people forced to flee or to leave their homes or places of habitual residence as a result of armed conflict during the past 11 years were scattered in different parts of Nepal. The main reason of the displacement was actual or perceived security risk.

People left their places of residence because of fear of general violence, violations of human rights or natural or human-made disasters and crossing an international border are considered as refugees and can claim protection and assistance under the 1951 Refugee Convention and can approach the UNHCR for help. However, IDPs have no such privilege, therefore they have to depend on their governments for the protection and assistance. Regrettably, often the governments either ignore or lack means to support and protect IDPs. Consequently, large numbers of IDPs remain at high risk of abuses, violence, malnutrition, diseases and stress, as observed in Sri Lanka (Brun, 2003), Nepal (Duijn, 2003; Tamang and Johan, 2006) and other many conflict-ridden countries (Curtis, 2001; Leux et al., 2000).

3.3 ARMED CONFLICT AND ENVIRONMENTAL SANITATION AND HEALTH

This section briefly discusses the relationship between armed conflict and environment and its effects on environmental sanitation and health of IDPs staying in urban areas of Kathmandu Valley. Based on empirical evidences, the paper argues that poor environmental sanitation and health of IDP is directly linked with environmental stress and population factors, which have played significant roles in creating underlying conditions for the armed conflict. Hence, the degrading environmental situation of Kathmandu Valley and poor health and sanitation conditions of IDPs are directly connected and affecting each other, which ultimately contributes to instability.

Local dynamics of resource use patterns are entirely shaped by power relations in Nepal. The 'winners take all' model practiced in Nepal is an example. It has been clearly observed that local elites hold almost all production resources and exploit poor and marginalized section of society (Upreti et al., 2008). Inequitable use of natural resources by powerful elites of village is depriving the poor people. A previous study of this author has shown that it was almost impossible for poor and marginalised people to get irrigation water in dry summer before the local elites (Upreti, 2001). Further, exploitation is not limited to physical resources. From the conflict perspective, irrational exploitation of human resources is a major cause of armed conflict.

Previous studies of the author of this book (Upreti, 2004a, 2006a, 2007b, 2006c and 2004e) demonstrate that, despite the several claims of the government, environmental and resource governance principles. processes and practices are extremely top-down, elite-centric, non-transparent and corrupt and therefore not able to address the environmental health and sanitation-related problems of IDPs. Government became inherently weak in mainstreaming and ensuring environmental/ecological issues and concerns in policies and plans, laws and regulations, strategies and decisions and actual actions at different levels within a good governance framework (i.e. consensus oriented, participatory, guided by rule of law, effective and efficient, accountable and transparent, responsive, equitable and inclusive) that led to a crisis in environmental sanitation.

The respondents shared their view that there are several consequences of the armed insurgency on their surroundings, sanitation and health and livelihood while they were staying in the slums of Kathmandu Valley. Most of the respondent IDPs explained that they suffer from lack of food, health facilities, enough drinking water and sanitation, legal and other physical protection. They were not able to exercise their economic, civil and political rights in the settlements. Particularly the elderly, children and women are suffering from lack of food and nutrients, medical facilities, drinking water and sanitations.

They had further explained that the IDPs in the study area were facing severe harassments and problems from the municipality authority and local host communities.

Shelter was one of the serious health-related problems observed in the study settlements. Several small, closely-attached dark thatches with congested spaces were illegally constructed on the banks of rivers, without having access to electricity, drinking water and public spaces. All of them were unsafe, as they were simply erected on fragile edges of both sides of the river banks. There was no proper ventilation in the houses, extremely congested spaces and no toilet facilities.

The pressure of IDPs was beyond the carrying capacity[9] of settlement areas, in terms of ecological services, open space and physical requirements because of their heavy concentration in a small fragile area.

The settlement areas had faced real problems of collection, management and disposal of solid and liquid waste. They dispose waste in the rivers, polluting the already polluted river. Bagmati and Manohara Rivers become almost dead in the dry season and remain the centre of waste disposal. The public frequently complains that the IDPs were responsible for pollution within and the surrounding areas of settlements and nearby communities. Settlements were too dirty and no one was interested in cleaning it up. The residents were not concerned with sanitation, health hazards and pollution in their areas. They simply ignored it.

3.3.1 Energy Difficulties

As settlements were being located in the city, they had to rely on electricity. However, they were not allowed to officially use electricity because of illegal settlement status. Ultimately, they use it illegally by connecting directly from the transfer lines, which is extremely risky. Such practices invite potential electric shocks, fire and other health hazards.

3.3.2 Security Tension

It was reported by the respondents that there are continuous tensions between local host communities and IDPs. Local people expressed that the petty thefts, gang fights, rapes, assaults and insecurity have sharply increased in the areas once the IDPs came and settled in the river bank. One local person[10] from the host community said, "*We are facing real security threats from the IDPs, I stopped waling from the settlement areas in early morning and evening. Numerous looting, grabbing of purses, watches and looting are occurring weekly. My house was theft twice. Police are not able to control these crimes. Rather, some of the police officers are helping them and getting share from the earning of criminals. Women and girls have completely stopped passing through the settlement areas. Until the illegal settlements of IDPs are dismantled and removed them from the Bagmati River bank and settle them in other areas, we do not feel safe*".

3.3.3 Congestions

The buildings and spaces inside the houses were too congested. Some families were also keeping pigs and poultry inside the house. There was a possibility of transmission of disease from animals to human beings.

3.3.4 Unsafe Drinking Water

The population in the settlements was seriously lacking in availability of adequate safe drinking water. The drinking water supply office did not allow the IDPs to access the water from its supply system. Hence, some of the IDPs did illegally puncture the water supply pipes and obtained the water. Others placed boring pumps to get water. However, the water pumped from the shallow boring is highly suspected as contaminated from the polluted water of Bagmati River. Children were severely exposed to pollution as they play in the polluted rivers.

3.3.5 Lack of Other Basic Services

The IDPs were facing a problem of accessing basic services such as health and education, and legal protection because of lack of their legal status. Extremely poor sanitation facilities and lack of toilets, direct disposal of human excreta and other solid and liquid waste in Bagmati and Manohara River have frequently caused various diseases such as frequent diarrhoea, dysentery, fever, jaundice, etc. Similarly, they were also not able to access social benefits provided by the state or municipality. Their traditional cultural values were threatened in the new settlement areas because they were not able to exercise these cultures.

3.3.6 Environmental and Health Related Problems

The settlements had also serious environmental problems because of destruction of vegetation cover, loss of biodiversity, soil erosion, damage of ecosystem functioning and pollution of the river and surroundings.

The respondents frequently reported that they were suffering from a large number of rats and public health officials said that the increased number of rats serve as disease-carrying vectors. However, the IDPs did not know about the disease-carrying vector and therefore they did not bother. Large numbers of poorly managed pig and poultry are also polluting in the settlement areas and disrupting local environment.

There were several health and sanitation-related issues and problems of the IDPs in the settlement sites and IDPs face a severe health crisis and the degradation of surrounding environmental service created social tension. The Liberian experiences documented by UNEP (2006) reveal that if these issues are not addressed promptly, it could lead to huge environmental and social problems. Hence, urgent attention is needed to address the health and sanitation problems faced by IDPs and their long-term rehabilitation.

The IDPs explained that displacement has made them poor and vulnerable because of their inability to meet their basic needs. Hence, they were facing severe impoverishment and suffering from societal stigmas, political restrictions, limited economic and wage-earning opportunity, insufficient access to required resources for basic needs and inadequate assistance. Consequently, displaced people exhibit disproportionately high levels of malnourishment, disease affliction, physical stunting and wasting, illiteracy and innumeracy, morbidity and mortality. They were highly vulnerable; once they were not able to get legal protection from the state. This case study indicates that risk, uncertainty and vulnerability were an integral part of IDP. In an interview, one leader of IDP stated, "*Once, we suffer from livelihood insecurity and psychological tensions, environmental and health considerations are secondary for us. Our first and foremost priority is to gain dignity, safe return home and re-establish normal life.*[11] "

3.4 LIVELIHOOD INSECURITY AND STRESSES

The displaced people were unable to meet their basic livelihood requirements because of being dissociated from their farming as the existing means of livelihood. They had faced severe impoverishment because of societal stigmas, political restrictions, limited economic and wage-earning potential, insufficient access to necessary resources and inadequate assistance. Consequently, they exhibited disproportionately high levels of malnourishment, disease affliction, physical stunting.

In the study area, the main livelihood basis of IDPs was wage labour. Some of them worked as street vendors; others worked as skilled labour in building construction. Some of them were engaged in poultry farming, pig farming and retail shops, and others were washing dishes in rich people's houses in the neighbourhood to sustain their livelihood.

The case study reveals that when IDPs left their homes, either by force or voluntarily, their social relations with their neighbours, friends or relatives were severely disrupted. Hence, they suffered from a deep grief and even trauma, which was also frequently observed in other conflict-affected countries (Orner and Schnyder, 2003).

Those IDPs who had better living conditions, prestige, name and fame, dignified lives in their native places are leaving with nothing but uncertainity and their helplessness future poses them severe psychological stress. Once there is a forced move from a dignified life to harsh condition, it incurs huge psychological loss to any individual (Palmer, 2002). The respondents expressed that it is more painful when responsible bodies such as government officials, political parties and organisations engaged in IDP issues ignore their problems.

Often they are treated badly by the government as well as the host community. Local people blamed them as land encroachers and source of insecurity. Therefore, IDPs were more frustrated and felt psychologically stressed from the behaviours of government staff and community members. Some of the respondents said that they felt insulted, humiliated and forced to think of suicide because of the behaviour of the KMC, government and host communities.

Human rights organisations were raising concerns of abuses of human rights, economic and political rights of IDPs (INSEC, 2007, 2005 and 2006; IA, 2005a and 2005b). One of the main concerns of IDPs in Nepal was protection of civil, economic and political rights and ensuring justices. Protection of displaced people was undermined in Nepal in the context of insurgency and counter-insurgency campaigns. They were victims of attacks by rebel groups as well as security forces. In Nepal, the rights of displaced populations are ignored.

The freedom of movement was one of the central rights in relation to internal displacement.[12] The implementation of the freedom of movement and the right to choose one's residence was especially important. Once people are internally displaced, their rights to return voluntarily and safety to their place of residence must be guaranteed. However, the IDP situation in Nepal clearly demonstrates that the rights of IDPs to return their homes were largely ignored at the policy level. Even after 22 months of signing of the CPA, the provisions related to IDPs stated in the agreement are not translated into action.

IDPs have a deep feeling of injustice. Reconciliation is the first and the most important step to cure this feeling of injustice and reintegrate them in society (Dhakal, 2004; ICG, 2005c; ICRC, 2005; IDD, 2005; Upadhaya, 2006). The famous saying of Nelson Mandela - 'we forgive but not forget' - is a basis of reconciliation for IDPs. However, the GoN has not yet come up with a package of reconciliation. The provision of Truth and Reconciliation Commission stipulated in the CPA has not yet been formed.

IDPs have often left their property, including house and land. Land was a major source of livelihood of the IDPs in Nepal and often their lands were either uncultivated or captured by others. Land being the main source of livelihood, regaining the land and cultivation was the main concern to secure their source of subsistence. Ensuring full access to their land and possession is an important step in the process of reconciliation, reintegration and rehabilitation (Upreti, 2006a; Aditya et al., 2006). The CPA had made provisions for returning the seized lands and property of people by CPN (M) but it has not yet fully implemented.

As many IDPs in Nepal were staying with their relatives, and depending on other people and only very few are residing in camps, depending on others makes them socially and psychologically insecure and vulnerable (Adhikari, 2006, Upadhaya, 2006). This feeling was further strengthened once they found negative attitudes of hosts, government and other organisations working on the issues of IDPs. It was also observed that many displaced people were hesitant to return to their homes because they had lost their property, houses, business. They felt insecure to return. Some of the IDPs were workers of ruling political parties, getting regular financial supports from GoN, I/NGOs sources by using their party's power and influences, therefore they did not want to return home. Interestingly, it was frequently reported in the media that some IDP leaders supported by influential political parties are earning millions of rupees in the name of IDPs from donors and INGOs and using them for personal benefit. Hence, the IDP issue became a highly politicised subject in Nepal and IDPs are used to undermine political opponents by both the CMN-M and the other larger parliamentary political parties.

Experiences of different conflict-ridden countries show that IDPs face several problems when they return to their community (Norwegian Refugee Council, 2006). Sometimes, they are perceived as supporters of the 'enemy' by the influential party in the community. In such a situation, they face continuous risks and threats. A hostile environment after their return to home/community can expose them to physical violence, capturing of their land and houses or persistent discrimination (UNHCR, 1997). Unless confidence and security are restored, the situation remains in a state of social instability.

Reconciliation and confidence-building measures are therefore important elements in any attempt to achieve lasting solutions for IDPs (Orner and Schnyder, 2003).

The IDP rehabilitation and recovery process seeks to prioritise interventions focusing on the psychosocial needs that arise in a situation of crisis. Psychosocial needs and problems refer to those problems and needs that have a psychological (referring to emotions, behaviour, cognition and individual coping resources) and a social (referring to the support mechanisms necessary for a collective coping process) origin (Palmer, 2002). On the contrary, the IDP situation in Nepal reveals that neither psychological nor social concerns are taken into proper consideration (Terres des Homes Nepal, 2005; Khatiwoda, 2004; Duijn, 2003; Dhakal, 2004, IDD, 2005; Adhikari, 2006). Political parties always look at problems from vested political interests and the IDP problem was no exception.

For children, family is the most basic unit of protection and a cornerstone of psychosocial support. When the children are involved, family members who are separated by displacement should be reunited as quickly as possible in accordance with Principle 17(3). In this process, children who are separated from family members need to be registered to facilitate tracing for reunification. Children need to be sheltered, cared and safeguarded against potential risks of trafficking and military recruitment (MacCormark, 2003). However, so far GoN did not take this issue seriously. Despite the continuous pressure from child rights activists and human rights organisations, GoN has not taken further steps.

Rehabilitation is one of the important elements of the long-term management of IDPs and making the peace process successful (Upreti, 2006a). It is not only a question of the infrastructure, but also a matter of reaching out to the hearts and minds of people for reconciliation (Burn, 2003; Curtis, 2001; Deng, 1999, 2001 and 2004). Long-term social and economic development, immediate needs and rehabilitation programmes must be envisioned to foster social cohesion, solidarity, tolerance and encouragement and maintenance of cultural, ethnic and religious diversities (Gomez, 2002; Holtzman and Nezam, 2004; ICRC, 2005; Leux et al., 2002). Once the political and security situation eventually allows IDPs to return home, they often encounter ruined property and infrastructure, lack of resource to meet the basic needs, as well as need for health, sanitation and education, livestock rearing, equipment and seeds for agriculture and lack of employment options. Consequently, they fall into a cycle of debilitating poverty (Orner and Schnyder, 2003; Moore and Shellman, 2002; Phuong, 2003). The Government of Nepal ihas not given priority to rehabilitate IDPS even after two years of signing of the CPA.

Return of displaced people can be viable only when conditions for their dignity and safety are assured, which include protection of their social, cultural and political rights, return of their assets and properties they lost and ensuring appropriate state help for resettlement and rehabilitation[13] (ICRC, 2005; Sinclair, 2002; OCHA, 2003). But, while examining the ongoing activities related to IDPs, it is hard to find encouraging progress. Politicisation of peace process and IDP is a glaring reality.

While managing IDPs, often relief and reconstruction efforts are focused on providing immediate shelter (ICRC, 2005). Reconstruction and relief interventions are essential for desperate IDPs who need immediate shelter and food. However, there should be long-term strategies focused on determination and implementation of realistic and permanent reconstruction plans for affected communities, tie up with rebuilding community confidence and support structures for local responsibility through participatory planning of reconstruction processes (Phuong, 2003; Leux et al., 2000).

The situation of the case study area in specific and IDP situation of Nepal in general demonstrate that IDP support should include not only food, non-food items, medicines and shelter but also measures to ensure physical safety and respect for human rights, including advising the government on drafting laws to protect specific rights of internally displaced persons, intervening to register the internally displaced, thereby entitling them to assistance, access to health care and education, as well as establishing monitoring mechanisms. Further, environmental health and sanitation should be an integral part of the long-term management and rehabilitation of IDPs.

3.5 VULNERABILITY AND RISKS IN A NEW URBAN ENVIRONMENT

During the focused group discussions and interviews, most of the IDPs expressed that they sufferfrom lack of enough means of livelihood, are exhausted and traumatized. They are separated from their community or family. They have no physical security or the necessary basis for subsistence. They live on the banks of the Bagmati and Manohara rivers full of insecurity, uncertainty and hardships. Because of this situation, they are highly vulnerable and at high risk.

It was observed in the case study sites that serious psychological problems and stress are part of the daily life of IDPs. Most common problems observed were:

- Feeling of isolation, frustration and helplessness,
- Emotional and psychological stress; and
- Feeling of revenge and retaliation.

The condition of children is worst in terms of sanitation, basic health and access to education as most of them are not enrolled in school and are consequently excluded from their right to health and education.

The elderly, children and women IDPs expressed their frustration, feeling of isolation and helplessness because of the human insecurities such as destruction or discontinuity in livelihoods, separation from their means of production, severe restrictions on mobility, disruption of social relations, hungry, lacking proper shelter and enough clothing, sick and children missing school. Their normal life was disturbed because of the separation from relatives and friends and loss of property and possession. IDPs frequently encountered emotional and psychological stress and trauma. All these emotional and psychological aspects had contributed to developing a feeling of revenge and retaliation in some IDPs, which can be a perennial source of conflict and tension in society and a threat to the ongoing peace process.

The IDP respondents of the in-depth interviews explained that they always felt risks and uncertainties. They are worried and thinking about what happened to their property and possession, when to regain them, what the government will do to assist them, when and how to re-establish relations. This situation forced IDPs to continue their life full of uncertainty, insecurity and vulnerability.

Once displacement is long, it develops into a situation of chronic insecurity and poverty, lack of opportunity for economic and social integration. Consequently, IDPs develop a very high sense of dependency and feelings of uncertainty and helplessness. In such a situation, IDPs do not know exactly what to do and often they wait for the government and aid agencies to decide their fate.

Experiences of other countries with IDPs show that IDPs are often excluded from participating in the political process as well as employment opportunities, unable to mange their property, and face harsh travel restrictions (Phuong, 2003; Moore and Shellman, 2002). They are socially excluded and face a heightened risk of sexual and physical violence. They are afforded limited access to education and healthcare. IDPs face impoverishment and destitution as a way of life[14] (Burn, 2002; Gomez, 2002; Holtz and Nezam, 2004; Sinclair, 2001).

Recalling his past situation in the home village, one respondent said, "*When we were living in our home area, we had greater mutual trust, cooperation in our community. All were ready to help each other for any individual and communal affairs. We had social safety-nets, mutual suppot and stronger ties among the villagers. We had developed resilience capacity in difficult circumstances. But when we left our communities, all these networks, solidarity mechanisms and social capital were broken and now we are facing such a grave situation*".[15] The work of MacCormack (2003) and Orner and Schnyder (2003) in different countries has also demonstrated a similar situation of IDPs. It is common elsewhere that in the a situation of displacement, it is not only hard to get basic needs and safety but also IDPs are exposed to life-threatening experiences, the tolerance ability of IDPs deteriorates and chance of suffering from psychological trauma including depression, frustration, pessimism, uncertainty, helplessness and hopelessness increases.

It is observed in the study areas that IDPs are highly vulnerable and impoverished. They were suffering from discrimination. They were experiencing significant deprivation and marginalization, loss of economic opportunities, breakdown of cultural identity, loosening of social and familial structures. The children faced interruption of schooling. They also suffered from increased poverty levels.

3.6 POLICY RESPONSE OF THE STATE TOWARDS IDP

The problems of IDPs were not yet taken seriously by the government of Nepal. It was an urgent need to address physical, social, cultural disruptions and livelihood insecurities faced by IDPs. Providing lip-service and uncoordinated, unplanned small occasional relief in a biased manner (giving only to the victim of one side) cannot address the widening problem of IDPs in Nepal. IDPs are in a vicious circle of losing physical, social and emotional aspects of their lives. Mere articulation of words of sympathy would not reduce the problems. The problems of IDPs are multidimensional in nature and therefore demand multidimensional solutions. Political, social, economic, environmental issues are attached to displacement. Therefore, a combination of humanitarian components, security, special legal provisions as well as immediate and longer-term needs should be addressed in a comprehensive and coordinated manner.

Currently the government, particularly the Ministry of Peace and Reconstruction has developed policy on IDPs. However, the government has yet to arrange instructional mechanisms, regulatory framework and operational procedures in translating policy into action and to address the IDP issues. All that the government is occasionally doing on IDP is limited mainly to providing some money to return home. However, it is ad hoc, incomplete, biased and consequently controversial. Some powerful IDPs, mainly displaced from CPN (M), are actively engaged in dealing with IDPs concerns and even sometimes politicising issues.

Box 3.1 Some general measures adapted for helping IDPs

- Emphasis on long-term development and not just short-term relief
- Emphasis on respecting social and cultural contexts
- Viewing traumatic experience as one of the stress-inducing aspects of life
- Encouraging a view of problems and solutions as belonging to the collective community
- Promoting reconciliation and reunion among separated members
- Addressing community prejudices and misconceptions about youth soldiers
- Creating a mechanism at communities to advocate for the needs of its children and youth
- Increasing community resources, facilities, and capacity to care for the returning people
- Training all concerned stakeholders to deal with the special needs of ex-combatants
- Rebuild needed infrastructures including education and health
- Train people to deal with the special needs of ex-child and young adult soldiers
- Work to make the community as self-sufficient as possible in dealing with these issues

The responsibility for managing IDPs primarily goes to government and local authorities. Disturbingly, however, IDPs find themselves in a vacuum of responsibility within the state and politicised for the vested political interests of powerful political parties.

Although government is primarily responsible for the welfare of IDPs, in the past few years the government has indicated that it is unwilling to take responsibility. The IDPs were separated from their normal support systems and mostly without identity papers issued by the CDOs of their respective districts, which are required to get small relief assistance form government or NGOs. Consequently, they were unable to get any formal assistance. This situation is also making IDPs susceptible to arbitrary actions and all forms of violence, exploitation, abuse, rape and recruitment into armed forces. In principle, displaced people have the same rights as all others citizens. However, in practice, they face discrimination. In fact, they need special protection and attention during their displacement, return, resettlement or reintegration.

Regrettably, IDPs of an ongoing armed conflict are often perceived by the government as a burden or added problem, even threat. In the past ten years the government has been one of the belligerent forces in the armed conflict. In the past ten-year history of the armed conflict, the Nepal government in the guise of security was creating terror and forcibly evicting or removing people from their home in the name of the supporters of the insurgents, ignoring the provisions of humanitarian law that prohibits the forcible removal of civilians from their residence. In the interaction with respondents, some victims of the state security force said that they had faced far more difficulties particularly when government's security forces viewed them as 'enemies of the state'. In dealing with IDPs, government during the past ten years of armed conflict did not respect international instruments such as the Geneva Convention. Nepal was unwilling to meet its obligations under international laws (AI, 2005; INSEC, 2006).

The CPA has made specific provision on IDP. Article 5.2.1 of the CPA states, *"Both parties express the commitment to allow without any political prejudice the people displaced due to the armed conflict to return voluntarily to their respective ancestral or former residence, reconstruct the infrastructure destroyed during the conflict and rehabilitate and socialize the displaced people into the society"*. However, this provision has not yet translated into action. If this provision is translated into practice and if the CPA is honestly respected, it could provide greater scope for addressing concerns of IDPs and helping to deal with the environmental health and sanitation problems associated with IDPs.

There is also urgent need to rehabilitate[16] the Manohara and Bagmati River banks by returning IDPs or settling them in proper manners in socially, economically and environmentally appropriate places. However, environmental dimension in IDPs mass settlements and camps is largely ignored so much that it leads to a crisis in terms of ability of these areas to sustain basic ecological and environmental services.

Immediate actions needed from the state, the municipality and the host communities to address environmental sanitation and health-related problems of IDPS are:

- Initiate environmental awareness campaign
- Establish environmentally sound support service (follow UNHCR's Environmental Guidelines, 1996 and 2005)
- Devise and operate a proper monitoring service
- Develop and implement environmental rehabilitation plan and action
- Provide proper waste management support to IDP communities and local people
- Supply of safe drinking water
- Support in return and reintegration of IDPs.

3.7 CONCLUSIONS

Displacement leads to adverse social and psychological consequences to the displaced people. As displacements are rooted in social and economic inequities and psychological dimension attached to it, remedies for IDPs should also come from broad social policies tied with the strategies for addressing root causes of the conflict, which address the psychological aspect of exclusion and injustice.

As IDPs are pushed out of their homes and forced to live in an alien place, often they have no control over their lives, they become victims to acute depression that exacerbates their trauma.[17] Their sense of powerlessness leads to increased despair, melancholia, extreme loneliness and greater distress.

Emotional and moral supports obtained by IDPs within a secure social setting dismantle when they have to separate from families, relatives and friends and seek refuge in different places. The displaced life demoralizes them and affects them physically, physiologically, socially and psychologically. Displacement disrupts social services and social relations; results in a loss or destruction of property and erosion of a person's social identity.

The decade-long armed conflict has created several negative impacts on health and sanitation, space and services such as education, drinking water and of IDPs staying in Kathmandu valley. Most of the negative environmental impacts are grounded in the governance problems, social and economic inequalities and environmental injustice and linked with the IDPs. Therefore, mitigating negative environmental impacts in urban areas and improving health and sanitation of IDP requires addressing underlying causes of environmental degradation. The CPA has opened avenue for addressing negative environmental impacts in Nepal.

Displacement is a social phenomenon that requires preventive strategies within the framework of human security that addresses the main causes of conflicts and displacement of individuals and groups. Social and economic development is the only means to avoid IDPs subjugation or permanent dependency on humanitarian assistance.

Environmental health and sanitation is one of the fundamental but often overlooked factors in dealing with IDP issues. Only attempting to deal with IDP issues based on the existing laws and regulations does not work in the case of IDPs. For example, if the Electricity Authority had supplied electricity and Drinking Water Supply Office had given potable drinking water service, the health and sanitation problem in the IDP settlement would not be so serious. But the state authority responsible for drinking water or electricity took a very controlling attitude instead of helping or supporting IDPs, which ultimately resulted in more health and environmental sanitation-related problems.

End Notes

1. See UNHCR, the State of the World's Refugees: A Humanitarian Agenda. New York: Oxford University Press, 1997, Page 99 for detail.
2. See http:www.idpproject.org/GlobalTrends 2004 for details on this tragic debate.
3. For example, approximately 24,000 people of 3,500 households of Rajapur areas of Bardiya District in June 2005 left their village and entered to Baharaich and Bachhya areas of India (See *Samaya Weekly*, Year 2, No 63, Ashad 17-23, 2062/1-7 July 2005) for the detail story).

4. The mission was led by Dennis McNamara, accompanied by Carmen van Heese from IDD and Romano Lasker from CRD.
5. Source – Global IDP Database, Norwegian Refugee Council.
6. The reason for such a high differences in the government figures is mainly its procedure of defining IDPs. Government recognises IDPs to those people who have registered in the District Administration Office (DAO) of the government and obtained certificates from there. But, people do not go and register with DAO because of their fear (as it is a local party in conflict) and mistrust (people do not believe on DAO).
7. This information was given by Durga Nidhi Sharma, Joint Secretary of the MoPR in the national workshop organised by National Human Rights Commission on 30 July 2008 at Yala Maya Kendra, Patan.
8. Personal communication with some of the donor representatives.
9. The study sites were small open areas in the both sides of Bagmati and Manohara river banks, which cannot sustain the existing number of population of IDPs.
10. Interviewed by the author on 20 May 2007.
11. Interviewed the respondent on 2 June 2007 in the settlement area but, upon his request, his name is not stated here.
12. Guiding Principle for Internally Displaced Persons, 2001, OCHA of United Nations.
13. See http://www.icrc.org/ for detail.
14. See http://www.fmreview.org/text/FMR/15/01.htm for details.
15. Interviewed on 2 June 2007 in the settlement area.
16. Rehabilitation is a full or at least partial restoration of degraded landscape and impaired ecosystem services to their stage prior to the arrival of IDPs.
17. http://www.safhr.org/refugee_watch20_voices.htm

Chapter 4

Hydro-conflict and Politics in Nepal: Links Beyond the Border[1]

4.1 THE CONTEXT

The water resource sub-sector is one of the major areas where a change in governing system, legal arrangements, bureaucratic reorientation and institutional reframing is essential in order to address the associated growing scarcity and conflict and meet the public expectation in the changed political context. This chapter discusses the dynamics of hydro-conflict in the changing political context and outlines the conditions and ways to address it in 'new' Nepal. New Nepal is the phrase frequently used in Nepal after the successful April movement mainly to reflect the expectation of people in terms of changes in the state's governing structures (e.g. federal governing system), process (meaningful participation of people in decision making of governing system) and outcomes (ensuring access of poor, marginalized and excluded people in economic, political and social security).

Since the political change of April 2006, the existing dominant power relations in the country have been altered. The CPN (M) emerged as one of the main power centres in the politics of Nepal. Consequently, the actions and behaviours of key players in Nepal's politics are now influenced and shaped by the changing power relations of the country. This has also been amply reflected in the water politics of Nepal. Now that the king has been suspended from the political process, people who enjoyed the protection and support of the king, and who were previously active in politics, now find themselves out of the mainstream politics and consequently not able to directly use state power and resources for their benefit from exploiting water resources (for example granting licenses, selecting particular companies for the construction, etc.).

Together with the changing political context, new institutional and legal provisions are emerging. The CPA has made some vague forward-moving proposals that relate to natural resources, including water. Article 3.1 of Section 3 'Political, social, economic transformation and conflict management' of the CPA states: "Adopt policies for protection and promotion of national industries and resources". Similarly, Article 3.1 states: 'Prepare a common development concept that will help in the socio-economic transformation of the country and will also assist in ensuring the country's economic prosperity in a short period of time'. These provisions are further reflected in the Interim Constitution, which will have some implications in future water resource-related policy. These implications would be: more investment from domestic sectors in water resource development, national consensus in taking decision about mega hydro projects, etc. However, at present all bio-physical, geopolitical and socio-economic aspects of water issues do not constitute the explicit priority of the new political actors; though they have vaguely voiced their opinions on how water resources should be developed in the new context that Nepal finds itself in.

4.2 CONCEPTS AND PERSPECTIVES

Though some scholars argue that water conflict is neither strategically rational, hydrologically effective nor economically viable (Wolf, 2004), the argument of rationality, effectiveness and viability often does not shape politically vested interest-based behaviour and the actions of major actors. Rather, special power relations shape the course of behaviour and actions leading to conflict. As far as Nepal is concerned at least, Nepalese hydro-politics and related conflicts mainly derive from vested political interest-based behaviour and the actions framed within the special power relations of main actors. Hence, the complexity of hydro-conflict cannot be reduced to the logic of strategic rationality, hydrological effectiveness, and economic viability; and, in so doing, ignoring the context of specific power relations and political dynamics.

The political system and subsystems of any nation not only frame policy, strategies and practices but also largely shape behaviour and the actions of its citizens. Similarly, the behaviour and actions of citizens influences national politics. Hence, the politics and behaviour of citizens are interrelated and reflected in various forms of power relations. Nepal's hydro-conflict has to be examined from this conceptual framework.

Politics can also be a source of mistrust, suspicion, injustice, exclusion, marginalisation, discrimination and hate, as well as a means of harmony, unity, cooperation and collective action – all these determine the course of action in conflict (both in resolving and escalating it) (Upreti, 1999 and 2007f). Hence, like all other areas, politics is influential in shaping and reshaping the destiny of sustainable water resource management and resolving hydro-conflict and addressing water scarcity (Upreti, 2007f). A critical examination of the political negotiations and renegotiations between different political actors (at both national and regional levels) provides a better understanding of how highly contested issues such as hydro-conflict and water scarcity are dealt with at national and regional levels.

4.3 AN OVERVIEW OF THE WATER CONFLICT IN NEPAL

Water conflict is not a new phenomenon in the world. The trans-boundary freshwater dispute database of Oregon State University has documented 1,200 cases from 1948 to 1999 (Wolf, 2004). Several studies (Ohlsson, 1995; Panos Institute South Asia, 2004; Phillips et al., 2006; Swain, 1996; Upreti, 1999; 2001; 2002a and 2007f) have amply demonstrated that water conflict and cooperation is an integral part of the social and political life of society. Environmental crises and hydro-conflict are major challenges of the 21st century. Nepal is no exception and is experiencing a large number of hydro-conflicts influenced by vested interests, trade-offs, power relations, norms, values and perceptions.

The growing population plus the factories and farms in Nepal all need more water resources. Therefore, competition amongst domestic consumption, industries and farms is increasing and turning into disputes. Water pollution is another strategic issue of conflict. We can see examples in Kathmandu Valley where all the river systems (Bagmati, Bishnumati and Manohara river systems) are almost collapsing because the river water is no longer useable. Conflict between the needs of population living upstream of river basins and that dwelling downstream is mounting. Water resource in Nepal is now becoming a highly sensitive political issue and a source of conflict. The Melamchi Megha Drinking Water Project is a prime example of such a conflict. Once the Melamchi Megha Drinking Water Project was started, local people affiliated with different political parties began to make several demands such as employment of local people, development of infrastructures and the project did not agree to fulfil all the demands of the local people and that virtually led to tension and conflict between the project and people. Consequently, they had to temporarily close the construction work on the site, which has caused delay in completion of the project.

Different kinds of water-related conflicts have been reported in Nepal (Upreti, 2004a). Source disputes, the sharing of water for different purposes (for example, use for drinking water, irrigation, water turbines), and the payment of compensation for damage caused while constructing canals and laying drinking-water pipes have frequently been reported. Similarly, conflict on responsibility of maintenance of irrigation and drinking water systems, the ambiguous roles and responsibilities of watchmen and their payments, and disputes among water users' associations/committees on their roles and responsibilities were other common water-related conflicts frequently reported in Nepal. In addition, damage caused by the overflow of water from canals and conflict, due to the ambiguous roles of water technicians and officials, were also common occurrences.

Earlier studies (Upreti, 2001; IMC, 1990; Pradhan et al., 1997; Upreti, 2007f) have shown that water conflict is a normal phenomenon – in the absence of a clear provision of water rights – if the same source is used for more than one purpose. The occurrence and intensity of such a conflict is especially high when water becomes scarce in the dry season. Inequitable and unreliable water distribution and the excessive use of water in the head section limits the supply (in terms of time and quantity) in the tail section and often causes frequent conflict concerning the irrigation system. This is particularly serious when several irrigation systems operate upstream and downstream with limited water availability. The demand for irrigation water is increasing due to the introduction of improved varieties of rice, winter crops and changes in the cropping systems. The cropping intensity and cropping patterns are also changing, together with technological innovations and the process of globalization. In periods of water scarcity, the frequency as well as the intensity of conflict is high. It was also noticed that conflict resolution over the two irrigation systems was easy if the same farmer is a user (having land in the command areas of these canals) of both irrigation systems. It is reported that the frequency and intensity of conflict is greater in joint managed irrigation systems than in ones fully managed by farmers (Gautam et al., 1992; IIMI, 1990; IMC, 1990). The main cause of conflict in such systems was an unreliable water supply to tail-end farmers during the winter and spring crop seasons, due to an inability to implement proper water scheduling (IMC, 1990; Upreti, 2002a).

Some studies have shown that agency intervention in existing irrigation and drinking water systems worsens the water supply and gives rise to numerous conflicts (Pradhan et al., 1997; IMC, 1990; Upreti, 2001 and 2002a). The improper design of structural work and the quality of the construction result not only in the inefficient delivery of water but can also lead to several conflicts (IMC, 1990). Technical matters, such as steep gradients of canals and laid pipelines, caused an excess of water in a particular area and an inequitable supply. Flat gradients also caused silt deposits and a reduction in water flow. Such technical difficulties also contributed to the occurrence of conflict. In the agency-developed systems constructed under contract arrangement, contractors are the major cause of conflict not only in new systems but also in the operation and maintenance of existing irrigation and drinking-water systems (Pradhan et al., 2000).

In Nepal, most of the farmers-managed irrigation systems (FMIS) practise some form of distribution rules and rotational water sharing, particularly in the peak water demand period. Therefore, they are effective in minimizing potential conflicts. Community coherence among the water users is high in the FMIS and community-managed drinking water systems, and therefore, community-managed systems are more effective in monitoring water distribution, maintenance and operation and in resolving conflicts, should they occur (Upreti, 2002a; Pradhan et al., 1997). In the case of agency-developed systems, users are generally unwilling to contribute to operation and maintenance (IMC, 1990; IIMI, 1990) because of the lack of any feeling of ownership and accountability. Within the particular irrigation or drinking water system, conflict is frequently observed between the tail-section and head-section users in sharing water, particularly concerning the amount used and the time period. Basically, water availability determines the occurrence and frequency of conflicts. Generally, conflicts in the head-section – unlike those in the tail-section – were not a result of the lack of water; on the other hand, conflicts in the tail-section, in winter and spring, were mainly due to water shortages. The magnitude of a conflict grows as the gap between the demand and supply of water increases. Unequal water distribution is generally linked to inadequate monitoring that allows greater access to head-section farmers. This is one of the major determinants of conflict concerning irrigation and drinking water (IMC, 1990; Upreti, 2001).

In general, socio-economic, agricultural, organizational and technical factors contribute to the emergence of conflicts at the local level, whereas political interference and interests are responsible more for political conflict. Availability, reliability, equity and seasonality of water supply determine the occurrence and intensity of conflicts. Earlier research (Upreti, 2002a; IMC, 1990) shows that there is a clear relationship between irrigation conflict and crop yields. Conflicts and cropping intensities are also positively related as both are affected by the availability of water (IMC, 1990). Nevertheless, it is not always predictable. In some cases, farmers changed their existing cropping patterns due to the scarcity of water and increased benefits, whereas in other cases their yields were decreased.

Local people use specific rules to determine the use of water. For example, if the water source is located on an individual's land, then they have full autonomy to use it themselves, but they have no authority to dictate who can use it for irrigation and how much to use within the community. One of the respondents of the research (Upreti, 2001) explained: *"A source owner uses a perennial water source located in his land whenever he likes. Only after he finishes his rice transplanting, then we get the chance to use this water source. But all community members share water from a common stream on a rotational basis"*. However, in the case of stream water, which is common to all members of the community, there is a rule that all community members have equal rights to use it on a rotational basis.

In several externally funded drinking-water projects, conflicts had erupted after a few years due to the scarcity of water and also because of the increase of population in the village. While designing these systems, technicians generally ignore the potential future need for water,[2] citing financial and technical reasons. Another major conflict in externally funded drinking water projects is the location of the tap stands. Due to the influence of politicians, or for their own hidden interests, technicians locate the tap-stand close to the houses of particular people (mainly rich and powerful – sometimes negotiated with a bribe), disregarding other people's protests. Similarly, sharing the source is another problem in such projects, as they are decided on the basis of technical justifications, thus ignoring the existing use patterns and the social context. Once the projects are built, based only on technical grounds without considering the people's opinion and need, local people may damage structures built in the source and cause the conflict to escalate.

There is also a growing debate about the hydrological effectiveness, economic viability and the managerial appropriateness of big versus small hydropower development projects, external investment in hydropower developments (who benefits and who loses), the risk factors involved and how to meet the nation's growing requirement of power. A group of scholars working in water issues, such as Dipak Gywali, Ajaya Dixit (2001), Bikash Pandey (1994), and others strongly argue for the development of less risky hydropower projects and consistently question the development of export-led large hydropower projects. On the other hand, some conventional hydropower engineers, water policy experts, planners and developers prefer the option of developing big hydro-power projects in order to export power to India. Some influential economists and politicians advocate the 'World Bank approach' of hydropower development (bigger projects) as the best solution to the economic development of the nation (Mahat, 2005). However, many others differ with this view (Pandey, 1994). In Nepal, construction of bigger water-related projects is often linked with corruption and malpractices. Latest examples of such malpractices are reported in recommending the external power development companies to construct a big hydropower project in Nepal. Government announced construction of 402 MW Arun III and 300 MW Upper Karnali Hydro Electricity Projects and formed a High-Level Committee to recommend the suitable hydro-power developers from among the 9 applicant companies for Arun III and 14 applicant companies for Upper Karnali. However, The High-Level Committee recommended granting both the projects to EMR Energy Company Limited (India). Hence, media covered the story of possible kickback and ill-intention of the Committee. The Parliamentary Natural Resource Committee has investigated the decision of the High-Level Committee.[3] The issue of corruption and malpractice in Nepal's water resource development (Upreti, 2001) is not different from the findings of the Robert Wade in administrative and political corruption in irrigation projects in South India (Wade, 1982). For example, details about the prevalence of corruption in the Asian Development Bank funded Irrigation Sector Support Project (ISSP) were documented widely in the past decades. The author has documented the details of corruption practices of the Asian Development Bank-funded 6-km-long irrigation development project called the Upper Andherikhola Irrigation System (UAIS) in Dolakha district with a total budget of 8 million. There already existed a farmers-managed irrigation system but the irrigation technician changed the alignment in some sections of the existing canal and abused the allocated fund. The corruption case was filed in the Distinct Administrative Office (Upreti, 2001).

Several factors contributed to the hydro-conflict in Nepal. These can be summarized in the following groups:

- Environmental concern versus economic concerns
- Water as basic rights (and every person has the right to access safe water) versus water as tradable commodity (subsequent water privatization debate)
- Interest in the construction of big, risky export-led projects versus focus on small domestic consumption-oriented and less risky hydropower development
- External (vested political and economic) interests versus internal need and interests
- Internal politics and power relations.

These factors are not mutually exclusive and complement each other in igniting the hydro-conflict. The degree and the intensity of influence in igniting the hydro-conflict depend upon the combination of various factors as well as spatial and temporal situations.

In cases of conflict related to water resource development, Nepal finds itself in a state of 'paradigm confusion' (confusion on ontology, epistemology and methodology). Consequently, the political economy of hydro-politics in Nepal is very much oriented towards the conventional wisdom of international development politics (Millennium Development Goals, Sustainable Livelihoods, empowerment, etc.) without critically analyzing them (merits, limitations, potentials, relevance, vested interests, inherent weaknesses, implementation capability of the state, etc.). Such 'confusion' is one of the main causes of the failure of planned development in Nepal (Pandey, 1999; Shrestha, 1997) and a perennial source of conflict (Upreti, 2001; 2002a; 2004a; 2007f).

4.4 REGIONAL DIMENSION FOR NEPAL'S HYDRO-POLITICS AND SOUTH ASIAN FRESHWATER CONFLICT

Several studies have amply demonstrated that India is at the centre of the South Asian hydro-conflict (Swain, 1996; Panos South Asia, 2004; Begam, 1987; Ohlsson, 1995; Crow and Lindquist, 1990; Islam, 1987), be it with Nepal, Bangladesh or Pakistan. Hydro-tension between India and Pakistan in sharing the water of the Ravi, Sutlej and Beas rivers of Pakistan and the Indus, Jhelum and Chenab of India was reflected by the Indus Water Treaty of 1990; controversy over water sharing of the Koshi, Gandak, Tanakpur and Mahakali rivers between India and Nepal and the disputes between India and Bangladesh on lower riparian rights are the precise reflections of power relations and political interests (Baillat, 2004; Swain, 1996; Wolf, 2004; Dixit and Gyawali, 2003).

Although some research findings have shown that transboundary water resources can serve as a means of cooperation (Wolf, 2004), Nepalese experiences of international water basins, especially with India because of its geo-position, is full of controversy, tension and political trade-offs. Nepal, surrounded as it is by India to the East, West and South, and the fact that most of the rivers flow from North to South (and given the virtually closed access to the northern border with China due to topography) has made Nepal totally reliant on India in terms of transport and market access, thus making Nepal's position extremely weak in negotiations over water and other issues. The compulsory reliance of Nepal on India is often used by India for its own strategic interests, which is not necessarily advantageous to Nepal.

For the Nepalese people, India's interests in dealing with Nepal, and with water resources in particular, are often equated with a 'Big Brother Attitude' or with 'hegemonic interests'. For example, the continued insistence of India to construct the Sapta Koshi High Dam in Baraha Area, irrespective of the constant objection and resistance of local people of more than 11 villages of Nepal, is cited as one of several examples of India's hegemonic attitude. Other prominent examples of inundation problems faced by the Nepalese people, because of dams constructed by India in the border regions, include Laxmanpur, Lotan Rasiawal Khurda and Mahalisager (Dixit et al., 2004). The Laxmanpur barrage is only 300 metres away from the Nepal-India border (pillar no. 19) and inundates 3,376 bigha (2247 hectares) of land, affecting more than 2,600 houses and a population of more than 1,50,00,174. Similarly, Lotan Rasiawal Khurda dam is located 200 metres away from the border (pillar no. 31 and inundates 33,000 hectares agricultural lands and 13km^2 of land and affects 100,000 people). Third, the Mahali Sagar dam built by India on the border with Nepal (25 metres away from border pillar 50) inundates 460 hectares of land and 1,000 families are affected (Ibid: 175, Table 3). These problems have long been raised by the government of Nepal with India at the very highest levels (e.g. the then King Birendra raised this problem with the then Indian Prime Minister Rajiv Gandhi in 1985 during the Dhaka SAARC Summit). As a result, a joint Standing Committee on Inundation Problems was formed to address this problem (Ibid). However, people affected continued to suffer from inundation problem despite the formation of the standing committee. This is one of the main discontents fuelling the Nepalese people's perception of India's 'big brother' attitude.

Nepalese water diplomacy with India is said to be the product of the shadow of shortsighted politics. In all the major political changes of Nepal has gone through (1950, 1990 and 2006), India has played a crucial role; it has also bargained hard on several occasions concerning Nepal's water resources. For example, after the political change of 1950, India and Nepal signed two treaties (Koshi in 1954 and Gandak in 1959) and then again two treaties after the political change in 1990 (Tanakpur in 1991 and Mahakali-Pancheshwor in 1996); all the treaties[4] on sharing water between India and Nepal are largely said to have been framed to India's benefit. There is a widely held opinion among the Nepalese people that the role of India in dealing with water resources of Nepal is deliberately orchestrated to serve its vested interests. Some Nepalese scholars even see India as a perennial source of water-related problems[5] for Nepal. Madan Regmi, representing this view, argues that Nepalese water diplomacy with India lies within the shadow of India's domination in all major political changes of Nepal (1951, 1990, and 2006). Unlike the Nepalese views, some Indian scholars argue that India is part of solution[6] of Nepal's water problem. Ashok Mehata, representing this view argues that India is not mainly the problem but largely the solution of Nepal's water disputes.

It is increasingly argued by 'rights activists' and 'critical analysts' in Nepal that the conventional paradigm of development adapted by Nepal considers water as a 'commodity' instead of as a basic right of people; this therefore is becoming a fundamental source of hydro-conflict.

4.5 CAUSES OF HYDRO-CONFLICT IN NEPAL

In reviewing the ongoing debate of water issues in South Asia and Nepal, the following can be cited as some of the main sources of water conflict.

4.5.1 Policy and Institutional Issues

My conclusions stemming from ten years of study of the interrelationship between resource conflict and political conflict and the political economy of resource conflict in centralistic, unequal, hierarchical social settings and exclusionary governing systems, confirms that the reductionist policy and institutional approaches of hydropower management, shaped and guided by technocratic engineering and economic interests, is the major cause of hydro-conflict (1999, 2001; 2002; 2004a). Similar observations have also been made by some Indian scholars (Mallik and Bandyopadhyay, 2004). The water resource policy of Nepal is full of confusion and inconsistency, highly politicized, bureaucratically orchestrated and technocratically manipulated to justify these contradictions and confusions. There is no consistent, coherent and long-term priority on how to effectively utilize available water resource for the economic development of the country. It is operating on an ad hoc basis, depending upon the interests of the governing political party or even invisibly controlled by the nexus of individual influential political leaders and external forces. Water resource institutions in Nepal are undermined by political trade-offs, corruption, overstaffing, incompetence and inadequacy in providing services to people. Several glaring examples include up to 16 hours of daily load-shedding and power cut, controversy in the Melamchi drinking water project, and the grand failure of the Arun II hydro-power project, to name just a few.

Professionalism of bureaucracy is almost absent in Nepal. For example, the government of Nepal frequently transfers officers dealing with India on water issues and brings in people with a lack of experience. This means that knowledge, experience-based competency and insights are not built up and/or go wasted. This is in contrast to their Indian counterparts, who have often worked in the same water-related issues for decades. This creates not only a knowledge vacuum and lack of institutional memory on the part of the Nepal, but also weakens its hand in negotiations with India.

4.5.2 The India Factor

India uses water as a 'means of political negotiation' and, therefore, trade-off in water resources is one of the main bases for this purpose. The discussion presented in Section 3 clearly demonstrates the factor of India in Nepal's hydro-conflict. The power asymmetry with India, surrounded on all three borders (the northern side being geographically nearly inaccessible in the present context) places Nepal in an extremely difficult position and is further constrained by the mentality of Nepalese politicians. Despite the strong reiteration of heavy rhetoric, almost all political parties so far fail to deal with India on a more equitable basis.

When there is a power crisis in Nepal, many Indian companies not only show their interest but also offer their commitment to provide electricity. For example, in December 2006, when Nepal had experienced power shortages and the Nepal Electricity Authority offered a solution to the crisis as routine electricity power cut, a private Indian energy company called Power Trading Corporation offered to provide 50 megawatts of hydro-power to Nepal within a month[7] but the promise was not fulfilled. However, many such offers have a strong element of interest in engaging in hydro-power development in Nepal. The recent selection of EMR Energy Limited to develop both Upper Karnali and Arun III Hydropower Projects of Nepal by the High Level Committee as an outcome of the nexus between them is an example of such interest (The *Himalayan Times*, 9 May 2007).

4.5.3 Choice of Scale of Development in Water Sector

Another major area of hydro-conflict concerns the scale of infrastructure in water resources development. There is a continuous conceptual as well as operational tension between (a) the preference for classical-large-scale export-oriented and externally-led water hydro-power development, and the construction of large -scale irrigation and drinking water projects and (b) domestically-led-small scale hydropower and other water-related infrastructure development, which are more sustainable, manageable, quick and effective.

Several overt and covert factors have contributed to this choice of scale of water resource development debate. They are not only linked with conceptual orientation, conviction and value systems but are also and more importantl, shaped by vested interests. The ongoing debate over the Melamchi mega drinking water project is one of the clear examples of the debate over scale. Some people argue that instead of opting for this mega project, the government should have rectified the issue of leakage in the existing water supply system of Kathmandu. Similarly, the government should facilitate conserving small sources and maximize their use, explore small sources and spouts, protect many dying sources, go for rainwater harvest. It has to explore all these possible options rather than going for extremely large projects which are financially external-dependent, technically too complicated, operationally too risky and managerially exclusionary (to be manage by external experts and technologists instead of consumers and users).

4.5.4 Diversity of Interests

The overt and covert interests in water resource development (be it hydropower development or the construction of irrigation systems or drinking water systems) often shape decisions. Ample evidence has demonstrated that such interests are not only sources of conflict and cooperation, but also a means of political negotiation and trade-off. In his study related to corruption, citing a vivid case of canal irrigation in South India, Robert Wade argues that administrative and political corruption is one of the major factors in pursuing bigger irrigation development (Wade, 1982). Similarly, several research findings and media reports have documented many cases of corruption in water resource development in Nepal (Thapa, 2002; Upreti, 2001). This is one of the main sources of conflict in Nepal. There are several actors engaged in water resources with their own vested interests in addition to the expressed or stated formal objectives. The following are the main actors engaged in water resource development with their own interests:

- Businessmen and traders with the main hidden interest of equipment sales and obtaining higher profits margins (which is mainly linked with manipulation and opaque and invisible negotiations with bureaucrats and politicians)
- Water resource bureaucrats (bureaucratic control of the projects, process and outcomes, collection of bribes and corruption[8])
- Environmentalists, who argue from the environmental perspective, which often ignores economic importance of the development of water resource infrastructures. Unlike in many cases in other (mainly western) parts of the world, Nepalese environmental activists often make their arguments based on their perceptions instead of findings of research. Hence, the credibility of their argument is often low. However, they are often able to

create larger interests in the general public and in some cases stopping construction of bigger projects or at least altering their original approach.

- International investors and donors often heavily influence the development of water resources in Nepal. These influences are either related to direct involvement in construction and development, sale of equipment and services, control decision making such as scrapping subsidies, the privatization of water services offered by the government or public company or through directly controlling politics.
- Political actors, (party politics and conceptual confusion about the long-term development of water resources).

4.6 ADDRESSING THE HYDRO-CONFLICT IN NEW NEPAL

As this beautiful country is in the process of transformation from war to peace, hopelessness and helplessness are also being transformed into expressions of optimism and ambitions for a prosperous new Nepal. The immense potential of water resources in the country forms a basis for such optimism and ambition. However, the logical question is whether Nepal can utilize the potential of water resources for economic development that benefit poor, marginalized, socially excluded, powerless and voiceless people or not. Can water-led economic development ensure social justice, equity and address those structural inequalities that exist in Nepalese society that constitute a perennial source of conflict and insecurity? Answers to these questions depend upon the following issues.

4.6.1 Public engagement

The events of April 2006 clearly demonstrated that the Nepalese people are capable of determining their own destiny and addressing the ever-growing issues of water scarcity and water conflict. In the past, one of the main sources of conflict and crisis in the water sector was mainly derived from the autocratic, top-down, techno-centric and exclusionary decision-making and the elite-centric, power-focused and selective benefit-capturing culture. As long as this culture exists in the water sector, crisis will exist side-by-side. Therefore, it is absolutely essential to re-examine a few fundamental questions such as who makes the choice, who makes decisions, who benefits and who suffers, and so move beyond the classical top-down exclusionary approach.

The ongoing state restructuring process and particularly the much anticipated federal political structure of the country will have great implications in changing the existing almost dysfunctional water bureaucracy and its exclusionary structures. Hopefully, this state restructuring will abolish the centrally controlled decision- making process and ensure public engagement in making any important water-related decisions and action.

4.6.2 New Foreign Policy and International Relations

As discussed in the above sections, Nepal's water resource management and hydro-conflict exhibits a very strong international dimension. Nepal's existing foreign policy is neither shaped by national strategic interests nor economic opportunities. Rather, it has traditionally been orchestrated, negotiated, manipulated, refined and reshaped by the vested interests of the palace and that of a few political elites. Hence, serious trade-offs, negotiations and bargaining over water resources have resulted in tension and conflict. Therefore, addressing water crisis and conflict in Nepal needs a wider vision as well as a conducive foreign policy and non-conventional ways of building relations, based on a more equitable and just basis. This, however, is not easy in a country where real actions have been diluted by rhetoric and false promises.

Nepal's foreign policy should be shifted towards economic diplomacy, targeting the promotion of economic collaboration, harnessing and promoting development of potential sectors such as water resources, tourism and information technology.

4.6.3 New Economic Development Policy and Institutional Arrangements

Challenges faced by the water resource sector in Nepal cannot be handled by the existing institutional arrangement and policy framework, simply because they are obsolete in addressing what are complicated issues. The water resource development policy needs to be integrated with foreign policy into a holistic vision. A new policy requires new institutional arrangements. One of the major institutional issues is the restructuring of the existing non-responsive and classical set-up of the Ministry of Water Resources and its related departments and offices. However, it is not possible to restructure the ministry in isolation and it has to be done as an integral part of a holistic bureaucratic restructuring. Redefining the existing governing system, ministerial and departmental arrangements, size, responsibility and accountability of the staff, their evaluation, rewards and punishment and placing them under the oversight of taxpayers of the country is necessary. Such reorientation is strongly related to the federal political structure of the country.

4.6.4 Human Security as New Orientation, Thinking and Perspective

Nepal needs new thinking and perspectives in regard to the development of the water resource sector. The conceptual orientation and broader framework has to be guided by the human security perspective. Human security is a holistic perspective, which goes beyond conventional notions of poverty alleviation or livelihood improvement at the individual level. It focuses on all aspects of security beyond the individual level and links with all aspects of livelihood of people. The following are integral parts of human security:

Energy security: New water resource management and development should be focused on addressing the energy needs of the country. Nepal is suffering from a lack of energy, which is negatively affecting all sectors (from industries to health to services). Lack of enough energy is also negatively affecting economic grown and generation of employment. Hence, the priority of the state should be to ensure a reliable supply of energy essential for domestic and industrial requirement. Diversity of energy sources such as hydropower, wind power, solar power, and power generated from bio-fuel and incineration is essential to meet future energy challenges.

Environmental security: Another important condition for water resource development and improving the overall development of the nation is to give due consideration to environmental security, which is often neglected in the development discourse. Environmental security implies not only the security of the surrounding environment but also the security of people staying in and around a particular area. New water resource development policy should acknowledge the necessity of the concept of environmental security in future water resource development. Environmental security is also related to environmental justice and environmental governance. Hence these issues should be integrated into environmental policy in federal Nepal.

Livelihood security: Livelihood security is another concept that needs to be brought into the mainstream in terms of Nepal's water resource development. Key actors need to understand the inter-relationship between livelihood security and water resource management, as they are closely interlinked. If water-related development projects and programmes are not able to contribute to the livelihood security of people, they will not get public support and they will fail simply on the grounds of public resistance, mistrust or the lack of ownership.

Rights, equity and social justice: The discourse on water resources now needs to focus on rights, equity and social justice. Rights-based and holistic approaches of water resource management and development, framed in terms of equity and social justice, are fundamentally important. Riparian rights, rights over usage (for example, prior rights for drinking water over irrigation or industrial use), and especially the rights of the indigenous community, including traditional or customary rights over water, are some of the common issues that are not only influencing the water debate (Pradhan and Pradhan, 1996; Benda-Beckmann et al., 1997) but also becoming sources of conflict and tension once they are violated by external interventions (Upreti, 2001). New rights-related issues, such as water as a basic right of people, are becoming increasingly important and, therefore, water should not be treated simply as a tradable commodity. Proponents of this school of thought argue that access, use, management and the control of water must be guided by equity and social justice. Hence, this issue must be sufficiently considered in any new water resource development policy and practice in order to overcome potential hydro-conflict.

4.7 BUREAUCRATIC REORIENTATION, POLITICAL COMMITMENT AND ACTION

The existing water bureaucracy is too ineffective, irresponsible, corrupt, politicized and is, therefore, not able to tackle the challenges faced by Nepal, particularly in regard to water resource management. The main political actors including the ministers are heavily engaged in spoiling the bureaucracy. They have abused their power and authority in damaging the bureaucracy. Hence, bureaucratic reorganization and reorientation is a precondition to effectively and efficiently managing available water resources in Nepal. This requires political commitment and sincere action. The restructuring of the state process is an opportunity for addressing the problems of bureaucracy.

4.8 CONSTRUCTIVE INTERNATIONAL ENGAGEMENT

The role of the international community is crucial in water resource development, particularly as regards the development of hydropower in Nepal. Multinational companies, mainly backed either by the government of their native origins or multilateral financial institutions such as the World Bank (WB), have shown interest in developing hydropower in Nepal. Once powerful countries are engaged in promoting particular multinational companies, they exert an unbearably high pressure on the Nepalese government. In such a situation, role and negotiation capacity of users and the communities go beyond their access and consequently hydropower development does not address their problems and only serves interests of international investors. The Nepalese history of water resource development is characterized by unfair international pressure and trade-offs. Continuity of such practices will implant conflict and tension in the water sector. Therefore the strategy of the international community, particularly the bilateral governments and the multilateral financial institutions like the WB, International Monitory Fund (IMF) and the Asian Development Bank (ADB) needs to be shifted from pressure and condition to facilitation/ harmonization to support economic development of Nepal through the utilization of available water resources. Nepal needs international actors to play a more constructive and supportive role in developing water resources that ensures that the concerns of people are met, and one that minimizes potential conflict and provides mutual benefits to all concerned actors. So far, the role of influential international actors such as ADB, WB, IMF and some bilateral donors in water resource development are seriously questioned in Nepal, particularly for their conditionality associated with assistance. For example, when the conditions posed by ADB to provide contract of distributing drinking water in Kathmandu Valley to a London-based private company was questioned by the then appointed Housing and Physical Planning Minister (she was from the CPN-M), the ADB in the first week of May 2007 threatened to cancel the loan assistance for the Melamchi Drinking Water Project.[9] This case has clearly demonstrated the clash of corporate interests and the public interests. In this case Bhandari (2007) writes, *"But still water supply services for Kathmandu Valley are being privatized as per ADB's loan conditionalities'* with the intention that *"water should be allocated and used by those who can best afford it"*.

International funding agencies often see the private sector as the solution of chronic drinking water problems in cities and seriously undermine the crucial role played by public sector and therefore pose different conditions to pursue privatization of drinking water (infrastructure development, operation, processing, distributions, etc.). The conditions posed in the Melamchi Drinking Water Project are vivid examples of this attitude of international actors. Pressure to pursue corporate interests often causes several economic, social and environmental negative impacts. Bhandari (2007) argues that the experiences of privatization of drinking water in Argentina, Hungary, Czech Republic, the Philippines (Manila), Indonesia (Jakarta) sponsored by World Bank and other international financial institutions demonstrate that they are not able to improve performance and meet the public needs. Instead, drinking water managed by public institutions in Cambodia, India, Thailand, Bangladesh, Pakistan, etc. are performing better than the drinking water managed by the private sector in manila and Jakarta (Bhandari, 2007). Hence the role of the international community, particularly the financial institutions should not be to pose conditions in developing water resources in Nepal but to assist this country to meet the growing energy and drinking water need.

4.9 LINKING WATER RESOURCE MANAGEMENT WITH SOCIAL RESEARCH

Water resource development and management in Nepal is not well grounded in social research and is almost entirely dominated by engineering and technical discourse. This approach to water resource management – that relegates social issues – has created enormous tensions and conflict during the planning and implementation of projects. Numerous examples can be cited from the history of bigger hydropower development or drinking water projects. There is a lack of systematic engagement in examining social, historical, cultural and economic aspects of local areas where bigger water-related projects are constructed. The sociological exploration of potential complications and consequent conflict are largely ignored in bigger water-related projects. Even if some social studies are made, they are often ad hoc, superficial and not able to bring future possible complications to light and offer ways to resolve them. Hence, a focus on social research – with especial emphasis on conflict Impact Assessment – should be an integral part of water discourse in Nepal.

4.10 CONCLUSIONS

The changing political context and the emerging new power relations in Nepal will have huge impacts on water resource management in general and in dealing with hydro-conflict. The interim government is a coalition of political parties with diverse interests, political orientations and objectives. In the past, water resource management and mismanagement was largely dominated by vested interests of different actors. One of the main actors in the government is the CPN (M), whose strategy has yet to be tested. In the past, water resource development was mainly shaped by vested interests and corruption; but to some degree this is likely to improve, given the increased scrutiny from the population, civil society and difference in interests among the major political parties. This situation will continue in the long term too.

The new situation that Nepal finds itself in will alter the existing approach of water resource management and hydro-conflict in the country. However, it depends upon:

(*a*) the transformation of thinking, behaviour and attitude of the major actors;
(*b*) the transformation of the political context (stability factor);
(*c*) the transformation of rules, policy and institutional arrangements;
(*d*) dynamic, robust and organic negotiations, and
(*e*) stable, progressive and people-centric power relations (which is possible).

The changing political context and altered power relations have brought tremendous opportunities and serious challenges for addressing water-related problems and the conflict in Nepal. If the emerging new political and social actors are able to use the opportunities brought about by political change, the water resource sector can greatly contribute to the economic development of the country. This will open up avenues for new forms of water-based relations with India and contribute to addressing tensions over water in the wider region of South Asia. But if the political actors of Nepal fail to use wisely the opportunities afforded to them and get entangled in vested interests and narrow party politics, as they did in the past, then they will fall into new challenges and more difficulties.

End Notes

1. This chapter is drawn form the paper presented at the Nepal Water Security Forum organised by The Silk Road Studies Program, Uppsala University, Sweden, at Hotel Radisson, Uppsala on March 27, 2007.
2. Engineers from the District Water Supply Office explained that they provide for future needs in their designs and estimates. However, in practice such provisions were not observed. Local people say that overseers refuse to consider the future water requirements of the community while constructing drinking-water projects in the village basing them on budgetary limitations.
3. See *The Himalayan Times* of 9 May 2007 for the detailed story.
4. The major water-related treaties with India were the Mahakali Treaty (signed in 1996 which includes also the agreements of two other dams already constructed by India: the Sarada barrage and the Tanakpur barrage, both on the Mahakali River), The Kosi River Treaty (1954) and the Gandak River Treaty (1959).
5. Madan Regmi from China Study Centre argued in this line in the interview with BBC Nepali Service on 10 February 2007.
6. General Ashok Mehata said this in an interview with BBC Nepali Service on 10 February 2007.
7. *The Himalayan Times*, 6 December 2006.
8. It is an open secret in Nepal that bureaucrats have to pay huge amounts to be posted in big infrastructure projects, customs and immigration offices, and even forest offices. Hence, their very first objective is to compensate what they paid for the senior bureaucrats and politicians and therefore corruption (rent seeking and bribe) is the first priority of their job. They can easily escape even from corruption charges if they have collected enough money to influence the mechanisms investigating corruption. Nepal's strange record of wining of corruption cases by almost all the alleged corrupt officials (politicians and bureaucrats) is a single most important evidence of how powerful corruption is.
9. See the *Himalayan Times* of 9 May 2007 for details.

Chapter 5

Public Legitimacy of Post-conflict Constitution Making in Nepal

5.1 INTRODUCTION[1]

The term 'post conflict' is quite contested in Nepal, particularly after the emergence of more than two dozen small armed groups and their engagement in violence and insurgency.[2] However, the operational definition of post conflict is 'a situation after the formal signing of the CPA on 21 November 2006 by the government and the CPN (M) to end the 10 years of armed conflict'.

The Constitution of a country is one of the powerful means to shape and influence the action and behaviour of its citizens. Attitude, behaviour and action of citizens at large ultimately determines the success or failure of any constitution. The two ways of interaction between the people and constitution and constitutional process are therefore the core of achieving durable peace and shaping the political culture of a country. Interaction between people and constitution in the form of legitimacy, ownership, accountability strengthens constitutional performance, whereas interaction between them in the form of feeling of exclusion, biases towards certain groups, protection of vested interests of elites at the cost of ordinary citizens, erodes a sense of belongingness, ownership, and ultimately public legitimacy of constitution.

The objective of this chapter is to explore the relationship between durable peace and political culture and constitution, particularly focusing on the specific question: in which way can a constitution-making process and the new constitution change the political culture of Nepal to restore durable peace and democracy in the country? Therefore, the discussion is focused on a psychological and sociological perspective rather than a specific legal framework while addressing this question.

The issues of achieving durable peace through a matured political culture are directly related to the broader social structure, political culture, level of awareness of citizen, commitment of state, behaviour of political and legal actors, and other many psycho-social factors such as perception, emotion, trust, expectation, aspiration, identity, etc. The culture of peace and constitutional life is therefore closely related and influenced by one-another and establishing a pattern of interaction between them is hugely complicated because it conjunctures multiple factors, such as economy, politics, religion, social structures.

5.2 SOCIOLOGICAL AND PSYCHOLOGICAL DIMENSIONS

Why did the constitution of 1990, once acknowledged as one of the best constitutions of the world, failed within 15 years of its existence and itself became a source of conflict? The political system, political culture and the constitution of any particular nation are closely interlinked, influenced and affected by one another. Ideally, the source of constitutions is people. However, pragmatically a lot of negotiations and renegotiations within a political context and actors beyond ordinary citizens of the country become the source of constitution. Therefore, politics is said to be the fundamental basis of law, economy, peace and social development. In case of the 1990s' constitution of Nepal, lack of proper understanding of the constitution and related legal provisions by a very large section of the Nepalese people on one side and glaring manipulations of constitution, laws and regulations by legal, political and social elite on the other side finally resulted in disowning of the constitution.

The constitution of 1990, its custodians, implementers, politicians and policy makers failed to address fundamental structural sources of inequalities such as caste, class, sex, race and religion-based discriminations. Further, issues of *Kamaya, Haliya* and other socially excluded communities did not get priority. Highly skewed land distribution, concentration of social services and allocation of the state resources in city centres and accessible areas, geographical discriminations also contributed to the failure of the system. People do not differentiate between political and legal issues if they are affecting their life and grossly interpret it as state failure. The 1990 constitution-making process itself was seriously questioned from the beginning by some political parties and critical constitutional experts and analysts. They argued that the 1990 constitution was not made by people; instead, it was made by social elites/lawyers and politicians and never endorsed by people or the elected parliament. Some political parties, including CPN (M) were, from the beginning, objecting to it and asking for the election of a constituent assembly to formulate a constitution.

In the history of the major political changes of Nepal (1951, 1990 and 2006), there were no fundamental changes in leadership, political culture and value systems, institutional and procedural mechanisms as well as bureaucratic culture and tradition. A clear lesson from these changes is that only popular political change without adequate changes in leadership, bureaucracy, institutional and legal arrangements did not bring about the desired socio-political transformation and political change in the country. Political institutions were mostly not able to deliver stable and legitimate democratic practices. The anomalies, frauds and unhealthy practices adopted in the time of elections not only eroded the trust of people but also established a culture of 'manipulation of election'.

The 1990 constitution was not translated into legal and political action appropriately. It was used as a means of both manipulation/exploitation and justice. Constitutional provisions make judges so powerful and consequently judicial autocracy prevails. If someone raises concerns about corruption and immoral issues related to judges, he or she has to face *Manhani*. A glaring example is the full court's decision to suspend the licence of senior advocate and Chair of Nepal Bar Association Vishwo Kanta Mainali for charging that he had undermined judges by saying that the post of judge is becoming a licence for corruption.[3]

The legal system of Nepal was so ineffective and inefficient that it took several years to decide simple cases filed in the court. The principle of 'justice delayed is justice denied' made many people negative towards the justice system in Nepal, which virtually created distrust towards the constitution.

Public perception and interpretation: irrespective of technical soundness and legal completeness of the constitution, it does not work if people do not perceive and interpret it in this way. The main problem of the 1990s' constitution was the feeling of constitutional exclusion by non-Hindu religious groups; radical political parties such as CPN (M) (objected the process of making constitution and asked for constituent assembly to write it), women (matrilineal citizenship) and Terai people (citizenship to Terai people). The 18 years of failed practices demonstrared that the West-ministerial winner takes all model of political system does not failed to function in Nepal. Hence, the constitutional provisions promoting 'winner-takes-all' political system therefore became a source of conflict (minority decides for majority[4]). Ultimately these activities developed a feeling of 'my country but not my state' of a large section of society (dalit, janajatis, socially excluded groups).

Attitudinal and behavioural factors of key actors are responsible for effectively translating the essence of any constitution into practice (such as judges, lawyers, bureaucracy). The Hinduisation process of nation-building based on a uniform state language, religion and identity has made unsuccessful attempts to homogenize the heterogeneous society with cultural, ethnic, linguistic, religious diversities (Upreti, and Adhikari, 2006). The four pillars of Nepal as a nation interpreted since the establishment of a unified Nepal in 1768 (1825BS) were:

(a) Hindu state,
(b) Hindu religion
(c) Hindu identity
(d) Hindu king.

This Hinduisation implanted a deep feeling of exclusion, discrimination, and injustice. The uniformity imposed by the state has also altered traditional practices in resource management and access to resources of indigenous peoples. Restrictions on the use of traditionally used resources because of declaration of protected areas in their ancestral lands and other regulations made them unhappy.

5.3 FACTORS DETERMINING SUCCESS OR FAILURE OF A CONSTITUTION

Based on the experiences of the 15 years of the constitutional process and political culture in Nepal, the following are identified as important variables in making the constitution a success or failure:

- Commitment,
- Efficiency and effectiveness
- Transparency
- Public perception
- Ownership and sense of belongingness.

We have learnt several lessons from the making, shaping, implementing and dumping of the 1990s' constitution in the context of the political process and the armed conflict in Nepal. One of the main lessons we have learnt is that irrespective of the legal soundness of any constitution, it cannot sustain if people do not own and protect it. Another lesson is that constitution making is not a legal issue. Rather, it is a social and political process and involves the psychological, interpersonal and political engagement of all stakeholders upon which it is executed later. If sustainable peace has to be achieved, intimate engagement of people in the constitution-making process is indispensable.

5.4 PUBLIC LEGITIMACY AND THE CONSTITUTIONAL PROCESS

It is learnt that social structure, political culture, level of awareness of citizens, commitment of state as well as psycho-social factors such as perception, emotion, trust, expectation, aspiration and identity influence constitutional peace. Hence, state and citizens have a collective responsibility to establish a positive pattern of interaction and legitimacy that ensures a sense of constitutional-belongingness, collective and individual ownership, accountability and a culture of peace and non-violence.

Two fundamental concepts are introduced to examine the pattern of interactions between people and constitution to achieve durable peace. These are vertical acceptance and horizontal acceptance. The notion of vertical legitimacy and horizontal legitimacy has been derived from the scholarly work of Baechler (2006). Vertical legitimacy means state, legal and other institutions, power-sharing arrangement and government structures, power sharing and exercise of power, laws and regulations, etc. (Harris and Reilly, 1998) whereas horizontal legitimacy deals with more socio-psychological: personal emotional issues such as a sense of belonging, trust, emotions, a feeling of ownership and accountability of the constitution and constitutional process, common vision and concerted efforts, cooperative behaviour, etc.

Major issues to be tackled collectively from the constitutional and political processes to achieve democratic peace are: democratisation of political parties and intra-party democracy; right to information; ensuring participation of all Nepalese people - women, dalit, janajatis, children, elderly people, disabled, youth and other socially excluded groups in the constitution-making process, accepting that constitution making is a part of the state-building process; addressing problems related to land ownership; effective management and rational utilisation of natural resources; progressive reform on education, health, and service sectors; judicial reform; securing rights of minorities; management and rehabilitation of internally displaced persons; truth and reconciliation (peaceful co-existence, trust, empathy and healing), ensuring justice (retributive justice: based on prosecution; restorative justice: based on mediation; administrative justice: based on disciplinary measures; truth commission: based on historical justice; and reparation: based on compensatory justice),

TABLE 5.1 : Constitutional Life and Public Legitimacy Continuum for Durable Peace

Vertical legitimacy (state structures, constitution, laws, etc.) →		
	High vertical but low horizontal public legitimacy • Controlling pattern of interaction between people and constitution • Low level of sense of belongingness • Lesser degree of trust in constitutional process • Weak emotional attachment of people towards constitution • Weakened feeling of identity • Low level of ownership and accountability • Low participation and democratisation • Rigid legal interaction • Legal domination over pluralism • Rigid definition and mono-poly of constitution • Assumption of constitution guides people's aspirations instead of peoples aspiration determines success of constitution	**High vertical and horizontal public legitimacy** • High sense of belongingness • High degree of trust • High emotional attachment • Strengthened feeling identity • High level of ownership and accountability • High level of legal performance of constitution • High integration • Pluralism well accepted • Dialogue-based interaction (assumes on effectiveness of constitution depends of dialogue-based interaction between constitutional provisions and people's aspirations (Expected from the new constitution of Nepal)
	Low vertical and horizontal public legitimacy • High risk of constitutional failure (as experienced in Nepal) • Eroding sense of belongingness • High degree of mistrust and distrust • Emotional distance of people from constitution • Increased feeling of denial of identity • No ownership and no accountability	**Low vertical but high horizontal public legitimacy** • Imbalance legal and social interaction leading to weak enforcement of constitutional provisions • Weak legal performance and in extreme cases anarchy
	Horizontal public legitimacy ——→	

Source: Adapted from Baechler (2006).

reconstruction and rehabilitation; redefining foreign and fiscal policies; reorienting development, reforming the security sector, modernising military and police forces, etc. Without addressing these issues and concerns; social and political contradictions existed in Nepalese feudalistic society, lasting peace and stable democracy cannot be achieved.

Developing a feeling of ownership in constitution making and change and transformation process is a fundamental precondition of success of the constitution, political system and democratic peace in the country. Instead of reducing essential processes and procedures of people's consultation, participation and intimate engagement in the peace process, constitution making and post-conflict transformation into mere political decisions, political leaders and decision makers must allow and ensure meaningful engagement of all concerned actors in the decision process and ensure the implementation of due processes and procedures.

5.5 UNITY AND BELONGINGNESS FOR A FUTURE FEDERAL NEPAL

This country has decided to go in for a federal political structure with the multi-party democratic system. The federal structure of the country was the outcome of the constant struggle of various political forces, civil society organisations and interest groups. Though the number and types of federal states in the country are not clear, some common elements are crucially essential to groom and bloom the multi-ethnic, multicultural and multi-linguistic country in a federal structure. Making a constitution by the 497 members of the Constituent Assembly is not difficult but the main challenge is to make the constitution-making process representative, transparent and owned by all people.

It is anticipated that provision of three levels of government, i.e. central federal-, regional state- and local governments will appear in the new constitution under the federal arrangement. Experiences of Switzerland, India, the USA and other many countries show that federalism is an effective means of managing diversities if implemented properly. In this respect, it is a great opportunity for Nepal to address the problems created by a centuries-old feudal, top-down and unitary state-governing system. Federalism is a concept that goes beyond a single constitutional or statuary provision and should be owned by every people, every community. Hence, belongingness and public legitimacy is a precondition to make federal system functional. Few factors or elements exist in this country that promote high public legitimacy, a high sense of belongingness, diversity as strength, not weakness, mutual trust and emotional attachment, a feeling of collective identity and ownership, a high degree of interaction and acceptance of pluralism. Federalism is a means of conflict resolution through power sharing. In this context, the distribution of powers is crucial and it has to be done in such a way that rights and responsibilities are clearly defined and that conflicts about who is in charge and who has the right to act and decide are properly dealt with. Balancing between self-rule and shared rule is therefore a crucial factor and the new constitution must be able to clearly handle these issues. Box 5.1 depicts the example of Switzerland how this country has managed federalism.

BOX 5.1 Power-sharing arrangement in Switzerland[5]

The Constitution attributes the central level with the following:

- Organisation of federal authorities
- Foreign affairs
- Army and civil protection
- Protection of the environment (shared)
- Principles for zoning (shared)
- National streets (highways)
- Energy policy (shared)
- Nuclear energy
- Postal services and telecommunication
- Monetary policy
- Agriculture (shared)
- Social security (pensions, invalids)
- Civil law, criminal law
- Civil and criminal procedure
- Customs
- Federal taxes
- Citizenship (shared)

Amongst others, the **cantons** have the following powers:

- Organisation of cantonal authorities (own constitution, own anthem, own flag)
- *Education*
- *Culture*
- *Police*
- *Relations between religion and state*
- Protection of nature and heritage
- Public health
- Cantonal streets
- Forests; water, natural resources
- Cantonal taxes
- Citizenship

Cantons attribute powers to the **municipalities** or communes. In Switzerland the cantons decide what powers their municipalities shall have. Municipalities normally have the following powers:

- Organisation of municipal authorities (limited)
- Kindergarden and primary schools
- Waste management
- Municipal streets
- Local infrastructure
- Local police
- Zoning
- Municipal taxes
- Citizenship

Especially the cantonal powers of education, culture, police, and the relation between religion and state are closely linked to identity. At the time of the adoption of the first federal constitution, most of all the role of religion in the state was fiercely disputed. A short civil war between conservative Catholic and more progressive Protestant cantons had preceded the adoption of the constitution. It would not have been possible to find a countrywide approach that would not have alienated parts of the population. By leaving the regulation of the relations between religion and the state to the cantons, the central level could avoid taking a decision in this sensitive field and could remain neutral. Cantons adopted different systems. For instance, the cantons of Geneva and Neuchâtel opted for a complete separation between the state and religion. The canton of Vaud, however, established very close links between the state and the Protestant church. Priests were even considered civil servants. Most cantons gave and give privileges, at least to the two main religious groups. The central level, however, assumed the role of protector of individual religious freedom and of guarantor of inter-religious peace.

Language is a slightly different example. In order to remain neutral, the central level adopted a policy of relative equality of linguistic groups. At the central level, today four languages are recognised as official languages. Three of the languages (German, French and Italian) have an equal status: for instance, all laws are published in the three languages, all language versions have equal validity. Romansh has a slightly disfavoured position; Romansh is used as official language only in relation to Romansh-speaking citizens. However, Romansh is also slightly favoured. The Confederation and the Cantons can adopt specific measures to protect this language.

The cantons have the right to regulate the use of languages at the cantonal level. "The Cantons shall designate their official languages. In order to preserve harmony amongst linguistic communities, they shall respect the traditional territorial distribution of languages, and take into account the indigenous linguistic minorities" (Art 70 II of the Constitution). In most cantons one language has an official status. However, three cantons recognise two official languages (Friboug, Valais, and Berne). One canton recognises three official languages (Grisons).

Source: Topperwin (2008).

Nepal is rich in ethnic and cultural diversities, religious tolerance, symbolic uniqueness, social platforms that bring people together, motivate them to work together, enhance mutual respect and trust. Mountain Everest, Lumbini (the birthplace of Lord Buddha), martyrs (e.g. Dasharath Chand, Dharma Bhakta, Ganga Lal, Sukra Raj, martyrs of April 2006 people's movement) are examples of the national pride of Nepal and Nepalese people at a national level. Similarly, there are several unifiers at the national, regional and local levels, such as leaders of social change (e.g. Shanka Dhar, Krishna Lal), river systems (e.g. Koshi, Narayani, Karnali) and lakes (Rara, Fewa, Rupa lake); festivals (*Lossar, Gaura-parba, Dhan-nach, Baisak-purnima, Dashain, Teej, Maghe-Sankranti, Chhath,* Christmas, etc.), places (e.g. Khaptad, Muktinath), customary practices and platforms such as *Samaj* of various caste and ethnic groups,

Guthi, which bring people together, create a common identity and promote a sense of belongingness. The new federal constitution needs to recognise and respect these diversities, tolerance, symbolic values and social-cultural forums. Sharing of power and collective decision making between different groups of people are the bases of the federal system. In the case of Nepal, our federal system must recognise and respect cultural, ethnic, linguistic and religious diversity and nationhood. Even if some of the local government units do not have enough cultural, religious, social, customary and symbolic uniqueness to bring people together, these local governing units can create some new collective identity (such as transport system, public space, etc.).

The size of the country does not affect the federal structure as many counties smaller than Nepal such as Belgium, Israel, the Netherlands, Switzerland, Austria have successful federal systems. They are successful because of respect of diversity and plurality. Hence, the major issue to make a federal structure of any country is not its size but the ways of managing diversities and practising tolerance and mutual respect. However, if diversity and plurality are not respected, the federal system does not provide the desired solution.

Each local government, regional/provincial/state government and federal government must protect and promote multicultural diversity, and address people's expectation of a fair, transparent, efficient, effective governance system.

5.6 CONCLUSIONS

Making new constitution functional and changing the existing political culture for durable peace in Nepal, clear provisions of ensuring democratisation of political parties (inner-party democracy), undeniable right of access to information; rights of Dalit, women, Madeshi, disables, minorities, children, youths, users and consumers; assuring linguistic, cultural, religious and individual freedom tied with citizens' responsibility; equitable access of Nepalese citizens to health, education and employment, transport, public services and other resources of the state; sustainable management and utilisation of natural resources (specifically water, land, forest, mines and minerals); infrastructure development (particularly focusing to remote and rural areas, which are often excluded from the process of globalisation and privation); respect of human rights and international human rights and humanitarian laws, national sovereignty and modernisation of security forces; guarantee of rule, and more important, honest and sincere implementation of the constitutional provisions into practice and active participation of Nepalese people in making a constitution are very essential. Ensuring both vertical and horizontal legitimacy is a precondition to make the constitution functional and owned by Nepalese citizens and to contribute to change in political culture for a peaceful Nepal. Political systems sustain trust, unlike economic systems which sustains efficiency and effectiveness. Therefore, building the trust of people towards a new constitution and a political system is the precondition for peace and stability.

It is not possible to promote horizontal legitimacy of constitution if it is not providing an avenue of creating a sense of belongingness, which is very hard compared to vertical legitimacy. Vertical legitimacy is often based on control and power sharing and in the context of developing countries like Nepal, it is often embedded with a feudalistic culture. If we reflect upon the perception of people excluded by the state, it is always expressed in 'my country but not my state' sentiment. Development of a feeling of common identity (common visions, collective response on external threats, feeling of equal fellow citizens' strengthened inter-personal relations, common spiritual sphere) is an important condition of increasing horizontal legitimacy. No matter how strong, legally-engineered and comprehensive the constitution, it will fail if people perceive it negatively. Therefore, formulating a constitution requires intimate engagement of people. Primarily, making a constitution is not the responsibility of lawyers, constitutional experts and judges. Their responsibility is to systematically arrange the issues and concerns raised by people during the time of the constitution-making process. One of the weaknesses of the 1990 constitution was the domination of legal experts (Upreti, 2006a and 2004a).

Post-conflict constitution making goes beyond reforming and introducing norms, regulatory institutions and procedures. It has to to deal with the recognition and protection of individual rights and making the obligations of the state to human rights and humanitarian laws, well-being of people, horizontal solidarity, nationalism and a feeling of belonging (Galtung, 1996; Harris and Reilly, 1998). When the constitution fails to justify, rationalize and legitimize public expectation and to overcome social contradictions, people become dissatisfied and ultimately disown it (Bhandari and Karki, 2005).

The main focus of all key actors (the government; political parties, civil society, bureaucracy, intelligentsia and international well-wishers of Nepal) should be concentrated to create an environment conducive for promoting horizontal and vertical legitimacy of the new constitution that promotes sustainable peace.

Lessons learned and experiences gained from the governing practices and exercising constitutional and judicial provisions for the past 15 years have provided an important basis for creating a new political culture.

The new constitution or judicial process must ensure healing, reconciliation (a process of addressing the legacy of the past violence and rebuilding the broken relationships), and reparation of victims.[6] The constitutional process in the changing political context must provide justice (retributive justice: based on prosecution, restorative justice: based on mediation; administrative justice: disciplinary measures, historical justice, and compensatory justice) to victims of the decade-long armed conflict (Upreti, 2006b).

Stabilizing democracy and reconciliation are interdependent and intertwined in shaping a peaceful societal system, particularly in a war-torn society (Bloomfield et al., 2004). Nepal is now entering a new phase of political transition of preparing a new constitution and therefore it is the right time to link reconciliation and democracy as part of restoring lasting peace and justice in the country. The new constitution must provide an avenue for people to promote legitimacy, express differences and dissatisfaction, recognize tradition and cultural diversity and finally, changing the constitution itself by people where needed. However, there are some powerful players in Nepal who directly or indirectly want to keep constitutional avenues for segmentation, exploitation and repression instead of integration, solidarity, social justice and pluralism. If the new constitution is not able to tackle these problems, it will not be able to create a conducive political culture and sustainable peace.

Promoting a sense of ownership of people toward the constitution depends upon, among others, economic and employment opportunities. If the constitution ensures opportunity for people to economically engage in productive activities, they feel a sense of belonging. Therefore, development (social, economic, infrastructure, etc.) should also be considered by the new constitution.

One of the main concerns of indigenous communities (*Janajatis*), Dalit and socially excluded sections of Nepalese society is fundamentally restructuring the exclusionary, hierarchical, top-down, elite and Chhetri-Brahmin-dominated state structure and governing system; respecting diversities in languages, cultures, values, traditions, religious faith, and social identifies; continuing access of indigenous peoples to natural resources they were using for generations; ending gender, racial, religious, ethnic, political and social discriminations must be addressed by the new constitution to achieve durable peace.

End Notes

1. A chapter is developed from the materials contained in a chapter of this author in the book 'Nepal Building New Road to Peace' edited by Baechler, G., Acharya, N., Dammann, P., Rajbhandari, R. and Upreti, B. R. (2008).
2. These armed groups are: Janatantrik Terai Mukti Morcha (Jwala Singh); Janatantrik Terai Mukti Morcha (Goit), Janatantrik Terai Mukti Morcha (Bisphot Singh), Madeshi Mukti Tiger, Terai Cobra; Python, Terai Baggi, Terai Army, Madeshi Virus Killers Party, Royal Defence Army, Gorkha Line Mukti Morcha, Liberation Tigers of Terai Ilem (LTTE), Kirat Workers Party (Udayapur and Khotang). In addition to these groups, there are also other criminal

gangs active in Terai (Chhotelal Sahani; Sanju Baba, Raju Singh Rathor and Munna Singh Groups), who operate from India.

3. See *The Himalayan Times* of 20, 21 and 22 September 2008 for details about the severe dispute between the Nepal Bar Association and Judges. Once the Judeges prohibited him for 6 months, the Nepal bar Association took a very strong stand against their decision and finally the judges withdrew their decision and both parties reached into negotiation.
4. In the election, less than 60 percent people cast vote and it is divided to different political parties and parties getting 35-40 percent of the total votes casted in election rules country leaving huge majority aside.
5. See Topperwin (2008), Introducing Federalism: Power-sharing, local self-government and electoral systems, for details.
6. According to the United Nations Declaration of Basic Principles of Justice for Victims of Crime and Abuse of Power, General Assembly Resolution 40/34, 29-11-1985, 'victims are persons, who individually or collectively, have suffered harm, including physical or mental injury, emotional suffering, economic losses and substantial impairment of their fundamental rights, through acts or omissions that do not yet constitute violation of national criminal laws but of internationally recognized norms relating to human rights'.

Chapter 6

Armed Conflict and Tourism in Nepal : Some Reflections

6.1 THE CONTEXT[1]

Nepal was in a unitary-cum-autocratic political system for centuries. The structural violence interwoven in age-old feudal socio-economic system, horizontal inequity and inequality in distribution and share of income and bad governance among others were the major barriers to include socio-economically deprived people in the mainstream economy and decision-making process. This caused prolonged, absolute poverty in the wider section of population at grass roots levels.

Though the popular people's movement in 1990 replaced a three decade-long unitary partlyless panchayat political system with multiparty democracy with a constitutional monarch, it failed to achieve political instability. Lack of structural equality in social, economic and political systems to fulfil the needs of grass roots levels in the national context for the next one and a half decades caused frustration in the masses. The CPN (M), capitalizing on the frustration of the socio-economically deprived masses, waged the armed conflict. The armed conflict continued for a decade (1996–2006). The conflict affected all major sectors and tourism was not an exception. However, not a single tourist was intentionally harmed or seriously injured or killed.

A number of conflict-related activities, like political strikes, state of emergencies, curfews, indefinite blockades, rioting,

Tourist Map of Nepal showing major tourist destinations

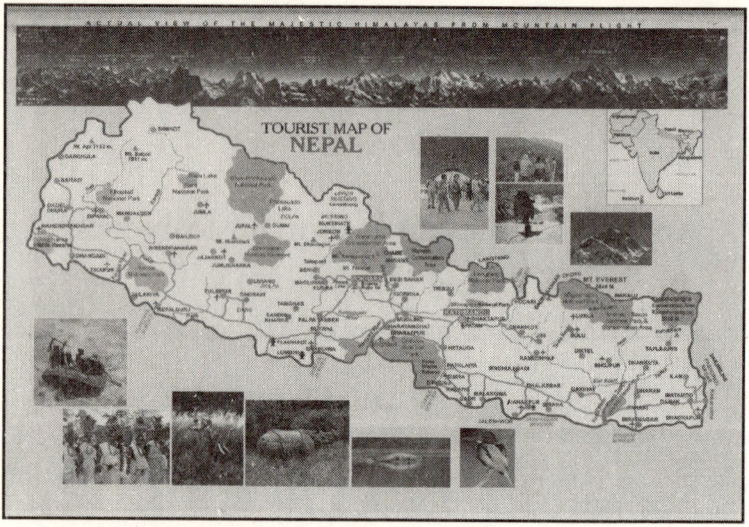

Source: Destination Nepal Travel Manual, 2008

intimidations, forceful shutdowns of big multinational and hotel companies, and consequences like negative travel warnings issued by the foreign affairs departments of tourist-generating countries and unrealistic media sensation (far from ground reality) created by national and international media became compelling reasons behind the dramatic fall in Nepal's image from a peaceful tourist land to an insecure destination. The escalation of armed conflict from the year 2000 onward resulted in a quick decline of tourist arrivals from 491,504 (the highest so far) in 1999 to 2,75,468 - the lowest in 2002.

The decreasing number of tourists negatively affected the tourism industry as many hotels, airlines and travel agencies closed down, which aggravated the unemployment situation and livelihoods resulting in irreparable damages to the tourism industry of Nepal.

However, the tourism industry adopted a number of response/coping strategies as celebration of Visit Nepal Year 1998, organization of familiarization trips taking high-level delegations in tourist generating countries.The Golden Jubilee

Celebration of the conquering of Mountains above 8000 metres, like Mount Everest in 2003 and Mount Cho Oyu in 2005, Destination Nepal Campaign 2002-03 and a number of press conferences, meetings and briefings among national and international medias relating to the tourism industry were held to recover from the effects of armed insurgency.

Nepal entered the post-conflict stage after signing the CPA by the Government of Nepal and the CPN (M) on 21 November 2006. With both sides' mutual agreement for a permanent ceasefire, it formally ended one decade of violent war, confining the Nepali Army and CPN (M) armed cadres within barracks and cantonments.

The tourism industry breathed a sigh of relief in the aftermath of the changed political context of Nepal and restoration of peace. The remarkable recovery[2] reflects the peace dividend to the economy that was nearly pulled apart by the decade-long conflict. According to Nepal Tourism Board (2008), flights to Nepal are packed; airfares and hotel rates remain on the upper side and there is a surge in the charge of porters and tour guides. New hopes have dawned upon people from all walks of society.

This chapter utilizes literature, publications, reports and printed data made available from tourism-related institutions, research centres and university libraries. These secondary sources of information are collected, analyzed and synthesized.

Tourism in Nepal has considerable scope for accelerating economic growth by exploiting its potential[3] resources. It is one of the major sectors of economy, which employs both rural and urban people. As a socio-economic activity, it touches the life of every Nepali one way or another. Its inherited nature and attributes have far-reaching trickle-down effects. According to the Hotel Association of Nepal (2007), the spending of one tourist benefits a minimum of 10 different parties through its cycling of expenses. This spending reaches both rich and poor people of the remotest areas of the country.

The lack of a sound tourism policy able to address new concepts of tourism, like sustainable and participatory tourism, inability for proper expansion and diversification of tourism products and resources in new areas and lack of effective mechanism to plough back tourism revenue in the local levels are few weaknesses in the tourism sector.

The concentration of infrastructure ownership in the hands of a few industrialized national or transnational corporations, local communities limited access to resources, commandeering of commons resources and inequitable distribution of benefits become compelling reasons to establish tourism as a non contributor to peace.

In the present context of globalization, tourism in Nepal, as in other destinations, brings opportunities for the economy, environment and society. The new and popular concepts of tourism, like eco tourism, sustainable and community-based tourism bring a lot of opportunities in terms of increasing awareness, knowledge, education, conservation and well being. It is a medium of fostering pride in cultural traditions and helping to avoid urban relocation by creating jobs locally and enhancing peace and prosperity.

The continuity of extortions from tourists, use of force if tourists are reluctant to offer donations, politicalization of labour unions in the tourism sector, a centralized tourism policy confining the benefits to urban-based key (elite) tourism entrepreneurs, limitation on community-based sustainable tourism development, pleasure-seeking and self-gratifying demands by tourists even in peaceful conditions, can be some threats visualized by tourism.

The undesired activity of preventing community welfare in the name of resource protection in sustainable tourism and increased transportation uses in tourism contributing to environmental degradation (pollution) and climate changes are also unavoidable threats in tourism.

6.2 CONSEQUENCES OF ARMED CONFLICT ON TOURISM

The decade-long armed conflict has both negative and positive consequences.

6.2.1 Negative Consequences:

Among the negative, the insurgency compounded with a number of conflict-related activities, like forceful closures of tourism enterprises, armed attacks at airports and hotels, indefinite blockades and strikes in between touristic points, extortion (forceful tax collection) from tourists by armed rebels became the convincing reasons for the loss in the image of Nepal as a tourist destination.

It ultimately resulted in the stopping of the growth of tourist arrivals and in the sudden decrease in arrivals during the second half of the armed conflict. These trends and different periods are clearly identifiable from Table 6.1 below.

TABLE 6.1: Tourist Arrival Trends During Armed Conflict in Nepal

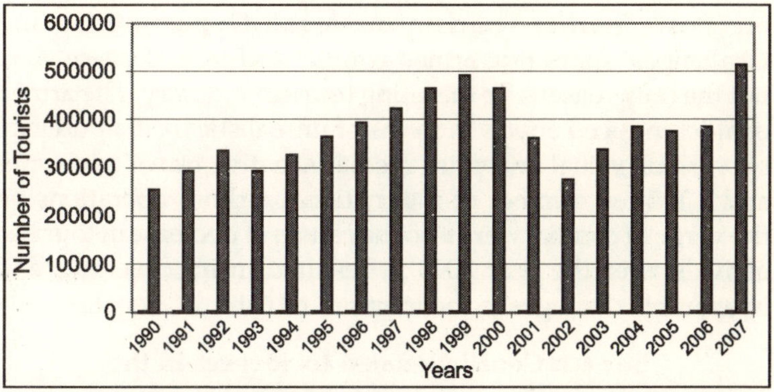

Source: Nepal Tourism Statistics, 2007.

The lowering of tourist arrivals affected tourism businesses mani-fold. There was downsizing and suspension of tourism-related operations and activities throughout the country, cutting of jobs, lowering of income of entrepreneurs and workers, and less emphasis on the encouragement of women participants as a matter of gender balance in the tourism sector.

Nepal lacks reliable tourism satellite accounts. According to the Nepal Association of Tour Operators (2004), the tourism sector lost revenue of around US$ 5 million due to the cancellation of 10 to 15 per cent bookings of tourists[4] during the first week of August 2004 following the CPN (M) blockade on Kathmandu Valley and "inaccurate reporting".

The tourism sector, in itscurrent transition phase in Nepal, is facing continued challenges in the post-conflict stage. The CPN (M) was found collecting forceful donations[5] both from tourism entrepreneurs and tourists at the entry points of trekking areas in Nepal. They even threatened[6] and beat[7] tourism entrepreneurs and tourists if they (tourists) are reluctant to offer donations demanded by the CPN (M) illegally. All tourism-related associations have been found to be quickly reactive in such a situation of the prevalence of crime in the tourism sector. The tourism associations fear that it could send out negative signals about Nepal to the international tourist markets.

Niroula (2008), in the proceedings of National Workshop on 'Post-Conflict Tourism in Nepal: Opportunities and Challenges' states that armed conflict and lack of peace were not the only reasons ffr the ailing tourism industry. The armed conflict induced effects in forms of unrealistic media publicity by various visual and print media, negative travel advisories and a limited number of international airlines operations on the verge of conflict were also the causes of decrease in tourists' arrivals after the year 2000. It resulted in irrecoverable and irreparable damages to the tourism industry in Nepal.

Box 6.1: Conflict-related Incidences in the Tourism Sector in Nepal

Date	*Places and nature of incidences*
Spring 2001	Starting of extortion (forceful tax collection) from Free Independent Travelers (FITs) by CPN - Maoist cadres at the entrances of every popular trekking routs like Annapurna conservation area (points at Besisahar/Birethanti/Beni) in western regions, Langtang national park (Dhunche) in central north region, Everest national park (Monjo/Jiri), Dolpa area (Dunai) in mid-western Nepal, Tumlingtar and Chitwan in southern central region.
September 2002 -	Begnas Lake Resort in Pokhara bombed with a heavy loss.
Oct 2002	Bombing at Visitor Centre of Annapurna Conservation Area. Project (ACAP) at Ghandruk, a popular tourist village famous for indigenous Gurung culture.

Mar 2003	Armed attack on Lukla airport, main gateway to Everest region in eastern Nepal resulting temporary halt of flights.
Sep 2003	Armed attack on Phaplu airport, eastern Nepal. Spring 2004 A weeklong blocked imposed by CPN (M) in Jiri, the gateway to Everest through surface.
June 2004	The only cable car tower connecting Prithvi highway to Mankamana, a popular pilgrimage for Hindu tourists, was destroyed.
16 August 2004	Four blasts took place inside the Soaltee Crown Plaza, a five-star hotel in Kathmandu. It resulted with immediate evacuation of 200 guests. It created a negative image of Nepal as a tourist destination.
17 August 2004	Forceful shutdown of 12 big multinational and hotel companies including Tiger Tops jungle lodge in Chitwan, Fishtail lodge in Pokhara, Hotels Sherpa, Malla and Soaltee Crowne Plaza in Kathmandu.
Year 2005 -	The cross-fire between the CPN (M) rebels and government led security forces at Lakeside of Pokhara.
Jan 2006 onward	Start of non-cooperation movement by CPN (M)-affiliated labour and trade unions of Hotel Yak and Yeti, a five-star hotel in Kathmandu demanding fair wages, other facilities and permanent status of temporary employees that resulted forceful closure for this hotel for many months.
Sep 2006 onward	Starting recollection of forceful donations from tourists from four major entry points in Annapurna Conservation Area.
Dec 2006	Hotels at Dhulikhel and Nagarkot, popular hill stations for tourists one hour's drive from Kathmandu, were forcibly locked by CPN - Maoist affiliated labour union for 3 days, demanding minimum wage standard to ensure fair treatment of employees.

Source: Upreti,and Upadhaya (2008)

6.2.2 Positive Consequences Along with Response/coping Strategies of Tourism Industry:

Nepal, like many other popular holiday destinations, does have its ongoing political problems, but it is remarkable to acknowledge that 4.35 million tourists have travelled to Nepal during a decade-long (1996–2006) armed conflict since 1996 when Maoist insurgency began (NTS, 2007).

Implementation of ten per cent service charge: A number of labour/worker unions affiliated to CPN (M), like Nepal

Tourism and Hotel Workers' Association, Nepal Independent Hotel Workers' Union and All Nepal Hotel and Restaurant Workers' Association came openly and strongly for the protection of tourism workers' professional rights and interests, establishment of an organizational climate and removing an unfair reward system.

As the result of continuous demand and struggle of those workers and unions during the armed conflict period, a joint agreement was signed between the Hotel Association of Nepal (HAN) and these associations on December 31, 2006. This agreement incorporated the implementation of 10% service charge from January 1, 2007 in all the member hotels (non-star to five-star categories) of HAN, putting an end to their more than two-decade-long dispute.

Peace-building endeavour by rural poverty alleviation through tourism: At a time when the country was embroiled in conflict, Tourism for Rural Poverty Alleviation Programme (TRPAP), realizing poverty as the root cause of armed conflict, was launched in September 2001 in six pilot sites (districts) of Nepal, which included altogether 48 villages, 28,337 households and 1,60,732 people as beneficiaries for a period of five years. Based on a pro-poor tourism programme, the major contributions of this tourism project include enhancing peace through alleviating poverty, empowering community through human resource development, providing credit facilities to economically disadvantaged groups in starting micro enterprises and generating income, developing tourism infrastructure,[8] formulating tourism-related model policies, plan and strategies and formulating site-specific tourism models.

Operation of Crisis Management Cell: The armed conflict period also marked the formation of a high-level tourism crisis response coordination committee headed by Ministry of Tourism, Culture and Civil Aviation in 2004. The committee later formed a crisis response action unit and crisis management cell (CMC) to offset negative dissemination of news to prevent and cope with the impact of unrealistic media hype by national and international media. Pradhan (2008) mentions The Crisis

Management Cell formed under Media Centre of Nepal Tourism Board started to prevent and cope with the impact of unrealistic media hype with the provision of its 24-hour information disseminating services from 2005.

Seasonal earning opportunity and prevention of the involvement in armed conflict: The trend shows that many semi-employed rural people during their free time from seasonal agricultural and animal husbandry work, rushed towards Kathmandu to get other seasonal jobs like porters, Sherpas, lead Sherpas, Sirdars, Trekking Cooks and kitchen support staff in many numbers. This definitely helped to divert the larger number of the rural people involvement in armed conflict, especially by providing alternative earning opportunities. In the post-conflict stage, a total of 85 expedition teams are granted climbing permits for spring season in 2008, which is up from 60 teams during the spring season last year. It is estimated that an expedition normally employs around 600 porters and 400 others as guides, cooks and kitchen boys during the time it stays in Nepal (MoCTCA 2008).

Marketing and promotion: The armed conflict period was also marked by some high profile international events: Visit Nepal Year 1998, Destination Nepal Campaign 2002–2003 and Mount Everest Golden Jubilee Celebration on 29 May 2003 (participated by 300 Everest Summiteers) and 50 years of ascend of Mt. Cho-ouy in 2004, one after another hand-in-hand with private sector tourism stakeholders. This helped tourism revive.

Trend of post-conflict tourist arrivals and its positive relationship with peace process: Krishna Regmi in his article[9] 'Rush on Himalayas as peace returns' mentions that lovers of mountaineering said the end of the conflict in Nepal had encouraged them to head for the Himalayas and climb the great peaks.

Nepal witnessed the first decreased tourist arrivals in April 2008 after the mainstreaming of the CPN (M) in the peace process in the last two years. There were 32,665 tourists arrivals in April 2008 compared to 33,024 arrivals in the same period in 2007, which is a loss by 1 per cent.[10] The visitors were suspicious of violence during the CA election in April 2008. This reveals, as Eric Neumayer (2004) also states, the unstable nature of tourism, which is highly sensitive to any uncertainties, especially conflicts. Any possibility of conflict and violence in both guest and host countries equally affect tourism on a global scale.

However, the total number of tourist arrivals grew by 11.15% during the first four months (Jan - Apr) in 2008, making it 1,28,802 from 1,15,881 during the same period in 2007.[11] The total arrivals in the first four months in 2007 and 2008 were more by 2.18% and 11.99% respectively compared to the same period in 2006 when Nepal was under conflict.

A message of peace has spread among tourists willing to visit Nepal due to the successful holding of the Constituent Assembly election and re-establishment of peace in the country. This has enhanced the possibility of Nepalese tourism in the world tourism market.

6.3 CONCLUSIONS

The armed conflict, which was less violent and destructive in the beginning till 1999, became violent and destructive from the year 2000 onward in the second half. The armed conflict changed its violent face and merged with people's peaceful movement during 6-24 April 2006 to fight against the direct rule of the king, which was in effect from 2001. There was the signing of the landmark CPA between the Government of Nepal and the CPN (M) on 21 November 2006.

Tourism in Nepal by nature is highly instable and sensitive to any political, social-cultural and economic factors. Nepal was vulnerable due to such uncertainties, with decrease in her tourists arrivals during the time of armed conflict The long history of armed conflict has had tremendous impacts on employment, poverty and displacement of the Nepalese people.

At a time when the country is in the transition phase with the peace process, conflict is still continuing although with changes in its nature, pattern and low gravity.

Armed conflict in Nepal is not only pathological but functional too. CPA is itself the result of conflict, which paved the way for the successful holding of CA poll with the ultimate goal of formulating a new constitution by the people for which the Nepalese people had been waiting since 1950, when it was promised by the state. The signing of CPA not only formally ended the decade-long armed conflict but also served as a vital tool for boosting the confidence of foreign tourists and potential investors in the tourism sector.

The tourism sector should be brought under the peace zone by the consensus of all political parties and declared a 'National Industry' to bring it under the essential services act and made free from any unforeseen uncertainties and crisis. This will help it to bring in the national development process. Tourism is a cross-cutting sector, touching all sectors, like education, local development, health, road connectivity and community development. Hence, tourism development should be incorporated in these processes.

The pressing need of sustaining peace in Nepal is directly associated with the economic opportunities in fundamental sub sectors of tourism, like trekking and hotel industries, mountaineering, wildlife and ecotourism, etc. The progress of these industries is directly and indirectly associated with enhancing livelihood opportunities, increasing income through foreign currency earnings, multiplying sales, financing of tourism management projects at local levels, diversifying of tourism entrepreneurships, stimulating infrastructure investments, enhancing living standards, contributing to local economies and increasing government tax revenues both in the short and long run.

Nepal's peace can be enhanced and prosperity can be promoted only by making tourism sustainable and participatory (pro-poor, pro-woman, pro-community). There should be the development of sound strategic packages for sustainable and participatory tourism.

While most of the benefits are claimed by outsiders and the upper elite, one of the examples in making tourism participatory is giving access to local people in tourism planning, programming and policy implementation.

End Notes

1. This section is largely drawn from the paper presented by Bishnu Raj Upreti and Pranil Kumar Upadhaya in International Conference on Research for Development in 2-4 July 2008 in Bern.
2. As one of the fastest growing sectors with 5,13,350 international tourist arrivals as the highest number in 2007 in the post-conflict era.
3. Rich natural resources/attractions, cultural heritage and unique hospitality of Nepali people.
4. *The Himalayan Times*, 27 August 2004 quoting the expression of the Nepal Association of Tour Operators (NATO).
5. Nepal Travel Trade Reporter dated Oct 29–Nov 11, 2007 stating the report of the Police Headquarter of Gorkha reports the forceful collection of a sum of Rs. 11,000 from a group of French tourist by the Maoist-affiliated Young Communist League (YCL) members in the northern part of Warpak in Gorkha district on Oct 24, 2007.
6. *The Himalayan Times* dated March 20, 2007 reports that the businessmen took to the streets after a group of Maoists severely beat up Mr. Hari Shrestha, owner of Hotel Woodland in Kathmandu.
7. *The Himalayan Times* dated Dec 7, 2007 has published the photograph of wounded Swiss tourist Stave Zinnerite who was beaten up by CPN - Maoist cadres on 6 December 2007 in the exit point of round Annapurna trekking route.
8. Tamang Heritage Trail in Rasuwa district in central north region and Chepang Hill Trail in Chitwan in Central southern region.
9. *The Kathmandu Post*, 21 April 2008.
10. *The Kathmandu Post*, 4 May 2008 under title 'Nominal decrease in tourist arrivals'.
11. Immigration Office, Tribhuvan International Airport (TIA), Kathmandu.

Chapter 7

Reorienting the Development Sector in the Post-conflict Situation in Nepal

7.1 RELATIONS BETWEEN CONFLICT AND DEVELOPMENT

Both modern economic development and traditional socio-economic systems exclude the poor people and ethnic minorities if the state is not responsive enough (Nayak, 1998). The Nepalese traditional social system is still deeply exploitative and so-called modern economic development has failed to address pervasive poverty, unemployment, underemployment, child labour, bonded labour, gender discrimination (Pandey, 1999). Poverty in Nepal is one of the major determinant factors of social exclusion, where a vast majority of population is below absolute poverty line. They are excluded from access to food for bare subsistence resulting in malnutrition, high infant mortality, and lack of access to basic facilities such as shelter, pure drinking water, primary health care, etc.

The upper social class often want to centralise power, resources and the decision process to maintain their hierarchical social structure. They have neither confidence over their actions (they always fear potential revolt from worst-off) nor do they believe in inclusive democratic practices (as they always want to be in power). They often fear for their social position and always show a defensive response to justify their exploitative actions. They directly or often indirectly attempt to block or hinder initiation of any social reform measures.

The exploitative act of the powerful elite creates silent tension, fear, mistrust, a feeling of injustice and resentment. Whenever oppressed people get opportunities to oppose such oppression, they act. This is one of the main reasons for the expansion of the Maoist conflict in Nepal as many oppressed people joined to oppose the ruling elite. Unlike the naïve belief of positive impacts of development interventions to well-being of the socially excluded, after decades of experiences it became apparently clear that such an intervention process often overlooked or excluded the most worst-off population (Upreti, 2002a; Shrestha, 1997; Pandey, 1999). Conflict has undoubtedly wide ranges of impacts on development processes and vice versa. Despite the long rhetorical policy of decentralisation, governance practices are yet strongly centralised. Reaching the fruits of the development to the poorest of the poor in remote rural areas is still difficult and slow (Seddon and Hussein, 2002). In this context, an important question arises regarding the donors' role in Nepal as well: What achievements have donor-funded development projects made in addressing inequality and social exclusion after several decades of their engagement? Why are they not able to ensure their development supports to address these issues? Why do they still want to continue the same regime if they are not able to achieve the stated goals? It is time for donors to rethink their development support strategies and practices and refine their approaches.

With reference to the development assistance programmes, the influence of donors lies in funding, which could influence the structures and process of conflict dynamics positively or negatively. Therefore, 'do no harm' should be the guiding principle of donors' development intervention in Nepal. Another important device of donors is diplomacy, which can be effectively used to reduce conflict. However, both these influential means are yet to be fully utilised to resolve the conflict in Nepal. So far, the unique characteristic of donors is to be sectoral, compete with each other on particular development issue, provide contradictory advice to the government and impose rigidity and conditionality in their assistances (e.g. to relinquish incentive systems, force to rise prices of basic goods and services like electricity and water that often lead to severe conflict). For example, the ADB-imposed conditions to abolish subsidy in agricultural inputs and reduce the number of food depots from Mid- and Far-Western regions have exacerbated the food crisis and fuelled the conflict. Such shortcomings have led to disillusionment of the public towards donors. Now it is time for the donors to re-examine their development assistance programme.

If someone looks critically at the overall performance of contribution of the internationally financed development programmes in addressing the root causes of the conflict, there can be a fundamental question. The obvious question would be: why is there no significant contribution of these programmes to address the root causes of conflict? These development assistance programmes were said to be focused on poverty alleviation, social justice, and empowerment of poor and marginalised people, support to fulfil the needs and rights of people, and so on. There is no significant achievement of these programmes to alleviate poverty, to overcome inequality and discrimination and to improve in governance even after so many years of donors' supports (since 1951) with such a huge amount of aids (more than 60 per cent of the total national development budget) and a large number of expatriates. Now it is time for the donor community to re-examine the impacts of their supports and redefine priorities, strategies, approaches and working procedures to address the root causes of the conflict.

The conventional development approach must be replaced by a conflict-sensitive development approach to contribute to realising a new Nepal. A conflict-sensitive development approach is needed to facilitate transformation of the state. It is too early to come up with a more concrete perspective, policy and strategy. However, it is right time to initiate the debate on new vision of development. Hence this paper attempts to bring some dimensions and perspectives of a conflict-sensitive development policy. Government of Nepal also has the responsibility to continue development efforts that address the structural causes of the conflict. Development programmes and projects in future have also to reconcile the social tension, promote harmony and equity that contribute to achieving the durable peace.

The objectives of this chapter are to identify the potential areas of development intervention that have created a feeling of injustices among the different sections of society and ways of overcoming them; and to identify measures that help in the smooth implementation of development programmes and projects and contribute to address structural causes of the conflict and promote peace. This chapter is mainly based on the literature review, consultation with key stakeholders and reflection of the experiences, knowledge and perspectives of the author (as this author is engaged in the field of development and social transformation for 28 years (1980-2008) and since 1996 more directly engaged in conflict research and analysis; conducting 'Peace and Conflict Impacts Assessment', risk assessment, security analysis; peace building initiatives; evaluating projects and programme from conflict perspective, training/orienting senior officials of the government, INGOs, NGOs and teaching conflict courses in universities and colleges in the capacity of university faculty, researcher, professional consultant and independent analyst). The perspectives, experiences and knowledge gained from these engagements are amply reflected in this chapter.

7.2 SOURCES OF THE ARMED CONFLICT

Table 7.1 shows an overview of the different sources of armed conflict.

TABLE 7.1: Summary of Potential Sources of Social Tension and Violent Conflict

1. Structural sources	2.International sources	3. Triggers and catalysts
• Political sources • Socio-economic (caste, class, religion-based discrimina-tions and inequa-	• Change in inter national context; • Interests of powerful nations (political, economic:	• Vested interests • Suddenly emerging situation (e.g. 1st June 2001 Royal massacre in Nepal)

lities; poverty and unemployment; social exclusion, etc.) sources,
- Geographical isolation
- Constitution and legal sources
- Ideological sources

natural resources- gas, oil, water and forest; historical legacy; religious; strategic and military).

- Failure of political leaderships,
- Psychological factors- revenge and retaliations
- Irresponsibility factor and culture of denial

7.3 THE BASIS FOR REORIENTING DEVELOPMENT

At the theoretical level, some important issues have been included in the Comprehensive Peace Agreement. Under Section 3, "Political, social, economic transformation and conflict management" it states, *"Both parties have agreed to formulate following programmes and policies for political, social and economic transformation and management of the existing conflict through positive means"*.

BOX 7.1: Issues Related to Development Included in the Comprehensive Peace Agreement

- Based on the decision taken by the meeting of the top leaders of the seven parties and the Maoists (schedule 6) on November 8, the CPA guarantees progressive political, economic and social transformation.
- Form the interim legislative – parliament, as per the interim constitution, the interim government shall hold election to constituent assembly elections by mid-June 2007 in a free and fair manner and make the Nepalese people feel their inherent sovereign right.
- No rights of state administration shall remain with the King. Bring the properties of late King Birendra, late Queen Aishwarya and their family members under the control of the Nepal government and use it for welfare purposes through a trust. All properties acquired by King Gyanendra by virtue of him being the King (like palaces of various places, forests and conservation areas, heritage having historical and archaeological importance) shall be nationalized. Determine the fate of the institution of monarchy by the first meeting of the Constituent Assembly through a simple majority vote.

- Promulgate the political system that fully comprehends the concepts of universally adopted principles of fundamental human rights, multiparty competitive democratic system, sovereign rights inherent in the people and supremacy of the citizens, constitutional balance and control, rule of law, social justice and equality, independent judiciary, periodic elections, monitoring by the civil society, complete press freedom, right to information of the citizens, transparency and accountability of the activities of the political parties, people's participation, fair, able and uncorrupted administrative mechanism.
- End the existing centralized and unitary state system and restructure it into an inclusive, democratic progressive system to address various problems including that of women, Dalits, indigenous community, Madhesis, oppressed, ignored and minority communities, backward regions by ending prevailing class, ethnic, linguistic, gender, cultural, religious and regional discrimination.
- End all forms of feudalism and prepare and implement a minimum common programme of socio-economic transformation on mutual understanding.
- End feudal land ownership and formulate the policies for scientific land reforms.
- Adopt policies for protection and promotion of national industries and resources.
- Adopt policies for establishment of civil rights in education, health, shelter, employment and food security.
- Adopt policies to provide land and socio-economic security to backward groups like the landless, bonded labourers, tillers, Haruwa-charuwa and other such groups, which are socio-economically backward. Adopt policies to take strict actions against the people who have worked in government positions and have amassed huge amount of properties through corruption.
- Prepare a common development concept that will help in socio-economic transformation of the country and will also assist in ensuring the country's economic prosperity in a short period of time.
- Follow policies ascertaining the professional rights of workers and increase investment on sectors, like promoting industries, trade and export and increase employment and income-generating opportunities.

Many of the provisions contained in Box 7.1 are directly related to development issues and they provide a framework for the development planning for new Nepal.

After the successful April movement, the 'Code of Conduct' (CoC) agreement between the Seven Party Alliance (SPA) and the Communist Party of Nepal (Maoist) on 26 May 2006,[1] had made specific provisions (Articles 9, 10, 11, 12 and 15) which are directly relevant to post-conflict space for development. Article 9 of the CoC states the provisions of allowing basic services and facilities for people to run smoothly; Article 10 highlights that any obstructions would not be created while carrying out regular public work and development work. Similarly, Article 11 mentions that both parties do not prohibit and obstruct the transportation of foodstuff, medicine, construction materials for development, and daily essential goods. Article 12 had made provisions for creating conducive environment for regular operation of schools, colleges, universities, health centres, hospitals and industries. Article 15 deals on prohibiting collection of donations and financial assistance in cash and kind against willingness of people.

Government of Nepal had established the Peace Trust Fund under the coordinatorship of Ministry of Finance to facilitate the post-conflict reconstruction and development and peace process. The donor agencies such as Switzerland, the UK, Denmark, Finland, and Netherlands are in support of the initiative. If it works properly, this arrangement could be one of the very few major conflict-sensitive development initiatives taken by the government of Nepal, which can directly contribute to post-conflict stability.

7.4 DEVELOPMENT AGENCIES AND APPROACH AT THE TIME OF THE ARMED CONFLICT

Until 2001, most of the development agencies were conflict blind in their approaches and strategies. They were opting for 'avoiding strategy' and trying to skip the conflict, either denying or ignoring it. Once the effects of armed conflict intruded their work and their existence fell into jeopardy, donor-funded projects and programmes started to rethink their development approaches, strategies and operational practices. By 2003, many of the development agencies started to critically examine the impacts of armed conflict in their development projects and programmes and vice versa. Issues of involuntary transfer of resources to the conflict became one of the prominent concerns. They started to examine the approaches and staffing structures and contribution of their development assistance to address social tension and violent conflict once the CPN (M) seriously questioned donor-funded projects in terms of their intention, operational style (lack of transparency, elite-centric staff composition, resource abuses, benefits captured by elites instead of reaching to intended beneficiaries, etc.). This concern ethically forced the donor community to review their very basic objectives of development assistance in Nepal.

The major donor countries providing development assistance to Nepal had formed a forum (called BOGs Group) to collectively respond to the development crisis. They came up with the 14-point Basic Operating Guidelines[2] (BOGs) to help in implementing their development projects and programmes (See Box 7.2). The government[3] and CPN (M) publicly expressed their commitment to respect the BOGs.[4] Similarly, the UN, Association of INGOs and NGO federation had also come up with their own BOGs that virtually covered almost all donor-funded development activities implemented in Nepal. These BOGs became valuable instruments not only for maintaining neutrality and reducing the risks of doing harm but also traced the root causes of conflict and building peace.

BOX 7.2 : Basic Operating Guidelines (BOGs)

Based on principles agreed internationally and in Nepal, we the undersigned have adopted the following Basic Operating Guidelines for all development and, where necessary, humanitarian assistance in Nepal.

1. We are in Nepal to contribute to improvements in the quality of life of the people of Nepal. Our assistance focuses on reducing poverty, meeting basic needs and enabling communities to become self-sufficient.
2. We work through the freely expressed wishes of local communities, and we respect the dignity of people, their culture,

religion and customs.

3. We provide assistance to the poor and marginalized people of Nepal, regardless of where they live and who they are. Priorities for assistance are based on need alone, and not on any political, ethnic or religious agenda.
4. We ensure that our assistance is transparent and we involve poor people and their communities in the planning, management and implementation of programmes. We are accountable to those whom we seek to assist and to those providing the resources.
5. We seek to ensure that our assistance tackles discrimination and social exclusion, most notably based on gender, ethnicity, caste and religion.
6. We recruit staff on the basis of suitability and qualification for the job, and not on the basis of political or any other considerations.
7. We do not accept our staff and development partners being subjected to violence, abduction, harassment or intimidation, or being threatened in any manner.
8. We do not work where staff is forced to compromise core values or principles.
9. We do not accept our assistance being used for any military, political or sectarian purposes.
10. We do not make contributions to political parties and do not make any forced contributions in cash or kind.
11. Our equipment, supplies and facilities are not used for purposes other than those stated in our programme objectives. Our vehicles are not used to transport persons or goods that have no direct connection with the development programme. Our vehicles do not carry armed or uniformed personnel.
12. We do not tolerate the theft, diversion or misuse of development or humanitarian supplies. Unhindered access of such supplies is essential.
13. We urge all those concerned to allow full access by development and humanitarian personnel to all people in need of assistance, and to make available, as far as possible, all necessary facilities for their operations, and to promote the safety, security and freedom of movement of such personnel.
14. We expect and encourage all parties concerned to comply strictly with their obligations under International Humanitarian Law and to respect Human Rights.

At the project level, several projects such as the Sahakarya Project[5] of the Canadian International Development Agency (CIDA), Livelihoods and Forestry and Rural Access Programmes of Department of International Development of the UK, Nepal Swiss Community Forestry Project of Swiss Agency for Development and Cooperation (SDC) were some of the pioneers in adopting a conflict-sensitive development approach and addressing root causes of the conflict. However, financial efficiency is always a source of contentions in donor-funded projects.

7.5 STRATEGIC REORIENTATION: CONFLICT-SENSITIVE DEVELOPMENT

The development sector in Nepal in general and development agencies in particular have been facing tremendous challenges. On one side, the more than five decades of Nepalese history of development is largely centralised, elite-based, exclusionary and has consequently failed and needs fundamental restructuring. One of the major causes of failure of the conventional approach of development is its limitation in addressing structural causes of the conflict. On the other side, expectations from people on the development sector to deliver services in the changing context are extremely high, therefore potential pressure from political process is huge. Hence, new vision, new strategies and new operational modalities are needed to meet the challenges.

Conflict-sensitive development requires conducive policy context, responsive institutions and committed actors in addition to political commitment and organizational culture. Effective implementation of conflict -sensitive development projects and programmes requires a positive attitude of the staff and organizational behaviour.

Conflict-sensitive development ensures incorporation of conflict-related concerns and issues in a regular project cycle (planning, implementation and evaluation). They provide methodology and conceptual orientation to minimise the negative effects of conflict and provide opportunity to generate new prospects for implementing development projects and programmes in the changing political and security landscape within which the development has to operate. Flexibility is one of the fundamental principles in implementing projects in a situation of escalated conflict. Conflict-sensitive development is a flexible, transparent and effective approach with functional modus operandi at all levels. Conflict-sensitive development framework provides these requirements, which are discussed below:

7.5.1 Conflict-sensitive project cycle

While visioning the conflict-sensitive development, the classical, centralised and controlled system of development planning by the National Planning Commission must be change. The USSR history shows that the centrally planned development model for local community was a means of control, which does not fit with the democratic norms and values. Hence, all local development programmes and projects must be planned, implemented, monitored, and evaluated locally. Once this point of departure is accepted in the development visioning, conflict-sensitive development planning can be accomplished at the local level, using concept of project cycle management.

It is essential to incorporate the concept of 'conflict-sensitive development' in all steps of project cycle. Analyse interrelationship and interaction between context, actors and cause of conflict and incorporate the outcomes of the analysis into each step of the project cycle (planning, implementation, monitoring and evaluations).

Conflict-sensitive planning has to be built on elements identified from the conflict analysis in relation to conflict *profile, causes, actors and the dynamics*. In recent years, the Peace and Conflict Impact Assessment[6] (PCIA) has been used as an effective planning tool for conflict-sensitive project design and formulation. It helps to understand the context where the development has to implement and the interaction between the contextual environment and the proposed development. This analysis ensures maximization of development for peace, and does not inadvertently exacerbate violence.

Conflict-sensitive planning involves understanding the context (using both a traditional needs assessment process and a conflict analysis), planning in a conflict-sensitive fashion based on the analysis of interaction between context and the proposed intervention and designing mitigation measures. So far, this important dimension is missing.

7.5.2 Social justice in development

Social inclusion should be the entry point for conflict-sensitive development. Social inclusion is a process of overcoming functional, institutional and policy barriers at macro and micro levels to increase the access of poor, marginalized and backward people to the development opportunities. Changes in incentive systems and improved capacity of the state and community are requisites of the social inclusion. Effective social inclusion leads to political, social and economic empowerment. Social inclusion must be a priority with a clear institutional mechanism and operational arrangement to ensure inclusion of the excluded, to address poverty, inequality, injustice and discriminations, and employment generation in the project area. Social inclusion is far wider than the approach of social mobilisation. When tangible benefits to poorest, landless and marginalized people are assured, several risks related to social tensions and potential manipulations by insurgents can be minimised.

A critical examination of the overall impacts of development programmes (Pandey, 1999; Shrestha, 1997; Upreti, 2004a) brings a fundamental question: why has development failed to address poverty and social exclusion, major structural causes of the conflict? The question directly points towards the performance of the government and development administration and governing system.

7.5.3 Conflict-sensitive Development Indicators in Monitoring and Evaluation

Conflict indicators are figures or groups of figures which, when monitored over time, tell about changes in situations or conditions of conflict. The use of indicators is common in order to better predict the intensity and prevent the negative effects of the violent conflict on development. Indicators warn of an incipient conflict and provide an opportunity to take measures to cope with it. Therefore, indicators are extremely important in conflict-sensitive works. Conflict indicators help development policy makers and professionals to examine the presence or absence of conflict factors and are used to monitor conflict situations (Leonhardt, 2000). In the following section, some examples of conflict indicators are provided. However, specific indicators depend upon the local context and dynamics of conflict, and therefore they have to be cautiously driven from the conflict situation itself.

TABLE 7.2: Examples of conflict indicators

Source of conflict	*Conflict indicators*
Mode of development interventions	• Negative impact to community (e.g. disparity and exclusion) • Introduction of unsuitable technology, inputs or knowledge • Favour to elite supportive social structures and processes • Benefit of development interventions only to certain people/groups • Top-down and non-transparent decision-making systems • Lack of meaningful participation of target groups in development
Failure of development interventions to address socio-economic disparities in their working areas	• Negative influence on or effects of policy change (e.g. abolition of fertiliser subsidy) • Social discriminations (caste, ethnicity, religion, gender, dalits, untouchability, etc.) • Contradiction with or marginalisation of local indigenous systems • Institutional failure in addressing structural causes of conflict (bureaucratic, top-down and controlling institutional arrangements)
Competition over natural resources	• Dispute in natural resources ownership and demarcation • Negative effects of external natural resources

	management projects to local community • Conflicting land-use goals (agriculture, conservation, forest, etc.) • Depletion of natural resources due to development interventions • Natural resources encroached by powerful people
Political exploitation of cultural and other differences	• Disrespect or repression of local culture and value by central authorities • Conflict over territorial rights • Conflict on use of language for education/ administration
Governance issue	• Exclusionary or unrepresentative local power structures • Low or no access to development resources to certain groups • Political discrimination to certain groups (e.g. indigenous people)
Pluralism and participation	• Lack of co-operation between communities • Absence or weak civil society organisations • Elite control of local media • Flow of resources (e.g. money) to fuel conflict • Autocratic leadership (domination) • Absence or abuse of rules/regulations
Channels of conflict management	• Poor performance of courts and semi-judicial bodies (corruption, influence of power, nepotism, etc.) • Contradiction of customary laws with state laws • Undermined roles of local mediators and indigenous conflict resolution mechanisms/ practitioners • Ignored conflict dynamics by development interventions
International engagement and influence	• Vested interests and contradictory approaches of donors • Legacy of past activities of donors • Resistant mindset of donors and their development staff

Legacy of violence	• Past history of conflict within and between community in development implementation areas • Use of development resources and institutions by warring parties in the past
Arm proliferation	• Flow of development project money to purchase arms by warring parties • Easy access to small arms and ammunitions • Engagement of development professionals in small arms deal.

Source: Adapted from Upreti (2006c:22-23).

It is essential to make sure that development agencies use conflict-sensitive indicators while monitoring and evaluating development projects and programmes. The following are some of the examples of indicators:

- Positive impact to community (e.g. addressing disparity and exclusion)
- Well-trained development practitioners on conflict-sensitive development
- Use of conflict-sensitive methodologies such as PCIA, conflict risk assessment, security management, etc.
- Introduction of locally suitable technology, inputs or knowledge
- Addressing unequal and elite-centric social structures and processes through development
- Benefit of development interventions to poor and marginalized people/groups
- Bottom-up and transparent decision-making systems and community engagement
- Meaningful participation of target groups in development
- Addressing social discriminations (caste, ethnicity, religion, gender, dalits, untouchability, etc.)
- Respecting local and indigenous systems
- Ensuring access of poor and marginalized people to natural resources

- Regeneration of natural resources from development interventions
- Respect local culture and value by central development authorities
- Increases co-operation between communities
- Strong civil society organizations
- Respect of local mediators and indigenous conflict resolution mechanisms/practitioners
- Addresses structural causes of the conflict
- Facilitate addressing the effects of conflict, such as rehabilitation and reconstruction, supporting conflict victims, etc.
- Fulfilling expectation of people at the time of frustration and anxiety by conflict
- Filling vacuum by continuing development activities and consequently keeping people engaged
- Incorporating conflict-related concerns and issues in a regular project cycle (planning, implementation and evaluation)
- Applying PCIA, conflict analysis (CA), Do-No-Harm and conflict risks assessment (CRA) in development projects and programmes
- Applying flexibility as one of the fundamental principles in implementing projects in a situation of conflict
- Training and equipping staff in Do-No-Harm principles (Anderson, 1999), conflict risk assessment and PCIA
- Development and implementation of operational guidelines (security instructions, Security Procedure Manual, Travel Tips, Responding to Violence in the Operating Environment, Crisis Management Guidelines, etc.)

These are some of many possible indicators, which could help to analyse conflict. But conflict indicators vary from project to project or programme to programme, and depend upon specific geographical and socio-economic contexts where such development interventions are in operation.

7.5.4 Incorporate PCIA in Development Administration and Management

PCIA is a planning and management tool in development programmes, which helps development practitioners, governments and administrators to mitigate conflict and promote peace. Based on a thorough understanding of the conflict, it provides a strategic framework for conflict prevention and peace-building work. It helps to identify the root causes of conflict and promote local capacities and opportunities for peace building within development programmes. PCIA helps to monitor and mitigate the potential negative consequences of a development intervention; assist to review existing good practice of development interventions, integrate conflict resolution and peace-building values in development programmes, emphasis codes of conduct to implement development interventions through a flexible approach to adapt to different types and stages of conflict, helps to coordinate a wide range of instruments and actors based on their comparative advantages; address security risks, promotes local capacities for peace and the structural root causes of conflict. It is essential to ensure that all development policies and strategies incorporate PCIA as compulsory development administration and management tool for bigger projects as Environmental Impact Assessment is practised.

- PCIA in the situation of conflict and post-conflict period is crucial to smoothly operate development, to minimise potential sources of conflict, to promote connectors and mainstreaming conflict-sensitive approaches in development. Therefore, PCIA should be an integral part of the project selection process (criteria, procedure, monitoring, etc.).

Steps in conducting PCIA

PCIA is a conceptual and methodological framework for comprehensive assessment of relationship between peace and development. Luc Reychler and Thania Paffenholz (2004) in their book entitled *Peace and Conflict Impact Assessment System"* (published by Field Diplomacy Initiative) provided an eight-step methodology for Peace and Conflict Impact Assessment. A short summary of eight elements of their methodology follows:

Step 1: Preparatory work: Awareness building on PCIA, obtaining commitment from concerned actors, clarification about the objectives of PCIA, agreeing on preliminary implementation plan, etc.

Step 2: Peace and Conflict Analysis: The second step is peace and conflict analysis, which forms a basis of further processes. Analyse both, the conflict and the peace-building context, both the macro conflict setting and the status of the peace-building process. Provide a short overall survey of the conflict and peace situation in the development intervention area and project future scenarios of conflict and peace-building situation.

Step 3: Peace deficiency assessment: Specify what conditions ideally tend to enhance peace building in a particular sector, programme, project, check the reality against this ideal framework, assess the missing links for peace building in order to eliminate the peace building deficiencies, assess the relevance and impact of the intervention.

Step 4: Mapping the intervention: Mapping the existing or planned development interventions (e.g. objectives and main activities lines, implementing agencies and actors, resource flow).

Step 5: Peace-building relevance assessment: Find out whether the overall direction of a programme or project (objectives and main activities lines, implementing agencies and actors, resource flow, etc.) is satisfying peace-building needs. Assesses how relevant a planned or ongoing development intervention is for reducing violence and building peace.

Step 6: Impact assessment: Assessing what kind of impact (real or potential) the conflict situation has or could have on an existing or planned development intervention (e.g. conflict related problems of the development intervention) and the impact of an ongoing or planned development intervention on the conflict and peace-building context (e.g. conflict and peace-related consequences caused by the development intervention). Different methodologies can be used for measuring impact, discussing problems and constraints linked to impact assessment.

Step 7: Recommendations: Provide recommendations on how to improve the peace-building relevance, conflict sensitivity and the peace added value of a development intervention. Offer concrete recommendations on how to incorporate a comprehensive, integrated PCIA in the routine planning, monitoring and evaluation of a project, programme.

Step 8: Post-step: It includes discussing the results, development of a joint action plan, writing the report and deciding on follow-ups and how to do an evaluation of the PCIA.

7.5.5 Apply Conflict Risk Assessment (CRA)

Conflict risk assessment is a concept, process, tool as well as strategy. It is a concept because it provides a powerful understanding of the conflict situation and level of associated risks. CRA is a process because it is not a one-time event and has to be continuously practised during the entire period of conflict, as a conflict situation is always dynamic and scale, intensity and patterns frequently change. It is also a tool forf analysing the degree, intensity and effects of conflict as it offers specific instruments to assess conflict. CRA is also a strategy because it is intended to minimise potential conflict risks to development and devise appropriate response options. Based on CRA, geographical areas of development can be categorised as very high, high, moderate, low and no risk areas. Similarly, demographic zones can also be identified based on CRA as highly sensitive, sensitive and normal.

7.5.6 Safety and Security Management

Safety and security of development staff is crucial at the time of conflict. Regular security analysis is crucial at the time of conflict. Keeping this need in mind, DFID and GTZ had established a 'DFID-GTZ Risk Management Office' at Kathmandu and appointed a special Risk Management Adviser during the time of armed conflict in Nepal to facilitate the security risk management. A similar arrangement was made by the Netherlands Development Organisation (SNV) and Canadian Cooperation Office (CCO) to minimise security risk to their staff. As an example, I am quoting the statement of DFID-GTZ risk assessment as *"Large-scale attacks by either side would delay return to negotiations. If the MB were to mount large-scale attacks, this would most likely occur in FW, East or eastern terai. If the SF were to mount large-scale attacks, most likely to be in Far West or Mid West. Current assessment: Probability of large-scale attacks by CPN (M) on SF or DHQs is low for the present. Probability of large-scale attacks by SF on CPN (M) in their heartland is higher"*.[7] Such observation and assessment provides development projects and programmes to devise their security management plan accordingly. Therefore, development security analysis and management must be an integral part of conflict-sensitive approach of development.

7.5.7 Addressing Root Causes as a Basis of Reorientation of Development

The development sector has to address concerns of landless, marginalized, indigenous and disadvantaged people. Implementation staff needs to be selected within the principle of inclusion from women, ethnic community, *dalit*, and poor. Similarly, priority should be given to community-level organisations, local clubs, and networks as local partners. Employing local poor people in infrastructure projects helps to reduce poverty and address structural causes of conflict.

Development agencies must adopt a policy of 'constrictive engagement to promote peace-sensitive activities'. They should also take affirmative action to ensure that the funding is fully invested to development programmes (poverty and discrimination alleviation, good governance, local people's capacity building and conflict management, etc.). Work on preventing a tendency to shift regular development budget to military expenditure. Opt for a flexible and learning-based approach, which ensures reorientation of development programmes to promote peace.

Implement development programmes in the remote areas that lack basic infrastructures. When properly supported, civil society organisations, CBOs and local NGOs work more effectively than other big organisations in empowering people and raising public awareness and properly mobilising scarce local resources towards poverty alleviation, good governance, and effective participation of the local people in development and social transformation. In this respect, pluralism in working approaches and partners is crucial.

Economic development and regional balances should be a crucial part of the reform process, which can be achieved through social inclusion and political reform. Social exclusion includes systems, mechanisms, processes, attitudes and practices that exclude individuals, groups, or communities from the political and economic decision-making process, basic means of livelihoods, social security and freedom that individuals have to have in a given social setting to organise and control their life (Bryne, 1999; Nayak, 1998). Therefore this system must be reversed to make the Nepalese polity inclusive. Similarly, centralism is a political phenomenon of concentrating all socio-economic, political and policy decision making in certain power centres (government structures, party structures or social structures) that must be changed through broader reform to promote social inclusion.

One of the major development reform agendas must be to eliminate the root causes of the conflict. This requires a drastic shift from the current perspective, regulatory and development frameworks, bureaucratic responsiveness and actual practices. Such reforms could mean breaking vested interests of political and bureaucratic elites, which is not possible unless major constitutional and civil reforms take place. Resistance from these elites based on false imagination and ambiguous logic, which has already been observed, is obvious in this transformation process. For example, radical land reform to provide a means of livelihood for landless people can be one of many agendas for social change.

Much has been said and written on decentralisation, representation, participatory democracy, people's rights, etc. but very little has actually been done so far. These concepts have to be translated into behaviour and action, which is not done. This needs new mechanisms, new thinking (for example, public hearing to select senior people in constitutional position), new procedures and concerted actions. Positive discrimination is essential to break the centuries-old inequalities. The current debate on the need of social re-engineering for social inclusion and affirmative action is the beginning of a paradigm shift.

The arrogance of war has developed military thinking in Nepalese society. Harassment of civilians, forced recruitment and state repression had left an utterly bitter legacy. If negative effects of this conflict remain in a latent stage, it could emerge and escalate when time, context and space become suitable. In such a situation there is always a great chance of re-escalation of conflict at the local level as terminal effects. To overcome terminal effects, three complementary strategies have to be adapted simultaneously. These are:

1. Transactional strategy: Efforts must be concentrated on local negotiation, and mediation (process of intervention in a conflict situation, of an acceptable, impartial and neutral third party who has no final decision-making authority but assists to negotiate an acceptable settlement of conflict) for the political accommodation and providing opportunity for peace enforcement (Galtung, 2000).
2. Structural strategy: Concentrate efforts on civil society building, especially in war-torn villages/communities. Roles of media, NGOs, local leaders are very crucial. In this strategy, local people and opinion leaders need mediation skills to develop accommodative behaviour to respect human rights and rule of law. This is particularly essential for ex-combatants. The Georgian

experience teaches that if ethnic fears and aspirations are not addressed by involving them in the reform process, it makes conflict transformation extremely hard (SEF/ KSI, 2000). Therefore, ethno-political dialogue is crucial in this strategy.

3. Transformational strategy: In all war-torn communities, it is absolutely essential to promote a dialogue between different fractions (of the past). Confidence building is a major challenge and efforts have to be concentrated to build confidence and trust to live together in harmony. Peace education, reconciliation and rapprochement must be an integral part of the social reform strategy.

The principal aims of all these three complementary strategies should be to promote trust, start economic reconstruction, social and political justice, demilitarisation and realisation of full security and healing of traumatised societies.

Basic Principles for reorientation of development:

- Reorienting development policies, strategies, programmes in meeting post-conflict challenges
- Creating equitable and sustainable opportunities for conflict-affected population (including former combatants) to rebuild their livelihoods and assist in restoring the rule of law, improving human security and achieving reconciliation
- Post-conflict stabilization, transition and recovery, and ultimately peace and development
- Flexibility, transparency and accountability in planning, implementing and evaluating development in a post-conflict situation
- Concerted and collaborative efforts amongst government, I/NGOs, local community
- Striking a balance between longer-term development goals (e.g. the achievement of Millennium Development Goals, poverty reduction strategies), and immediate developmental need of conflict-affected population
- Link post-conflict development with the national defence policy, foreign policy and national constitutional provisions.

The conflict-sensitive development policy in a post-conflict situation needs to integrate development with disarmament, demobilization and reintegration, which often takes place in a situation characterised by insecurity and lawlessness, poor or badly functioning economies, and a lack of social services and social tension. Post-conflict recovery should be a prime focus of conflict-sensitive development.

Conflict-sensitive development strategies must synchronize all development programmes and projects implemented by development agencies, including the UN, bilateral and multilateral agencies, INGOs, national NGOs and government agencies to ensure smooth implementation of broader recovery and development programmes.

Ensure cooperation of major players in post-conflict development. Development programmes are unlikely to succeed without full cooperation and the firm commitment of the political and development actors within and outside state structures. Building trust and cooperation between political and development actors and the general public is crucial and strategic focus of conflict-sensitive development must be concentrated in these areas.

The post-conflict development should focus on:

- Flexible and responsive programmes are designed and implemented as part of a larger strategy to build sustainable recovery and peace that relates to political, social, economic and security dimensions
- Post-conflict stabilization, peace-building, conflict prevention, reconciliation and economic recovery processes
- Rebuilding the social fabric and community networks, creating and reinforcing equalities, human capacities and social capital
- Priority focus of the programme must be on extremely vulnerable, young men and boys, women and girls, ex-combatants and militias, disabled, IDPs, and people in deprivation traps
- Addressing gender-based violence, suffering war trauma

Developing infrastructure and the services necessary for

economic activities (e.g. transportation and communication networks, electricity supplies and banks) and production (e.g. factories and agriculture-based employment, micro credit cooperatives)

Successful development intervention in a post-conflict situation is that which ensure basic principles of conflict-sensitive development and for that existing institutional arrangements are not enough to address the wide-ranging difficulties faced by the Nepalese people in the post-conflict period. Hence, new arrangements are needed in terms of development administration and planning, resource allocation, implementation and monitoring.

Post-conflict monitoring and evaluation should focus on integrity (accountability, professionalism, and corruption control) in addition to regular domains of monitoring and evaluation. Constantly monitor at the national and local level whether concerned parties are redirecting their political commitment to pursue the development goal for peace, stability and democracy. Monitoring and evaluation must focus on a broad and long-term commitment of development actors and make sure that resources previously used for military purposes are sufficiently redirected in reconstruction and recovery, social reconciliation and the strengthening of the rule of law.

7.5.8 Priority in Reconstruction and Rehabilitation

The focus of conflict-sensitive development in the changing context has to be in rural reconstruction and rehabilitation to promote equity-based livelihood basis and well-being of the poor, marginalised and conflict -affected people, economic growth and poverty reduction. Restoration of basic infrastructures and social capital, public services and community-based services should be a priority in a post-conflict situation. Employment and income generation through rural roads and community water supply and sanitation, community development, institutional capacity building and empowerment of socially excluded, marginalised sections of society are some of the important activities that can contribute to peace building and stability. The main objectives of reconstruction and rehabilitation are:

- to promote both security and development
- to provide a framework for comprehensive peace-building strategies
- to contribute in socio-economic recovery programmes, security sector reform, and programmes to re-establish and strengthen the rule of law

7.5.8.9 Issues to be Considered for Conflict-Sensitive Development

Focus on social inclusion: Social inclusion is a process of overcoming functional, institutional and policy barriers at macro and micro levels to increase the access of the poor, marginalized and backward people to development opportunities. Changes in incentive systems and improved capacity of the state and community are requisites of social inclusion. Effective social inclusion leads to political, social and economic empowerment. Social inclusion must be a priority of the development sector with a clear institutional mechanism and operational arrangement to ensure inclusion of the excluded, to address poverty, inequality, injustice and discriminations, and employment generation in the project area. Social inclusion is far wider than the approach of social mobilisation. When tangible benefits to the poorest, landless and marginalized people are assured, several risks related to social tensions and potential manipulations by insurgents can be minimised.

New development policies: Development policy and practices in the new political context have to start with addressing concerns of the landless, marginalized, poor, indigenous and disadvantaged people. Development programmes not addressing these concerns in the changing context will face tremendous difficulties at the midst of implementation, as public expectation is too high. Development programmes therefore have to strengthen and expand the initiatives which address issues and concerns of marginalized, socially excluded and disadvantaged groups within the framework of conflict-sensitive development.

Staff selection: Implementation staff have to be selected locally from women, ethnic community, *dalit*, and poor, where possible reflecting the proportion of the population. The development strategy in the changing context must engage community-level organisations, local clubs, and networks as main partners of development.

Accepting basic principles of conflict-sensitive development: Flexibility, transparency and accountability are the fundamental principles of conflict-sensitive development. Hence, the new development policy and strategy must ensure provision of these principles in modus operandi and project management levels. This modus operandi of the development programmes needs to be responsive to adjust in the changing political situation.

Use tools and techniques of conflict study: Conflict analysis (CA), conflict impact assessment (CIA), conflict and peace impact assessment (PCIA) and conflict risks assessment (CRA) must be made compulsory in designing and implementing big development projects and programmes and regular project performance monitoring system, yearly reviews and periodic evaluations. PCIA provides methodology and conceptual orientation to minimise the negative effects of conflict, build harmony and provide opportunity to generate new prospects for peaceful coexistence in the changing political and security landscape within which the project has to operate. Development policy and programmes should also incorporate Do-No-Harm principles (Anderson, 1999). Development professionals must get training in all these methodologies.

Any organisation working in conflict zones can influence the conflict dynamics positively or negatively. The positive or negative influence can be examined by the notion of connectors (those activities which positively influence the conflict dynamics, prevent fuelling the conflict) and dividers (those activities which negatively influence the conflict dynamics and consequently contribute to escalate conflict). For example, working with the poorest people in a transparent and accountable way helps to positively influence the conflict dynamics. On the other hand, resource captured by elites, concentration of development activities in accessible areas, biases towards certain power groups, manipulation or misuse of rules and regulations to justify ill intentions of power brokers, abuses of project resources and other mal-practices are some examples of the dividers.

Information and communication: In the changing political context, a strong development project information management system at the local level must be promoted. Project information system should reflect local power structures, social relations, conflict scenarios and trends, conflict and security risk mitigation measures taken, development project resources reach socially excluded people and benefits obtained from the project and lessons learnt for future adjustment. Sharing with and learning from other development projects and programmes should be an integral part of the new strategy of the development sector.

Operational guidelines: New development policy and strategy should make provision for conflict-sensitive operational guidelines such as security instructions and procedure manual, crisis management guidelines, conflict impact assessment guidelines to minimise perceived and actual conflict-related risks of development actors.

Conflict monitoring: Regular conflict monitoring must be an integral part of the core work of managers of development programmes and projects. From the risk management perspective, risk-related information gathering, management and communication is crucial, particularly for the first few years of new political setting. Hence, establishment of a mechanism of getting feedback and suggestions is essential. Competency of the development staff on conflict risks assessment, conflict monitoring, risk mitigation and peace building, security behaviour, early warning is crucial.

Focus on training and capacity building: A proper understanding of conflict and security situation, and appropriate skills of dealing with it are the key factors for successful implementation of a project in the conflict and post-conflict situation. Training in conflict and security risks assessment, conflict monitoring, risk mitigation, trauma counselling and evacuation, Do-No-Harm, peace building, dealing with different actors of conflicting interests is essential.

Policy of affirmative action: Take affirmative action to ensure that the development funding is fully invested to development programmes (poverty and discrimination alleviation, good governance, local people's capacity building and conflict management, etc.)

Exchange of information: Exchange of experiences in governance, conflict management and peace-building practices from different parts of the world is important at the time of conflict. Opt for a flexible and learning-based approach, which ensures reorientation of development programme to promote peace.

Focus on research: Analysis of cultural and socio-psychological dimensions of conflict is important. Research and documentation of indigenous conflict resolution practices and their contribution to peace building and social harmony, their relation with culture, religion, economy and history and role of customary laws in conflict management should be an integral part of a conflict-sensitive approach. Research also needs to focus on in-depth sociological exploration of the background (economic, cultural, social, religious, educational, gender, caste/ethnicity, etc.) and their interrelations with motives and perceptions of people involved in conflict. This type of rigorous analysis helps the government, donors and organisations involved in conflict management to design appropriate development interventions.

Conflict management capacity building at local level is an important strategy. The potential of local organisations to resolve conflict at local level needs to be supported. Promotion of practical, action-oriented learning-focused participatory conflict management methodologies[8] is essential for conflict-sensitive development.

Planning a coherent approach to conflict prevention and peace building in situations of violent conflict is extremely essential. Reinforcing civil society for peace building and reconciliation, support to traditional institutions engaged in promoting human rights and conflict management training is essential.

7.6 CONCLUSIONS

A new vision, new policy, new strategy, new institutional arrangement, new methodological approaches and a fresh perspective on development is absolutely essential to make the development sector responsive and contribute to New Nepal. Adopting conflict-sensitive development approaches is one of the main options for policy makers to maximise the contribution of the development sector in achieving sustainable peace, social harmony and living standard of the Nepalese people.

In future, any development project must: (a) address root causes of the conflict and structural inequalities; (b) build trust, cohesion and harmony in the community; (c) develop community resilience to cope with the adverse impacts of conflict; (d) create space and opportunities for peace building, (e) ensure visible benefit from the project to socially excluded and marginalized people and make sure that they are included in the decision-making process; (f) prevent possible widening of gap between rich and poor and avoid discriminations; (g) make sure that development interventions are not introducing new conflicts and tensions; and (h) ensure that resources are not captured and manipulated by elites or warring parties. This is possible through incorporating PCIA into development programmes and projects.

Nepal's peace process has paved the path for broader socio-economic and political transformation. However, transformation is successful only when economic and political stability is restored. Conflict-sensitive development intervention in a post-conflict situation is one of the best means to restore economic stability. Development intervention can be both a source of tension or stability, depending upon the approaches and strategies employed in operation. Hence, making development programmes conflict sensitive is a prime condition to achieve economic recovery and stability. Based on the contents presented in the preceding sections of this chapter, a general framework for conflict-sensitive policy guidelines has been presented here.

End Notes

1. A National Monitoring Committee on the Ceasefire Code of Conduct was active to monitor the violation of code of conduct but now it has been dissolved after signing the Comprehensive Peace Agreement.
2. Basic Operating Guidelines are a 'set of measurable working principles' codified by 10 donor agencies to ensure aid impartiality and access to the needy section of society in the context of the ongoing armed conflict in Nepal. It has proved to be an effective instrument to protect operating space for development. It is based on international humanitarian principles and legal standards to protect staff of development agencies and conflict-affected population.
3. In July 2005 government recognised BOG and publicly expressed its commitment to respect it whereas on 22 December 2005, the CPN (M) accepted the BOG through a public statement.
4. The BOGs were adopted by 10 development agencies representing Canada, Denmark, European Commission, Finland, Germany, Japan, the Netherlands, Norway, the United Kingdom and Switzerland in October 2003. Australia formally joined the group as a signatory to the BOGs in March 2006.
5. *Sahakarya* is a bilateral project of the Government of Nepal (GoN) and the Canadian Government, represented by CIDA. The executing agency is the Canadian Centre for International Studies and Cooperation (CECI), an NGO based in Montreal, Canada, with agreements with the GoN to operate offices and projects in Nepal. This is a five-year project (2003-2008). Sahakarya is implemented in partnership with 21 district-based NGOs for the health component and 20 second tier organizations/ lead CBOs for the economic component.
6. PCIA provides methodology and conceptual orientation to minimize negative effects of conflict and provide opportunity to generate new prospects for functioning of market in the changing political and security landscape within which the agricultural markets has to operate.
7. Conclusion of the risk assessment made by Risk Management Advisor of DFID-GTZ Risk Management Office in his assessment report entitled "Risk overview as at 29 Sep 2003".
8. Interactive Conflict Management is one of such methodologies designed by this author (Uperti, 2003).

Chapter 8

Legacies and Consequences of the Armed Conflict in Nepal

8.1 INTRODUCTION

In this chapter, a brief discussion on legacies, effects and consequences of the armed conflict is presented. The scale, intensity and the dynamics of the conflict varied during the period of 10 years of the armed conflict. Different parts of the country were affected differently, therefore the impacts of the conflict were also different in different places in different time periods.

The focus of this chapter is on the post-conflict assessment of impacts. The armed conflict has created enormous impacts on environment, economy and society. However, a comprehensive assessment of the impacts of the armed conflict in various sectors has yet to be made and it will demand a considerable amount of time, effort and financial resources. The objective of this chapter is to discuss the various consequences and impacts of armed conflict on development, natural resources, and society.

This chapter combines different methods, such as review of research reports, documents, discussion papers, books and journals related to environmental/natural resources conflict; consultations and discussions with selected environmentalists, policy makers and practitioners, representatives of different political parties, bilateral and multilateral organizations, INGOs and non-governmental organizations; rapid field assessment in Chitwan, Nawalparasi, Kaski, Myagdi and Mustang districts to assess the impacts of the armed conflict on environment and biodiversity. In addition, information collected from Bhojpur, Rupandehi, Dang, Pyuthan, Rolpa and Dolakha districts by the author for earlier study have also been included in this chapter. The perspectives, experiences and knowledge gained by the author have also been reflected in this chapter.

The impact period in this chapter covers the entire duration of armed conflict in Nepal from February 1996 to Nov 2006 and a year of transition period after signing of the CPA on 22 November 2006. This period was used to define the cut-off point. However, where relevant, the assessment also covers until August 2007.

The armed conflict had not only eroded the social capital existing in the community but also severely disrupted the relation in communities. Indigenous forms of social networks and institutions, which glue the society together are divided, causing the decline of both binding (relation within communities) and bridging (link between communities) social capitals, which is very difficult to rebuild. Putnam (1993) in his book entitled *Making Democracy Work* highlights the fundamental roles of trust in the democratisation process. Social trust in the context of democracy is one of the most important elements of social capital. Social capital is an important feature of society reflected in social network, norms, trusts and faith. It is essential to promote civic engagement, public participation, mutual learning, concerted action to achieve negotiation and political stability.

Access and control over natural resources are historically embedded in the feudalistic socio-cultural structure of the Nepalese society. Different researchers, scholars and practitioners have analysed the causes and consequences of the armed conflict in Nepal (Bhattarai, 2003; Duijn, 2003; Hutt, 2004; ICG, 2005a; ICG, 2005b; Upreti, 2004c; ICG, 2006a; IDD, 2005; Karki, and Seddon, 2003; Upreti, 2006a; Misra, 2004; Nickson, 2003; Panday, 1999; Pokharel, 2004; UNDP, 2004; Upreti, 2004a). Similarly, different tools and techniques, and analytical frameworks have been used in assessing the conflict (Aditya et al. 2006; Anderson, 1999; Austin and Bruch, 2000; Brabant, 2000; Conflict Prevention Network, 1999; Cutts and Dingle, 1998; Leonhardt, 2000; OECD, 2001; UNHCR, 1996; Upreti, 2003c).

8.2 IMPACTS OF ARMED CONFLICT AND NATURAL RESOURCES AND BIODIVERSITY[1]

Numerous studies around the world have documented the evidences of relationship between the armed conflict and natural resources (Upreti, 2004a & b; Austin and Bruch, 2000; Blom et al., 2000; Blom and Yamindou, 2001; Cuny and Hill, 1999; Dabelko, 2000 and 2001; Global Witness, 1998 and 2001; Gurr et al., 2000; Hart and Mwinyihali, 2001; Hatton et al., 2001; Hillmann-Smith and Smith, 1997; Homer-Dixon, 1994; Jacobs and Schloeder, 2001; Shambaugh et al., 2001; Kalpers, 2001; Matthew et al., 2001; McNeely, 2000; Plumptre et al., 2001; Squire, 2001; Tarasofsky, 2000; UNEP, 2006; Terfon, 2001; Wabbes, 2000). Asian, African and South Asian conflicts have demonstrated that conflict itself is a 'resource' for politicians, professional troublemakers and power players (UNEP, 2003a and 2003b; Terfon, 2001; Wabbes, 2000; UNEP, 2006) for gaining political strength, for accumulating wealth or using it for other

TABLE 8.1: Number of Incidences and Attack in the Natural Resources Sectors

S.No.	*Year*	*Frequency of attack*	*Remarks*
1.	1996	10	• The number of attacks in the natural resources sector presented here is based on the reporting in the newspapers and some reports, therefore it may go beyond this number if the attack cases of remote areas were not accessible. • Natural resource sectors cover land, forests, agriculture, environment
2.	1997	15	
3.	1998	21	
4.	1999	25	
5.	2000	22	
6.	2001	26	
7.	2002	103	
8.	2003	56	
9.	2004	99	
10.	2005	35	
11.	2006	7	

Source: Compiled from Newspapers, reports and other sources.

advantages. Further, armed conflict blooms in a power vacuum. Post-conflict environmental assessment by UNEP (2003b) in Afghanistan concludes that improving livelihoods of local people is strongly linked with the protection of environment and sustainable management of natural resources.

Table 8.1 demonstrates that the high frequency of incidences and attacks were in the year 2002 followed by 2004. The reasons ffor high intensity conflict in 2002 and 2004 were end of the ceasefires and resumption of active war.

The issues of minimizing the effects of war and armed conflict on environment and natural resources became more prominent when the United Nations celebrated the International Day for Preventing the Exploitation of the Environment in the War and Armed Conflict on 6th November 2002. In his foreword, Dr Ahmed Djoghlaf, Executive Secretary of UNEP Secretariat of the Convention on Biological Diversity writes, "*The conflict afflicting the Democratic Republic of Congo has alone caused the death of more than three million people. In his report on the causes of conflict and the preservation of sustainable peace in Africa, the United Nations Secretary General noted that 'since 1970, more than 30 wars have been fought in Africa, the vast majority of them intrastate in origin. In 1996 alone, 14 of the 53 countries of Africa were afflicted by armed conflict'. The Secretary General identified the illegal exploitation of natural resources as a major cause of the conflict in Africa. Indeed such natural resources as oil, minerals, metals, timber and diamonds have been coveted by various parties including regional parties and been the source of conflict particularly in Africa* (Shakya and Chitrakar, 2006:24).

Numerous studies have been completed in assessing the relationship between armed conflict and environment, conservation and natural resources across the world. The study of Blom and Yamindou (2001) in Central Africa, the work of Blom, et al. (2000) and Buckles (1999) in different parts of the world; studies of Budathoki (2003), Oli, (1998), Upreti (2007a) and Chazee (2003) in Nepal; study of Conservation International (2001) in Guinea and Togo; work of Global Witness (1998) in Angola and Liberia (2001); work of this author (Upreti, 2002a; Upreti, 2002b; Upreti, 2000b) in Nepal; study of Hart and

Mwinyihali (2001) in Sub Saharan Africa have shown the strong relations between armed conflict and natural resources, biodiversity and environment. Similarly, biodiversity of Mozambique was seriously threatened by the armed conflict (Hatton et al., 2001). National parks and conservation areas of Garamba National Park of Democratic Republic of Congo were seriously affected by the civil war (Hillman and Smith, 1997). The same thing happened in protected areas of Ethiopia (Jacobs and Schloeder, 2001). Homer-Dixon (1994) in his work has established a clear relationship between environmental scarcity and violence. Biodiversity of Sub Saharan Africa was heavily impacted by the armed conflict (Kalpers, 2001). Matthew and Upreti (2005) clearly demonstrated that demographic pressure creates stress in existing natural resources and that ultimately provides a fertile ground for insecurity and violence. Matthew et al. (2001) argue that protection of environment at a time of war and violent conflict can lead to peace and it can be one of the effective means of achieving it. Studies of Plumptre et al. (2001) in Rwanda and Squire (2001) in Sierra Leone have shown that civil war seriously affects biodiversity if special efforts are not made.

A study of Trefon (2001) in the Democratic Republic of Congo on impact of war on population and environment; various studies of UNEP in Iraq (2003a); Afghanistan (2003b), Liberia (2006) and Lebanon (2007) have extensively documented the impacts of civil war and armed conflict in different aspects of environment such as industrial and urban areas, agriculture, water resources, costal and marine resources, and other natural resources. The Panel of Experts of the United Nations had made a comprehensive documentation of illegal exploitation of natural resources in war torn Congo (United Nations, 2001).

The author of this paper has conducted several studies on impact of armed conflict on environment and natural resource, and resource conflict and its inter-relationship with governance, political system and armed insurgency in Nepal (Upreti, 1999; Upreti, 2000a; Upreti, 2001; Upreti, 2004b; Upreti, 2004d; Upreti, 2004e; Upreti, 2004f; Upreti, 2005; Upreti et al., 2005; Upreti, 2006c). A study of Wabbes (2000) in Democratic Republic of

Congo has identified the role of international community in conserving environment and biodiversity during the time of war. The work of Winterbottom and Neme (1997) in Sub-Saharan Africa has identified the possible environmental flashpoints for violence.

Several studies have extensively documented the negative impacts of violence, civil war and armed insurgency on environment, conservation, biodiversity, natural resources and society (Cuny and Hill, 1999; Dabelko, 2000; Dabelko, 2001; Global Witness, 2004; Global Witness, 1999; Gurr et al., 2000; McNeely, 2000; Myers, 1996; Schwartz et al., 2000; Shambaugh et al. 2001 (trampled grass); Tarasofsky, 2000; Uvin, 1998; World Wildlife Fund, 2000). Most of these studies and analyses have covered wider reasons and different social and environmental issues. However, one conclusion is common, i.e. environment and natural resources are means of peace building if due attention is given by the concerned actors.

The Biodiversity Support Programme[2] (a consortium of WWF, the Nature Conservatory and World Resource Institute) coordinated by World Wildlife Fund US to promote conservation of the world's biodiversity had extensively documented the impacts of armed conflicts and civil wars on biodiversity in different countries. This programme has vividly demonstrated several negative impacts of armed conflict and civil wars on biodiversity and natural resources.

The natural resource sector as a whole suffered from various problems during the time of the conflict. The concerned authorities of the environmental and natural resource sectors were not able to execute rules and regulations. The psyche of staffs working in these sectors was heavily affected by insecurity, fear, mistrust and suspicion that ultimately affected the performance to accomplish their roles and responsibilities. Visiting field, monitoring and control of illegal trading of wildlife and forest resources were seriously constrained. The natural resource sector was almost under the control of either PLA or military.

The main issue of difficulty was 'one-state-two regimes' situation (Upreti, 2006c) once the CPN (M) had formed the

United People's Council (the CPN (M) Government) and declared the Common Minimum Policy and Programme. The natural resource policies of the CPN (M) and the government of Nepal were contradicted. They had also issued a 'Forestry Directive' and 'autonomous forest policy' as parts of 'Directives for running the People's Government' (*Janasatta Sanchalan Nirdesica*).

Widening rural-urban inequalities, increasing internal displacement and migration, shifted priority of the government to security and fragile stage of private sector are severely undermining the government's integrity and posing a serious question on its intention. The Tenth Five-Year Plan was presented as a major development response to address the root causes of conflict. It had offered a comprehensive poverty reduction strategy and identified priority areas. However, it failed to deliver the promises made and the escalated armed conflict was blamed for its failure. However, mal-governance (weak, ineffective and corrupt governing practices), politicisation of development administration, shifting blame to others and weak commitments were also equally responsible for the weak delivery of the Tenth Plan. The recently developed three-year interim plan has focused on transition and post-conflict stability. However, its effective implementation is yet to be observed.

A study by Dinesh Poudel, Stephen Keeling and Dil Raj Khanal (2006) documents evidences of rampant corruption in the forest sector. They wrote, '*the poor governance of this valuable resource has led to widespread illegal exploitation of Nepal's forest products by powerful groups and individuals for financial gain and by local communities for their subsistence. ...Forestry related corruption has had a significant negative impact in this sector, leading to over-exploitation of commercial forest species*'.[3]. Increased political compartmentalisation and interference in bureaucracy is seriously undermining principles of good governance and people's hopes and aspirations for positive change are quickly shattering. Corruption related to natural resources during the time of armed conflict and civil war is not new and unique for Nepal. It is a common phenomenon in conflict-ridden countries (Global Witness, 2004).

Another major setback to the conflict and political power struggle was the local governance structures. The CPN (M) strategically weakened local bodies and consequently made them dysfunctional and filled up this political vacuum by their local *janasarkars*. In 2002, the then government knowingly or unknowingly helped the CPN (M) in their efforts to create a political vacuum. The government neither conducted local elections nor extended the tenure of the existing elected bodies when the local governments completed their term. Instead, the government assigned responsibility of the elected representatives to civil servants that virtually ceased the principle and spirit of local government. The CPN (M) emerged even stronger in absence of the local government and maintained a high degree of control. Consequently, the office-bearers of the government offices at local levels (except teachers and health workers) were withdrawn from the villages. For example, 39 police posts in Rolpa were reduced to 2 in 2000 and 23 police posts of Rukum were reduced to 2 in 2000 (Seddon and Hussein, 2002).

The CPN (M) had expanded its influence in large parts of the remote areas where presence of state was rare. The government officials working in Dang and Ropla, while discussing with the study team, explained that it was not possible to go to the field and implement programme activities. The government officials were not able to collect revenue and regulate the forests in the CPN (M)-influenced areas.

The armed conflict was also used as an easy excuse for inaction, ignorance or even to legitimize the wrong-doing (for example, not controlling corruption in forestry sector) (Poudel et al., 2006). A study conducted by the author in 2005 on impacts of conflict on NARMSAP reveals that malpractices and lack of accountability and responsiveness were very frequent and every inaction or even wrong action was simply linked with conflict (Upreti et al., 2005).

8.2.1 Consequences of the Armed Conflict on Forest Resources

Forest area, one of the main bases of biodiversity, was the main battlefield during the armed conflict. Most of the CPN (M) shelters were also in the forest areas. Hence, forests became the centre of war strategy and fighting action that ultimately led to biodiversity loss and deterioration of natural resources. Conservation or management-related activities in the forest areas from the government became virtually nil. This situation is not unique to Nepal but widely prevalent in other conflict-ridden countries too. An assessment of the environmental situation in Afghanistan by UNEP (2003b) shows that governance of protected areas was nearly dysfunctional in many national parks and wildlife reserves.

Forestry was one of the major hard-hit natural resource sectors from the armed conflict (Matthew and Upreti, 2005a; Khanal 2006; NSCFP, 2007; Upreti, 2007c&g). Forest-based resource transfer to expand insurgency and using forests as a battlefield had serious negative implications and created many complications in management of forests. CPN (M) used the forests for their strategic purpose: to hide, train people's liberation army, and operate insurgency. State security forces also used forests for their strategic purpose during the time of the armed conflict. Such tactical use of forests by the warring parties ultimately posed several security concerns for forest users and disturbed many people's livelihoods and management function of the forest (Khanal, 2006; Upreti, 2004a). Total value of damaged property of Ministry of Forest and Soil Conservation is estimated to be Nepalese Rupees 354.5 million[4] during the time of the armed conflict. In addition, the armed conflict had several impacts in community forestry. Many CFUGs were threatened, forced to remain inactive or dissolved; bank accounts of some of CFUGs were suspended or ceased and some community forests were captured by insurgents and state security forces (Khanal, 2006). CFUG's autonomy was challenged or seized during the time of the armed conflict (Upreti, 2007c&g; Upreti et al., 2005). State security forces had declared many forests as "no go zones", which had severe negative implications on management of forests and livelihood of CFUGs.

The then government handed over several community forests to security forces, which ultimately created conflict between the security forces and local forest users groups.[5] It is documented that during the time of conflict, 35,608 hectares of community forest of 48 places of 38 districts were made available to the army by the then government, and declared many community forests as 'military training areas'. Further, the military had encroached additional of more than 50 community forests managed by CFUGs in 16 districts (Khanal, 2006:14). The Armed Police Force has also encroached and controlled many community forests without the consent of CFUGs. The military had launched a series of Aerial Attacks in many forests, suspecting that the insurgents are hiding in these forests, which might have caused negative effects to forest biodiversity and management.[6] Chief District Officers as the representative of the government (as per the request of security forces) declared many forest areas of 16 districts as no go zones and issued propitiatory orders. In some cases, even local military barracks had directly imposed prohibition orders in forest areas (Khanal, 2006). In the time of the 'direct rule of the king (1st February 2005 to March 2006), the Zonal and Regional Administrators glaringly interfered with community forests. The Regional Administrator of the Far Western Region imposed a ban on timer trading from community forests suspecting that the timber traders might have paid a donation to CPN (M). The ban on trading of timber from community forests was imposed in all districts of Far Western Region, all districts of Janakpur Zone, Udayapur, Rautahat, Ilam, Jhapa, Morang, Makawanpur and Sunsari districts. In many cases, timbers from community forests were seized by security forces arguing that timber was one of the main sources of income of CPN (M). Mostly affected districts from this action were Ilam, Udayapur, Makawanpur, Sindhuli, Dang, Surkhet and Dadeldhura from Inner Terai and *Churiya* areas.

Similarly, CPN (M) imposed a prohibition order in many forests in their zones of influence to minimise potential risks of information of their activities reaching to the security forces. Large areas of national forests were under the influence of CPN

(M) and they used forest-based products for sustaining and expanding their insurgency.

Irrational exploitation of the expensive medical herbs, e.g.,*Yarsagumba (Cordyceps sinensis), Chiraito (Swertia Chiraita), Jatamasi (Nardostachys grandiflora), Kutki (Picrorhiza scrophulariiflora), Bikhama (Aconitum palmatum), padamchal (Rheum emodi), Panchaunle (Galearis stracheyi), Sunpati (Rhododendron anthopogon), Sughandhawal (Valerina wallichii)*, was rampant once CPN (M) took policy of imposing tax on transaction of forest products in their zones of influence.

The CPN (M) had imposed a 'war tax' (*Yuddha kar*) for transaction of forests products with contractors buying forest products from forests. For example, they had imposed a 15-65 per cent tax on forest products in all districts of Rapti Zone, 35 per cent in Sankhuwasasa district, 5 per cent in Dolakha district, 15-50 per cent in Ramechhap district, 10 per cent tax in timber trading in Far Western districts, 40 per cent in Kailali district, 30 per cent in Terathum, 20 per cent in Banke, 40 per cent in Bardiya and 10 per cent in Ilam and Jhapa districts.[7] Further, they had collected up to rupees three hundred thousand as tax on medical herbs from Humla district, rupees 62 per cubic ft. of wood or Rs.2,500 per tractor load in Udayapur.They were also directly engaged in transaction of some expensive forest products such as Yarsagumba (*Cordyceps sinensis*) (e.g. in Baglung district they purchased it from collectors and sold by themselves) (Khanal, 2006; Upreti, 2007c). As a consequence of the CPN (M) control in forests, the national revenue from the forest sector was sharply reduced. For example, the total revenue collected from the forest in FY 2059/60 was 3,82,29, and 911 was reduced to 2,30,57,420 rupees in the fiscal year 2061/62 (Khanal, ibid: 28).

CFUGs were heavily targeted from both sides. A total of 15 CFUGs' executive members or workers were abducted or tortured and one of them was killed by CPN (M) whereas 14 CFUGs' executive members or workers were abducted or tortured and one of them was killed by the state security forces (Khanal, 2006). The major forms of attack were abduction, arrest, detention and assassination.

TABLE 8.2: An overview of attacks in the forestry related infrasturcutres in the districts by CPN (M) during the time of armed conflict

Situation of attack (number of district)	*Development Regions →*					
	Eastern region[8]	*Central region*[9]	*Western region*[10]	*Midwestern region*[11]	*Far-western region*[12]	*Total*
Districts attacked	16	17	13	13	8	67
Districts not attacked	0	2	3	2	1	8
Total districts	16	19	16	15	9	75

Source: Department of Forests, 2007.

The situation of 'one-state-two regimes' (Upreti, 2006b) appeared once the CPN (M) formed the local *Janasarkar* (local government). The principles, procedures and practices of the local *janasarkar* were fully contradictory with the government of Nepal. The CPN (M) had categorized forests into National Forests, Community Forests and Production Cooperative Forests, and started to work in this concept of management regimes.

TABLE 8.3: Damage of forest offices by district

S.No.	*Districts*	*No. of Inci-dences*	*Types*		*Description of Damage*
			Ilaka/ DFO	*Range posts*	
1.	Sankhuwa sabha	5	0	5	Destruction of document, furniture, damage of door and window.
2.	Solu-khumbu	3	2	1	Destruction of document, furniture by fire outside of building.
3.	Okhald hunga	6	1	5	Destruction of document, furniture, damage of door.
4.	Morang	7	1	6	Destruction of document, furniture, damage of door and window, other materials, damage up to Rs.10,00,000. One

					building is completely destroyed.
5.	Bhojpur	6	2	4	Destruction of document, furniture, damage of door and window, damage up to Rs 4,00,000.
6.	Siraha	8	2	6	Destruction of document, furniture, damage of door and window, Partial damage of building, other materials, One motorcycle, damage equivalent to Rs. 600000 and cash Rs. 4515.
7.	Ilam	8	1	7	Destruction of document, furniture, damage of door and window, Partial damage.
8.	Udayapur	5	1	4	Destruction of document, furniture, damage of door and window loss of personal material.
9.	Terathum	5	1	4	Destruction of document, furniture, damage of door and window, Partial damage, abduction of staff.
10.	Taplelung	2	1	1	Destruction of document, furniture, damage of door and window, abduction of staff.
11.	Khotang	2	1	1	Destruction of document, furniture and other official material.
12.	Saptari	1		1	Destruction of building by fire.
13.	Sunsari	4	2	2	Destruction of document, furniture, damage of door and window by fire.
14.	Panchatar	2	1	1	Destruction of document, furniture, and partial damage of building.
15.	Jhapa	1	1		Destruction of document.
16.	Dhankuta	1	1		Destruction of building by bomb blasting.
17.	Rasuwa	3		3	Destruction of one range post building and Destruction of document of others.
18.	Rautahat	4	1	3	Destruction of document, furniture by fire.

19.	Rame-chhap	2		2	Destruction of document, furniture, and complete damage of two buildings.
20.	Sarlahi	8	3	5	Destruction of document, furniture, 2 motorcycles and complete damage of one building and kitchen room. Rs. 24,000 loss in fire, visitors' station of DFO Sarlahi was also damaged.
21.	Dolakha	3		3	Destruction of one building, document and furniture.
22.	Makwan pur	10	4	6	Destruction of two buildings and document, furniture, and loss of personal material of staff.
23.	Mahotari	4	2	2	Destruction of one building, office document and furniture.
24.	Nuwakot	4	2	2	Destruction of one building and office document, furniture.
25.	Sindhu-palchok	10	4	6	Destruction of documents, furniture, and partial damage of buildings.
26.	Sindhuli	10	2	8	Destruction of 6 rooms, 3 buildings, document, and furniture.
27.	Chitwan	12	5	7	Destruction of one building, document and furniture and partial damage of buildings.
28.	Kavrepa-lanchok	8		8	Partial damage of building and destruction of document and furniture.
29.	Dhading	3	1	2	Destruction document, furniture and one Jeep. Partial damage of building.
30.	Parsa	2	1	1	Destruction document, furniture and loss of one Motorcycle.
31.	Bara	3	2	1	Destruction of 1 building of six rooms, document and furniture.
32.	Bhaktapur	2	1	1	Partial damage of two buildings and destruction of office document and furniture.
33.	Lalitpur	1		1	Partial damage to building.
34.	Dhanusa	1	1		Destruction of Golo Ghar by fire.

35.	Kathmandu	1	1		Diffusion of bomb by security force before blast.
36.	Synjha	6	3	3	Destruction of 4 buildings, document, furniture.
37.	Rupandehi	9	3	6	Destruction of document, furniture.
38.	Baglung	5		5	Destruction of two range post building, office documents and materials with partial damage to 1 building.
39.	Myagdi	7	1	6	Destruction of one range post building, loss of office material, and document and field materials. Partial damage to district forest office including office material.
40.	Palpa	3	1	2	Partial damage of ilaka forest office with document and material, destruction of office document by fire in two range post (one range post was on rented house)
41.	Parbat	6	1	5	Destruction of office document and office material by fire in all range posts. Due to bomb blast damage of building equivalent to Rs.22,000.
42.	Arga-khhachi	3	3		Destruction of DFO building, Pick-up van after hijacking, and of office document and material by fire in Ilaka forest office.
43.	Lamjung	4	1	3	Complete Destruction of 3 range post buildings and one Ilaka forest office.
44.	Kapilbastu	10	4	6	Complete destruction of 4 range posts and 2 Ilaka range posts, and partial damage to one range post.
45.	Tanahu	6	1	5	Complete Destruction of 2 range post buildings, partial damage in 2 range posts and destruction of official document.
46.	Gorkha	4		4	Partial damage to building and

					destruction of furniture and document.
47.	Gulmi	6	2	4	Complete destruction of 1 range post, hijacking of 1 pick-up van, and destruction of document by fire.
48.	Nawalparasi	17	5	12	Destruction of one pick-up van, 2 ilaka buildings, 7 range posts, 2 tractors and document.
49.	Kaski	2	1	1	Destruction of document and furniture due to fire and partial damage in nursery building.
50.	Rolpa	4		4	Destruction of document, furniture and other office materials.
51.	Salyan	4	2	2	Complete destruction of two office buildings and document and material.
52.	Surkhet	13	2	11	Complete destruction of 3 range posts and one ilaka building, documents, furniture and one motorcycle.
53.	Rukum	6	1	5	Partial damage to office building in loss of material and document.
54.	Banke	10	5	5	Complete destruction of 4 range post buildings and destruction of office document and material.
55.	Bardiya	13	7	6	Complete destruction of 3 range posts and destruction of office document and material with furniture.
56.	Dailekh	4	2	2	Complete destruction of 2 range post buildings and destruction of document, furniture and material.
57.	Dang	6	2	4	Destruction of DFO building with weapon, document and furniture, Destruction of 3 range post buildings and damage to document and furniture.
58.	Mugu	4	2	2	Destruction of two buildings

					and fire on document and furniture.
59.	Jajarkot	3	2	1	Partial damage to building and fire on document and furniture.
60.	Jumla	1	1		Partial damage to building and fire on document and furniture.
61.	Pyuthan	4	1	3	Destruction of 2 buildings and fire on document and furniture.
62.	Kalikot	4	1	3	Destruction of one range post, partial damage on one and fire on document and furniture.
63.	Dadeldhura	8	3	5	Destruction of 4 range post buildings and fire on document and furniture.
64.	Doti	5	1	4	Partial damage to Ilaka office and fire on document and furniture.
65.	Baitadi	6	2	4	Destruction of 2 buildings and fire on document and furniture.
66.	Bajura	2		2	Partial damage on building and fire on document and furniture.
67.	Darchula	6	1	5	Partial damage and fire on document and furniture.
68.	Achham	9	2	7	Destruction of DFO building, including all office document and material with computer and partial damage on range post building fire on document and furniture.
69.	Kailali	12	5	7	Destruction of 5 range post buildings, partial damage of 7 buildings, fire on document and furniture.
70.	Kanchanpur	13	4	9	Destruction of buildings and fire on documents and furniture.
	Total	382	120	262	

According to the study of Dil Raj Khanal, 14 people associated with community forestry were abducted and killed by the state and 15 people by the CPN (M) (Khanal, 2006: Annex 1.1 and 1.2: 59). It was also reported that more than eighty thousand (80,635) hectares of forest mainly from the Terai region have been encroached upon in Nepal in the past two decades.[13] Dang, Banke, Bardiya, Kailali, Kanchanpur, Bara, Parsa, Chitwan and Rautahat were the main target of the encroachers. The Rising Nepal, referring a member of the Parliamentary Committee on Natural Resource writes, "*...powerful politicians were involved in deforestation in the name of rehabilitating the freed Kamayas and landless squatters*" (*The Rising Nepal*, 28 September, 2007).

The main impacts of the armed conflict on forest have been summarised as follows:

- CPN (M) has stopped selling timber from community forestry. They were also forced to adopt their policy, which contradicts with the operational plans of CFUGs.
- There was growing smuggling of timber from the government forests (often the smugglers pay bribe to insurgents and forest officials if they are caught).
- Dual tax to be paid by community/local people to the government[14] and the CPN (M) on timber and non-timber forest products. It was estimated that the Ministry of Forest and Soil Conservation is looking at 40 billion rupees annually from failing to manage non timber forest products.[15]
- Approximately 166 types of medicinal herbs from the Nepalese mountains are used for medicinal purposes. The estimated annual transaction of the medical herbs is around 2.5 billion rupees. Unsustainable harvesting of the expensive medicinal herbs such as *Yarsagumba*,[16] *Chiraito, Jatamasi, Katusi, Bikhama, padamchal, Panchaunle, Silajit, Sunpati, Sughandhawal*, etc. by smugglers by paying tax to the insurgents as the state is not able to regulate and control non timber forest products which are available in remote mountains controlled by CPN(M).
- Security forces cleared forests around their camps for security reasons without considering any implications.
- Forest range posts supposed to regulate forests are either closed or shifted to secure places and therefore open access in many areas.
- Danish Embassy stopped funding to the Natural

Resource Management Sector Assistance Programme (NARMSAP) implemented in 38 districts of Nepal and consequently it has to be closed by the government.

- A large number of forest user groups' operational plans expired, and the forest users were not allowed to harvest in their forests. This had a negative effect on the community relying on income from the forests.
- Forest staff were not able to work efficiently because of the insecurity caused by the conflict. They are confined to working in the district headquarters and its vicinity,
- The military took over office buildings of forest offices (e.g. DFO Dolakha).

Some of the agencies working in the conservation and forestry sectors have started a very innovative approach to cope with the conflict situation and were able to continue their activities at the time of escalated conflict. WWF has made special working procedures to work in the conflict environment. NSFCP was another natural resource management (NRM) project working in a conflict-sensitive programme management approach. The Rural Access Programme worked in a Safe and Effective Development Approach. Livelihood and Forestry Programme (LFP) was another NRM organisation to develop new and innovative approaches to address root causes of the conflict. Pro-Poor and Social Inclusion Strategy (PPSIS) was one of the many innovative procedures. Basic Risk Management, Gender and Social Inclusion, Livelihoods and Social Inclusion, Social and Geographical Auditing, etc.) were other frameworks and methodological procedures developed by LFP to work in the situation of conflict. Box 8.1 illustrates the PPSIS:

BOX 8.1: Main Features of Pro-Poor and Social Inclusion Strategy of LFP

Active targeting of poor and excluded:

- Categorising poor and excluded (P&E) households based on their economic well-being and social identity
- Allocating resources and designing of livelihoods and social empowerment interventions specific to the needs and priorities of different categories of the P&E

Inclusive targeting:

- Balancing the targeted activities specific to the P&E with other activities that are of benefit to the general communities
- Ensuring that all members of communities are aware of why targeting is important and how the identification of targeted households and communities takes place where active targeting of P&E is taking place
- Ensuring increased awareness and sensitisation within communities, especially among elites, about the needs and priorities of the P&E.

Focused on field-level interventions to ensure:

- Inclusion of P&E in user groups through membership
- Effective participation of P&E in decision-making processes
- More equitable access of P&E to forest and other natural resource products derived from user groups
- More equitable access of P&E to financial, political and social benefits derived from participation in user group's initiatives.

Monitoring against Livelihoods and Social Inclusion framework:

- Monitoring against the three domains of change in the lives of the P&E (i.e. access to assets, services and capabilities; voice, influence and agency; and rules of the game)
- Maintaining a disaggregated level of data (against economic conditions and social identities based on gender, caste and ethnicity)
- Monitoring against the context.

Source: Upreti (2007c).

Forest is one of the major natural resources in Nepal and largely contributing to generation of national revenue, providing environmental services and livelihood basis for a large number of people. On the other hand, forest is not only politically, economically and socially one of the most contentious areas because of various interests and benefits but also highly affected by the armed conflict as most of the times warring parties use forests as a battleground as well as means of continuation of fight. Hence, a comprehensive study on forest focusing on commercial timber and NTFP is essential.

8.2.2 Consequences of the Armed Conflict on Biodiversity and Wildlife

The established relationship between the armed conflict and degradation of genetic resources is largely unknown. Hence, only some impressionistic observations are made here and a comprehensive study is essential to explore the impact of armed conflict on genetic resources. The following are general observations:

- Land mines placed in various parts of the country could be potentially affecting growth and composition of genetic resources as it has chemical contamination in soil.
- Big fights in the biodiversity-rich areas had destroyed genetic resources.
- Security forces had fired in the forests and intensified aerial bombarding, suspecting hiding of insurgents. These fires and bombarding had damaged flora and fauna as well as polluted the surrounding environment.
- Severe disruption of farming systems and seed flow mechanisms.
- Disturbance of works of organizations devoted to the conservation of genetic resources might have also negatively affected the genetic resources.

The negative impacts of civil wars and armed conflict on genetic resources and biodiversity are widely documented. The case of Sierra Leone was documented by Squire (2001) and the case of Liberia, Cambodia and Burma was extensively documented by Global Witness (2004). Similar documentation of the case of Nepal is essential to find the actual loss of genetic resources and biodiversity during the time of the armed conflict.

Illegal wildlife trading was rampant during the time of armed conflict. It had caused different categories of effects. The first category of effect was the alteration (reduction) of wildlife from poaching. For example, several numbers of rhinoceros, elephants, and tigers were killed during the time of conflict. The second category of effect was related to alteration of biodiversity composition. The third category of effects was habitat destruction. The fourth category of effect is related to the livelihood disturbance of communities around parks and protected areas.

The illegal wildlife trade in Nepal is operated by a strong and large network of smugglers and accomplished through various trade routes. The recent episodes of red-sandalwood arrests very clearly demonstrate the complications and power of smugglers. The Southern region of Terai is home to the Bengal tiger, the one-horned rhino, the Asian elephant, and many other smaller mammals. They are restricted to the five national parks and wildlife reserves of the region. This region is highly susceptible to the illegal hunting, poaching and illegal trading of wildlife to India. Similarly, the Northern Himalayan region of the country bordering with Tibet, China, and India shelters a number of high-altitude species, including the snow leopard, Tibetan antelope, black bear and blue sheep.

The Southern trading routes are connected to a number of commercial centres and are linked to many Indian towns and cities located along the southern, eastern, and western borders of Nepal. Illegal trading of wildlife goods to India is quite known. The Red-Sandal-Wood scandal has revealed that custom check posts of the state in border areas rarely check illegal trading of wildlife and plants. The most frequently traded items were tiger bones, bear gall bladders, common leopard skins, rhino horn, musk pods and shahtoosh wool (Shakya and Chitrakar, 2006). The primary urban centres where wildlife goods are traded are Nepalgunj, Kohalpur, Biratnagar, Birgunj, Raxaul, and Kakarvita, and Katmandu. Delhi and Motihari (Bihar) are some of the main Indian cities where wildlife related goods were sold either locally or to export in other countries.

The northern region of Nepal is less accessible because of poor infrastructures (communication, road, etc.) that became favourable for poachers to kill animals and transport (by porters or mules) to the Tibetan border. In the north, wildlife are poached and hunted in both within and inside and outside protected areas. Major wildlife poached in North were snow leopards, black bears, musk deer, blue sheep, Tibetan antelopes, Rhesus monkeys and red pandas and otters. Some of the common northern trade centres are at Taklakot, Kodari, Gola, and Panchthar.

Prevention and control of illegal wildlife trade is crucially important at the time of armed conflict and transition period. Illegal wildlife and NTFP trading is one of the major concerns for Nepal. It is the second largest in terms of transaction, after narcotics. Nepal is being used as a transit point. It is a hard-hit sector because of gaining a big amount of money by the armed rebels with less risk from the trades. Illegal traders provide money to armed groups and continue their business in the areas where government control is weak. So, illegal trade of NTFP and wildlife was one of the main easy sources of money for the rebels. The Terai reason is still facing rebellion from different armed groups (more than a dozen of such groups are active). Hence there is a danger of obstruction of the work of biodiversity and forest organisations from these groups and potential for such exploitation is high in near future.

TABLE 8.4: Wildlife casualities 1996-2006

Species	*Total Killed 1996-2006*		
	Causalities	*Natural*	*Total*
Rhino	128	128	256
Tiger	7	33	40
Hog-deer	1	13	14
Wild Buffalo	1	10	11
Red Panda	0	3	3
Monitor Lizards	2	0	2
Musk Deer	5	15	20
Swamp Deer	1	1	2
Cheetal	21	25	46
Elephant	4	17	21
Samber	0	7	7
Leopard	1	27	28
Leopard Cat	0	4	4
Jharal	0	13	13
Barking Deer	0	6	6
Tortle	0	2	2
Python	0	6	6
Wild boar	0	3	3
G. Crocodile	1	3	4
Black Buck	0	7	7
Peacock	0	2	2
Bear	0	2	2

Source: WWG data sheets, 2007.

Table 8.3 demonstrates that several important wildlife species have been killed during the time of armed conflict. However, the respondents explained that there were large numbers of wildlife killed during the time of the conflict but they are not properly recorded and counted. Jose Kalpers (2001) documents that often three categories of people (professional poachers and hunters, armed groups and local people) involved in poaching and hunting in conflict-ridden Sub-Saharan Africa. Professional poachers and hunters were engaged for commercial purpose whereas armed groups and local people were engaged for their livelihoods. The Nepal's poaching case is also not much different from the Sub-Saharan Africa in terms of category of people involved.

It is essential to have a comprehensive assessment of all 16 protected areas to find the actual loss of biodiversity, loss of habitat and economic valuation and other long-term impacts of the decade-long armed conflict. It is often argued that restructuring of parks is essential to make them more effective in new Nepal. Some of the main issues raised in this debate are: role of military in protecting park, park-people conflict and its politicisation, contested claims on benefits of parks to local people, engagement of local people in management of park (shifting from stakeholders to share holders), contribution of parks to achieve sustainable peace (in line with the concept of peace park). All these issues have to be thoroughly analysed and come up with some informed conclusions.

The need and relevance of military engagement in park is under intense debate in Nepal since signing of the CAP between the government and the CPN. The involvement of military in park is questioned by some of the scholars, analysts, and politicians linking with downsizing military as a part of the security sector transformation. Earlier the palace had controlled the military. The conservation sector was heavily influenced by interests of the palace. After the exit of the king from power, the dynamics of the military in conservation changed. It was also realised that the relation between park administration and military leaders deployed for the park is tense. Hence, a through analysis of this issue is needed which would contribute to security sector reform and settling this contentious issue of engagement of military in park with technically and managerially sound basis.

8.2.3 Consequences of the Armed Conflict on Agriculture

The main problem in agriculture was 'one-state-two regimes' situation (Upreti, 2006b) once the CPN (M) had reinforced its own governing structures (local, district and regional *janasarkars*) and United People's Council (UPC). The UPC declared the Common Minimum Policy and Programme including natural resource policies, which had seriously affected the existing system of land and agriculture. On the issues of land and agrarian reform, the Section IV, point 26 of the Common Minimum Policy and Programme of UPC states, "*the agrarian revolution is the basic foundation of the New Democratic/ People's Democratic Revolution. Therefore, the main policy of agrarian revolution shall be to abolish the feudal, semi-feudal and bureaucratic capitalist production relations in the land and develop national capitalist relations, of which 'land to the tiller' shall be the main policy tenet. In other words, the lands owned by feudal, bureaucratic capitalists and various Guthis (a type of feudal ownership by social and religious institutions), in the places where the old reactionary power structure have been smashed, shall be seized without any compensation and distributed to landless and poor peasants, and the tillers shall be made the owners of the land. In case of rich and medium level peasants, their lands shall not be seized but ceiling shall be imposed on them keeping in mind the ratio of availability of land and population. In the places where old state structure has not been totally smashed or people's state power has not been founded as yet, only reformative measures shall be taken in the initial stage, according to which ceilings on lands shall be implemented, tenurial rights of tenants shall be guaranteed, the rate of land rent shall be reduced and made one-third, interest rate of credits shall be reduced, Guthi lands shall be turned into 'raiker', i.e. governmental lands etc*". This statement clearly demonstrates the CPN (M)' perspective on production relation, which was contradicted with the general policy and practices in government of Nepal.

Land was one of the most contested natural resources during the time of armed conflict. Land is symbol of power, prestige and social status in the villages for long time. Reason being that power brokers and local elite controlled large areas of valuable land resources by using their networks and connection with state power centres and traditional power structures. Consequently, land remained as one of the major means of exploitation as well as main concern of CPN (M). Hence, land became most prominent target of CPN (M). Hence, CPN (M) evicted many local landlords and village elites from their village and captured their lands. In the CPN (M) controlled areas, they distributed the lands of landlords to poor people but the poor people were not able to utilize because of fear from security force. Local landlords were not able to cultivate their lands and consequently the scarce land resource is under utilized.

Previous studies (Blaikia et al., 2002; Seddon and Hussein, 2002) show that in rural areas 20 per cent people were wealthy landowners and peasants and remaining 80 per cent people experienced livelihood insecurity and risks. The lives of women, girls and children were more threatened from the conflict, as they live in chronic poverty and social insecurity. Livelihoods of poor, marginalized and socially excluded people of Nepal involve a constant struggle for their survival because of lack of their control over and access to productive resources, weak social capital and networks, lack of stable or regular source of income, etc. (Seddon and Hussein, 2002). The CPN (M) slogan 'land to the tillers' has gained wider sympathy of tenants, poor farmers and marginalized people. Reason being that the capture of land from landlords became an integral part of the CPN (M) tactical strategy in their strong hold areas. In a study of this author (Upreti, 2005a&b), many key informants[17] explained that most of the big landholdings were either directly controlled by CPN (M), or exerting pressure over tenants to stop paying contractual payments to landlords.

In the CPA, there is a clear provision of returning of the land captured by the CPN (M), which is not yet fully implemented. In the coming years the land issue will be centre of political debate once the constitution making process begins and once the federal structures materialize. Therefore, a comprehensive study of land resources linking with the state restructuring and the notion of 'scientific land reform' stated in both the CPA and Interim Constitution is crucially essential.

Land is going to be the centre of debate and contention for the coming decade. The issues of scientific land reform will be a major agenda of political parties in their political struggle for survival, potential resistance from landlords and international financial institutions on land reallocation in one side and organised demands from landless, tenants and poor farmers backed by communist parties on the other side. Hence, land conflict in the changing political context is a major issue to be considered by agencies working in conservation and natural resources/environmental areas. This study should address some pertinent issues related to land resources. However, even a separate in-depth study beyond this proposal may be required to cover all relevant issues related to land resource.

8.2.4 Consequences of the Armed Conflict on Parks and Protected areas

The ongoing armed conflict has direct impacts on the management of protected areas. The Nepal Army deployed for the protection of the national parks and wildlife resources was mobilized for counter-insurgency operation that resulted into lack of enough security protection. The weak security of the protected areas has been abused by the smugglers, poachers, hunters and other unauthorized persons. The insurgents were influential in some of the protected areas (for example, Khaptad National Park, Makalu Barun Conservation area, etc.) and therefore park authorities were not able to manage and regulate parks.[18] The attention and priority of the state shifted form protected areas to manage the war that ultimately leads to lack of resource to manage protected areas. On the other hand, because of the security restrictions, poor people who base their livelihood in forest resources are deprived. Five Rhinos were killed at the time of state of emergency in 2001 in Bardya National Park alone. In Lantang National Park, slaughtering of Musk Deer by poachers has been reported.[19] Prior to CPN (M) attacks on PA infrastructure, there were 112 guard posts positioned throughout Nepal's PAs. By 2002, this number had been reduced to 34, a 70% reduction (Yonzon, 2004).

Further, specific consequences such as: (a) loss of unique habitats for wildlife within ecosystems once the vegetations for such specialized habitat are destroyed; (b) loss of plant resources having medicinal values once the forests are used as battlefield; and (c) severe disruption of conservation activities leading to intensified unsustainable exploitation once the law and order is breakdown by the armed conflict, have been realised from the ten years of armed conflict.

National parks and wildlife reserves were one of the frequent targets of the insurgents mainly because of

(a) being located in geographically isolated areas,
(b) engagement of the military in parks and reserves as targets of the insurgents,
(c) rebels' interpretation of park-people conflict as outcome of the restriction and denial of access of poor people on the livelihood-based resources by park authority, and
(d) perception of rebels towards parks and reserves as recreation centres of royal families.

The following Table 8.5 presents the physical damage in park infrastructure during the time of the armed conflict.

TABLE 8.5: Park-related Physical InfraStructure Damaged during the Period of Armed Conflict

S.No.	*Name of the parks*	*Number of infrastructures damaged*	*Estimated values of damage in million rupees*	*Damaged infrastructures*
1.	Chitwan National Park	8	4.00	Range posts, staff quarters and offices
2.	Bardiya National Park	9	3.65	Range posts and offices
3.	Shey-Phoksundo National Park	9	3.70	Visitor's centre, store, head office, staff quarters
4.	Rara National Park	5	1.70	Range posts, guard posts and view tower

5.	Khaptad National Park	1	0.40	Range post
6.	Langtang National Park	3	1.45	Guard post and range posts
7.	Makalu-Barun National Park	4	0.90	Head office and sector office
8.	Shivapuri National Park	4	1.51	Ticket centre, range posts, guard post
9.	Shuklaphanta Wildlife Reserve	9	2.775	Offices and range posts
10.	Koshitappu Wildlife Reserve	2	0.60	Range post and guard post
11.	Parsa Wildlife Reserve	1	0.40	Pratappur post
12.	Dhorpatan Hunting Reserve	2	0.86	Dhorpatan office building and Maikot post
13.	Sagarmatha National Park	No	No	No damage to physical infrastructures
14.	Kanchanjunga Conservation Area		NA	Seized communication sets, computers and other equipments from Lelep project Office
15.	Annapurna Conservation Area	15	12.30	Office buildings and other properties of main office and area offices destroyed
	Manaslu Conservation Area	NA	NA	NA
	Total	57	20.195	

Source: Department of National Park and Wildlife Conservation[20] (2007), Upreti, (2007g).

Most of these infrastructures were damaged by bomb blasts, fire and physical break-up. Once the national parks and wildlife reserves were under attack from the rebels, officials, security personnel and operating staffs were not able to perform their normal duties; often they had to move to secure places. Using this situation of vacuum, thefts, damage to property, poaching and illegal hunting were also increased. There is serious concern among the conservationists about the political interference in technical issues related to conservation. Some conservationists consulted during the study vehemently expressed their dismay about the interference by 8 parties on technical issues related to conservation. The army had cleared a large area of the forests in different parts of the country, arguing that these forests carry security risks. Similarly, they had also cleared community-managed forests, agriculture fields (sugarcane, maize and other tall or thick crops). A study estimates that the forest damage by the army in reconstruction of the demolished post in SNP cost 60 million rupees (Shakya and Chitakar, 2006).

The priority of the then Royal Nepalese Army (the name changed to Nepal Army after the successful people's movement of April 2006) was to fight insurgency than to protect biodiversity. Therefore they had abandoned some of the security posts of national parks and reserves and consolidated in certain strategically important areas. For example, in the Shivapuri National Park (SNP) the army pulled 15 of 21 army posts to prepare for the possible attack by the CPN (M). Once, the security forces moved away, the security vacuum was conducive for the CPN (M) to intensify their activities.[21]

The Annapurna Conservation Area Project (ACAP) was most seriously affected by the armed conflict since its start in February 1996. However, more serious effects of the conflict were observed after 2001. Once the CPN (M) declared their regional autonomy, the situation in the ACAP became more complicated. Among the 9 autonomous regions formed by CPN (M) based on the language and ethnicity, ACAP fell under two autonomous regions (Myagdi and Mustang districts under Magarat Autonomous Region and Manang, Kaski and Lamjung districts under the Tamuwan Autonomous Region). The Tamuwan Autonomous Region was declared on 28 January 2004 and the Magarat Autonomous Region was declared on 9 January 2004). The Tamuwan Autonomous Region was controlling all the mountainous regions between Kali Gandaki to Budhi Gandaki Rivers and the Magarat Autonomous Region, which occupies all the mountainous territory between from the river Kali Gandaki to Bheri Rivers. This arrangement had a direct impact on operating ACAP. Failing to meet the requirement of the Autonomous government of the CPN (M), ACAP has to close its field offices (Area Conservation Offices, Ghandruk-Kaski, Lwang, Sikles, Bhujung and Lamjung and their subsidiary branch offices were closed). Further, Berethati, Dhampus, Dhiwang, and Chasu of Kaski districts were evacuated to Pokhara and tourist information and checking centre located at Tal of Manang district were shifted to Chame, the headquarters of Manang district. The check post at Bhulabhule of Lamjung was shifted to Beshisahar and Tatopani of Myagdi and Ghorepani check posts and the staffs were shifted to Pokhara. In the year 2002, CPN (M) had burnt all the belongings of the office of ACAP located at Ghorepani in 2002 and asked the project staff to stop their work. Once the autonomous regions were operational, CPN (M) asked to implement the rules of autonomous region in the local conservation area management committees of ACAP. Well-known conservation management groups of ACAP economically, psychologically and organizationally suffered from the armed conflict. This project was seen by the rebels as a means of fulfilling royal interests.

BOX 8.2: Dysfunctional grass root sorganizations in ACAP

Focused group discussions at Ghandruk (Kaski) and Sikh and Ghar (Myagdi) reveal that local mother groups, youth and father groups, tourist business groups, community forests users groups and conservation management committees became almost dysfunctional once CPN (M) forced to cease their activities. Most of the mother groups had withdrawn their deposits from the group funds and used for domestic consumption. Fear, insecurity and perceived risks had compelled grass roots committees to obey the instructions and orders of the insurgents. ACAP staff were not able to visit field and their activities were completely stopped. In this way, grass roots organizations became dysfunctional during the time of the armed conflict.

The target of CPN (M) to ACAP [managed under the then King Mahendra Trust for Nature Conservation (KMTNC)] was mainly because of its perceived affiliation with the royal palace, as King Gyanendra had controlled KMTNC for long time and his son was assigned as patron once he became king. CPN (M) cadres had consistently argued that the tax collected from ACAP goes to KNMTC for the use of palace instead of country's treasury. They also raised the issue of non-transparency in ACAP. The CPN (M) cadres perceived that the ACAP has not provided any benefit to poor and marginalised people, its staff consumes resources in the name of conservation and people and spying against CPN (M). Interestingly, the general public in Ghandruk areas also perceived that ACAP is for the rich and better-off people. They cited ACAP's flexibility to give unlimited access to cutting trees for hotels but restrict the access of poor people to forest for firewood as an example of such biases. It was also understood that the then KMTNC Act has made especial privileges to KMTNC (the name changed to NTNC after people's movement in 2006). Hence, the then KMTNC was seen as a special royalist organisation.

During the field study and interaction with the people of Gahndruk (Kaski) and Ghorepani (Myagdi), they told the study team that the service provided by ACP was going to local elites, owners of hotels and travel agencies but not to the poor, marginalised and socially excluded. ACAP has focused its activities on tourist routes and people engaged in tourism. People from far remote areas felt that they were excluded and not getting benefits from ACAP. Man Bahadur Vishwokarma (48 years, from Ghandruk VDC, Ward No. 8) said, "*We did not get any benefit from ACAP so far. Rich powerful people who have connection with ACAP are getting benefits and we poor people are excluded. Some time people like you come, ask different questions and return back but nobody takes our concerns seriously. ACAP is not for poor, marginalised and Dalit like me*".

TABLE 8.6: Damage caused in NTNC and ACAP areas

Name of the Office	*Date*	*Description of damages*	*Cost estimate (Rs.)*
NTNC Central Office	2000/10/31	Damage due to bomb blast in the building	91,371/05
NTNC Central Office	2006/3/21	Damage due to bomb blast in the building	1,36,570/80
ACAP Main Office, Pokhara	2001/7/6	Office Building destroyed partially	2,92,636/12
ACAP Main Office, Pokhara	2001/7/6	Loss of property	5,02,083/-
ACAP Area Conservation Office (ACO), Bhujung	2002/5/2	Office Building destroyed partially	53,650/-
ACAP- ACO, Bhujung	2002/5/2	Loss of money and property	9,33,615/-
ACAP- ACO, Ghandruk	2002/11/8	Office Building completely destroyed along with the materials present in the building	37,00,000/-
ACAP- ACO, Ghandruk	2002/11/8 2003/9/20	Loss of money and property	13,97,925/80
ACAP- ACO, Lwang	2003/9/30	Training Building completely destroyed	5,13,396/41
ACAP- ACO, Lwang	1999/12/29 2001/7/4 2001/12/16 2003/9/20 2003/9/30	Loss of money and property	18,00,947/27
ACAP- ACO, Siklesh	2000/11/6 2003/12/9	Loss of money and property	31,13,371/98
NTNC Biodiversity Conservation Centre, Sauraha,	2004/2/1	Hero Honda Motorcycle, Blue plate 66 1 0979 taken away	85,850/-

Name of the Office	*Date*	*Description of damages*	*Cost estimate (Rs.)*
NTNC Biodiversity Conservation Centre, Sauraha	2004/4/13	Hero Honda Motor cycle, Blue plate 66 1 0983 taken away	85,850/-
NTNC Bardiya Conservation Programme, Betani, Bardiya	2004/12/1	Office Building and other materials destroyed due to bomb blast	7,30,000/-
TNC Bardiya Conservation Programme, Betani, Bardiya	2006/1/18	Captured hilux pick up Ba.3 Cha.1889 and was damaged when returned	1,50,000/-
Manasulu Conservation Area Project, Gorakha	_	Destroyed during the conflict and transitional period	8,16,600/-
Shree Suklaphanta Conservation Programme, Majhagaon, Kanchanpur	2004/12/1	Balero Camper Ba.4 Cha. 4075 destroyed by firing	16,12,140/-
Shree Suklaphanta Conservation Programme, Majhagaon, Kanchanpur	_	Window glasses of Training Building destroyed	45,100/-
		Total Cost (Rs.)	160,61,184/08

Source: NTNC, 2007.

Table 8.6 clearly indicates the target of CPN (M) on ACAP and the enormous negative impacts of the armed conflict on its functioning. Interestingly however, ACAP activities in Mustang district were not much affected. The reason was the absence of CPN (M) activities in this district.

Bardia National Park (BNP) was not much affected by the armed conflict until 2001. Security patrol by the then RNA was intact and it was said that illegal poaching of wildlife was also not intensive. Since, June 2001, CPN (M) intensified their activities in the park and the military and park administration withdrew several park guards from their posts.[22] On 6th December 2001, CPN (M) had attacked and destroyed the army's guard post in Gola VDC. The CPN (M) had controlled the Babai Valley and posed serious threats to army patrols. Consequently, army patrolling virtually stopped and that led to an increase in illegal poaching and logging. The military and the park guards had avoided regular patrolling of the park since the CPN (M) destroyed the guard post of Bardiya National Park on 6th December 2001.

Chitwan National Park (CNP) was well equipped with 44 army command posts to protect the park. But as a consequence of the armed conflict, the security posts were reduced to 9 by 2002. Though 7 unified command posts were located in Kasara, Khagendra Malli, Sauraha, Banakatta, Bagai, Bhimle and Khoriya Muhan. In Gazapur and Kolhuwa, they were not able to protect wildlife poaching. It is reported that there is a strong and active network of poachers. A total of 89 Rhinos were killed between 1997 to 2006 in CNP (Shakya and Chitrakar, 2006:140). A serious problem of poaching of the rare Asiatic one-horned rhinoceros, *(Rhinoceros unicornis)*, is observed in CNP. Poachers hunt them for their valuable horns. Yakche Lama, a predominant wildlife smuggler, was arrested in 2006. It was claimed that he has possessed 20 horns of the Asiatic one-horned rhinoceros. Chief Conservation Officer Shiva Raj Bhatta believes that he must be the ringleader of a larger network of smugglers. The park has apprehended more than 200 people involved in poaching. They are behind bars in different locations of the country, including the District Jail in Chitwan. Shakya and Chitrakar, (2006) write that 'Ranger Vishnu Prasad Thapaliya of the Chitwan Head Office, Kasara, explained that the official population record of rhinoceros was 544 in 2000 but that figure has dropped to 372 rhinos in the past five years'. It was revealed that the park has confiscated 7 horns and seized two tiger hides and 4 kg of skeleton in 2005 from poachers. According to Ranger Thapaliya, a vehicle used by the traffickers, two motorcycles, caches of arms and NRs 473,100 in cash were also seized.

Kanchanjunga Conservation Area (KCA) was also severely affected from the armed conflict. All government offices, including area police station, border administration office and customs office located at Olangchun-Gola VDC, except the post office, health post and schools, were displaced from the area. Similarly, the police stations at Lungthung and Ghunsa of Lelep VDC, Tapethok and Yamphudin were evacuated because of the conflict. All the displaced police stations were relocated to the district headquarters in Taplejung. The displacement of the customs office and security posts had increased illegal smuggling.

The security forces were not able to patrol since the second week of April 2003. CPN (M) had used the KCA as one of their concentrated areas in the eastern hills. KCA was also used by CPN (M) for their labour camps (e.g. construction of road in Lelep VDC). In March 2002, the CPN (M) visited the head office of the Kanchenjunga Conservation Area Project located at Lelep and had demanded donation. Once the project rejected their demand, tension between the CPN (M) and KCAP overtly mounted. CPN (M) had also demanded ten per cent of the KCAP development budget from DDC and again it was rejected by the project. Consequently, CPN (M) seized the project's communication set, solar panels, library belongings, computers and other equipments and asked the project staffs to resign from the project. Then the project stopped its activities and terminated 17 staff members. Once the project was not able to operate due to the armed conflict, illegal poaching and deforestation sharply increased. The activities of poachers quickly expanded and they were coming from up to Sikkim of India and the Dentang region of Tibet (Shakya and Chitrakar, 2006).

Local people view that poachers from Dentang of Tibet and Sikkim often came to the KCA for hunting. Shakya and Chitrakar (2006:43) wrote, *"The villagers claim that the security personnel from the headquarters are also involved in illegal hunting of wildlife. They have seen the army patrol at Yamphudin, killed two deer. The locals further claim that 2 years ago CPN (M) killed a blue sheep at Yangma"*. Illegal collection of herbs such as pakhanbed

(*Bergenia ciliata*), jatamansi (*Nardostachys grandiflora*), bikh (*Aconitum ferox*), padamchal (*Rheum australe*) from the upper regions of the conservation area was frequent and they were exported to India. Irrational exploitation of Lokta (*Daphne bholua*), a shrub for pulping paper in large volume has resulted intendangered stage.

Dhorpatan Hunting Reserve (DHR) was also suffered from the CPN (M) insurgency. They had destroyed five guard posts between 1998 and 2000. The Reserve had to move its office to the district headquarters of Baglung. Pressure to staff for donation was frequent and intense. Hence, the reserve staff stopped visiting sites and concentrated on the district headquarters. Consequently, illegal poaching sharply increased after the sanctuary office was relocated. The smugglers used snares to catch the blue sheep and musk deer. A rough estimate of people engaged in DHR indicates that smuggling of *yarshagumba* (*Cordyceps sinensis*) cost about Rs. 30 million annually (Shakya and Chitrakar, 2006).

Khaptad National Park[23] (KNP) was almost under the full control of the CPN (M) in the later stage of the conflict. It is located in a relatively isolated area compared to other parks, as 5 to 6 hours are required to reach the human settlement areas. However, it also faced social tension with local communities. The 'Intermediate region development committee' declared by the government[24] itself became a source of tension. Hence, the park authority had established an inquiry office to deal with the voice of people and to compensate for local people residing in the intermediate region. However, it is not functional. The park staff, ranger and game scouts of the park had to move to Silagadhi, the headquarters of Doti district due to the conflict-related risks. Only game scouts and non-gazetted staff were kept in the headquarters of the park at Khaptad. Once the CPN (M) formed District *Janasarkar* (people's government) comprising parts of all four districts covered by the KNP and buffer zone, the operational complications started. The District People's Government forced the park authority to implement its regulations. The local people were using KNP for pasture to their herds during summer (Jestha to Bhadra) and this continued even after the establishment of the park with payment of rupees 10 for a buffalo, 5 for a cow, 3 for a goat and 5 for a horse. But that arrangement was also disturbed after the intensity of conflict.

Koshi Tappu Wildlife Reserve (KTWR) was also under the attacks of CPN (M). They had burnt official documents, furniture, communication set and other equipments of the security posts. CPN (M) often accused park staffs were spying for the army. The Koshi Sarokar Samuha (Koshi Concern Group) became active against the Reserve. Later, majority of the members of the Koshi Sarokar Group was mainstreamed in the CPN (M) insurgency.

Langtang National Park (LNP), covering a geographical territory of 1,710 sq. km. located in Rasuwa, Nuwakot and Sindhupalchok districts, was under the heavy influence of CPN (M). The CPN (M) intensified their activities in the park districts and surrounding districts, viz. Rasuwa, Nuwakot, Dhading, Sindhupalchok and Kavre that had direct effect in the park. It is prohibited to hunt the Tibetan Antelope found in Tibetan landscape and in the park region. However, the traffickers smuggle the fur[25] of Tibetan Antelope via the way of Rasuwagadi. Hunting is mainly done with firearms like guns and riffles. With the escalation of the armed conflict, the army has withdrawn half of its security posts working for the protection of the park. The evacuated security posts were Magenabot, Dhokachet, Dhimba, Langtang, Thulo Syaphru and Briddim of the Rasuwa district. In the record of the Rasuwa District Administration Office, only two persons had obtained the licence for keeping weapons. In the Langsisha area of the National Park, illegal hunting of musk deer and Danphe (lophophorus) are frequently reported. The main problem of the national park is illegal export of Lokta (bark), a raw material to produce Nepalese handmade paper. This problem highly prevails in Chandanbari, Cholangpari and Mangche areas.

Manaslu Conservation Area (MCA) was also one of the most affected by the armed conflict. Poaching sharply increased in MCA after the eruption of armed conflict. The most widely poached animals were the Himalayan black bear for its bile and the musk deer for their aromatic musk pods. Poachers used rifles snares for entrapping these animals. Illegal collection of expensive herbs such as *panch aunle, nirmasi, yarshagumba* and *ban-lasun* was frequent in MCA during the time of armed conflict. Though the CPN (M) did not levy tax on collection of herbs to local people, they imposed tax and collected donations from unauthorized Tibetan traders active in herbs trading in the MCA.

Parsa Wildlife Reserve (PWR) was severely affected by the conflict, particularly in 2005. It was reported that the CPN (M) had installed land mines at several places in the reserve. Explosion of landmines in 22 November 2004 killed 5 staff of the Reserve (two rangers, two scouts and one driver) while patrolling reserve areas in a vehicle. Since then, patrolling of the Reserve was suspended for a long time. Illegal logging and poaching was frequent in the Reserve during the period of conflict. In the year 2002, 14 offenders were arrested. Poaching of the golden monitor lizard, *suna gohoro*, (*Varanus flavescens*), illegal excavation of boulders and sand, logging timber, trafficking of herbs was quite frequent.[26]

In Rara National Park (RNP), tension between park authority and local people escalated because of the damage caused by large numbers of the wild pig (*Sus scrofa*) to local community. As there were no settlements inside the Park after resettling of 600 residents of Rara and Chhapru villages in Bardia district, tension was only between park authority and with communities residing outside the park. The armed conflict had further exacerbated the tension. Seven security posts deployed for the protection of the RNP became gradually dysfunctional after the series of attack form the CPN (M). The first attack was on 13 December 2001 in the Southern post of the army at Jhyari and consequently the deployed security force and the armed forest guards were fled. Then the CPN (M) destroyed the post of armed forest guards at Baunpani (on 12 January 2002) and Faka (4 August 2004). The entry post of the forest guards at Bhulbhule was destroyed on 3 April 2002. Wildlife poaching significantly increased since the evacuation of security posts. Snaring of 40 to 50 ghoral and musk deer were hunted annually. In addition, wild boar, danphe, kaliz, dove, and partridge were frequently killed inside the park for the use of meat. Hunting of wildlife was escalated since 2000. Often wildlife were killed once they came outside the park boundaries. However, illegal hunting inside the park increased once the security posts were dysfunctional. Shakya and Chitrakar (2006: 113) quote Warden of the park, "*when the posts were deployed in every corner of the park, nobody performed such activities. Now, they are hunting at will. We can't do anything to stop them*".

Since 2001, the CPN (M) had destroyed all security posts[27] of the Shuklaphanta Wildlife Reserve (SWR). In the absence of security patrolling, the poaching of spotted deer and swamp deer was frequent, particularly in the Indian borders. The hunters and poachers use boats to cross the Mahakali River and freely hunt in the Dodhara Chandani area of the Reserve. The local people estimate that more than 50 animals have been hunted from the above-mentioned sectors (Shakya and Chtrakar, 2006). Earlier, Jaya Krishna Goet, leader of the one fraction of Janatantrik Terai Mukti Morcha (JTMM) was leading a Koshi Sarokar Samuha (which was formed to deal with the problems arises from the Koshi Dam and KTWR). He was not happy with KTWR and this may create difficulties in KTWR if the political situation in Terai deteriorates.

Shey-Phoksundo National Park (SPNP) was also severely affected by the 10 years of armed conflict. Up to now, it suffers from lack of proper management. CPN (M) destroyed different security posts (Sumaduwa post on 3 April 1997, the Palam headquarters on 28 June 2002). The CPN (M), evacuated the park personnel and torched the office premise, detonated a bomb and destroyed the office. The series of CPN (M) attacks had led to the gradual withdrawal of Tuen, Chhepka, Palam, Rigmu, Sulighat, Raha and Aankhe posts and concentrated in Dunai, the district headquarters. Once the security posts were withdrawn, poaching and illegally smuggling of wildlife became common without any restrictions. The government was unable to control poaching and illegal trade of wildlife. CPN (M) occasionally captured some smugglers (45-60 persons) but released them after penalizing or imposing a fine. "*We have imposed monetary penalties as per the directive of the party. Cadres in the district are directly monitoring and supervising the park. Previously, the activists at the village level were delegated the responsibilities but they were ineffective. Since our party is inclined towards attaining economic benefits from the park, it is seen as a priority zone*", said, District Committee Members of the CPN (M) Pawan (Shakya and Chitrakar, 2006:186). Shakya and Chitrakar reports, "*The CPN (M) have devised a tax system to collect money according to the species of wildlife that has been poached. A penalty of 30% tax, without physical action, is imposed on traffickers of rare wildlife such as the snow leopard, clouded leopard, musk deer and yak, amongst other species. DCM Pawan explained, 'A tax of NRs 500 for one pod from the musk deer and 30% of the amount, equal to the quantity of hides and bones of the leopard is levied. Smugglers of Chinese origin smuggle the valuable wildlife. Our party believes that Nepalese nationals have more rights to Nepalese wildlife than foreigners'*" (Shakya and Chitrakar, 2006:187).

In several places, park authorities have shifted local people from their resident area (for example, people of Suklaphata were shifted once the park was extended. Similar shifting happened in Bardiya. In Padampur area of Chitwan, park authority has shifted people from their areas). Great potential exists in these areas for conflict to erupt once the issue is either politicized or some other factors trigger this debate again. The long existing park-people conflict and people-wildlife conflict in national parks and wildlife reserves will create many problems if these issues are not resolved properly.

Sagarmatha National Park (SNP) also did not suffer much from the armed conflict compared to other parks. The CPN (M) attacked the army barracks at Saleri, the district headquarters in 2001. CPN (M) had also exploded bombs and looted a bank in Lukla that could have affected the functioning of SNP. On 22 November 2004, the CPN (M) abducted three staff of SNP in Khotang and seized official documents. After the 2001 State of Emergency, the existing four army security posts were merged citing security reasons. This was very favourable to the illegal hunters, poachers, loggers and herb smugglers. Patrolling virtually ceased and activities of poachers and illegal loggers sharply increased. The musk deer was one of the prime targets of the poachers in SNP areas.

Surprising enough, there were no physical attacks in park areas after August 2004, except in ACAP. Further, there was no physical damage occurred in Sagarmatha National Park during the time of conflict. In terms of intensity of escalation of the conflict more numbers of incidences occurred in 2002 and 2004.

Often it was reported in the field and consultation process that during the conflict period military structures placed in the parks and protected areas were not able to protect wildlife because of their priority in counterinsurgency. Hence, illegal hunting and loss of biodiversity and habitat increased, mainly because of the lack of priority of the military. However, quantifying the habitat and biodiversity loss requires further assessment.

Placement of anti-personal landmines became one of the serious challenges in management of conservation and natural resources in Nepal, as they are massively placed in forests areas without proper marking. Placing anti-tank and anti-personal landmines is common in war-torn countries. The human population, domestic animals and wildlife were seriously threatened by landmines in Angola and Mozambique (Kalpers, 2001). Nepal is no exception. Though CPA contains provision of landmine clearance, no concrete action has been taken so far.

The National Parks and Wildlife Conservation Act 1973, Forest Act 1993, Environment Protection Act 1997 and the Customs' Act are some of the principal acts dealing with the wildlife protection in the country. The Wildlife Conservation Act legalizes protection of wildlife of the country. This Act also enables the Government of Nepal to designate the various categories of protected areas: national parks, reserves, conservation areas, and buffer zones. This Act makes it illegal to possess any wildlife trophy without a certificate. Any person wishing to import or export a trophy must obtain permission from the government. The Act enables a prescribed officer to arrest any person committing any offences under the Act and impose penalties. Convictions for poaching and/or dealing in trophies can sentence the offender to 15 years imprisonment. Protection of wildlife within designated protected areas has been managed solely by the DNPWC. While forests, biodiversity remaining outside the mandate of National Parks and Wildlife Conservation Act (DNPWCA) are managed by the DoF under the legal provisions of The Forest Act 1993. The Forest Act provides a framework for the management of forests and forests-based resources in Nepal. Conflicts between the Wildlife Act and the Forest Act are visible when wildlife crosses the boundaries of protected area and enters neighbouring national forests.

Environment Protection Act 1997 is primarily concerned with ensuring that the environmental impact of all proposals is considered before starting any development activity. This Act also contains some provisions applicable to wildlife protection. This Act empowers the government to establish environment conservation zones at any place within Nepal that has rare wildlife; a ban could also be imposed on prescribed activities within this zone. The rules applying to the Act prohibit any person from buying, selling, trading in, hunting or causing harm to any wildlife in an environment conservation zone. The Act also requires the applicant to consider the impact of the proposal on wildlife. Nevertheless, there are some confusions and contradictions among these acts.

Local Self Governance Act 1999 is the latest Act mandating local governments (CCDs, VDCs and municipalities) to decide local issues related to natural resources which sometimes contradict specialised and thematic Acts, such as Forest Act or DNPWCA.

8.2.5 Consequences of the Armed Conflict on Water Resource

Though the direct impacts of armed conflict on water resource was less visible compared to forest, or biodiversity, the water sector has also faced several difficulties and challenges during the time of armed conflict. Investment in water resource was severely disturbed. Exploitation of water resource for hydropower, irrigation, drinking water, recreation and industrial uses were limited because the unfavourable political environment and security risks. Investors and entrepreneurs were not confident and able to take risk risks. The constructions of the ongoing hydropower projects (Kaligandaki, Mid Marsyangdi, etc.) and drinking water projects (e.g. Melamchi mega-drinking water project) were frequently disturbed. Water sources in various places were polluted by the war. In many places, drinking water supply systems were disturbed. The CPN (M) and the state security forces cut drinking water sources in several places or they were damaged in attacks and counter-attacks. Comprehensive assessment of impacts of Nepal's armed conflict on water resources is needed to explore level, scale and intensity of negative (or positive if any) impacts. Chapter Four has discussed in detail the conflict and its relation with water.

There has been very little documentation of the impacts of the armed conflict on water resources. In the changing context, it is extremely essential to have proper information on the damage of water-related structures and their causes, public response, etc. Hence, this study has to focus on both surface and ground water, (including assessing conflict on various areas such as ground water, drinking water and arsenic contamination, irrigation, lake, river rafting and recreation, hydro-power generation, flooding, erosion and trans-boundary water management). This assessment will provide basis for long-term planning and comprehensive management as well as contribute to the state restructuring process.

8.2.6 Environmental Concerns in the Cantonments

When the decision of establishment and operation of the cantonments for People's Liberation Army (PLA) was made, no consideration was given to possible environmental damage. Neither UNMIN, nor GoN nor CPN (M) gave enough attention to minimise potential and actual negative environmental impacts while deciding the sites for the cantonment. The sole reason for deciding cantonment sites was political. Therefore, some of the PLA camps are located in some of Nepal's most sensitive environmental areas. Forests are almost the sole supplier of the energy needs of cantonments.

A recent unpublished PLA Camp impact study report of UNP[28] entitled 'PLA Fuel wood Extraction Endangers Nepal's most Crucial Environmental Sites' states, *"Of the 28 total cantonments, approximately 21 are located in forested areas. Moreover, the 12 camps for PLA Divisions 3, 4, and 7 have been established directly within restoration target areas, identified by the Government of Nepal (GoN) and various donor agencies as the highest priority environmental sites in the country.*[29] *Despite the sensitive nature of cantonment locations, PLA energy needs are almost exclusively dependant on Nepal's leading cause of deforestation – illegal firewood extraction. Six of seven central cantonments rely on unregulated firewood collection for food preparation. PLA representatives from Division 1 - 4 estimated their combined consumption at nearly 1,500 tons per month. Taken as a whole, the 35,000 combatants in residence could require up to 2,100,000 tons of fuel wood each month.*[30] *If extraction continues at current rates, Nepal's natural resource base will lose its most important assets"* It further states, *"In the case of the Kailali cantonments, PLA cadres are housed in close proximity to the mere 1.5 kilometres of forest cover that facilitate the migration and genetic dispersal of critically-endangered species like the Royal Bengal Tiger. Without key areas like this, scientists estimate that tigers in Nepal will be genetically extinct in just ten years."*[31]

It was reported by local people during the field visit in Chitwan that nearly 9 hectares of forest was cleared to construct basic camp facilities in Division 3 in Jutpani VDC, Chitwan District. Further, the cantonment has to rely on fuel wood from the nearby forests. Mr Ganesh Bahadur Parajuli, resident of Chainpur VDC-5, Gotheshwor, Chitwan district and user of CFUG said, *"It took 25 years for us to develop this community forest but it is going to be destroyed within a year. I am seriously hurt by the deforestation in our community forests in the name of cantonment'.*[32]

Users of local community forests Mr. Prit Singh Karki (district chair of FECOFUN) and Mr Min Bahadur Karki from Chainpur VDC-5, Gotheshwor agree with the remarks of Mr. Parajuli. Mr. Prit Singh Karki further explained that logging was massive at the beginning of establishment of cantonment but it was stopped once an all-party meeting decided to give identified trees to built cantonment. It was decided to establish the Basu Smriti Brigade Cantonment in the Kankali CF and Pratap Smriti Brigade Cantonment in Kankali + Amritdhara + Ajingare community forests. However, users were not informed about the establishment of these cantonments in their community forests. Mr Bodh Raj Adhikari from Kumroj VDC-3, Chitwan district also explained the massive logging of *sal* and *asna* (both are considered as good quality wood) trees in the cantonment sites.[33]

Mr Yam Bahadur Thapa from Kawashoti VDC-5, of Nawalparasi district residing close to one of the cantonment sites had expressed similar observation and frustration about the logging. He further explained that the wild animals are occasionally killed by army and police from their areas. The capturing of piglets of Bandel (wildboar) and selling it @ 300-400 per animal in this area is common during April to June. Majhi, Mushahar and other marginalised groups are not getting benefits from buffer zone provisions. The landless and encroachers protected by political parties are real threat to natural resource and conservation in Nawalparasi district.

It is surprising to note that there are no environmental considerations given by any agencies (governmental, non-governmental, or donor agencies) working in environmental field while developing cantonment infrastructures: road construction, housing, water and electricity supply, play grounds, provisional stores, etc.

The main and satellite cantonments are lacking sufficient medical facilities, clean drinking water supply, sanitations, sufficient foods, poor housing, etc. In the rainy season, they suffered from rain and in winter season from cold. Some of the PLA were killed by the fallen trees. In one cantonment, PLA found massive numbers of poisonous shakes and they killed 700 at a time. Hence, the environmental consideration for the PLA is nuisance in such a misery situation of cantonment.

Investment in infrastructure and development in all the cantonments are huge and they are linked with electrical grids, roads and basic water, and sanitation facilities. This indicates basis for long-term settlement in the cantonment areas. Hence, it is realised that the current cantonment sites will turn to permanent settlements despite the provisional or temporary arrangement was the spirit of CPA.

Nevertheless, there is not only a negative environmental story in the cantonment sites. The UNDP quick assessment report states, *"The PLA has taken measures to mitigate environmental degradation. Specifically, each camp site has maintained a certain degree of tree cover in order to prevent erosion and solar panelling is in use at several sites. When possible, the PLA has sought to avoid unnecessary deforestation. For example, nearby open spaces, rather than forested areas, are favoured as helipads. Since the rhino poaching incident on January 2nd, PLA soldiers have also conducted joint patrols in the Udayapur Community Forest near Jutpani VDC, Chitwan (Division 3)"*. These positive aspects need to expand in other cantonments and the GoN, UNMIN and CPN (M) have to encourage such activities.

High pressure on forests to supply energy need of the cantonment sites can be reduced by other alternative energy sources like biogas, solar panel system or cooking stoves. Even if part of the energy needs is to be fulfilled from the forests, it can be managed by supplying legally-harvested fuel wood from appropriate forest sites. Conservation organizations need to take initiative by engaging with the local Cantonment Management Committees to incorporate remedial measures to reduce their negative environmental impact. In some cantonment sites, PLA has started mitigation measures to address environmental degradation in the cantonment sites (for example, maintained a certain degree of tree cover in order to prevent erosion, helipads built on open areas instead of forest area and use of solar panels for energy). PLA soldiers have conducted joint patrols in the Udayapur Community Forest near Jutpani VDC, Chitwan (Division 3) since the rhino poaching incident on January 2, 2007. These positive aspects need to expand in other cantonment and the GoN, UNMIN and CPN (M) have to encourage such activities.

An in-depth study of environmental implications of PLA cantonments will provide better knowledge and reality-based context to mitigate negative impacts, prevent long-term negative consequences and devise prevent measures for future. Therefore, the government must take this issue seriously.

8.2.8 Major Attacks on Protected Areas and Natural Resources

This section briefly presents the major incidences occurred in the conservation, biodiverusty and natural resources. On 16 December 2006, the CPN (M) and SPA agreed on the interim constitution. On 21 November 2006 the SPA and CPN (M) signed Comprehensive Peace Agreement and 10-year rebel insurgency was ended. On 24 April 2006 the then King Gyanendra surrendered power and agreed to reinstate parliament after street protests. GP Koirala was appointed as prime minister. On 22 November 2005 the CPN (M) and SPA agreed on a common platform for restoring democracy.

On 11 August 2004, Motor cycle (no 66-1-297) provided PCP-UNDP used in Bardia National Park was taken away by CPN (M) from East- West Highway and a Toyota Jeep was destroyed by setting on fire. On 27 July 2004 a quarter of Assistant Warden & Amaltari Sector office of Chitwan National Park was destroyed by setting on fire. A Motor Boat donated by WWF was set on fire. On 27 June 2004: Jarnali post of Chitwan National Park was destroyed by setting on fire. On 21 May 2004 Bhurigaon post, Motipur post, Parewa odar post and Sainabar post of Bardia National Park were destroyed by being sett on fire. On 23 April 2004: Dhoba post of Chitwan National Park was destroyed by being set on fire. On 5 April 2004: Ramche Range post of Langtang National Park was destroyed by fire. On 16 March 2004 the Jhilmila post of Suklaphata Wildlife Reserve was destroyed by fire. Two government staffs and 9 civilians were killed in mine blast planted by CPN (M) on the way of Baba Tal where one Pickup Jeep (No. Ba Jha 3851) was also destroyed. On 8 March 2004 Lamichaur sector post -2 of Chitwan National Park was destroyed by fire. On 16 February 2004: Pratappur post of Parsa Wildlife Reserve was destroyed by fire. Similarly, on 11 January 2004 aMotorcycle of Chitwan National Park was damaged.

On 18 September 2003 Alche post of Shivapuri National Park was destroyed by being set on fire. On 15 September 2003 the Cha Gaon post of SNP was similarly destroyed. On 24 August 2003 the Arjuni post of Suklaphata Wildlife Reserve was destroyed by fire. On 25 February 2003: Bhagalpur Guard post of Koshi Tappu Wildlife Reserve was destroyed by fire. Staffs from the post were pulled to HQ. On 24 February 2003: Patheri Range was of Koshi Tappu Wildlife Reserve completely destroyed by fire. On 6 November 2002: Dadreni post-Dibya Nagar of Chitwan National Park was destroyed by fire. Mitsubishi Pickup van No 66-1-253 was destroyed by fire.

On 13 October 2002, Chepang post of Eastern sector of Bardia National Park was destroyed by using explosive materials. On 18 September 2002, the Ticket counter and guard post of Chisapani sector of Shivapuri National Park was destroyed by setting on fire. Dhap Guard post of Sindhupalchowk, Haibung VCD-4 was also destroyed Staffs from the post were pulled to park HQ. On 5 September 2002 Kutumsang Range post of lchok VCD-9 of Langtang National Park was destroyed by setting on fire. Staffs from the post were pulled to park HQ. On 26 June 2002 five houses of Palam HQ of Shey Phoksundo National Park were damaged by setting it on fire. All the staff were merged to Suligadi sub HQ.

On 26 April 2002, Tempathan Guard post of Langtang National Park was destroyed by setting on fire. All the staff Tempathan sector were merged to HQ. On 22 April 2002, two houses of Champapur Guard post of Suklaphata Wildlife Reserve were destroyed by setting on fire. Staff from the post were pulled to park HQ. On 4 April 2002 all the official documents of Makalu Barun National Park were damaged by setting on fire and captured. The sector office of Hatiya Staffs from the post were pulled to district HQ, Khanbari. On 3 April 2002, two houses of Bhulbhule Rangepost of Rara National Park, Dolpa were damaged by setting on fire. Staffs from the post were pulled to park HQ.

Similalry, on 3 April 2002 all the official documents of Dhorpatan Hunting Reserve were destroyed by setting them on fire and captured the Reserve HQ. Consequently, Staff from the post were pulled to Baglung District HQ. On 3 April 2002, Toijom (Jagdulla) post of Shey Phoksundo National Park was destroyed by setting it on fire. Consequently, Protection unit was merged in HQ and become vacant. On 1 April 2002 the Asneri post of Eastern sector of Bardia National Park was damaged by setting fire. Consequently, protection unit was merged to HQ. On 28 March 2002 all official documents from Yamphudin sector of Kanchanjunga Conservation Area were destroyed by setting them on fire and a radio set was taken away. All the staff of the sector had to move to District headquarters at Taplejung. On 21 March 2002, four Canoes of Gola post, Bardiya of Bardia National Park were destroyed by setting on fire and the staff were beaten. Canoes were used for patrolling.

On 8 March 2002, about 500 cubic ft. of sal timber was looted by a group of unknown people from the Manaughat Depot of Bardia National Park. The logs were collected by the Bardia National Park during monsoon flood. On 22 February 2002: All the official documents including furniture and other materials were destroyed by setting on fire and capture sector office-Tamku of Makalu Barun National Park. All the park staff were moved to district HQ, Khandbari. On 15 February 2002 all the official documents of Makalu Barun National Park was destroyed by setting on fire and captured HQ based on Seduwa, Taplejung. On 12 January 2002, Dadi Chaur post of Rara National Park was destroyed by setting on fire. The protection unit was merged with HQ. On 3 January 2002: Jhyari post of Rara National Park was destroyed by setting on fire.

Targetting natural resources-related structures continued in 2001. On 24 November 2001, Dhakka Range post, Beldandi Range post and Badanikheda Range post of Suklaphata Wildlife Reserve at Kanchanpur were completely destroyed by setting on fire. *All the staff were merged with Reserve HQ.*On 23 November 2001, Tarapen Post of Extension Area of Suklaphata Wildlife Reserve was completely destroyed by setting on fire. On 10 December 2000, Chescan sector office of Makalu Barun National Park was destroyed by setting it on fire. All the park staff were stationed at district HQ, Khanbari. On 13 February 1996 - CPN (M) started armed insurgency aimed at replacing the constitutional monarchy with a communist republic.

8.3 ADDRESSING CONSEQUENCES OF THE ARMED CONFLICT ON NATURAL RESOURCES

Literally, recovery is a process of returning to a normal situation or becoming even stronger after an unusual or difficult period of time. In the situation of severe negative impacts of armed conflict on biodiversity and conservation, natural resources and environment, the recovery goes to three levels, i.e. mental or psychological recovery, recovery of physical infrastructures and organizational capacities and competencies. A rapid response plan and early recovery plan are simultaneously used in this document.

The past decade of armed conflict has obstructed effective implementation of natural resources, conservation and environmental strategies. The quick impact study reveals that conflict has seriously affected the management capacity and the existing implementation procedures; it has destroyed physical infrastructures and hindered the motivation of main actors who were active in the areas of natural resource management, conservation and environment.

Nepal has been in the midst of a shaky transition for more than 10 years from armed conflict to peace. This transition will remain until the national and local elections are held successfully following the new constitution developed by the Constituent Assembly. This means that transition will remain for another three to four years. The transition period is characterized by instability, confusion, contradiction tension, uncertainties, frequent shift of priorities, encounter of unanticipated consequences and so forth. The state focus during the transition period will mostly be concentrated in successfully conducting constituent assembly election, preparation of new constitution followed by national and local elections. Hence, conservation of biodiversity, mitigation of negative environmental effects of the decade-long armed conflict, addressing problems and difficulties arising from the conflict and post-conflict situation will obviously get less attention, if there is no constant and systematic engagement of conservation organizations and people working in this field to bring issues into attention and action. One of the best ways to engage in this crucially important issue is to collectively develop an early recovery plan bringing governmental and non-governmental actors together and implement it jointly. However, this prescription is not easy and therefore a concerted effort from conservation organizations is a precondition to move forward. This brief 'quick recovery plan' highlights some of the activities to be implemented during the transition period. Onceconcrete efforts are made collectively, the current situation can be converted into a great opportunity for addressing the problems and difficulties faced by the conservation sector during the time of conflict.

The main objectives of this quick recovery plan are: to identify areas of immediate actions that are needed to prevent the situation from further deterioration in biodiversity and natural resources, and to provide framework and basis for conservation organizations to take immediate action to promote recovery in biodiversity and natural resources. The following guiding principles help in devising a recovery plan:

- Focus on psychological (mental) recovery, reconstruction of infrastructures and recovery of organizational capacity and competence
- Immediately address urgent issues to minimize further damage
- Reorient policies, strategies, programme activities in restoring loss and mitigate negative impacts during the transitional and post-conflict period
- Mobilize local stakeholders in recovery action as principal partners of conservation
- Contribute to post-conflict stabilization, recovery and peace
- Maintain flexibility, transparency and accountability in post-conflict recovery plan, implementation and evaluation
- Initiate concerted and collaborative efforts between government, I/NGOs, conservation agencies and local community
- Link post-conflict recovery plan with the broader priority of post conflict reconstruction, reintegration and reconciliation of the state.

During more than ten years of the armed conflict, the natural resource sector was severely threatened in this regard, However, there were two major actors, i.e. CPN (M) rebels and the state security forces. In the CPN (M) influenced areas, they were controlling natural resources issues (e.g. decisions relating to regulating, harvesting and imposing taxes and levies). Local people and conservation organizations had to deal with only single rebel force. However, the current situation in 2007 is more complicated from the perspective of managing natural resources (mainly forest and protected areas) particularly in Terai because of emergence of more than a dozen of militant and fringe arms groups, who often rely on forests and protected areas for financing their armed activities but not demonstrating responsible behaviour towards biodiversity, environment and natural resources. Local people and conservation organizations have to face pressure from all of them.

8.3.1 Risk Assessment in Natural Resources

Risk assessment in the context of this paper is an attempt to consider the risk factor more systematically in term of threats, vulnerabilities and response measures to reduce threat and or vulnerability (Brabant, 2000) in conservation, natural resources and environmental sectors. The attempt of this paper is to highlight risk reduction strategy to minimize the negative impacts of the armed conflict and address potential threats and uncertainties existed in this sector. As Nepal is in transition, there are several social, political, economic, security and environmental risks in the foreseeable future. Some of the environmental, natural resource, conservation-related risks are presented here as:

- Politicisation of natural resource and environmental sectors leading to a dysfunctional operating system,
- Ignorance or no-attention attitude of the government and political parties to crucial issues, such as addressing environmental concerns sin the new constitution,
- Less priority to this sector in terms of allocation of budget, human resources, policies and planning,

- Illegal and or irrational exploitation of valuable flora and fauna in protected and non-protected areas by different vested interest groups, such as armed groups of terai, illegal smugglers and illegal traders, etc.
- Encroachment of forests and biodiversity reach areas by internally displaced people, land-grabbing by smugglers, and professional trouble-makers,
- Shift of priority of donors and international community to post-conflict reconstruction and rehabilitation leaving environmental sector alone or less attention
- Mounting wildlife animal conflict and or park-people conflict (there are already several flashpoints and unresolved conflict in Bardiya, KTWR, etc.).
- Lack of staff in government offices or demotivation of staff because of politicisation, biases and unfair-transfer,
- If political issues of various groups such as women, dalits, Madhesis, Janajatis and minorities are not settled, political instability increase and consequently environment sector suffers,
- Tussle and power struggle within and between political parties, ministries and department leading to inaction or inappropriate action.

Hence, Nepal's environment, conservation and natural resources are highly vulnerable in the coming few years with high risks.

8.3.2 Rapid Response Actions

Reactivating and functioning of management of organizations responsible for conservation, environment and natural resources in the field is one of the immediate areas of support and recovery. Restoration of public confidence and trust and boosting of morale of staff working in conservation field is crucial. Accomplishing the tasks detailed in management plan and improving management functions of conservation organizations requires responsive policies, pragmatic strategies, adequate resources and a favourable political environment.

The rapid response plan has two parts, i.e. activities related to prevention and preparedness, and activities related to restoration, mitigation and recovery. Though it is difficult to draw a clear demarcation line between the two categories, they are complementary and supplementary to each other.

Related to prevention and preparedness

a) Awareness through conservation education, media mobilization (for example, collaboration with local and national media in production and telecasting/airing conservation documentaries), policy dialogues at local level,

b) Intimate engagement with political parties to make sure that they include 'biodiversity and environmental concerns in their policies and assisting political parties in defining 'conservation policy'.

c) Proactively engage in making sure that new constitution made by the Constituent Assembly adequately incorporates conservation and biodiversity concerns.

d) EIA and Conflict Impact Assessment (CIA) must be a precondition to establish industries in the surroundings of parks to minimize the negative effects of industrial waste in conservation and potential for conflict respectively.

e) Some provisions of DNPWCA, Land Act and Forest Act are still either contradictory[34] or overlapping. Hence, immediate action for reconciliation has to be started.

f) Collaborate with and support to communities for taking action on preventing habitat destruction and conservation of biodiversity and genetic resources. It is possible only through concerted action by mobilizing the local community.

g) Initiate activities to protect and promote indigenous knowledge and skills on biodiversity and natural resources available at local level.

h) Strengthening indigenous conflict management institutions and procedures and actively engage them in managing park-people conflict.

i) A clear strategy on anti-poaching operation is urgently needed. Implementation capacity of existing anti-poaching operation is constrained by lack of physical and logistical facilities such as raincoats, sleeping bags, tents, compass, binoculars, phone and functional radio-sets, etc. Make sure availability of functional logistic equipments. Insurance for anti-poaching monitoring staff may be an additional motivating factor to control poaching; with minor repair it can be operational.

j) Establish community-based biodiversity registration and monitoring mechanisms as concerted efforts all organisations working in conservation.

k) So far, the poorest people and marginalized indigenous community are much less benefited from the Buffer Zone arrangement in terms of participation, benefit sharing and decision making. Hence, immediate actions to ensure full participation of poorest people, marginalized indigenous community in benefit sharing and decision making are required.

l) Redefining engagement and role of military in parks is essential. There is intense debate on this issue and therefore DNPWC needs to clarify the needs, relevance, level and scale of engagement of army (in which level, where and how much strength is required, if needed). There are cases of latent conflict between the warden (head of the park) and the chief of the local army barrack, reflecting a situation of 'two lions in one den'. Addressing this perennial source of conflict is to keep senior warden in position than the military head in the barrack under the overall responsibility of the warden.

m) Immediate initiatives are needed to form a 'River Authority' to regulate and or control urban waste disposal in rivers. For example, urban wastes from Munglin and Narayanghat areas are disposed in Narayani River that is polluting the aquatic ecosystems.

n) Poaching is becoming a lucrative business and therefore expanded its roots from Tibet to India and internationally. It is strongly connected with national and international power centres. Hence, controlling poaching requires national focus and it is not possible to control alone by

DNPWC or any other single department. Help of parliamentary committees is crucially important and therefore conservation organizations need to closely work with related parliamentary committees and continuous engagement with political parties.

o) Link tourism, ecotourism and nature conservation through public-private-partnership arrangement between government-conservation sector and corporate sectors.

p) Jointly establish a 'Best Conservation Award' to annually award to the most conservation-sensitive business persons in collaboration between private-corporate and conservation sectors.

q) Initiate religion-based conservation and tourism in collaborating with the religious groups and inter-faith organizations. For example, Lumbini can be an example of this type as Buddhist people form around the world want to visit Lumbini one time in their life. Many other religious conservation sites can be promoted in this way.

r) A functional collaboration mechanism is needed to mobilize hotel and tourism sector in promoting conservation of biodiversity and natural resources. The representatives of hotel and tourism sectors active in conservation areas are willing to collaborate for this aim (guidance, facilitation and right tracking is needed to avoid undermining conservation goal).

s) Reactivate and strengthen community based anti-poaching operation mechanisms (including local communities of buffer zones, park authority and local administration, where appropriate).

t) Proactively engage in minimizing the negative effects of industrial wastes in the river around the park areas, For example, the wasted produced by the Bhrikuti Paper and Pulp Industry and beer factory in Nawalparasi and Chitwan districts are disposed in the Narayani River and conservationists claimed that it has seriously affected the wildlife and aquatic animals.

u) Improvement in communication is urgent and therefore

providing mobile phone to surveillance staff could help as walky-talky is not functioning well in the park areas.

v) Strengthening and refining 'information collection and information purchase system' (ICIPS) practiced by park authority to control poaching and illegal exploitation of conservation resources (natural resources and biodiversity).

w) Identify poor people residing to the surroundings of the parks and protected areas who are abused by poachers and illegal traders for their survival and create livelihood opportunities for them, and ensure that anticipated benefits reach the poor and marginalised people through constant monitoring and refining procedures of buffer zone management committees and forest users committees.

x) Initiate immediate action to return the community forests encroached upon and property of users taken away by security forces to communities. Thousands of hectares of community forests were given by the government to the security forces or captured by them (Khanal, 2006: Annex 1 and 2). Working with parliamentary committees, FECOFUN and security forces is essential.

y) Uncontrolled logging was observed in different parts of the country.[35] ACAP and concerned agencies need to minutely look the logging situation in their working areas and initiate necessary action to address the problem.

Related to Mitigation, Recovery and Support

a) There is strong pressure on forest resources for supplying fuel wood for PLA and IDPs. Therefore, supplying fire-wood in regulated ways, supplying kerosene or alternative energy sources, installing solar power and biogass system for fuel can reduce pressure on forest resource. Further, promoting energy saving mechanism and techniques (e.g. improve cooking stoves, solar panel system) is essential.

b) Some of the rehabilitation and recovery activities need direct financial support, for example, rebuilding damaged infrastructures or rehabilitating range posts and game posts, reinstalling communication systems. It is urgent to effectively carry out the conservation and protection activities and therefore providing financial support to local and national conservation agencies for rehabilitating these structures should be priority.

c) Controlling poaching: The UNEP study (2003) of Pamir-e-Buzurg Wildlife Reserve found that illegal hunting can be controlled even in the situation of armed conflict if commitment is there. The call of Afghan Transitional Authority to control hunting was taken positively in this area because of its sincere commitment. Hence, an important aspect of controlling poaching is commitment from the concerned authority. Better coordination at the central level and mobilisation of local people in the field help to control illegal activities.

d) Illegal encroachment of forest and conservation areas and public lands is increased and immediate action to protect encroachment is essential. Collaboration with local community is needed to achieve this objective.

e) Landmine clearance: The UNEP assessment in Afghanistan (2003b) shows that anti-personal landmine is one of the major challenges in post-conflict situation.[36] Cleaning landmine is almost a pre-requisite for developing conservation-focused and nature-based tourism and protecting livestock and wildlife. In the case of Nepal, UNMIN is actively working according to the provisions of the Agreement on Management of Arms and Armies between UN, Government of Nepal and CPN (M). Joint Mine Action Group composed of different civil society organisations with the support of UNICEF is also engaged in this issue. Hence, DNPWC and DoF have to closely work with them in making sure that landmine, explosive residues of war (ERW), Un-Exploded Ordnance (UXO) and Improvised Explosive Devices (IEDs), placed in protected areas and forests.

f) Focus on psychological, psychological recovery: One of the important tasks to be undertaken is psycho-social counselling to the conflict victim people working in conservation, biodiversity and forest sectors who are suffering from fear, insecurity, trauma and other many problems. The armed conflict has also negatively affected the morale of the staff working in remote and difficult areas. Hence, immediate action is needed.

g) Strong monitoring and coordination is a precondition to make the early recovery plan of action successful. Monitoring and coordination ensure availability of human and financial resources; operational procedural issues; and backstopping for the implementation. Some of the activities proposed in this document are not possible to execute without proper coordination. Coordination with UNMIN and its mine clearance team to identify IEDs/landmines placed in forests and conservation areas is one of several examples of this precondition.

h) Regular Conflict analysis (CA), Conflict Impact Assessment (CIA), Conflict and Peace impact Assessment (PCIA) and Conflict Risks Assessment (CRA) are crucially important at the time of conflict and situation of post-conflict transition. If these techniques and methodologies are used in designing and implementing conservation activities and in project performance monitoring system, yearly reviews and periodic evaluations, they will greatly contribute to achieving the intended results from the quick recovery action.

8.3.3 Post-conflict Impact Assessment on Environment and Natural Resources

Nepal is undergoing a major state restructuring process with federal governing arrangement. The number, size and geographical and demographic details of each federation are still unknown. These will be known once the new constitution is developed by the Constituent Assembly. In the public debate so far, availability of natural resources has been considered as one of the important criteria for deciding federal states. Once the position of federations is clear, a daunting task remains:

formulating policy, strategy and laws and regulations related to environment, natural resources and conservation. Accomplishing this task requires comprehensive information on impacts of armed conflict and ways of mitigating them. This study has to contribute in this state restructuring process and therefore it has to go beyond the narrow focus of study looking only to the existing provisions and arrangements.

The comprehensive study needs to apply both qualitative (e.g., in-depth interviews, case studies, observation, focus group discussion, PRA) and quantitative methods (chemical analysis, survey, etc.) and use of primary and secondary source of information. The primary information has to be collected from the comprehensive field assessment and wider consultation with the concerned stakeholders. The secondary source of information needs to be gathered from an intensive review of national and international literature.

The following components are proposed:

1. Intensive literature review of relevant documents on environmental impacts of armed conflict on environment, biodiversity and natural resources.
2. Field research: Field assessment representing mountain, hill and terai, Terai Arc Landscape, Sacred Himalayan Landscape, cultural heritage, national parks, wildlife reserves and protected conservation areas. If assessment of all 16 protected areas is made, it will cover most of the aforementioned issues/areas. The field work has also to cover all the proposed thematic areas (such as urban environment, environment-industry relation, land, forest and water resources, agriculture, pollution, wildlife and protected areas, and environmental governance and institutional arrangements),
3. GIS-based conflict mapping for Nepal.
4. Chemical analysis where appropriate.

This assessment has to focus on the following three stages of analysis:

a) Conflict analysis: covering structures, actors and dynamics of the armed conflict.
b) Response analysis.

c) Exploration of strategies and option.

These three areas have been elaborated upon in Table 8.7:

TABLE 8.7 : An Overview of focus of conflict assessment

Areas of conflict assessment	
A. Structures of the state related to conflict	A1 Security A2 Political A3 Economic A4 Social A5 Environmental
B. Actors: armed groups (state and rebels), IDPs, local population, political parties, human rights and humanitarian organizations, conservation organizations, donors, development agencies, etc.	B1 Interests B2 Capabilities B3 Agenda B4 Incentives B5 Relations
C. Dynamics	C1 Trends C2 Triggers C3 Scenarios
D. Impacts and consequences	D1 Wildlife and protected areas D2 Water resources D3 land resources D4 Forest resources D5 Mines and minerals D6 Environment • Solid and hazard waste • Water and air pollution • Soil contamination • Urban environment D7 Landmines, small arms and explosive devices D8 Internal displacement D9 Environmental/resource governance and institutions D10 Others
Stage 2 Response analysis	2.1 Mapping of state response 2.2 Mapping of international response 2.3 Mapping of policies and strategies 2.4 Mapping of peoples response

	2.5 Assessing impact on conflict and peace 2.6 Mapping of the potentials of natural resource as basis for defining federations
Stage 3 Strategies and options for restoration and recovery and preparedness and prevention	
	3.1 Policy options 3.2 Strategies 3.3 Areas of action 3.4 Institutional arrangement 3.5 Legal conditions

Source: Adapted from DFID 2002; Upreti, 2006d and 2005a.

These are sequential stages and make complementarity in analysis and preparing a restoration plan. A thorough analysis of conflict focusing on the socio-political structures; attitude behaviour and action of key actors (both internal and external) of the conflict and impacts/consequences of conflict provides solid ground for assessing response strategy of the actors, which ultimately leads to preparing a strategy and options for future intervention in the sustainability of environment and natural resources.

Not much is known about the relationship between mines and minerals and conflict in Nepal. No in-depth study has been made so far. Hence, an exploratory type of work in this area has to be part of this project, which will provide basis for further in-depth study.

There is a wider agreement on the severe negative impacts of the armed conflict on environment and some arguments of potentials of environmental sector in building peace and achieving stability and security. However, the degree and intensity of negative impacts and ways of maximising potentials of environmental sectors in building peace and security are not known. Environment also covers a very wide range of potentially overlapping areas. Hence, this study has to focus on the impact of armed conflict on the following:

a. Solid and hazard waste

b. Water, air and noise pollution (river pollution, drinking water pollution, etc). It was observed that the dead bodies of the people killed in the attacks such as Pili, Beni, Solukhumbu, and Dang were thrown away in water sources, rivers and forests and the decomposed bodies were creating pollution around the deposed areas.

c. Soil and land contamination

d. Urban environment

- o Urban contamination,
- o Factories and plants,
- o Solid waste and dumping sites (so many difficulties observed during conflict, particularly in Kathmandu Valley).

Use of landmines was common practice of the CPN (M) and security forces to hurt the other side during the time of the conflict. The CPN (M) had extensively placed landmines in the routes of security forces and the security forces did the same. There is lack of information on how many landmines are placed, where, and when by whom. Realising the severity, clearing landmines was also included in the CPA but it did not start yet. Similarly, small arms and light weapons have proliferated in Nepal. Illegal arm trading from India is becoming lucrative business these days. However, a full assessment is needed to know the actual situation and find a solution. The assessment of landmines requires close coordination with UNMIN, Nepal Army, CPN (M) and DoF and DNPWC.

It is widely reported in the media and expressed by analysts and researchers that environmental governing institutions are severely affected by the armed conflict. Their institutional capability has highly deteriorated. However, a critical assessment of components of governance, such as transparency, efficiency, effectiveness, inclusion, participation, institutional responsiveness, and their relations with armed conflict has not been made so far. This study has to focus on these issues.

This study has also to focus on the effective application of rules and regulations, as well as on ways of increasing people's participation in managing conservation areas. A quick impact study conducted by our team found that poor people of buffer zones are not getting expected benefits from the existing buffer zone management system. Hence, in the changing context it is essential to explore ways on how the poor and marginalised people could benefit from the buffer zone management system.

A decade-long armed conflict has had enormous impacts on people, society and environment including internal displacement. It is important to examine the relationship between armed conflict-induced displacement and environment. The settlements of internally displaced persons (IDP) in and around the forest areas have great negative impacts on environment. Similarly, environmental sanitation and health is a major issue in the IDP settlement areas. Hence, a comprehensive assessment is essential.

The Terai region has become most violent during the entire period of transition (2006-2007) and it has created serious insecurity. The Nepal Police has categorised eight districts[37] of the Terai region as "highly sensitive" and other 13 Terai districts[38] as sensitive. Media reports and cursory observations have highlighted the irrational exploitation of natural resources and obstruction of conservation and biodiversity sectors. However, there is no in-depth study of the impact of Terai violence on environment, biodiversity and natural resources. Hence, especial focus on this issue should be part of the assessment.

It is often argued that the livelihood of poor and marginal people of the remote and rural areas has been seriously affected by the armed conflict in Nepal (Upreti, 2006a and 2004b; Upreti and Adhikari, 2006; Seddon and Hussein, 2002; Seddon and Adhikari, 2005). Hence, a comprehensive assessment of how and in which way the livelihoods of poor and marginalised people are affected by the conflict is needed.

Policy is essential in building local capacity in managing natural resources, conservation and environmental areas. The post-conflict situation is entirely different, therefore business as usual type of thinking and action cannot address the new challenges. Hence, the study has to identify parameters, institutional arrangements and methodological framework to deal with new challenges that have emerged from the past ten years of armed conflict and the political changes in the country.

Donors and the international community have important roles in realising the need for new policy, institutional arrangements and methodological procedures to address these new challenges. This study has to address all challenges in the new context so as to provide a basis for the reorientation of conservation, natural resources and environmental policy focusing on the new state structures of the country.

Illegal trading of wildlife is one of the main challenges in conservation sector. So far there are several authorities (DNPWC, Custom Department, Police, DoF, etc.), which deal with illegal trading of wildlife and plant genetic resources but there is a lack of coordination between them. Consequently, they are ineffective in controlling the illegal trade. Hence, a more coordinated mechanism is needed. Creating CITIS Authority could be one of the pragmatic options but it is not clear how it works. If one agency is responsible for controlling poaching, verification mechanisms (e.g. whether animals and plants under CITIS arrangement smuggled are from Nepal and or India or other countries), intelligence mechanisms (strengthening intelligence in transit points and identifying smugglers, etc.), dealing with transboundary issues (animal migration and movement, illegal trade, collection and sharing of information) and bio-piracy and illegal gene trading, illegal trading will be effective. Hence, a comprehensive study is needed to work out ways to address these issues.

8.4 HUMAN RIGHTS VIOLATIONS

During the last 11 years of conflict, this country faced serious damages not only in terms of infrastructures but also human side in the form of killing, abduction, displacement, people with injuries and associated psychological effects. According to the MoPR the total economic cost of conflict is more than five billions rupees (5004494000) and the cost required form the rebuilding infrastructure is nearly 4 billions (3813756000). However, it is not possible to calculate the cost of damaged caused in human aspects.

According to the 2007 Human Rights Year Book report of INSEC, 930 people are disappeared during the time of the conflict and out of that 825 were disappeared by the state and 125 people were disappeared by the CPN (M). Similarly, the same report documents the killing of more than 13300 people. Children, women, innocent people are victims of the conflict.

TABLE 8.8: Women and Children Killed by the State and CPN (M) during the Time of Armed Conflict

S.N.	*Year*	*Number of women killed by*		
		CPN (M)	*State*	*Total*
1	1996	0	1	1
2	1997	1	2	3
3	1998	1	37	38
4	1999	3	44	47
5	2000	8	17	25
6	2001	8	25	33
7	2002	35	238	273
8	2003	21	138	159
9	2004	53	205	258
10	2005	49	89	138
11	2006	14	24	38

S.N.	*Year*	*Number of children killed by*		
		CPN (M)	*State*	*Total*
1	1996	–	3	3
2	1997	–	–	–
3	1998	2	19	21
4	1999	3	16	19
5	2000	10	9	19
6	2001	10	5	15
7	2002	32	91	123
8	2003	32	29	61
9	2004	58	42	100
10	2005	35	28	63
11	2006	9	4	13

Source: INSEC, Human Rights Yearbook, 2007

Until 1997, only a few incidences of attack on children were observed. The number of killing of children has increased since 1998. The highest numbers of children were killed in 2002 followed by 2004. The trend of killing is similar in the case of children and women (Table 8.8). Large numbers of killing of both children and women were in 2002 and 2004. Other years having higher numbers of killing were 2003 and 2005.

TABLE 8.9 : Number of People Killed by the State and the CPN (M)

S.N.	*Year*	*Number of children killed by*		
		CPN (M)	*State*	*Total*
1	1996	22	59	81
2	1997	16	32	48
3	1998	75	334	409
4	1999	141	328	469
5	2000	219	180	399
6	2001	390	243	633
7	2002	1337	3266	4603
8	2003	646	1217	1863
9	2004	1113	1606	2719
10	2005	709	815	1524
11	2006	286	313	599

Source: INSEC, Human Rights Yearbook, 2007

The intensity of conflict was high in the years 2002 and 2004. In 2002, a total of 4,603 people were killed followed by 2,719 people in 2004. The reason for high intensity of armed conflict was the breakdown of ceasefire and termination of peace talks of 2001 and 2003 respectively, which resulted in heavy fights between the state security forces and the CPN (M) fighters.

Though it was difficult to find the year-wise data of disappeared people, the geographical distribution of disappeared people presented in Table 6.3 shows that the state has done away with an extremely higher proportion of people compared to the CPN (M). In 2004, Nepal was ranked as the number one country in the world to make its own people disappear(INSEC, 2007).

While visiting Nepal (23-26 January 2005), the UN High Commissioner for Human Rights Louise Arbor issued a press statement highlighting the severe human right crisis. The

TABLE 8.10 : Disappearance of People by the State and the CPN (M)

S. N.	*District*	*Disappeared by CPN(M)*	*State*	*Total*	*S*	*District*	*Disappeared by CPN(M)*	*State*	*Total*
1	Jhapa	-	6	6	29	Tanahu	-	10	10
2	Ilam	6	-	6	30	Gorkha	-	20	20
3	Panchthar	-	2	2	31	Lamjung	-	8	8
4	Taplejung	-	1	1	32	Syangja	1	3	4
5	Morang	4	6	10	33	Kaski	-	12	12
6	Sunsari	-	7	7	34	Rupandehi	-	2	2
7	Bhokpur	-	3	3	35	Baglung	-	4	4
8	Sankhu wasawa	1	1	2	36	Myagdi	=	1	1
9	Saptari	-	8	8	37	Dang	5	70	75
10	Siraha	-	7	7	38	Pyuthan	-	3	3
11	Udayapur	-	2	2	39	Rolpa	18	43	61
12	Khotang	3	1	4	40	Salyan	-	27	27
13	Okhaldhunga	-	1	1	41	Rukum	6	23	29
14	Dhanusha	1	1	2	42	Banke	15	88	103
15	Mahottari	1	1	2	43	Bardiya	16	183	199
16	Sindhuli	-	7	7	44	Surkhet	2	18	20
17	Ramechhap	1	9	10	45	Jajarkot	3	14	17
18	Rautahat	3	6	9	46	Dailekh	-	6	6
19	Parsa	4	-	4	47	Dolpa	-	4	4
	Chitwan	5	23	28	48	Jumla	-	4	4
20	Makawanpur	-	7	7	49	Kalikot	-	17	17
21	Lalitpur	-	6	6	50	Humla	-	4	4
22	Kavre	-	16	16	51	Kailali	1	17	28
23	Bhaktapur	-	6	6	52	Achham	-	1	1
24	Kathmandu	-	35	35	53	Kanchanpur	-	15	15
25	Dhading	4	34	38	54	Dadeldhura	-	1	1
26	Sindhupal chowk	3	9	12	55	Rasuwa	-	1	1
27	Nuwakot	2	22	24		Grand total	105	825	930

Source: INSEC, 2007.

statement says, *"I would warn the leaders of the insurgency not to misread development in the wider world nor to believe that they can operate outside of the law."* A series of reports of Amnesty International (Nepal: Killing with Impunity, 20 January 2005; Nepal: State of Emergency Deepening Human Rights Crisis, 1st February 2005 and Nepal: A Long Ignored Human Rights

Crisis Now on the Brink of Catastrophe, 18 February 2005) highlighted the worst human rights situation of Nepal.

The Secretary General of the UN has repeatedly expressed his concerns about the crisis of Nepal. He issued several statements concerning the crisis. One of the statements (issued on 23 December 2004) amply demonstrates his worries about the deteriorating situation of Nepal. It states, *"The Secretary-General is deeply troubled by reports of an escalation of fighting in Nepal and of continued grave human rights violations. The conflict is undermining democracy and human rights and seriously hindering development activities. Reports that human rights defenders in Nepal face grave threats to their safety and security are very disturbing. The safety and ability of the National Human Rights Commission and all human rights activists to carry out their essential work should be guaranteed. In that regard, the recent signing of a Memorandum of Understanding between His Majesty's Government of Nepal and the Office of the High Commissioner for Human Rights is a welcome step. The Secretary-General once again calls for an urgent cessation of fighting and the initiation of dialogue between the Government and the Communist Party of Nepal (Maoist) with the participation of all political and civil forces. He stands ready to assist such a national effort"* (Upreti, 2005a: 7).

Similarly, Amnesty International in its statement of 19 December 2004 stated, *"The heightened threats occur as the international community reacts to the human rights situation with growing alarm. The UN Working Group on Enforced or Involuntary Disappearances (WGEID) concluded a visit to Nepal on Tuesday having received more reports of disappearance cases than from any other country in the world"* (Upreti, 2005a: 7).

Secretary-General of the International Commission of Jurists (ICJ) while visiting Nepal said on 30 November 2004, *"We are deeply concerned about the escalating and gross human rights abuses being committed by both sides of the conflict in Nepal. Addressing the breakdown of the rule of law cannot wait for a peace settlement. On the contrary, urgent steps can and must be taken to protect non-combatants, halt the spiralling descent into lawlessness and build the confidence for a political process"* (Upreti, 2005a: 7). According to the reports of globally reputed organisations such as ICG,

Amnesty International, the situation is further worsening after the royal takeover (AI, 2005a and 2005b; ICG, 2005).

Though the controversy on the actual number of internally displaced persons (IDP) persists, large numbers (ranging from some 25,000 in government statistics to 200,000 claimed by the non governmental sector) of IDPs are the product of armed conflict and their return, rehabilitation, resettlement, reconciliation and reintegration is yet to fully materialise. The growing phenomenon of displacement has numerous economic and social implications for host communities. Pressure in the existing basic infrastructure (such as roads, water supplies, sanitation, waste management and housing infrastructure); increasing competition for unskilled labour market and irrational exploitation of scarce natural resources of the host areas and consequent mistrust and conflict are some of the immediate effects of the internal displacement.

8.5 INSECURITY AND FEAR

Criminal activities are frequent in the study areas. Such criminal actions are in the form of small-armed groups or organised criminal groups. Robberies, petty thefts, abductions, killing, threats are some of the frequent crimes observed in the study area. Often state security forces are not able to control crimes and make people feel secure. Criminals are using the messy security situation and fragile transition as opportunity. People are in a situation of trauma from the combined effects of worsened transitional security and the resultant fear of the last decade of the armed conflict. When insecurity and fear persists in community, promoting reconciliation and reintegration encounters difficulties. Revealing truth and healing requires building confidence and trust. However, building trust and mutual respect, wilful participation and collaboration in facilitating reconciliation and reintegration is not possible. Therefore, addressing the situation of insecurity and fear at local level is one of the pre-conditions for reconciliation and reintegration.

Small arms and light weapons[39] had massively proliferated in Nepal during the time of the conflict (Upeti, 2006a). Illegal arm trading from India was becoming a lucrative business during this time. The legacy of the illegal arms trading during the last 10 years has continued and even increased in the Terai, which is posing serious security challenges. Landmines and Improvised Explosive Devices (IED) were common practices during the time of active armed conflict. Now, children and ordinary people are suffering from the left out landmines. Residual effects of small arms and landmines have greatly contributed to maintain and enhance community insecurity and obstructing confidence-building process.

Social stigmatisation and marginalisation of conflict victims (single mother with unidentified husbands' children with unidentified fathers), wounded people, etc. are still not getting a positive attitude towards conflict victims and survivors. It was reported that many women and girls were forced to have sex with fighting forces and became pregnant. However, once the fighting forces were transferred, the pregnant women were left alone. Families and society badly treated these mothers with unidentified husbands. The child is not accepted in society and thus and their lives become increasingly difficult. Wounded people, widows, children and wives with unidentified fathers and husbands are suffering from social stigmatisation, as a larger portion of Nepalese society is still patriarchal, feudal, traditional and superstitious. Providing justice, reparation and psychological rehabilitation to these especial groups of people is crucially important to promote reconciliation and reintegration.

BOX 8.3: Erosion of Social Capital

An appreciable regular practice of concerted social actions by community members such as regular cleaning repairing of trails, maintaining irrigation canals and drinking water sources, rotational grazing, financial and physical help of the members of community suffered from natural calamities or social problems were some of the examples of social capital existed in Pawoti Village Development Committee of Dolakha District. However, after the escalation of conflict, these concerted social actions are disturbed, members of society are divided and spirit of collective action is dead.

In the interaction with local people, it is known that conflict victims severely suffered from psychological troubles; from sleeplessness, talking while sleeping or terrible dreams. It was said that some of the people, particularly women, directly victimised during the time of the armed conflict are suffering from a series of mental difficulties such as pessimism, lack of interest, tiredness, and depression, loss of interest in life and consequently leading to depression. If trauma and resulting depression are not properly taken on board during the reconciliation and reintegration process, rebuilding of society is not possible. When ex-combatants/soldiers lack self-confidence and support, they may feel isolated. This can mark the beginning of a tendency to take the law into one's own hands; the consequence may be a reversal of reconciliation/reintegration and nullification of prospects for creating a harmonious society. One of the major challenges to be tackled for facilitating reconciliation and social and political reintegration is addressing a widely prevalent problem that requires technical skills, constant efforts and materials and non-material resources.

The ten years of armed conflict have severely damaged social organisation and relation patterns of Nepalese people that had existed for a long time. These social orgnaisations and relation patterns were instrumental to maintain harmony and reconciliation. Social gatherings, collective social works, cultural activities, public religious ceremonies and platforms, local social networks, etc. are some of the examples of social capital. Reviving some of these capitals is crucially important to make the R and SPR successful.

Local people are confused, frustrated and even angry with the worsening security and political situation. The participants of the focus group discussions frequently expressed their dismay, confusion and anger for the political insecurity, chaos and inaction in social and economic reforms. They were citing their higher expectations of positive development on political stability, successful completion of constituent assembly election, improving security situation and getting justice done to conflict victims and survivors. Once local people are hopeless and frustrated, it is extremely difficult to make reconciliation and social and political reintegration successful.

Conflict-induced displacement in Nepal is becoming a major concern. A recent study by the author on the relationship between IDPs and environmental issues in one of the IDPs settlement in Kathmandu Valley shows that there is severe negative impact on environment and health of IDPs (Upreti, 2007a). However, there is a need ffor a broader study to look upon the holistic analysis of IDPs and its impact of natural resources and environment.

It is realised that the local community was full of fear, mistrust, and insecurity during the time of the active armed conflict. The elderly, children, women, youth had a feeling of helplessness. Positive thinking was eroded and social psychology of the society was shaped by war, fights and killing. Communal harmony, trusts and social bonds were severely eroded (Upreti, 2006a).

A quick public perception on impacts of armed conflict in their society was documented from local communities of Chitwan, Nawalparasi, Kaski, Myagdi and Mustang districts during the field work from 12 to 25 August 2007. Responses of more than 300 people during the perception assessment are summarised as bellow:

- Insecurity: fear, anxiety, suspension, intimidation, distrust and frustration
- Rapid displacement (physical, political and social) at both levels (forced and voluntary displacement)
- Deep polarisation of society (ethnic, political and other divide)
- Breaking of traditional bonds and social relations
- Erosion of trust and credibility of government because of its failure to provide security
- Ruining of their livelihoods and earnings
- Disturbance on exercising their religious, customary and social activities
- Restriction on access to health, educations and other basic services

- Physical violence (abduction, physical injuries, killing, sexual abuses, etc.) and damage of properties
- Psychological effects (tension, shock and mental disability)
- Restriction on mobility
- Obstruction in social and economic development of their areas.

Local people reported that gender roles and social relations in the villages had drastically changed in the conflict-affected areas (Upreti, 2006a). Because of displacement of male people from the villages, the conventional roles of men and women have changed. For example, women have started to plough land in absence of their male members of family, which was culturally forbidden. Women are also engaged in other functions previously performed by male members such as representing in meetings and discussions, attending funerals, dealing with outsiders (e.g. security forces or insurgents). This has empowered women but also added the extra work burden to them in the community. The number of single women has increased due to the armed conflict. Majority of them have difficulty in securing access to government compensation, basic rights and resources such as land, public services, etc.

Significant reduction of public services (health, education, transport, market, employment, etc.) was observed during the time of the Maoist insurgency, mainly due to the fear and insecurity, reduction of transport of goods because of the blockade, *bands*, general and transport strikes, curfews and restriction on mobility. Similarly, dead bodies of the people killed in the areas of attacks such as Pili, Beni, Solukhumbu, Dang, etc. were thrown away in water sources, rivers and forests and the decomposed bodies were creating pollution around the deposed areas.

One of the severe consequences of the armed conflict was the livelihood insecurity of conflict-affected people. The notion of livelihood is complex in its scope, nature and understanding. Generally, livelihood comprises the capabilities, assets (both material and social resources) and activities required for a means of living. Livelihood is sustainable when it can cope with and recover from stresses and shocks and maintain or enhance its capabilities and assets both now and in the future, while not undermining the natural resource base (Chambers and Conway, 1992). Livelihoods of Nepalese people become better when:

a) They have access to basic rights established through international conventions. If they access to high-quality education, information, technologies and training and better nutrition and health;
b) Supportive and cohesive social environment;
c) Secure access to, and better management of, natural resources;
d) Better access to basic and facilitating infrastructure, and financial resources; and
e) A policy and institutional environment that supports multiple livelihood strategies and promotes equitable access to competitive markets for all (DFID, 1999).

But the current livelihood situation of poor, marginalized and socially excluded people of Nepal based on these criteria was highly insecure and vulnerable.

Employment generations, ensuring access to means of production and provisions of safety net measures are some of the main responsibilities of the state towards its citizens, particularly to the poor, landless, marginalized, women, dalit,

TABLE 8.11: Number of Households and Food Sufficiency Situation

Household characteristics (food insufficiency situation)	*Total no. of holdings*	*Number of land holding*
Total holdings	3364139 (100%)	26700 (100%)
Sufficient to feed household	1337965 (39.8%)	1728 (6.5%)
Not sufficient to feed household	2026174 (60.2%)	24972 (93.5%)
• 1-3 months insufficient	439592 (21.7%)	755 (3%)
• 4-6 months insufficient	877362 (43.3%)	2250 (9%)
• 7-9 months insufficient	342039 (16.9%)	2275 (9.1%)
• 10-12 months insufficient	357544 (16.6%)	19633 (78.6%)

Source: CBS 2004 (Table 2.32, Pp-104-107)

disables. However, despite the vulnerable state of the poor and marginalized, Table 8.11 shows that the state has refrained from discharging these responsibilities.

If the state has failed to secure food for more than 60 per cent of households and more than 16 per cent households of Nepal have food insecurity all round the year, where is the responsibility of the state to secure livelihoods of its citizen and how they feel the ownership of state? When the state is refraining from its responsibility, citizen will be further alienated, which potentially leads to conflict.

8.6 CONSEQUENCE ON DEVELOPMENT

The 10 years of armed conflict of Nepal shows that there are several negative impacts of conflict on development. The negative impacts of conflict on development are widely reported (Upreti, 2006a; Gersony, 2003; Howel et al., 2005; Hutt, 2004; Kumar, 2004; Matthew and Upreti 2005a) and special tools and techniques of analysis have been documented.[40] All development interventions do not necessarily contribute to achieving the stated objectives. They may have fuelled conflict directly through imposing different conditions or creating cleavage in community and/or indirectly through involuntary transfer of resources, information or disturbing local mechanisms. Therefore, every development programme/project has to critically examine their positive and negative contribution to conflict.

Destruction of basic development infrastructure, such as VDC buildings, range posts, bridges, roads, schools, electricity, drinking water, telephone, etc. is widespread. After the ceasefire break in August 2003, the CPN (M) in different districts informally announced, 'no development without political settlement'. Serious violation of human rights from the warring parties, using villagers as human shield and arbitrary arrests of general public were common across Nepal (AI, 2005a and b; INSEC, 2005). United Nations Working Group on Enforced and Involuntary Disappearance on 1st March 2005 stated that in 2003-2004 Nepal scored highest in the world for new cases of disappearance.

It has been globally observed that development contributes both positively and negatively (Anderson, 1999). It involuntarily transfers resources to fuel conflict, creates high but unfulfilled expectations of people, different approaches adopted by development agencies lead to confusion, contradiction and conflict in community, its interventions ruin indigenous systems. Similarly, it has been observed that external development interventions concentrate on accessible area that develops feeling of exclusion of people and ultimately non cooperation and even revenge. Donor-funded development projects create perception of inequality and grievances due to the use of expensive vehicles, computers, better pays and expensive life style of project staff, which provides evidences or at least feeling that international aid serves the privileged group instead of needy poor. Donor-dominated development projects create dependency and decrease government incentives to mobilise internal resources and distorts local production and exchange system. In the case of Nepal's development practices, it is often observed that development aids provided by the international community has contributed to conspicuous consumption of elites of Kathmandu and accessible areas and very little has trickled down to the rural poor. In addition to these general negative impacts of development, there could be several specific sectoral impacts of violent conflict on: migration and internal displacement; people's livelihoods; public services; health, education; transport; market; employment; agriculture and forestry; tourism and others.

Similarly, there could be several negative impacts of conflict on development. Conflict increases insecurity. It pulls development budget for security expenditures, disrupts development services and distracts people from development activities. Another devastating negative effect of conflict is destruction of development infrastructure. It also abuses rights of people to take part in development activities.

Conflict not only creates negative impacts but also positively contributes to development sector. Conflict empowers marginalised and excluded people and helps to develop a sense of self-identity (e.g. Dalit movement, Terai movement, Janajati movement), enhances conflict sensitisation, strengthens feeling of group responsibility for community building and exerts pressure to decrease discrimination and forces for social reform. Similarly, it creates new opportunities (Upreti, 2007g).

Development also positively contributes to transform conflict or minimise negative effects of conflict on society. It rise awareness and facilitate empowerment of target population. It addresses the root causes of conflict. It promotes economic activities and contributes to reduce poverty. It offers peace-building activities. It supports advocacy and networking organisations to end conflict and resortore peace. It promotes

TABLE 8.12: Damages of Physical Infrastructure during the Armed Conflict

S.N.	*Ministries and constitutional commissions*	*Damages worth*	*Cost required for reconstruction*
1	Local Development	596446000	161722000
2	Water Resources	342703000	297243000
3	Health and Population	417000	130130000
4	Forest and Soil Conservation	354461000	377123000
5	Education and Sports	20960000	44984000
6	Agriculture and Cooperatives	260755000	00
7	Industry, Commerce and Supplies	18123000	15064000
8	Environment, Science and Technology	3209000	00
9	Information and Communication	741555000	145166000
10	Culture, Tourism and Civil Aviation	134747000	26550000
11	Physical Planning and Works	25174000	19746000
12	Land Reform and Management	12187000	00
13	Defense	24799000	00
14	Finance	4666000	2270000
15	Home	2428646000	2428203000
16	Women, Children and Social Welfare	230000	00
17	Supreme Court	27489000	165555000
18	Election Commission	2946000	00
19	Office of Attorney General	201000	00
20	Public Service Commission	4780000	00
21	Total	5004494000	3813756000

Source: Ministry of Peace and Reconstruction, 2007.

access of poor people to development benefits and helps to develop skills of target population to resolve conflict.

Development infrastructures damaged during the time of armed conflict: It is extremely difficult to find the actual quantity and types of infrastructures damaged by the decade-long insurgency in the country. However, the following are some of the main categories of infrastructures damaged during the period of armed conflict:

Table 8.12 shows the estimate of the value of damage of property during the time of the armed conflict and the amount needed for the reconstruction of the damaged infrastructures. The total destruction was estimated at about 5 billion rupees worth, out of which 3.8 billion rupees is required to reconstruct and the damages worth of 1.2 billion rupees has already been reconstructed. Damage of physical infrastructures was one of the main strategies of the CPN (M) during their 'people's war'. Even they have targeted infrastructures related to basic services such as health, education, drinking water. Most of these offices were damaged while CPN (M) raided district headquarters, or scattered attack on the individual offices.

End Notes

1. This section is an outcome of the post-conflict environmental assessment, which was funded by the United Nations Environment Programme - Regional Office for Asia and Pacific (UNEP-ROAP). I would like to thank WWF Nepal and UNEP for giving me the responsibility to conduct assessmsnt on impact of armed confilcit on biodiversity and natural resources.
2. See www.BSPonline.org for detail about the Biodiversity Support Programme and its publications related to impacts of war on biodiversity.
3. See VEFOR: Options for Forest Verification, June 2006 Issue 'Country Case Study No. 10 entitled Forest Product Verification in Nepal and the work of the Commission to Investigate the Abuse of Authority' for details.
4. *The Himalayan Times*, 14 May 2007.
5. For example, Kuwepani CFUG filed a case against Rajpur Barrack Dipayal in Supreme Count of Nepal. See Supreme Court Bulletin, Year 9, No, 23, Issue 109, 2057 for the decision of the Supreme Court.

6. For example, massive aerial bombarding in the community forests areas of bordering between Nawalparasi, Arghakhanchi, Palpa and Tanahun by military immediately after the attack of Beni, the headquarters of the Myagdi district by CPN (M). Consequently, the fires in these forests remained for weeks. Similar attacks were made by the military in many hilly and mountain districts during the time of armed conflict.
7. See Khanal (2006) for details.
8. Districts attacked by CPN (M) in the eastern region are Sankhuwasabha, Solukhumbu, Okhaldhunga, Morang, Bhojpur, Siraha, Udayapur, Ilam, Tehrathum, Taplejung, Khotang, Panchthar, Sunsari, Saptari, Jhapa and Dhankuta.
9. Distracts attacked by CPN (M) in the central region are Rasuwa, Rautahat, Ramechhap, Sarlahi, Dolakha, Makawanpur, Mahotari, Nuwakot, Sindhupalchowk, Sindhuli, Chitwan, Kavrepalanchowk, Dhading, Parsa, Bara and Bhaktapur.
10. Districts attacked by CPN (M) in the Western region are Syangja, Rupandehi, Baglung, Myagdi, Palpa, Parbat, Arghakhanchi, Lamjung, Kapilvastu, Tanahun, Gorkha, Gulmi, Nawalparasi.
11. Districts attacked by CPN (M) in the Mid-Western region are Rolpa, Salyan, Surkhet, Banke, Bardiya, Dailekh, Dang, Mugu, Pyuthan, Kalikot, Jajarkot, Jumla.
12. Districts attacked by CPN (M) in the Far-Western region are Dadeldhura, Doti, Baitadi, Bajura, Darchula, Accham, Kailali, Kanchanpur.
13. See *The Rising Nepal* of 28 September 2007 for detail.
14. In the Fiscal Year 2003-2004 26.6 million rupees were collected by the government as revenue from NTFP but last year only 15.9 million rupees only.
15. Reported by *Nepal National Weekly*, 1st May 2005, Vol. 5, No. 37.
16. The brokers severely exploit local collectors. For example, brokers pay 80 thousands rupees (app. 1127 US $) per kg but they sell it on 1.5 to 2 million rupees (2113 to 2817 US $) per kg.
17. The respondents were ordinary farmers; small growers; traders and marketers as well as rural landlords and local elites who left their villages due to insecurity and stayed in Kathmandu. The interview with them was conducted in 2006 January-February.
18. See *Samaya Weekly*, *Nepal Weekly* and *Himal Fortnightly* for the detail story on how CPN (M) are controlling the protected areas. These news magazines have also reported that government staff are absent in some of the parks or reserves since 2 years.
19. Different issues of *HakkahakiPatrika* (an environmental magazine

published by the Nepalese Forum of Environmental Journalists) have extensively reported the terrible impacts of the ongoing armed conflict on environment, natural resource and protected areas.

20. The details of the damage record compiled by DNPWC (2007) weres provided by Yuva Raj Rgmi, Chief Warden of Makalu Barun National Park on 11 July 2007.
21. In the Shivapuri National Park (SNP) the CPN (M) destroyed six security posts at Rolche, Chisapani (16 September 2003), Dhap, Cha-gaun, Kakani (28 September 2003) and Pharsechaur.
22. Before starting the armed conflict, the RNA had 15 security posts (Harre, Chepang, Betahani, Asneri, Dhakaiya, Rammapur, Parewa Wodar, Sainabar, Amreni, Gola, Danavtal, Badhi, Babai Valley, Eastern Chisapeni and Thakurdwara) in the BNP. There were also 15 guard posts run by park administration (Chepang, Betahani, Thumani, Rammapur, Sainawar, Bhurigaun, Motipur, Lalmati, Karnali Chisapani, Banjariya, Banakhet, Khairapur, eastern Chisapani and Thakurdwara). The advancement of the CPN (M) movement forced the army to reduce its posts to five from 15 (Eastern Chisapani, Thakurdwara, Karnali Chisapani, Rammapur and Harre). Bardiya park administration withdrew six posts.
23. It is spread over 130 wards of 22 VDCs of 4 districts with approximately 16 thousand people inhabit the area.
24. The 1569.84 sq. km area of Achham (6 VDCs), Bajura (2 VDCs), Doti (5 VDCs) and Bajhang (9 VDCs) districts was declared as intermediate region in 1995. The intermediate region comprises 20 community forests organized by 17 consumer groups.
25. The fur of antelope is used to produce expensive shawls.
26. In the year 2001, 14 offenders were arrested in the Reserve, 13 for illegal logging and 1 for poaching of a chital. In 2002, 11 offenders were arrested for 6 cases of illegal logging, 1 for poaching a chital, 1 for poaching a golden monitor lizard, *suna gohoro*, (*Varanus flavescens*), and 3 incidents of illegal excavation of boulders and sand. In 2003, there were 11 incidents of logging timber, 1 poaching of a Suna gohoro, 1 incident of herb trafficking and 5 incidents of sand and boulder trafficking. Offenders of 13 incidents were jailed. In 2004, 13 incidents were recorded, including 9 cases of illegal logging, 1 of poaching, 2 of herb trafficking and 1 of boulder trafficking. Within the last year, 2005, perpetrators of 2 herb trafficking and 2 logging offences were arrested.
27. On 23 November 2001, two posts at Tarapur were torched. On 24 November 2001, they set fire to Dhakka, Beldandi and

Wadanikheda range posts. On 22 April 2002, they burnt down Champhapur security post and on 21 August 2003 Arjuni post and on 16tMarch 2004 the Jhilamila post were destroyed.

28. This study was conducted by UNDP Energy, Environment, and Disaster Mitigation Unit in January 2007 as a part of a multi-agency assessment of the seven central cantonment sites for the Communist Party of Nepal-Maoist (CPNM) People's Liberation Army (PLA).
29. See (i) Government of Nepal - Ministry of Forest and Soil Conservation. (2004). *Terai Arc Landscape: Strategic Plan 2004 - 2014.* Kathmandu, Nepal: Ministry of Forest and Soil Conservation; and (ii) Dinerstein, E., Louckes, C., Heydlauff, E., Wikramanayake, E., Bryja, G., Forrest, J., Ginsberg, S., Klenzendorf, S., Leimgruber, P., O'Brien, T., Sanderson, E., Seidensticker, J., Songer, M. (2006). *Setting Priorities for the Conservation and Recovery of Wild Tigers: 2005 – 2015. A User's Guide.* Washington, DC: WWF for detail about the priority environmental sites.
30. Calculation based on 5 people requiring 10 kg of firewood a day ration.
31. Dinerstein, E., Louckes, C., Heydlauff, E., Wikramanayake, E., Bryja, G., Forrest, J., Ginsberg, S., Klenzendorf, S., Leimgruber, P., O'Brien, T., Sanderson, E., Seidensticker, J., Songer, M. (2006). Setting *Priorities for the Conservation and Recovery of Wild Tigers: 2005 – 2015. A User's Guide.* Washington, DC: WWF.
32. Interviewed with Mr Ganesh Bahadur Parajuli, Mr. Prit Singh Karki (district chair of FECOFUN and Mr Min Bahadur Karki from Chainpur VDC-5, Gotheshwor on 18 August 2007.
33. Interviewe with Mr Bodh Raj Adhikari on 18 August 2007.
34. For example, Section 20 of Land Administration Act, 1967 prohibits cultivation of any land area which has been used since time immemorial as a road, highway, grazing land, waterholes, public resting hut, cemetery, graveyard and any other land area or servitude land which has been used for public purposes. on the contrary, there is no provision in the Schedule 2 of Rule 4(1) of WRR to have entry permission to perform religious practices and funeral rites/rituals in reserve area (Belbase and Thapa, 2004).
35. The study team observed uncontrolled logging in the *Deurali Danda* (border between Ghandruk and Sikha VDCs) areas during the time of field study (12-25 August 2007) and some parts of Rolpa district (28 June to 1 July 2007).
36. For details see the Section 4 of the UNEP (2003b).

37. Bara, Parsa, Rautahat, Mahottari, Dhanusha, Sarlahi, Siraha and Saptari districts.
38. Jhapa, Morang, Sunsari, Makwanpur, Chitwan, Nawalparasi, Rupandehi, Kapilbastu18, Dang, Banke, Bardiya, Kailali and Kanchanpur districts.
39. The United Nations Institute for Disarmament Research (UNIDIR) defines small arms and light weapons as all conventional weapons that can be carried by an individual or by a light vehicle. These weapons do not require an extensive logistical and maintenance capability. Small arms include pistols, rifles, sub-machine guns, machine guns and ammunition. Light weapons (in addition to small arms) include: small-calibre cannons, grenades, landmines, mortars, light anti-tank weapons, anti-tank mines, shoulder-fired anti-aircraft missiles and ammunition.
40. The detail can be found in the book entitled 'Conflict Management in Natural Resources: A Study of Land, Water and Forest Conflicts in Nepal' (Upreti, 2001), Development in Conflict: A Seven Step Tool for Planners (2001), Conflict Impact Assessment: A Practical Working Tool for Prioritising Development Assistance in Unstable Situation, (1999) and Working with Conflict: Skills and Strategy for Action (2000).

Chapter 9

Women's Role in Nepal's Peace Process[1]

9.1 THE CONTEXT

Transformation of Nepal's conflict into durable peace and democracy requires not only sensitively dealing with the existing fragile transition situation and concrete delivery of peace dividends to conflict victims, survivors but also acknowledging the potential of women's contribution and involving them in the process of peaceful decision making.

In general, peace refers to the state of social, psychological, physical, and spiritual well being of an individual. However, in the context of Nepal, peace is a state of restoring normal relations between people and between institutions directly and or indirectly affected by the 10 years of armed conflict, leading to well being. Achieving peace requires inclusion of women and an appropriate process that deals with the past and envisions a better future by generating hope and aspiration. It can be achieved by getting the process right, having a gender-sensitive approach in the monitoring mechanism, sincere implementation of understandings and agreements, appropriately dealing with past and ensuring transitional justice and rule of law, guaranteeing transitional security, holding free and fair elections, proper facilitation of disarming, demobilizing and reintegration and restructuring of the security sector.

Nepal is in a fragile transition to peace. This country has experienced severe armed insurgency for a decade. The major causes of the conflict were related to structural inequality, exclusion and discrimination (caste, class, gender, geographical), concentration and abuse of power, poverty and unemployment, failure of state governing system, and ideologies. The armed conflict not only took the lives of more than thirteen thousand people and caused damage to infrastructure worth billions of rupees but also paved the path for transformation of a feudal, centralized, monarchical unitary state into a modern, inclusive, federal republican state.

Nepal's peace process is in fact widely praised for its fast and substantial progress. However, it has not only been equally criticised for its failure to deliver the promises made but also for adopting exclusionary practices (not properly involving women, Dalits, Janajaties and other concerned stakeholders in the process) (Upreti and Ghimire, 2008).

Success of peace process depends upon the right process, right representation of concerned stakeholders and translation of the promises made into action and the external cooperation (Upreti and Karna, 2007). So far, leaders have shown willingness to make peace process successful but failed to internalise the need of widely expected inclusion of women and other stakeholders, recognising the importance of process element and providing peace dividends to the Nepalese people (Upreti, 2008a; 2008b; 2008c). Instead, they have been whole-heartedly involved in the power struggle and vested political interest. In this paper I am limiting the discussion mainly to the various issues of women's participation in the peace process.

9.2 ROLE OF WOMEN IN PEACE PROCESS: INTERNATIONAL PRACTICES AND SUCCESS STORIES

Experiences around the world have demonstrated that women can play important roles in all elements of the peace process, such as: (a) implementation of UNSCR 1325, (b) crisis management, (c) negotiation and conflict management, (d) peace talks and agreements, (e) post-conflict transitional management (transitional security and transitional justices and (f) post-conflict reconstruction and rehabilitation.

Women could play a crucial role in the peace process. The experiences of various war-ridden countries have proved that women's qualitative engagement is crucially essential to make the peace process successful. Several examples and success stories are documented on the contribution of women in peace building and post-conflict reconstruction[2] in various parts of the world (Upreti, 2006a; Rehn & Sirleaf 2002; Baechler et al., 2008; ICG, 2006, Bloomfield 2003; Agustiana & Pakpohan 2004 and Anderson 1999).

If we look at the history of women's initiations to promote peace, women have demonstrated novel examples. One of the prime examples is International Congress of Women (popularly known as ICW) where more than a thousand people gathered in the Hague in April 1915 from the European countries entangled in the First World War with the specific aim of ending the bloody war. They vehemently demanded to end the war and universal disarmament, and more important, they demanded creation of a non-partisan international agency to mediate in inter-state conflict (Rehn and Sirleaf, 2002). This means they must have already envisioneded a UN-like body in 1915.

A comparative study conducted by International Crisis group (ICG) in Sudan, Democratic Republic of Congo and Uganda concludes that "*women can make peace agreements and post-conflict efforts more viable, effective and practical by engaging in a wide verity of actions, including but not limited to participating in peace talks; rehabilitating children associated with armed groups; convening people across conflict lines to discuss common concerns such as access to clean water; and advocating budget priorities that emphasised social services rather than military expenditures*" (ICG, 2006:1). This statement clearly demonstrates the potential of women in peace building. However, internalisation of strengths of women in the peace process is largely ignored.

Similarly, a comprehensive study of women's role in peace building was conducted by UNIFEM, entitled 'Independent Experts' Assessment on the Impact of Armed Conflict on Women and Women's Role in Peace Building-Progress' (Rehn and Sirleaf, 2002). The publication coming from this study has extensively documented the role of women in building peace and the difficulties women faced from the wars. Several examples and individual stories documented in this study give a comprehensive understanding of women's contribution in restoring peace.

The thematic assessment on women's role in peace building in Central Sulawesi and North Malhku (Agustiana and Pakpahan 2004) demonstrates that women are not only conflict victims or combatants but also peace builders, decision makers and peace leaders. Some of the women organisations, such as (i) Central Sulawesi Group of struggle for Women's Equality located in Palu and Poso (ii) Poso Women's Cooperation Forum (iii) Poso Women Empowerment Office (iv) Central Sulawesi Women and Children's Care Activists Group (v) Dorkas Women's Cooperatives in Kawua, (vi) Women's solidarity in Palu (vii) Indonesian Women's Coalitions played an important role in peace building.

Similarly, the Resolution 1325 unanimously passed by the Security Council of the UN in 31 October 2000 has provided a strong framework for dealing with women, peace and security. It gave a clear perspective and areas of focus to mainstream a gender perspective into the peace process by acknowledging the fact that civilians, particularly women and children, are adversely afflicted by armed conflict.

The UNIFEM took the lead in facilitating the implementation of the Resolution 1325. In 2002 it had published a very comprehensive report entitled "Women, War and Peace: The Independent Experts' Assessment on the Impact of Armed Conflict on Women and Women's Role in Peace building", which analyzes the disproportionate impact of armed conflict and violence on women and children and explores the ways and procedures for involving women in the peace process. This is one of the important documents that provide information on how the changing nature of violence is affecting the dignity of women as the increasing use of rape as a weapon of war.

One of the main messages of this report is that peace agreements work better when women are involved in the peace process. Based on extensive reviews and documentation, it highlights that a critical mass of women, and not merely token representation, in negotiation and peace talks not only improves the quality of agreements reached but also equally or even more important, increases chances of implementing peace accords.

Rwanda experienced terrible genocide in the mid-1990s and created a humanitarian crisis with grave human rights violation. The population composition (74 per cent women and 26 per cent men) of the country was altered by the genocide and it has still not fully recovered (54 per cent women and 46 per cent men). Women were instrumental in coping with this tragic reality. Hence, it developed a new legal framework and established a 'Gender Desk' within the Ministry of Law' to deal with the issues related to impacts of war on women. With the constant effort of this Desk, the Rwandan government had made inheritance and marriage laws. Further, from the constant efforts of women the Justice and Reconciliation Committee (JRC) had added women members in its structure. There was serious criticism of the JRC that it had female judges to look into women cases and humiliation to female witnesses. Now, Rwanda is one of the few counties having a high percentage of women in parliament and other state structures (the election completed after the genocide was able to elect more than 48 per cent women in the parliament). Various small and large initiatives of women held bring a large portion of women in parliament. One of them was AVEGA (an association of widows of Rwanda genocide). It became active not only to help conflict victims but also to protect women and in political participation.

The Mano River Union Women's Network for Peace was another novel initiative started by women from Guinea, Liberia and Sierra Leone who was successful to influence at political level in the three countries. It was working both at grass-root and national and regional level. It was one of the instrumental forces to end the war in Sierra Leone. Because of its strength, the Mano River Union Women's Network for Peace became part of the Federation of African Women's Peace Networks (FERFAP), who is collaborating with UNIFEM and other organisations for building peace in Africa.

In Somalia, women were constantly struggling to include in the political structures and they were able to obtain 25 seats of the 245 seats in the Transitional National Assembly. In East

Timor a 30 per cent quota was assigned for women in the new parliament and 267 women candidates took part in the election.

In Afghanistan the American government was insisting on participation of women in peace process. Women's issues were placed at the top of the agenda. Media were also mobilised to highlight the role of women. Continuous efforts are still ongoing to ensure the mainstreaming of gender in various ministries and projects, and ensuring that the new constitution guarantees equal rights for men and women. The economic and physical security of Afghan women is clearly linked to peace and security in Afghanistan itself, as well as to its economic growth.

Several initiatives of women have contributed to achieving peace in their countries. A good lesson can be learnt from the work of Women in Black (a Serbian women peace group) who organized peace-loving women and came to peaceful street protest (they silently stood in front of government offices with play cards to denounce violence and calling for peace) despite the coercive response of the government and they became successful to make government listening to their voices. WNIFEM in collaboration with other international organizations awarded them the Millennium Peace Award as recognition of their hard work to establish peace in their country. The AVEGA (an association of Rwandan widows) not only provided psychological support to the conflict victims but also raised a constant voice to address the detrimental impacts created by the genocide to society.

Women were important actors of peace in Northern Namibia (Becker, 2003), building peace and resolution of conflict in Morogoro Region of Tanzania (Lihamba, 2003), prevention of conflict and promotion of peace in Central African Republic (Mathey et al., 2003), Somalia (Mohamed, 2003) and Burundi (Ntahobari, and Ndayiziga, 2003).

Africa is also well known for the involvement of women in traditional mediation practice in resolving conflicts. Women had very actively engaged in traditional mediation of the conflict in Cameroon (Ngongo-Mbede, 2003).

Women have played a very constructive role in healing and reconciliation in the conflict in Zimbabwe (Ranger, 1992). The work of Schmidt (1997) on women's role in healing the wounds of war in Zimbabwe is notable. UNESCO (2003) has extensively documented women's role in peace-building in Africa particularly focusing to cases on traditional conflict resolutions practices.

A study of by Miriam Agatha Chinwe Nwoye from Department of Philosophy and Religious Studies of Kenyatta University of Nairobi Kenya have extensively documented[3] role of women in Africa. She argued that in view of the innate qualities of women and their position in society, women can and must be actively involved in conflict prevention and resolution, peace process, as peace envoys and delegations.

9.3 ANALYSIS OF THE EXISTING NEPAL'S PEACE PROCESS

Though the CPA reaffirms the commitments to the 12-point and 8-point agreements, and 25-point code of conduct between the seven parties and the CPN (M); decisions taken during the meeting of the top leaders of the seven parties and the Maoist on November 8 along with other agreements, understandings, code of conducts and letter sent to the United Nations stating identical viewpoints by the CPN (M) and the Nepal government; the implementation process in either weak or selective (Upreti, 2004a; 2006a).

It has also pledged for progressive restructuring of the state by resolving prevailing problems related with class, ethnicity, regional and gender differences, and reiterated firm commitments to civil liberties, Universal Declaration of Human Rights 1948 and other international humanitarian laws and values and principles of the human rights, press freedom, rule of law. The implementation of these commitments is also partial. On the Article 1.3, it states that 'both the sides shall issue directives to all the agencies under them to follow and implement this agreement immediately. However, the agencies under them have only partly respected these provisions of the CPA.

In the Article 3.7, CPA states provision of land reform 'End feudal land ownership and formulate the policies for scientific land reforms' and in the Article 3.10, it states, 'Adopt policies to provide land and socio-economic security to backward groups like landless, bonded labourers, tillers, Haruwa-charuwa and other such groups, which are socio-economically backward'. Land has been one of the source prime sources of unequal power relations in Nepalese society and women are the victim of land-based power structures (Ghale, 2008) but no action has been taken so far in implementing the Article 3.7 of the CPA.

Management of PLA and their integration into security structures and democratization of Nepal Army is becoming one of the few main controversies and problems in peace process as this sensitive but important issue is very much used as a bargaining tool by political actors. The Article 4.4 of the CPA states, 'The interim cabinet shall form a special committee to carry out monitoring, integration and rehabilitation of the Maoist combatants' and the Article 4.7 states 'The cabinet would control, mobilise and manage the Nepali Army as per the new Military Act. The interim cabinet would prepare and implement the detailed action plan of democratisation of the Nepali Army by taking suggestions from the concerned committee of the interim parliament. This includes works like determination of the right number of the Nepali Army, prepare the democratic structure reflecting the national and inclusive character, and train them on democratic principles and human rights values'. However not much has been done so far in this important element of peace process (Upreti and Karna, 2007).

The human rights section of the CPA (Article 7.1.3) states, 'Both parties express their commitment and state that necessary investigation will be undertaken against any individual involved in violating the rights mentioned in the agreement and action will be taken against ones that are found guilty. Both parties also ascertain that they will not protect impunity and along with it, the rights of the people affected by the conflict and torture and the families of the people who have been disappeared will be safeguarded'. This provision is not fully implemented.

The above brief review of implementation of provisions

stated in the CPA clearly shows that a lot has to be done to make the peace process successful in Nepal. One of the main causes of the weak action could be lack of participation of women in the decision and implementation process.

9.3.1 Content

The content of negotiation and peace talks and provisions of agreements and understanding must address specific issues of women, children, elderly people, and conflict victims.

Making the peace process successful also requires promoting accountability for war crimes committed against women. Ensuring justice and re-establishing the rule of law in society is essential for achieving peace in society.

In any peace process, participation of women makes it sustainable and reduces possibility of inadequate outcomes or failure of entire process.

Any peace process should be able to address specific problems of different groups of conflict victims. They can be grouped into (a) families of people killed, (b) abducted people and their families, (c) internally displaced people and their families, (d) missing people and their families, (e) injured or wounded people, and other generally affected people. Similarly, different age and gender groups of conflict victims such children, adult, old elderly people and women require specific focus. Dealing with the problems related to these conflict victims requires special efforts. Representation of women in making decisions related to these people is utmost essential.

Women's role is in reconciliation is crucial. Reconciliation being a process of process of searching for justice, healing, and forgiveness, pattern of cooperation and coexistence, women could play important role in these issues by helping conflict victims to address their needs, fears, and aspirations and rebuilding the broken relationships. Women could be equally important to facilitate reintegration of conflict victims. Reintegration is a complex psychological, social, political, and economic process of mainstreaming conflict victims as active members of either their communities or new communities and becoming active producers in civilian life, where women could play a fundamental role. Women have to be involved in the repatriation- rehabilitation-resettlement package because they know the need of women, children more than their male partners do.

9.3.2 Structures

As observed in different negotiations of violent conflict in different parts of the world, a fully mandated, strong, committed, and gender-balanced negotiation team is one of the important operational factors in making negotiation successful. Further, support of major stakeholders (civil society, political parties, women activists, dalit, business community, expert groups, etc.) becomes crucial. Unless there is a clear mechanism to bring local concerns and voices of people into the peace process, elite-centric gender-blind composition of negotiation and peace process team cannot ensure sustainable peace process.

Article 8.4 of the CPA contains important structures required for making the peace process successful. Some of them are: The National Peace and Rehabilitation Commission, the Truth and Reconciliation Commission, the High-level State Restructuring Recommendation Commission and other mechanisms as per the need to implement this agreement, the Interim Constitution and all the decisions, agreements and understandings reached between the SPA,, the Government of Nepal, and the CPN (M) (8.4). While forming these structures, proportional representation of women enhances chance of making peace process successful. Ensuring key stakeholders' inclusion in these structures (such as Dalit, Madeshi, Janajaties, conflict victims) is a key to make peace process a success.

If I examine the physical involvement of women in the negotiation and peace talk team and nominated a list of facilitators in the paste, it is quite discouraging. No single woman was assigned or trusted to be the facilitator. In the first round of peace talks two respected male facilitators were assigned but no additional female members included in the facilitators team. In the second time peace talks there more were added in the previous two but all men. Again in the third time

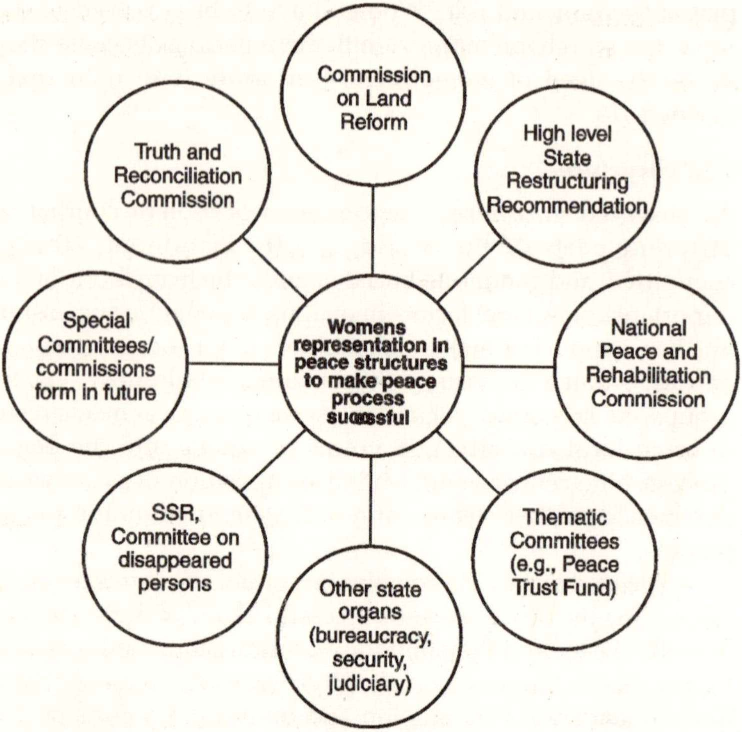

FIGURE 9.1: *Women's Qualitative and Informed Participation in Possible Peace Structures*

talk five members facilitator (rather observer this time) team was formed by the government but no woman included again. Similarly, there were no women negotiators from both sides in peace talks except in first part of the 2003 peace talks where government had appointed one woman as member (see Table 9.1) but her role was quite limited.

9.4 PROBLEMS, CHALLENGES AND WAYS AHEAD

Nepal's peace process in general and the participation of women in the peace process in particular has faced several problems and challenges. The patriarchal social structures and power relations are obvious in hindering meaningful and qualitative participation of women in Nepal's peace process. In fact, key political decision makers never realized the importance of

TABLE 9.1: Composition of the Negotiation Team and Facilitators in Nepal's Peace Process

1. Peace Talk team 2001:	2. Peace Talk team 2003
1A. The Government Side:	**2A. The Government Side:**
Mr. Chiranjivi Wagley Convenor	Mr. Badri Prasad Mandal Convenor
Mr. Mahesh Acharya Member	Mr. Ramesh Nath Pandey Member
Mr. Chakra P. Bastola Member	Mr. Kamal Prasad Choulagai Member
Mr. Vijay K. Gachhadar Member	Mr. Narayan Singh Pun Member
Mr Narahari Acharya	Dr. Upendra Devkota Member
	Ms. Anuradha Koirala Member
	=========================
1B. The CPN (M) Side:	(Once the government was changed on 4 June 2003, new PM Surya Bahadur Thapa appointed new negotiators)
Mr. Krishna Bahadur Mahara Convener	Dr. Prakash Chandra Lohani, Convenor
Mr. Top Bahadur Rayamajhi Member	Mr. Kamal Thapa, Member
Mr. Agni Prasad Sapkota Member	**2B. CPN (M) side:**
	Dr. Baburam Bhattarai Convenor
	Mr. Ram Bahadur Thapa (Badal) Member
	Mr. Krishna Bahadur Mahara Member
	Mr. Dev Gurung Member
	Mr. Matrika Yadav Member
	=========================
	Once the government was changed on 4 June 2003 and new PM changed negotiators the Maoist also refined it as:
	Dr. Baburam Bhattarai Convenor
	Mr. Krishna Bahadur Mahara Member
Facilitators 2001:	**Facilitators 2003:**
Mr. Padmaratna Tuladhar	Mr. Damannath Dhungana
Mr. Damannath Dhungana	Mr. Padmaratna Tuladhar
	Mr. Shailendra Kumar Upadhyaya
	Mr. Karnadhwaj Adhikary

3A. The Maoist team (10 May 2006)	**3. The 2006 Negotiators The Government (19 May 2006):**
Mr. Krishna Bahadur Mahara Convenor	Mr. Krishna Prasad Sitaula Convener
Mr. Dinanath Sharma Member	Mr. Pradip Gyawali Member
Mr. Dev Gurung Member	Mr. Ramesh Lekhak Member
	Observers:
	Mr. Padmaratna Tuladhar
	Mr. Damannath Dhungana
	Mr Laxman Prasad Aryal
	Mr Devendra Raj Pandey
	Mr Marhura Prasad Shrestha

Source: Compiled by author from different sources.

qualitative engagement of women in decision-making structures of peace process

Another problem lies with the women themselves. Nepalese elite women are too divided (politically, socially and psychologically). Most of them are heavily guided by the parties' political agenda at the cost of common interests. I am not arguing that political party worker women should not work for the interest of their party. My argument is that they have to be bold enough to come for common cause. For example, two women were presented as the candidate of Vice President Election in CA. However, both of them were used as tool for bargaining. Neither the women CA members from all parties nor the civil society leaders stood firmly behind them. Women CA members themselves did not vote to women candidate. One can argue that it was special situation or there were efforts but not successful. May be! Nevertheless, I am not convinced with these logics. All women of this nation should stand behind this as women are half of the population of the country and they have the right to be one of the seniormost positions of the state. The Presidential election clearly showed the attitude of decision-maker men towards women as they were not ready to unanimously accept a female president. Even the candidate of Vice President given by two parties was made a victim of power struggle.

9.3.4 UN Resolution 1325 and its implementation in Nepal

Implementation of UN Security Council Resolution 1325 is extremely weak in Nepal mainly because of the following reasons:

- Lack of awareness about the content of the UN Security Council Resolution 1325 at the political and decision-making level
- Lack of realization or internalization and of importance of women in peace process by the politicians
- Patriarchic, feudal, exclusionary socio-cultural system that gives direct benefits to political elites, who are strongly dominating all the decision making structures.
- Competition, non-collaboration, revelry or party political affiliation among the elite women that limit them to fight common cause.

9.4 FUTURE ROLE OF NEPALESE WOMEN IN MAKING PEACE PROCESS SUCCESSFUL

The CPA 2006 and the USCR 1325 have to be whole-heartedly accepted as a strategic framework and operational guideline to promote women's role in making Nepal's peace process successful. In future women have to be involved actively in content, process and structures of peace process, which is discussed in the following section:

9.4.1 Women in content of the peace process

Dealing with conflict victims such as killings, disappearance, torture, forced donations, threats of attack, arrest and violation of human rights in general and gender-based violence (rape, molestation, unwanted pregnancy, sexual abuses, etc.)

Victims are displaced, ex-combatants or and ex-soldiers, physically and mentally injured, children, women, elderly and disabled, or other people who are directly and or indirectly affected by the armed conflict, etc.

Women play a crucial role in promoting reconciliation and reintegration. Women can greatly contribute in addressing the suffering, pain and tragedies of the conflict victims, developing their confidence, bringing communities together. It is crucially important to provide justice and develop harmony by promoting a better understanding among the conflict victims: developing confidence, re-establishing mutual trusts and deepening understanding between former enemies. Special inherent qualities of women (called womanhood) greatly help in achieving reconciliation and reintegration and contribute to a lasting peace in Nepal.

The government had formed a committee to address the issue of disappearance but not much progress has been made so far. Similarly, the government has also made agreements with several identity groups such as Nepal Federation of Indigenous Nationalities (NEFEN), Chure Bhabar Ekata Samaj, Madeshi Janaadhikar Forum, National Badhi Rights Struggle Committee, etc. However, constant monitoring and follow-up of the implementation of these agreements where women have a direct stake is required.

One of the urgent areas of support needed for conflict victims is psychological counselling at local levels. They are profoundly suffering from trauma, stress, fear, and hopelessness. Reviving their hope for the future requires psychological counselling. Improvement of psychological health and social well being of individuals exposed with the ten years of violent conflict takes considerable time and efforts of psychological counselling. Developing a sense of belongingness and normalization of daily life of people requires a feeling of security and constant efforts for a long time. Hence, mobilization of capacity and commitment of women in facilitating community normalization process is utmost essential.

Women can play a crucial role in the following major pillars of Nepal's peace process:

a) Proper execution of the power-sharing arrangements,
b) Constant monitoring of peace process,
c) Sincere implementation of the understandings and agreements reached in the past,
d) Ensuring transitional justice and rule of law,
e) Guarantying transitional security,
f) Facilitating the disarming, demobilizing and reintegration process,

g) Promoting security sector restructuring,
h) Implementation of reconciliation, rehabilitation, recovery, and reconstruction,
i) Managing and or addressing public expectation and frustration,
j) Obtaining international support.

9.4.2 Women in Facilitating the Peace Process

So far, Nepal's peace process is extremely weak and even I have argued that Nepal's peace process is 'without processes'. Nepal's peace process can be successful only when it makes the 'process right'. To make the process right means inclusion of main stakeholders of peace process in decision-making (e.g. women, Dalits, Janajatis, conflict victims, displacement), balancing confidentiality and transparency, getting approval of decisions that have far-reaching consequences, proper documentation of the decisions, being accountable to sincerely implement decision, etc. Experiences of other conflict-ridden countries show that when women are involved in decision, the quality of decisions and their implementations are better (ICG, 2006).

Women, elderly people, and children face more difficulties by not implementing or partly implementing the CPA where the complications arise mainly from not respecting process or following inappropriate process. Women and children are at risk. Women working on hard issue of peace agenda such as taking impunity issue, human rights violations, etc. are at personal risk.

9.4.3 Women in Structure of Nepal's Peace Process

The political change of 2006 and progress achieved afterwards at the theoretical and operational level have changed the gender-based power relation in Nepal once the Interim Constitution has made provision for having at least 33 per cent women in the state structures. However, a strong psychological resistance exists at decision making leave to accept this provision. Despite the resistance, very positive progress has been observed in the CA election (see Tables 9.2 and 9.3)

TABLE 9.2: Party-wise Gender Composition of Members of Constituent Assembly

S. No.	Party Name	Candidate Female	Candidate Male	Total	Elected Female	Elected Male	Elected Total
1.	Communist Party of Nepal (CPN (M))	43	197	240	24	96	120
2.	Nepali Congress	26	214	240	2	35	37
3.	Communist Party of Nepal (UML)	27	212	239	1	32	33
4.	Madhesi People's Rights Forum, Nepal	3	100	103	2	27	29
5.	Tarai Madhes Loktantrik Party	4	90	94	1	8	9
6.	Sadhvawana Party	4	83	87	0	4	4
7.	Janamorcha Nepal	28	175	203	0	2	2
8.	Nepal Workers and Peasants Party	27	71	98	0	2	2
9.	Independent	42	774	816	0	2	2
10.	Rastriya Janamorcha	15	107	122	0	1	1
11.	Rastriya Janshakti Party	14	184	198	0	0	0
12.	Rastriya Prajatantra Party	22	210	232	0	0	0
13.	Samajwadi Prajatantrik Janata Party, Nepal	7	43	50	0	0	0
14.	Nepal Rastriya Bikas Party	0	13	13	0	0	0
15.	Socialist Party of Nepal	0	5	5	0	0	0
16.	Rastriya Janamukti Party	8	76	84	0	0	0
17.	Rastriya Prajatantra Party Nepal	8	196	204	0	0	0
18.	Communist Party of Nepal (Unified)	10	126	136	0	0	0
19.	Communist Party of Nepal (M.L.)	11	105	116	0	0	0
20.	Rastriya Janata Dal	0	8	8	0	0	0
21.	Communist Party of Nepal (United)	6	49	55	0	0	0
22.	Nepal Samata Party	2	12	14	0	0	0
23.	Dalit Janajati Party	1	49	50	0	0	0
24.	Nepal Sadhvawana Party (Anandidevi)	13	91	104	0	0	0
25.	Communist Party of Nepal (United Marxist)	5	43	48	0	0	0
26.	Communist Party of Nepal (Marxist)	1	7	8	0	0	0

27. Hindu Democratic Party	0	4	4	0	0	0
28. Nav Janawadi Morcha	1	14	15	0	0	0
29. Nepal Rastriya Janakalyan Party	0	3	3	0	0	0
30. Rastriya Bikas Party	0	21	21	0	0	0
31. Muskan Sena Nepal Party	2	32	34	0	0	0
32. League Nepal Shanti Ekata Party	0	10	10	0	0	0
33. Nepal Janavawana Party	0	2	2	0	0	0
34. Nepal Shanti Kshetra Parishad	1	2	3	0	0	0
35. Rastrawadi Yuwa Morcha	1	4	5	0	0	0
36. Liberal Samajwadi Party	0	3	3	0	0	0
37. Nepali Janata Dal	10	30	40	0	0	0
38. Nepal Rastriya Lokatantrik Dal	1	1	2	0	0	0
39. Rastrawadi Ekata Party	2	0	2	0	0	0
40. Janamukti Party, Nepal	0	3	3	0	0	0
41. Sa-Shakti Nepal	6	0	6	0	0	0
42. Rastriya Janata Dal Nepal	0	17	17	0	0	0
43. Shanti Party Nepal	4	8	12	0	0	0
44. Nepal Janata Party	2	23	25	0	0	0
45. Lok Kalyankari Janata Party Nepal	2	32	34	0	0	0
46. Mongol National Organization	0	17	17	0	0	0
47. Nepal Samyawadi Dal	0	1	1	0	0	0
48. Federal Democratic National Forum	2	43	45	0	0	0
49. Nepa: Rastriya Party	1	5	6	0	0	0
50. Nepal Lokatantrik Samajbadi Dal	0	11	11	0	0	0
51. Nepal Sukumbasi Party (Loktantrik)	3	8	11	0	0	0
52. Nepal Dalit Shramik Morcha	0	1	1	0	0	0
53. Chure Bhawar Rastriya Ekata Party Nepal	1	21	22	0	0	0
54. Tamsaling Nepal Rastriya Dal	3	19	22	0	0	0
55. Nawanepal Prajatantrik Dal	0	2	2	0	0	0
Total	369	3577	3946	30	209	239

Source: Election Commission, (2008); Ghale (2008), Table 7.4.

Table 9.2 shows that 369 out of 3,577 were women candidates. The percentage of women in the total candidacy was low (10.32 per cent); however, the percentage of wining was high (18.30 per cent) compared to their male counterparts (5.3 per cent). This indicates that women are more popular and they could win if given the opportunity but they are not given enough opportunities.

TABLE 9.3 : FTTP Party-wise Candidates Constituent Assembly

S. N.	*Party*	*Total Candidate*	*Women (No)*	*%*	*Janjati (No)*	*%*	*Madhisi (No)*	*%*	*Dalit (No)*	*%*
1.	CPN (UML)	240	26	10.8	65	27.1	65	27.08	2	0.8
2.	Nepali Congress	240	25	10.4	62	25.8	51	21.2	1	0.4
3.	CPN (M)	240	42	17.5	85	35.4	68	28.3	16	3.3
4.	RPP	237	25	10.5	77	32.5	67	28.2	3	1.2
5.	Janamorcha Nepal	214	29	135	47	21.9	54	25.2	26	12.1
6.	Rastriya Janamorcha	125	14	11.2	32	25.6	16	12.8	12	9.6
7.	CPN (United)	142	10	7.04	68	57.8	14	9.8	4	2.8
8	MPRF	105	3	2.8	20	19	96	91.4	0	0
9	TMLP									
10.	Sadhbhawana Party	93	5	5.3	20	21.5	87	93.5	0	0
11.	Rastriya Janashakti Party	201	14	6.9	59	29.3	48	23.8	6	2.9
12.	RPP (Nepal)	207	9	4.3	55	26.5	50	24.15	2	0.96
13.	Nepal Sadbhawana Party (A)	105	12	11.4	17	16.1	88	83.8	10	9.5
14.	CPN (ML)	120	12	10	15	12.5	28	23.3	10	8.3
15.	Nepal Majdoor Kisan Party	98	27	27.5	33	33.6	34	34.6	6	6.1
16.	Rastriya Janamukti Party	84	8	9.5	71	84.5	10	11.9	6	7.1

Source: Dahal and Kaphle (2008); Ghale (2008), Table 7.5.

Table 9.3 shows that political parties are not yet liberal towards providing opportunities to women in politics. The three big parties were not willing to fulfil the constitutional provisions of providing 33 per cent to women. Among the big three parties, the CPN (M) gave only 42 candidates out of 240 (17.5 per cent), the CPN (UML) gave 26 candidates (10.8 per cent) and the Nepali Congress gave 25 women candidates (10.4 per cent). Nepal Peasant and Workers' Party is comparatively better in providing more opportunities to women (by giving 27 out of 98 candidates (27.5 per cent).

Women have to be included, at least as per the provision of the Interim Constitution, if not possible to represent on proportional basis at present, in the following actual and potential state/peace structures:

- Cabinet and council of ministers
- Commission on Land Reform
- Security Commission and or National Security Council
- Security Sector Restructuring or other related committees,
- Committee on Disappeared Persons
- Special Committees/commissions form in future
- Local Peace Committee
- Administrative Restructuring Commission
- Thematic Committees (e.g. Peace Trust Fund)
- National Peace and Rehabilitation Commission
- National Planning Commission
- High-level State Restructuring Recommendation Commission
- Bureaucracy, Security and Judiciary structures
- Political party structures

It may not be feasible to involve women in the above-mentioned potential or actual structures if political decision makers use the existing legal, institutional and operational frameworks. Therefore, it is essential to identify what factors are obstructing to include qualified women in these structures and change them.

The ICG comparative study (2006) of conflict-ridden African Countries shows that women play a crucial role if they are given the formal responsibility. In Sudan, a country with more than four decades of war, Dr Anne Itto, State Minister in Government of national Unity and Mary Kiden, Minister for Gender, Social Welfare and Religious Affairs played important roles in the peace process. In Nepal, for example, if a woman heads the Ministry of Peace and Reconstruction, the outcomes may be different and hopefully positive.

9.5 CONCLUSIONS

So far the state has not properly internalised and acknowledged the women's crucial role in the peace process and therefore not provided substantial responsibility. One of the main reasons of this response is the masculine mindset, a true reflection of feudal, patriarchic society. Women themselves have also indirectly or directly contributing to this mindset.

Women are half of the population of the nation, therefore they are half of the solution of the country. It is also inappropriate to argue that women's role alone brings about peace and stability in Nepal. However, meaningful participation of women in the peace process can definitely contribute to achieve it.

Nepal needs to learn and internalize from the experiences of other countries where women have greatly contributed to peace building, peace operation, reconstruction, rehabilitation, resettlement, reconciliation, resettlement reintegration, and repatriation (6R).

To make Nepal's peace process successful qualitative engagement of women in content, structures and process of peace process is essential. The peace process being part of the political process; women's engagement in the broader political process can only ensure their representation in the peace process. Hence, these two components should go together.

It is realised that to makie the peace process gender sensitive, inclusive and productive, it is essential to accept the CPA 2006 and the UNSCR 1325 as the guiding framework and consider the following:

1. A comprehensive mapping of women's engagement in peace process with the detail documentation of areas of their focus or specialisation, available human resources

and their competency, etc. that provides a basis for making availability of women for specific structures.

2. Promotion of young female professionals in the areas of peace. So far only few women leaders are available for participating in peace-related structures.
3. Invest in gender budget analysis of government and international investment in peace process to ensure that the resources rich to needy women and children.
4. Assess the existing situation through evidences (collection and analysis of information with gender specific indicators) that how and to what extend the GoN policies, programmes, and service are directed to women victims of armed conflict and how much women are engaged in such service. That gives sound basis for redirecting the services towards needy victims.
5. Map out the existing situation of positions held by women in state structures, assess the legal provisions that hinders women's inclusion in state structures. Similar assessment is also needed at the level of political parties, semi-governmental agencies.
6. Constitutional provision of inclusion of women (33 per cent) in state structures gives a strong basis to include women in peace structures but women needs to further develop thematic speciality or bring the subject matter experts on board instead of appearing of few popular women figures everywhere. Affirmative action in favour of women may be needed for some time in specific structures that are crucially important for make the peace process a success.
7. The women should not focus only on participating in the structures but also and equally concentrate on the content of the peace process, such as exerting pressure on government to allocate more resource on girls' education, access of girls on health and education, establishing ownership of land to women, gender mainstreaming in post-conflict programmes.
8. UNSCR 1325 is still largely unknown to wider population. I suspect even many senior politicians;

bureaucrats and women professional may not be well familiar with the provisions of SCR 1325. Hence, massive awareness rising is essential.

Collaborate with men (at least begin with gender-sensitive male members of society) to widen the effects of women's work on peace process.

End Notes

1. This chapter is based on the paper presented at the national seminar on Women in Constitution organized by Women for Peace and Justice (Core Committee) at Kathmandu, 18-19 August 2008.
2. For example, see The Role of Women in Peacebuilding and Reconstruction: Lessons from Rwanda, East Timor, and Afghanistan held on 6 March 2003 (Council on Foreign Relations) http://www.state.gov/s/p/rem/2003/18759.htm for detail.
3. For details see http://www.afrikaworld.net/afrel.chinwenwoye.htm (retrieved on 2 August 2008).

Chapter 10

Security Systems Restructuring in Nepal

10.1 THE CONTEXT

Transformation of Nepal's conflict into durable peace and democracy requires sensitively dealing with the existing fragile transition and concrete delivery of peace dividends to conflict victims, survivors, ensuring transitional security and more important, restructuring of the security systems of the country.

Achieving peace requires getting the process right, monitoring mechanism, sincere implementation of understandings and agreements, appropriately dealing with the past and ensuring transitional justice and rule of law, guarantying transitional security, holding free and fair elections, proper facilitation of disarming, demobilizing and reintegration and restructuring of security sector, providing peace dividends and implementing reconstruction.

The CPA, Agreement on Management of Arms and Armies, promulgation of the Interim Constitution, completion of the verification process[1] of the PLA by a Joint Monitoring Coordinating Committee[2] chaired by UNMIN; successful completion of the Constituent Assembly (CA) are some of the major building blocks for security sector restructuring (Upreti, 2008a). After the decade-long armed conflict and two years of messy, ad hoc and tense negotiations and renegotiations between major political forces of Nepal, this country is now at the crossroads and gradually moving from transition to transformation, hopefully to achieve stability, peace, prosperity and democracy.

Nepal's peace process is in fact widely praised for its fast and substantial progress. However, it is also criticized for its failure to deliver the promises made, not following due process and unable to deal with transitional security and resistance to materialize security system restructuring (Upreti, 2008b).

Success of Nepal's peace process depends upon the right process, translation of the promises made into action and effective undertaking of the SSR (Upreti, 2008c & d). So far, leaders have shown a willingness to make peace process successful but failed to internalise the need of widely expected inclusion of women and other stakeholders, recognising the importance of process element and providing peace dividends to Nepalese people (Upreti, 2008b & d). Instead, they wholeheartedly involved in power struggle and vested political interest. In this paper, I am limiting the discussion, mainly the various issues of women's participation on peace process.

The objective of this chapter is to quickly examine the immediate security situation and initiate a constructive debate on the long-term need of security sector restructuring in the changing political context.

The CPN (M), one of the signatories of the CPA (other one was the then government) has now been leading the government[3] and therefore there is no existence of two parties as stated in the CPA. Hence, the new government needs to make all the provisions of the CPA as the programme of the state in consensus with other major political parties.

10.2 IMMEDIATE CONCERNS: TRANSITIONAL SECURITY

In any war-torn country, one of the major challenges after signing the peace agreements is maintaining the security situation. Though the term 'post conflict' is contested in Nepal, particularly after the emergence of several small armed groups and their engagement in violence, the operational definition of post conflict is 'a situation after the formal signing of the CPA on 21 November 2006 by the government and the CPN (M) that ends armed conflict and parties earlier engaged in fights, violence and war start to implement the provisions of the agreements'. The transitional security of Nepal, particularly in Terai[4] is severely challenged by small armed groups such as Janatantrik Terai Mukti Morcha (Jwala Singh); Janatantrik Madesh Mukti Morcha (Goit), Janatantrik Terai Mukti Morcha (Bisphot Singh), Madeshi Mukti Tiger, Terai Cobra; Python, Terai Baggi, Terai Army, Madeshi Virus Killers Party, Royal Defence Army, Gorkha Line Mukti Morcha, Liberation Tigers of Terai Ilem (LTTE), Kirat Workers Party (mainly Udayapur and Khotang). In addition to these armed groups, there are other criminal groups active in Terai (Chhotelal Sahani; Sanju Baba, Raju Singh Rathor and Munna Singh Groups are few of many others mainly operating from India), rural areas and towns and creating severe insecurity and violence. This is serious immediate security concern that state has to address.[5]

Nepal is in critical transition because of power struggle among the coalition parties, severely weak law and order, violent activities of interest groups and extremely weak performance of the government. General strikes, closures (even some time indefinite closures), blockades are routinely observed across the country and often they turn violent (blazing vehicles, smashing or destroying public and private properties, humiliating travellers, etc.). In August 2007, 19 different groups[6] had called 55 *bandhs* and blockades in Nepal. This is an example of severe problem of transition. Violent clashes between different political wings of various political parties are more frequent creating further insecurity. The government is not able to provide security to front line workers of the government working in the high-risk areas.[7] The triple bombs blast in Kathmandu on 2nd September[8] and Kapilvastu massacre of 16 September 2007 are two glaring examples and concrete evidences of the worsened security situation in the country. Severe clash started in Kapilvastu district on 16 September, which took the lives of more than 2 dozens people. Many more people are still unaccounted and more three thousands people were displaced. This quickly spread to neighbouring districts and almost turned into communal and religious conflicts. Series of killing, bomb blasting, kidnapping, attacks, looting, extortion and strikes and blockades have created full of insecurity, fear and helplessness in the country.

For more than one and a half years, the Terai region become increasingly insecure and violent, particularly after the promulgation of the Interim Constitution that did not address the issue of proportional representation election system and federal state structure raised by Madeshi people. Recently, the Nepal Police have declared eight districts namely Bara, Parsa, Rautahat, Mahottari, Dhanusha, Sarlahi, Siraha and Saptari as "highly sensitive" and other 13 Terai districts namely Jhapa, Morang, Sunsari, Makwanpur, Chitwan, Nawalparasi, Rupandehi, Kapilbastu,[9] Dang, Banke, Bardiya, Kailali and Kanchanpur districts as "sensitive" areas. It would be very difficult to smoothly implement any conservation, natural resources or environmental programmes in Terai region is security situation if not improved. Open border is becoming a haven for illegal arms traders and smugglers. Open borders have greatly contributed to organise and expand several militant and fringe groups, most of whom have no political base, popular support and clear organizational structures. Therefore, they do not fall under the category of political force.

10.2.1 Violence crime and insecurity

Nepalese people are seriously suffering from insecurity and violence. The phenomenon of criminality-led insecurity, such as kidnapping of children, murder and attempted murder, rubbery, illegal trafficking of arms and ammunitions, human trafficking, drugs abuses and trafficking, atrocities, murders, killings, massacres, forced displacement became serious (Upreti and Nepali, 2006). This phenomenon, particularly from Terai is growing, particularly after signing of the CPA.

10.2.2 Emerging Security Dilemma: Youth Mobilised in Coercion by Political Parties

The transitional situation is getting further complicated after creation of the coercive nature of organisations such as Young Communist League[10] (YCL), Youth Force (YF) and *Madesh Rakshya Bahini* by political parties. The official justification of need for creation of such forces by political parties does not match with the actions. The only legally defined institutions have coercive rights such as police, army and private security system approved by the government. However, these organisations are operating without any legal mandate, which consequently weakens state security apparatus, creates parallel functioning and adds insecurity. Any one can easily understand that coercive forces created by political parties serve their vested interests. Once powerful political parties have created such coercive forces, a severely weakened police force (by politicisation or political protection) cannot contain them. Hence, Nepal's security situation is facing a dilemma.

10.2.3 Political Protection, Impunity and Security Threats

Transitional security always suffers from political protection of criminals and criminal groups, political mobilisation of criminals and impunity to the wrongdoers for political interests and fear of victims to publicise the crime because of security threats.[11] Taking undue advantage of the transitional situation is always the domain of powerful elites (politicians, businesspersons, bureaucrats, security personnel) and mostly they directly or often indirectly engage in activities that create security problems. Further, impunity is a serious problem in transition. 'No legal actions' to the persons recognised by Mallik and Rayamajhi Commissions as guilty are two glaring examples of how Nepalese politicians want to deal with impunity. Without addressing impunity, improvement in security is extremely difficult.

10.2.4 Responding to Immediate Security Challenges

The issues discussed in Section 10.2 clearly demonstrated the immediate security challenges and problems. If political actors are willing to ensure transitional security, they need to address the issues discussed in Section 10.2.

10.2.4.1 Strengthening police forces

One of the main responses to address violence crime and insecurity is to strengthen the police force. Strengthening the police force means making police well equipped (providing required equipments), resourceful (physical facilities, etc.)

professional (competency, commitment, dynamism, ethics, knowledge, skills, information), maintaining neutrality (operate based on the motto of police not on the interests of home ministry officials or home ministers and parties associated with them) and accountable to people instead of to the home minister.

10.2.4.2 Controlling small arms and light weapons

Needless to say, illicit trade and use of small arms and light weapons (SALW) is not only intensifying the ongoing civil wars and armed conflicts in different parts of the world but also severely hindering the post-war reconciliation and reconstruction efforts. The International Action Network on Small Arms (IANSA) describes that small arms are in fact the weapons of mass destruction. It is extremely difficult to find out the actual amount and types of small arms and light weapons illegally produced, traded and used in different countries. Furthermore, due to unwillingness of the state to actively participate in disarmament and controlling SALW in conflict-ridden countries, the situation is becoming more complicated.

Massive production, illegal trafficking and misuse of small arms and light weapons (SALW) are fuelling the armed conflict and civil wars and severely undermining the peace process in many countries (IANSA, 2003). Nepal is one of these countries severely suffering form proliferation of SALW (Upreti and Nepali, 2006). Proliferation of SALW in Nepal and their implications on security systems, challenges posed are serious concerns to achieve transitional security.

Proliferation of SALW is also related with rampant poverty, chronic unemployment, severe discrimination and accumulated injustice and hatred. When these issues are not addressed by the state, people join the illicit business of SALW, as it gives earning as well as power. Estimates of the black-market trade in small arms go up to $ 10 billion a year and more than 639 million firearms exist in the world today, of which 59 per cent are legally held by civilians.[12] Abuses of small arms and light weapons are more pervasive and horrendous in conflict-ridden countries and causing enormous effects to ordinary people including abduction, death, injury and forced displacement, forcing people to be human shields, sex slaves, etc. North Atlantic Treaty Organisation Panel III divides small arms into three groups, i.e. (a) personal defence weapon, (b) an individual combat weapon and, (c) a medium support weapon.

Globally floating small arms are not much expensive, easily available and easy to use. According to the estimate of Inter-American Development Bank, direct and indirect costs of small arms violence in Latin America range from $140 to $170 billion per year. The Independent Small Arms Survey 2002 documents that every day, more than thousands of people are killed by small arms. It is reported that about 1 million weapons are lost or illegally trafficked each year and hundred of thousands are lost from government bodies themselves. Per minute, one person loses his/her life from the misuse of SALW in the world, (IANSA, 2004).

An estimated 70,000 small arms and light weapons fell into the hands of armed groups in Congo during the conflicts of 1993-1999. More than half of the SALW circulated in this period are still in circulation, causing serious threat to peace and security in the country. Even in Nepal, it is estimated that more than 10 thousand small arms are illegally disseminated in the society.

According to a report (called Shattered Lives) of Control Arms Campaign, the five permanent members of the UN Security Council, France, Russia, China, the UK, and the USA account for 88 per cent of the world's conventional arms exports. Arms Control and Disarmament Agency of USA highlights that Iraq alone imported armaments costing around 50 billion US dollars during the period of several years (1983 to 1990) (Banerjee, 2000). It is interesting to note that 85 per cent of total import of arms in Middle East is shared by the five Permanent Members of the UN Security Council (IANSA, 2003 and 2004).

It is now the response of state to combat small arms flow. Combating illegal proliferation of small arms requires the lead role of the government and support from political parties, civil society, experts, international community and citizens as a whole.

10.2.4.3 Maintaining neutrality and promoting accountability

If security and bureaucracy are not allowed to operate in their professional norms in accordance with the legally defined mandate, combating insecurity and achieving stability and democracy is impossible. One of the main challenges of this situation is to maintain neutrality of security forces and make them accountable. It has to come from both the security forces themselves and politicians. Civil society can work as a watchdog.

10.2.4.4 Promoting community security

Achieving transitional security requires full support and cooperation from the community. A collaborative approach (collaboration between security forces, local politicians, community members, media and intellectuals) is crucially important to achieve transitional security. Security forces need information, physical and moral support to combat crime, violence and other security challenges.

10.3 LONG-TERM PERSPECTIVES: DEVELOPMENT OF A COMPREHENSIVE SECURITY POLICY AND SECURITY SYSTEM RESTRUCTURING

The following are components of a comprehensive security policy

- Human security approach
  - o Social security: health education, drinking water
  - o Economic security: employment and poverty
  - o Food security
- National security
  - o Army
  - o Police
  - o Intelligence
- Non-conventional security issues
  - o Environmental security
  - o Energy security
  - o Information security

The security sector is defined differently by different people in different contexts. OECD defines security sector as those state institutions, which have a formal mandate to ensure the safety of the state and its citizens against acts of violence and coercion (OECD, 2004; cited in Kumar and Sharma, 2005). Security Sector Reform is a common concept globally used in post-conflict literature. However, in the context of Nepal, the term 'security sector or system restructuring' (SSR) is more relevant as it has to be a part of the broader state restructuring. SSR is a process of transforming the organizations having legitimate authority to use or order the use of force such as police, army, paramilitary, local security units, intelligence and other legally defined arrangements (Greene, 2003). Changing roles, responsibilities and actions of security actors in a changing context in consistent with democratic norms, values and principles of good governance are some of the basic elements of SSR (Schnabel and Ehrhart, 2005).

Fundamental principles of SSR are civilian control and parliamentary oversight of security apparatus, right sizing and modernization and professionalisation of security forces, respecting rule of law, facilitating war to peace transition, within the broader national security policy (Upreti, 2006d; OECD, 2004; DFID, 2002). SSR is a concept of total reform in the shortcomings and weaknesses of security sector, new vision and neutrality that demands honest commitments and impartiality from both civilian government and security professionals. Appropriate trainings (both military and human rights, capacity building and technical competence), mainstreaming security issues into development policy and programme, delicate balance between confidentiality and transparency, strong coordination and operational mechanisms, relationship between military and civilian, building public awareness, strengthening constitutional and legal frameworks, periodic review of performance of security sector and strengthening of independent oversight mechanisms (e.g. public complaint bodies like human right commission, auditor general, legislative and judicial bodies) are some of the important elements of SSR (Baldwin, 1997; Ball, 2002, Aditya et al., 2006; DFID, 2003; Ebo, 2003).

Restructuring of the security sector is not only related to security aspects but also with social, political, economic, international and development[13] issues. Security sector restructuring or transformation has to address policy, legislative, international relations; structural and oversight issues set within standard democratic principles and values (Upreti, 2003e, 2007b; DFID, 2003 and 2002). The classical security approach mainly focuses on legal monopoly of state to use the security instruments and security force for safeguarding people and national security specifically to defend against external threats. Further, the conventional notion of existence of military force is to prepare for, prevent and engage in war (Walt, 1991) and army, paramilitary and police forces, intelligence and secret services are used for this purpose. This conventional state-centric approach of security operation is narrow and ignores the modern notion of security that relates with the holistic framework of human rights, livelihood security, environmental security, energy security in other words broader human security with people's rights for dignified life (Upreti, 2006a and 2004a; Baldwin, 1997). Hence, democratic governance is a central element of security sector restructuring (Kumar and Sharma, 2005; Upreti, 2003a & b; Aditya et al., 2006). This is a seriously lacking issue in case of Nepal.

Clause 4.7 of the Section Four of the CPA has mentioned the democratization of Nepal army. It states, "*The cabinet would control, mobilize and manage the Nepali Army as per the new Military Act. The interim cabinet would prepare and implement the detailed action plan of democratization of the Nepali Army by taking suggestions from the concerned committee of the interim parliament. This includes works like determination of the right number of the Nepali Army, prepare the democratic structure reflecting the national and inclusive character, and train them on democratic principles and human rights values*".

Similarly, Article 144 (3 and 4) of the Interim Constitution has stated similar provisions. Hence, the new political context has clearly envisioned restructuring the existing army structures. However, neither the CPA nor the Interim Constitution is able to visualize the comprehensive need of security sector restructuring which includes a holistic approach, i.e. developing national security policy (by complementing International relations, defence policy, and economic policy; establishing a supreme and powerful national security apparatus such as national security council), reforming intelligence, restructuring army, police and other security apparatus. Isolated effort of restructuring of one component of security sector alone cannot produce expected result and therefore need to opt for a holistic approach.

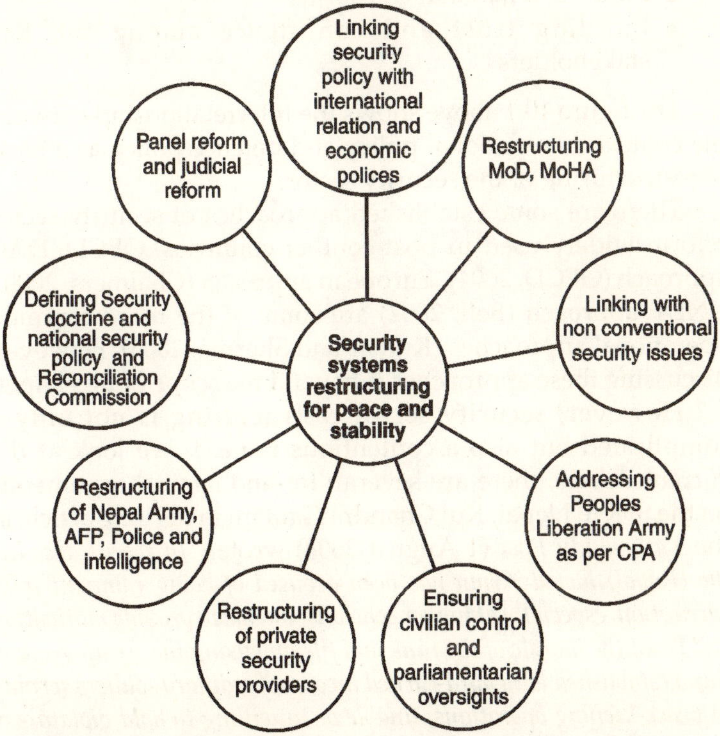

Figure 10.1: *Major components of security system restructuring*

Often the need ffrsecurity sector restructuring arises from:

- Transition from war (civil or inter-state) to peace
- Fundamental political change in the country
- Unanticipated security related crisis faced by the country
- Regal or gradual process of change

In any of these situations, important interrelated bases are:

- The context of the country (economic, political, security, etc.)
- International relations policy of the country
- National dance policy of the country

Further, in addition to these fundamental elements, there are two important operational elements of SST. These are:

- Building a national consensus
- Building trust and confidence among the key stakeholders

The figure 10.1 above shows the interrelationship between the context, international policy and defence policy as a basis of restructuring of the security sector.

There are some established approaches of security sector reform widely used in post-conflict countries. OECD/DAC approach (OECD, 2004), European approach (Chalmers, 2000), UNDP approach (Bell, 2002) are some of the more common operational approaches (Kumar and Sharma, 2005). However, discussing these approaches is beyond the scope of this paper.

However, security sector restructuring is not only a complicated but also a contentious issue. If we look at the current debate, there are several 'for-and against-arguments' on the SSR in Nepal. Kul Chandra Gautam in his long article in the *Kathmandu Post* (1 August 2008) wrote, "*In recent decades, the (Royal) Nepal Army has been accused of being rampant with corruption, especially at higher echelons; unable to provide motivation and boost the morale of the rank and file; misusing the Army Welfare Fund established with hard-earned income of ordinary soldiers serving in peace-keeping operations; unable or unwilling to hold violators of human rights within its ranks accountable, and frequently openly expressing contempt for political parties and civilian leadership. On the other hand, it has been a mark of NA's professionalism and sensitivity to the winds of political change that, although accused of being "royalist", it has not attempted to intervene in Nepal's dramatic political transition in the past three years, leading to the abolition of monarchy and coming to power of CPN (M) through elections. It is worth noting that in similar circumstances, elsewhere in the world, it is not uncommon to see a restless military staging mutiny, bloodshed and acrimony, if not outright coups d'etat"*. He is in favour of SSR.

However, one of the recently retired senior military officers Dilip Rayamajhi wrote a counter article in the News Front (11-17 August 2008). He wrote, *"The concepts of demobilisation, disarmament, reintegration, rehabilitation, security sector reforms, reconstruction, etc. are some of the cosmetic concepts which the UN chalks out from time to time in bold underlined letters like DDR, SSR. These abbreviations or acronyms may sound very effective in making peace but they have not been as successful as projected in their literatures. In most cases the failure is linked to the imposition of western standard processes without proper understanding of the culture, traditions and socio-political environment of the conflict torn area. These processes usually follow the maxim 'short term peace at all cost' and 'short term peace eventually will foster lasting peace' even though it may raise dire consequences for the future. For example in the case of Nepal, it seems that the UN and other western institutions want an early unconditional integration of CPN (M) combatants with the NA as an easy way out without due consideration of the future consequences. This is very much reflected in Mr Kul Chandra Gautam's article on the subject posted in the August 1, 2008 issue of the Kathmandu Post"*. His conclusion was that integration of PLA into NA is a political gambit to weaken the national army in the name of peace. He also projects that the integration process is taken further positively it could bring serious consequences. He further writes, *"It is time for us to unite for peace and not to waste our energies in the pursuit of an outdated ideology to fulfil one's political ambition"*. This article is a clear example of resistance to accept the reality and vehemently argue against the implementation of SSR in Nepal.

10.3.1 Defining National Security and International Relations Policies

Step 1: Analyze security sector

- Prioritize core needs and challenges
- Identify weaknesses and constraints
- Explore opportunities and potentials

Step 2: Formulate new policy, institutional and legislative framework based on the identified opportunities and potentials,

Step 3: Translate policy, institutional arrangement and legislative framework into action

The new security policy of Nepal should not be limited to conventional security paradigm practised by this country and must cover the new paradigm that includes:

- National defence
- International relation
- Territorial security
- Human security
- Environmental security
- Livelihood security
- Information security
- Energy security
- Space security

Even the current debate on security policy includes a good governance framework, and economic and development policy of the state. Conventional security is not enough to provide security to a nation and its people, especially in the developing countries. The Brandt Commission (1980) and Olaf Palme Commission (1982) have amply highlighted this issue. The Geneva Centre for Democratic Control of Armed Forces (DCAF) has vividly established a relationship between reform of security system and development by embedding reform of security sector into human development and helping poverty reduction and expanding options for life of poor people (Brzoska, 2003). Hence, Nepal needs to reorient its security sector according to the new security paradigm that builds upon the above-mentioned essential elements.

10.3.2 Restructuring Security Sectors

A holistic approach to restructuring of security systems is essential for the durable peace and democracy in Nepal. Successful restructuring of the security sector depends upon the internalization of holistic approach of security sector restructuring. This means:

- Developing new national security policy (defence and international relation)
- Redefining National Security Council (NSC), the existing arrangement of NSC is too narrow
- Restructuring of Ministry of Defence
- Restructuring of (a) Nepal Army; (b) Civilian police and (c) Armed police
- Redefining state intelligence (both security and civilian structures)
- Redefining and strengthening of overseeing bodies (parliamentary, judicial and human rights bodies)
- Integration of qualified CPN (M)'s 'People's Liberation Army in appropriate structures
- Successful implementation of reconciliation and reintegration of security forces from both sides [state and CPN (M)] in modernized and transformed security structures of the state.

All these components of the security sector are interrelated and complementary, and therefore reforming one and leaving others unchanged cannot be effective to meet the requirement of modernization, professionalisation and democratic governance of security components.

One of the fundamental points to be realized by the Nepalese people in general and political parties in particular is that national security and international policy must be developed by consensus (there should be in-depth study, serious discussion and wider interaction among and between political parties while formulating these policies) but once they are finalized, these policies must be the outcome of a consensus and common to all political parties; they must not change every time different political parties come to power.

National Security Council (NSC)

The National Security Council in the past never worked or used for the internal political purpose. Even the provision of the NSC in the Interim Constitution is not able to reflect the spirit of principles of national security management. Hence, a comprehensive NSC is essential and it has to be formed in consensus among the political parties.

Ministry of Defence (MoD)

For decades, MoD was under the shadow of the palace and acted as a rubber stamp to give acceptance to the decisions made in the military secretariat in the Narayanhiti royal palace or military headquarters. But according to the principles of modern security systems management, MoD is the civilian authority to control the military. Hence MoD has to have the full authority over the military. While undertaking the SSR, strengthening of MoD should be an integral component.

Ministry of Home Affairs (MoHA)

MoFA is responsible for homeland security or day-to-day security management of the state. Police forces, prison, border, intelligence and general administration are some of the main components of MoHA. Therefore it has a great responsibility. According to SSR principles, MoHA have to closely coordinate with other security-related agencies and should operate under the full supervision of the parliament.

Nepal Army

NA is the most important, quite complicated and wrongly debated (without properly understanding the dynamics) institution in the context of the peace process in Nepal and therefore presented in this section at length compared to other security providers (e.g. police).

The history of the Nepal army is seen by many as an important contributor in the state-building process. The success of King Prithivinarayan Shah in uniting several petty states into one Nepal was made by the army. Historically, they were in the forefront to resist external security threats. The Military Act 2063 (BS) has highlighted the reasons for the very existence of the Nepal Army. It states: protection of the independence, sovereignty, national integrity and national unity of the nation are the major directives of operation of military. However, there is a debate against this claim, saying that the military alone cannot protect the independence, sovereignty; national integrity and national unity to ensure provide security.

In the modern state, the security apparatus, bureaucratic apparatus and judicial apparatus are three fundamental permanent pillars of any state governing system. The Army is the major actor in the security apparatus. These three structures provide basic services to citizens of a country. It is not possible to democratically govern a country without modernizing, professionalizing and establishing accountability of these fundamental state apparatuses. The Nepal Army is being one of the very important components of the security sector; its transformation in the changing political context is highly expected by both political actors and citizens of the country.

While discussing the restructuring of Nepal army, four areas are crucial. These are:

1. Rule transformation (laws and regulations; guidelines, norms and values, etc.)
2. Content transformation (training, orientation, issues, structural arrangements, etc.)
3. Procedure transformation (behaviour and action, operational style, use of symbols, etc.)
4. Relation transformation (civil-military relation,[14] media policy; balancing transparency and confidentiality; accountability and civilian control and parliamentary oversight; human rights, etc.)

Transformation in these four crucial areas in the management and operation of the Nepal army is an integral part of the broader security sector of Nepal, which provides a sound example of state restructuring for new Nepal.

Existing Areas of Engagement of Nepal Army[15]

1. Safeguarding territorial integrity
2. Mobilization during the internal conflict
3. Development work such as construction of roads, bridges and other vital areas
4. Nature conservation such as deployment of military in parks and reserves
5. Disaster management and responding to crisis
6. Participation in UN peace-keeping operations
7. Security of palaces[16] and V/VIPs

8. Rescue and recovery: mainly helicopter service in natural calamities and other disasters
9. Protection and security of vital areas such as airports, boarder areas, security of banks and fund transfer, telephone towers and relay stations, and other relevant areas
10. Limited provisional emergency medical services to general public through Chhauni Military Hospital, Kathmandu.

These areas of engagement should be redefined, reoriented, combined, modified or reduced, based on the comprehensive assessment of the Nepal Army, considering the changing context of Nepal and international security dynamics. Some of the existing areas of engagement of the Nepal army are not needed in the changing context. There is an emerging debate on why the army should be engaged in national parks and reserves as the modern concept of people-park-partnership is more sustainable and effective.[17] A large number of army deployed in the security of places and the royal families earlier is not needed once the monarchy is abolished from Nepal. The engagement of security in development work such as construction of road and other infrastructure is also an issue of debate on economic and social grounds. Proliferation of small arms has rapidly increased during the period of armed conflict (Upreti and Nepali, 2006) where army can play more concrete role to control. These are only some examples and definitive areas of engagement can be defined only after the comprehensive assessment of NA by the technical committee.

Basic principles of restructuring of Nepal army

- Nepalese people as the ultimate source of power
- Accountability
- Transparency
- Inclusive representation
- Rule of law and human rights
- Social justice and good governance principles
- International provisions and standards

Right Size of Nepal Army

The actual size of the Nepal army depends upon several factors. Some of them are:

- Long-term national security policy
- International power relations and Nepal's position in this context
- Economic feasibility of the state, as it is one of the expensive institutions[18]
- Possibility of mobilizing alternative security arrangements (e.g. military training to eligible citizens, mobilizing paramilitary)
- Major areas of engagement to be categorised as:
  - o must be engaged,
  - o better to engage and
  - o less important to engage
  - o No need to engage
- Other factors

The CPA and the Interim Constitution have clearly stated to redefine the size of Nepal Army. There are several arguments against and in favour of reducing the existing size of Nepal army (the total strength of 91,444 persons[19]). There can be three options:

- Downsizing of the existing strength
- Upsizing of the existing strength
- Keeping the existing strength.

Arguments for keeping the existing strength (or not drastically downsizing)

- Reducing the existing size seriously imbalances the command and control strengths particularly in senior positions
- Need for deterrence in case of unexpected external interference
- Serious problems occur in nature conservation
- Affects development work carried out by Nepal army
- Alters contribution in UN peace keeping operations

- Affects in disaster management and risqué operation
- Affects security of V/VIPs
- Affects protection of vital areas such as airport security, security of banks and fund transfer, telephone towers and relay stations
- Affects jail security
- Requires strengths if internal conflict escalates.

Arguments for downsizing the existing strengths of NA

- The expansion of the existing military size into double during the past 10 years was precisely because of the Maoist armed conflict and this strength is not needed after the end of the CPN (M) armed conflict.
- Nepal, a poor country can not sustain this big size of military,
- Some of the conventional areas of military engagement are not needed, such as palace security, parks and reserves security,
- Nepal can not militarily confront or compete with the giant neighbours irrespective of the large size of Nepal army as they are massively large in size and technologically highly advanced,
- If needed to deter, Nepalese citizens have to be train.

Further, the down sizing of army is vehemently coming form the CPN (M). CPN (M) leader Prachanda in his first public appearance in the Prime Minister's official residence[20] said that Nepal needs only about twenty to thirty thousands army to provide military training to all eligible Nepalese people and security of the nation in his view is the responsibility of all citizens of the nation. This argument principally contradicts with the CPN (M) arguments to integrate all their PLA into state army.

In case of downsizing

If downsizing is agreed upon, the general criteria for downsizing are:

- Termination of all persons within 6 years on a phase-wise basis who have completed their legally defined pension period.

- Termination of those officials who have bad record of human rights abuses.
- Termination of all who have a record of punishment and disciplinary action.
- Accepting the unaccepted resignation of those who have submitted resignation during the time of the armed conflict.
- One-time decision for premature pension retirement (one or two years before the normal pension time depending upon the size to be reduced).
- Not filling the vacant positions created because of the completion of pension period and other means (exception may apply in some crucial positions),.
- Golden handshake package, where appropriate.
- Other appropriate criteria defined by the government.
- Transferring the interested officials to police force and other appropriate places.

Social Reintegration and Other Options for Nepal Army

If and when the decision is made to reduce the existing size of the Nepal army, they have to be integrated in society. The existing standard procedure and package of reintegration practised by Nepal Army has to be continued as the obvious option. However, if the downsizing is going to happen on a relatively large scale, the following are potential areas of engagement:

- Exploring the possibility of placing in the new arrangement of the permanent peace keeping force of UN. However, it requires especial efforts of government to convince the UN to recruit their peace-keeping force from Nepal
- Adjusting in private security sector: industrial security, security of public institutions, etc.
- Engage in skill-based occupations, income generation
- Creating a special force for post-conflict reconstruction and development

- Assigning civilian roles in the government structures where appropriate
- Other relevant options.

Establishment of a Technical Committee for Restructuring of Nepal Army

Both the CPA and Interim Constitution have outlined the responsibility of the interim cabinet to prepare and implement the detailed action plan for democratization of the Nepali Army by taking suggestions from the concerned committees of the interim parliament. However, during the entire period of interim government (late November 2006 to early August 2008) the PLA-NA debate was merely used as a bargaining tool by political parties to strengthen their own political position rather than implementing the provisions of CPA and Agreement on Management of Arms and Armies. If political parties want to constructively work in this issue, they need to form a technical committee composed of PLA leaders, Nepal Army officers and experts to assist parliamentary/CA committee and the government. This committee has to work out all necessary details and overcome technical complications in transforming Nepal army and integrating PLA. This committee needs to continue until the complete transformation of security sector.

Right Time for Restructuring of the Nepal Army

Though no substantial work in this area has been started, debate has already been initiated; a small initiative such as revising the Military Act has been completed by the former parliament. The whole effort so far has been focused on military, leaving the holistic framework of transformation to the security sector. Both the CPA and the Interim Constitution have to some extent opened the avenue to start work on SSR. However, it is extremely difficult to come up with a clear proposal of SSR on how to go about it. Nepal is relying on the existing national defence policy, international policy and economic policy, which are most probably going to fundamentally change after the promulgation of the new constitution formed by the Constituent Assembly. Hence, it is more appropriate to fully implement SSR after the promulgation of the new constitution by the CA. The following strategy is useful to initiate SSR:

During the Time of Constitution Making:

- Achieving commitment and consensus at political level
- Debate and discussion relating to the broader state restructuring
- Analyzing the security sector (what changes, how, when, where, by whom, options, risks, opportunities and challenges, resource required, etc.). This has to be done by the 'Technical Committee' and expert team.
- Ensuring the incorporation of fundamental principles of operation of security systems in the new constitutional provisions
- Providing a conceptual framework for the creation of modern, professional and democratically operating security apparatus
- Preparing the ground work and implementation of preparatory actions

By the elected government after the promulgation of new constitution

- Preparation of a comprehensive SSR package
- Execution of actual security sector restructuring according to the new constitutional provision.

Armed Police and Civilian Police Forces

The basic principles of restructuring of the police force are the same as of the army, as discussed in Section 3.2.4. However, the police force is engaged in day-to-day management of security, therefore its operational system should be more flexible, more transparent, and more accessible to general people. The SSR must ensure these provisions.

Whether we need the Armed Police Force (AFP) as a separate security provider institution or the specialised functions within the civilian police can perform some of the tasks of APF and some of them by army, is the domain of the SSR process. AFP was created mainly to counter the armed insurgency waged by CPN (M). The tasks of APF became more prominent mainly because of the CPA, which was contained NA in the barrack. But once NA resumes its tasks and civilian police force is strengthened, relevance of APF may be less significant. However, it has to be thoroughly assessed by the technical committee before coming to any conclusion.

Civilian police is the sole of local security. Our police force is severely demoralised, brutally politicised, and blatantly abused for the vested interests of powerful elites such as Home Minister of his/her political parties, smugglers, criminals, traders and business tycoons. Professionalisation of police force, increasing its existing size and capacity, improving quality of work is crucially essential and it possible only when politicisation of abuse of police is stopped and their neutrality maintained.

The recent revolts within both police organisations in different parts of the country have forced us to ask the several questions: Why did mutiny start in a much-disciplined organisation? Why did government respond positively at the first mutiny by appreciating the police involved in thisact and the officials of the Ministry of Home Affairs entered into an agreement with the revolting police and to filful their demand and later when the mutiny started in other districts the government took repressive approach just contrary to the earlier agreemnt? Why were all attempts made from the police organisations and the government to justify this was simply an indisciplined act of some junior police officer? Why was an independent inquiry not accepted despite the demand of civil society, experts and even some political parties? This case gives ample justifications to go for the restructuring of the police force and good governance in police organisations.

State Intelligence Mechanisms

Intelligence mechanisms Nepal are nearly dysfunctional. The department of intelligence service of Ministry of Home Affairs is merely a means of employing supporters and helpers of home ministers. Intelligence is a specialised function and ordinary people cannot perform it. How can a political cadre or ordinary people or a forcefully employed home minister perform this specialised task? Even DMI (Department of Military intelligence) of NA was not able to demonstrate its ability in intelligence {particularly when CPN (M) made high profile attacks in district headquarters such as Beni). One of the prominent examples of failure of intelligence of Nepal is the royal massacre of 1 June 2001. The SSR package has to deal with the intelligence mechanisms.

Parliamentary Oversights

In the framework of SSR, parliament plays a crucial role. Hence, parliamentary supervision is an integral part of the modern operation and management of security systems. The widely accepted definition of the parliamentary oversight is, *Tthe legislature exercises parliamentary oversight by passing laws that define and regulate the security services and their powers and by adopting the corresponding budgetary appropriations. Such control may also include establishing a parliamentary ombudsman or a commission that may lunch investigations into complaints by the public'* (DCAF, 2003:22).

DCAF and Inter,Parliamentary Union (2003) have identified the following important oversight functions of the parliament:

- Approve, reject or propose amendments to security policies and defence-related laws
- Initiation of parliamentary debate
- Seek explanation form the government
- National consultation of security issues
- Research
- Adopt and oversee budgetary provisions related to security
- Authorise or end state of emergencies
- Approve or reject government proposals on important issues such as international treaties, alliances and sending security forces abroad; appointment of high level security personnel; procurement of major arms, etc.
- Monitor and evaluate national defence and security policies and programmes through parliamentary hearing

or inquiry; independent performance assessments, establish audit mechanisms, etc.

In the parliamentary oversights of security systems, range of actors collaborates with together such as parliamentarians, political parties, civil society, researchers and parliamentary ombudsperson.

Addressing People's Liberation Army as per CPA

CPN (M) is constantly arguing to form a new national army by combining both PLA and NA. Though Maoistshave not made public details of how to form a national army, they have raised this issue very strongly. Further, the mistrust between the CPN (M) and Nepal Army persists.[21] The tension between the CPN (M) and NA is clearly observed from the expression of the head of the NA. The Chief of the Army Staff Rookmangud Katuwal on 6th January 2007 at the time of the departure to a week-long official visit to China said, *"Nepal Army is Nepali People's army that is paid for by the people themselves. So the national army should not be kept under any isms, ideology and political motivation. It should be competent, professional and disciplined, impartial and obedient to the order of the military chain of command. Nepali army is in favour of finding a lasting solution to any problem. That's why long-term impacts should always be considered while seeking solution to current problems. We believe that stability and sustainability can be gained only through a democratic system. And a force is required at national level to guarantee stability"*. In response, CPN (M) suprimo Prachanda very angrily expressed his reaction at a personal level against the army chief (in a big mass meeting at Tundikhel). Senior leaders of CPN (M) publicly expressed their dismay on several occasions. Such a crisis of confidence mounted because of lack of sincere implementation of the provisions of the CPA. Further, increased mistrust between CPN (M) and Nepali Congress mounted continuously, which was vehemently and blatantly reflected in the process of formation of the new government. The CPN (M) became the largest party from the election of CA, which political parties were not anticipating. Consequently, the power relations of the country changed. When the monarchy was abolished by the first meeting of the CA, CPN (M) envisioned the Nepali Congress Party as the centre of feudalism and therefore their long-term political enemy. On the other hand, the Nepali Congress Party started to suspect CPN (M) as an autocratic totalitarian political force working for establishing the people's republic. The public expressions of other parties after the CA election amply demonstrate their mutual suspension. That was blatantly demonstrated in the election of the president and even more prominently in the election of prime minister (15 August 1008) once NCP use MoD and NA as tool of bargaining and a strategy to psychologically widening the gap between the CPN (M) and NA. It is extremely difficult to transform security sector in general and Nepal Army in particular without reaching a national consensus at the political level. The national army, being a permanent important state structure, does not belong to any particular party or political group and therefore strengthening the national army is athe collective responsibility of the citizens of Nepal. However, once Prachanda was elected Prime Minister, he has declared that he is no more the supreme commander of the PLA and even other PLA leaders elected in the CA left their PLA position. This was one of the main sources of contention. This was also a strategy of confidence-building measures.

UNMIN verified 19604 PLA staying in the cantonments as qualified, which are eligible candidates for the integration if they meet the standard criteria to be defined by the government.

CPN (M) has repeatedly publicly expressed that the existing size of the army is not necessary for Nepal and it has to be reduced. It will be difficult to justify the argument of CPN (M) to incorporate a substantial number of the PLA in the army as it will expand the size of the army. Hence, the downsizing means lesser number of PLA integration in the army. However, the determination of actual size is political decision but it should be based on the sound technical basis.

There is also a strong public argument that the PLA is the ideologically indoctrinated political cadre of one party and how they can be professionally neutral. The statements of Army Chief and Dilip Rayamajhi, a recently retired senior military officer, mentioned elsewhere in this paper have clearly indicated this position.

Criteria of Selection of PLA for Integration

The government needs to decide selection criteria based on a thorough discussion with senior officials of PLA and Nepal army and experts. However, the following can be a general basis for selection to integrate in national army from the verified PLA:

- Giving up the party membership (neutrality principle)
- Physical fitness
- Meeting the standard selection criteria
- No record of human rights abuses
- Inclusiveness and representative - caste, geographical regions and sex
- Individual choice of PLA, whether he or she wants to join the army or opt for other options

PLA qualified the verification process and met the selection criteria for national army needs to be integrated into NA, according to the provisions made by the government based on the political consensus. However, those disqualified PLA staying in the cantonments but not meeting the criteria for integration into national army need to be adjusted in other areas or to be disarmed, demobilized and reintegrated in society. Disarming is a process of handing over of the arms used by individuals to the authorities who are responsible for the safe storage, redistribution or even to the destruction of those arms (Gleichmann *et al.*, 2004). Demobilization is a act of either disbanding arms unit, reducing the number of combatants or an interim stage before reassembling entire armed forces (ibid:15). Reintegration is a social and economic process by which ex-combatants acquire civilian status and gain access to civilian forms of work and income (ibid: 15).

The CPN (M) leaders have so far outrightly rejected the classical notion of disarmament, demobilization and reintegration (DDR). Their interpretation of DDR is an approach to apply for the defeated rebel force. However, the agreement between the government and the CPN (M) on management of arms and armies and involvement of UNMIN[22] in the ongoing management of arms and armies is an integral part of DDR. Further, DDR does not apply only to defeated rebel force but also to state security force, irrespective of wining or defeating if the existing size is decreased.

Qualified PLA verified by UNMIN have to be adjusted in other potential areas such as APF, civilian police, intelligence, or integrated into society. For those who want to return to civilian life it is essential to develop their capability to economically sustain livelihood, re-establish social relations, diffuse toxic memories and live a normal life. This requires special provisions that are not discussed in this paper.

Further, once the government decides to integrate the registered PLA in Nepal Army based on the above criteria, those who do not meet the criteria have to adjust in different areas such as:

- Place in industrial security
- Engage in skill-based occupations (by providing training, resources and conducive environment)
- Adjusting in private security sector:
- Placing for security of public institutions,
- Creating a special force of post-conflict reconstruction and development
- Assigning civilian roles in the government structures where appropriate
- Border security
- Other options.

Dealing with Private Security Providers

Private security providers are emerging and adding a new dimension in the security sector. They are becoming an important part of the security systems and therefore it has to be dealt with in the broader national security concerns. Several private security companies are operating in Nepal to provide security and protection of persons and properties. Their services are not always associated with arms and are often defensive instead of offensive to cater to the general level of security services to the private sector, NGOs, INGOs and individuals.

So far in Nepal they are mainly involved in physical protection, close protection as bodyguards and helpers, surveillance, risk assessments. Hence, a clear policy that supports national security and complements the state security system is needed and the SSR has to deal with this issue.

Border Management

So far, border management is the most neglected but crucially important issue in Nepal and therefore it has to be fully considered in the national security policy. Border management is the combination of techniques, tools and procedures in administering borders that includes handling of people crossing the borders and goods, patrolling and controlling illegal entries and regulating legal process. In border management, the following key actors are engaged:

a. Border guards
b. Immigration services and officials
c. Customs officers

Often crimes, corruption, illegal trading of small arms and light weapons, human trafficking are common border-related illegal activities and controlling these activities requires special knowledge, skills and procedure. SSR has to deal on these concerns.

Panel Reform

In the broader security systems, restructuring penal reform is also an important element. The conventional notion of penal system has been changed and prison reform is becoming one of the major concerns in the field of security issues. Hence, broader SSR needs to include penal reform as an integral part.

Judicial Reform

Effective SSR is not possible without a responsive, accountable, impartial and transparent legal and judicial system. The media has reported every day the poor performance, delay in giving justice, corruption, etc. in the field of judiciary. Hence, it must be dealt with in the broader SSR process.

A comprehensive review of existing treaties, international

conventions and legal provisions is essential.

10.4 CONCLUSIONS

Organized crimes and insecurity will continue and even further expand with activities like extortion, abduction, robbery, looting, narcotics smuggling, rape, girls trafficking, hunting and smuggling of rare animals (e.g. musk deer, valuable furry skin, tiger bones, rare herbs, woods) if the state is not proactive enough to deal with transitional security, if parties continue their coercive youth mobilisation in the name of YCL or YF. Hence, addressing transitional security requires the collective responsibility of government, political parties, security actors, civil society, media and community.

Improving transitional security is only a short-term strategy and it needs long-term security policy of the nation. The long-term security policy of the nation has to consider at least coming 5 decades of the possible security scenarios in the region and international level. Restructuring of security apparatus (army, police, intelligence), ministries (home and defense), National Security Council should be guided by national security doctrine and policy, international relations and economic policies with a strong provision for civilian control of the security sector and proper supervision from the parliament.

The security sector in general and security providers in particular are often used as a bargaining tool for vested political and individual interests. If such practices are continued in future, it is not possible to restructure security systems.

Exchange of intelligence information by establishing 'regional network of information sharing', cooperation among the authorities of the nations in the region, collaboration between the state and civil society are other areas to be considered in controlling SALW.

The government should realise that SSR is not only its private domain and civil society, experts and researchers, citizens, security providers have to bring together to develop ownership.

End Notes

1. A total of 19,604 people have been qualified from the UNMIN verification process.
2. For details about the Joint Monitoring Committee, see the decision (SC/8942) of 5622nd Meeting (PM) of the Security Council of UN.
3. Mr Puspa Kamal Dahal, 'Prachanda' was elected as Prime Minster by the parliament on 15 August 2008. He was presented by CPN (M), CPN (UML) and Madeshi Janaadhikar Forum as a common candidate and backed by other 16 of 25 small political parties and therefore obtained 464 votes (78 percent) out of 577 parliamentarians voted in the election. Nepali Congress leader and 3 time-PM Ser Bahadur Deuba lost the election by obtaining votes from only his party and Rastrya Janamorcha Nepal, Rastrya janasakti Party, Nepal Workers and Peasants Party and CPN (Unified) abstained from the voting (They had all total 14 members who were not voting in the election).
4. For detail about the terai violence and insecurity, see International Crisis Group Asia Report No 136 published in 9 July 2007.
5. The Terai region has increasingly insecure and prone to further violent conflict. The Nepal Police had declared eight districts namely Bara, Parsa, Rautahat, Mahottari, Dhanusha, Sarlahi, Siraha and Saptari as "highly sensitive" and other 13 Terai districts namely Jhapa, Morang, Sunsari, Makwanpur, Chitwan, Nawalparasi, Rupandehi, Kapilbastu, Dang, Banke, Bardiya, Kailali and Kanchanpur districts as "sensitive" areas.
6. The groups calling *bandhs* and blockade were: (i) businessmen, (ii) CPN (M) affiliated organizations, JTMM (JS), Limbuwan, Chure-Bhabar Pradesh Ekata Samaj, Madeshi Peoples Right Forum, Madhesi Revolutionary Front, Madhei Tiger, Conflict Victims, Local communities, different wings of 7 parties, Independent students groups, transport Unions, Dalit and janajaties organizations, Tamang Autonomous Region Democratic Front, United Tharu National Liberation Front and other groups (See OCHA report of August 2007 for detail).
7. For example, assassination of frontline government staff and local-level politicians of mainly hill origin in Terai by different armed groups is growing and state is not able to ensure security and safety in nation. Within six months (March to July 2007), more than 7 people were assassinated by different armed groups (the people killed were Ram Brikshya Yadav, VDC secretary by Cobra Group; Basudev Paudel (trainer) by JTMM Goit Group, Nava Raj

Bista (engineer), Purna Singh Pradhan (overseer) Arun Prasad Jaisawal (fireman) and Ram Hari Pokharel (VDC secretary) by JTMM-Jwala Singh Group.

8. On Sunday, the 2nd of September 2007 at 16:15 hours 3 bombs were blasted at crowed public places of Sundhara, Balaju and Tripureshwor where 2 school children and one ordinary woman were killed and more than 26 people including a 2-year-old child were wounded. The so-called People's Army and Terai Army' took the responsibility.
9. Though the Nepal Police categorized the Kapilvastu District in second category of high-risk area, the killings and violence erupted in different villages of Kapilvastu district on 16 September 2007 posed a serious question on their risk assessment ability. The violence erupted once the Abdul Mohit Khan (member of Loktantrik Madhesi Morcha and leader of Village Defence Committee, which was formed by the then Royal Nepal Army to fight against the CPN (M) during time of the active war in 2004-2005) was killed by unidentified people. Immediately after the killing of Mr. Khan, his supporters started to indiscriminately attack people, burnt their houses. More than 2 dozen people were killed, many more are still missing and more than five thousand people displaced. One of the main causes of the Kapilvastu massacre was the arms provided by military to Village Defence Committee to fight against the rebels which were not returned back even after signing of the CPA, despite the repeated urge of human rights activists, researchers and local leaders.
10. On the occasion of CPN (M) leader selected as the first elected Prime Minister of the Federal Democratise Republic of Nepal (he is the second communist prime minister after the late Mana Mohjan Adhikari) the CPN (M) declared to demilitarise YCL. This provision came as a result of the 7-point agreement reached between three parties to go for coalition government. However, it is yet to see how CPN (M) fulfils its promise of changing YCL behaviour and actions.
11. For example, media again brought the issue of non-reporting of high profile ransom-led kidnappings once daughter (a 10th class school girl) of Dr Uppendra Devkota was kidnapped by a notorious criminal gang and Dr Devkota, unlike previous victims, brought the case to the police. Once a professional criminal gang (Siddhartha Lama, Krishna Rai alias 'Bijaya', Raju Thapa and Keshav Darlami Magar and Hem Bahadur Magar) kidnapped the girl, Nepal police in cooperation with the victim family succeeded

in arresting one of the 5 members of the gang Hem Bahadur Magar alias 'Hemanta' ak 'Gore' and brought before the media on 13 August 2008 (see the *Himalayan Times*, 14 August 2008 for details).

12. See Fact Sheet, Bureau of Arms Control, Washington, DC, 2005 and http://peacejournalism.com/ for details.
13. The relationship between security sector and development has been extensively discussed by the report of the Club of Rome in early 1970s (Meadows et al., 1972), Brandt Commission (1980) and Olaf Palme Commission (1982).
14. See Huntington, Samuel P, (1957), *The Soldier and the State: The Theory and Politics of Civil-Military Relations*, London: The Belknap Press of Harvard University Press for the detail about the conceptual basis of civil military relations.
15. Information obtained from Army Command and Staff College on 19 January 2007.
16. After the historic declaration of the Parliament on 18 May 2006 to suspend the monarchy, the then government decided to use police instead of Nepal Army for the security of palace and the first meeting of the Constituent Assembly on 26 may 2008 decided to completely abolish the monarchy. Though the government of Nepal gave 50 military officers for the security of the ex-king, the NA engagement is not needed.
17. For details about this debate see Upreti, B.R. (2007), Crisis beyond the Battlefield: Quick Impact Assessment of the Armed Conflict on Environment and Biodiversity in Nepal. Kathmandu: World Wildlife Fund.
18. If the government is not able to provide enough resources required to meet the high standard of army, having a big number of army alone cannot achieve the desired result. Rather, it brings several problems within the organisation.
19. The figure obtained from the Army Command and staff Colleague on 19 January 2007. The caste-wise distribution of 91444 people working in the Nepal Army is: 8901 are Brahmin, 37764 Chhetri, Thakuri 3706, *Janajatis* 22000, Madeshi 5122, Newar 5821, Dalit 5655, Muslim 13 and 2462. In terms of gender disaggregating, 1025 are women and remaining are men.
20. Prachanda, chairman of the CPN (M) appeared in public after the first summit meeting between the Seven Party Alliance and the Maoists at the Prime Minister's official residence at Baluwatar in Kathmandu on Friday, June 16, 2006 and first time publicly express his opinion about the size of Nepal army and since then other CPN (M) leaders have repeated the same.

21. For details see the *Kathmandu Post*, 7 January 2008.
22. UN Security Council passed a resolution on 23 January 2007 to operate UN Mission in Nepal for a year where more than 186 arms monitors and around 600 persons in total will work in different part of the country.

Chapter 11

War-to-peace Transition in Nepal[1]

11.1 THE CONTEXT

The decade-long armed conflict came to an end once the CAP was signed in November 2006. The present situation is the outcome of a series of understanding, negotiation, compromises and agreements between major political forces of the country. The main objectives post-conflict war-to-peace transition management have to be rebuilding local social relations, building and strengthen mutual trusts, ensure justice, revitalise social capital that entail emergence, promotion and strengthening of local association, community participation, collective accountability, enables collective censure of violence, promotes feeling of security and common identity and reduces fear. This strategy has to consider three steps (immediate, medium-term and long-term engagement) and two levels (national and local levels).

Nepal needs a comprehensive post-conflict strategy in the spirit of CPA and wider consultation with concerned stakeholders (conflict victims, political parties, and civil society and donor agencies). National Planning Commission, all ministries, departments and national NGOs have to internalise and incorporate post conflict strategy into their programme activities. A large portion of Nepal's population is suffering from the armed conflict during the last eleven years in the country. The Nepalese people need to develop confidence, capacity and willingness to be part of national strategy that requires systematic and continuous efforts.

A gender-responsive post-conflict response strategy has to be a priority area of entire process and special attentions needed from the central level. Creation of a Gender Auditing Group at the central level (and even at local level) by representing gender specialists, women activists, government representative and concerned stakeholders with special mandate is essential to ensure gender-sensitive post-conflict reconstruction programme.

One of the main challenges in the post-conflict situation is misuse of external resources in the form of duplication, abuses, disproportional allocation and non-transparent use. Therefore, proper coordination with donors, INGOs and ministries, mobilisation of required resources and appropriate allocation of available resources (equity-oriented resource allocation) is the responsibly of the central government. Inter-ministerial coordination is crucially important to allocate and mobilise financial resources to implement reconciliation and social and political reintegration strategy. A separate unit in each ministry and department is essential to ensure smooth coordination, monitoring and proper allocation of resources. Successful post-conflict reconstruction reconciliation and reintegration require different institutional arraignments and regulatory provisions, which is the responsibility of the central level (the government and parliament).

The twelve-point understanding between the SPA and the CPN (M) reached on 22 November 2005 paved the way for resolving the ten years of armed conflict and transformation of the state. This understanding states, *"The long struggle between absolute monarchy and democracy in Nepal has now reached a very grave and new turn. Establishing peace by resolving the 10-year old armed conflict through a forward-looking political outlet has become the need of today. Therefore, implementing the concept of absolute democracy through a forward-looking restructuring of the state has become an inevitable need to solve the problems related to class, caste, gender, region, etc. of all sectors including political, economic, social and cultural, bringing autocratic monarchy to an end and establishing absolute democracy. We make public that, against this existing backdrop and reference in the country, the following understanding has been reached between the seven parliamentary parties and the CPN (M) through different methods of talks"*. The success of popular people's movement was the result of this understanding.

Fundamentally, the 12-point understanding had two vital components, one: bringing autocratic monarchy to an end and the second: restructuring of the state. They became successful in the first but they are still struggling to realise the state restructuring, which is basically related to solving centuries-old problems related to class, caste, gender, region, etc. in the country and ensuring political, economic, social and cultural rights of people. Until and unless the second part is not ensured proper democracy will not be established in Nepal.

The non-violent people's resistance movement (popularly known as *Janaandolon*) of 6-24 April 2006 defeated the autocratic and feudal regime. Every strategy of the king to survive his regime failed on the mid night of 24 April 2006, when the king finally gave up power to people. In a televised speech he said, *'Realizing the people's movement and seven party alliance's roadmap we have revived the House of Representatives which would help resolve the national problems, including violence…'*.[2]

This movement was the collective aspiration of all Nepalese people. People from all walks of life such as women, marginalized groups, ethnic communities, disabled, youth, children students, housewives, labourers, peasants, workers, street-vendors, business people, retailers, peace and human rights activists, journalists, lawyers, scholars and researchers, poets, writers, school teachers, university professors, doctors, nurses, shoe makers, tailors, government employees, technicians, artists, film actors and actresses, politicians were participated in the movement. The greatest achievements of this movement was to end the autocratic rule of the king and bringing the SPA in power that paved way for reaching the agreement between the SPA government and the CPN (M). However, the weakness from the political side appeared when the political leaders failed to realise the people's aspiration and perceived that changing ruling elites is the will of people participating in the people's movement.

The 8-point understanding reached between the CPN (M)

and SPA on 16 June 2006 was another fundamental step in ending armed conflict and restoring peace in the country. The point four of the 8-point understanding is crucially important basis. It states, "*To form an interim constitution, constitute an interim government accordingly, to announce the date for elections of the Constituent Assembly (CA), to dissolve the House of Representatives on the basis of consensus and after making alternative arrangements, and dissolve the 'people's governments' formed by the CPN (M) on the basis of 12-point understanding between the SPA and the CPN (M), the spirit of the preamble of the ceasefire code of conduct and by guaranteeing the people's rights acquired from the people's movement of 1990 and the recent historic people's movement*". However, the parties making the eight-point understanding were not able to fully implement them and consequently it had provided a ground for mistrust and affecting the peace process adversely.

Conflict resolution, conflict management, conflict transformation, peace process, state restructuring, democratisation of security forces, management of arms and armies, constituent assembly, federal state structures, inclusive state are some of the quite frequently used phrases in the contemporary debate in Nepal. Every phrase is heavy enough to write a book. Among them I am discussing here mainly managing the peace process, which is often used in the current political discourse to refer to the transitional political situation.

Peace is a state of mind. Peace refers to the state of social, psychological, physical, mental, spiritual and physiological well being on an individual and therefore it is referred to state of mind. Once, one or more of the external or internal factors disturb, obstruct or hinder the well being related to one or more of these factors, peace is not observed. If I use this conceptual definition of peace, the situation of Nepal for a long time was not really peaceful. However, the decade-long fight between CPN (M) and the state and subsequent by-products have created an enormous insecurity, fear, nervousness, anxiety in Nepalese society. In this context therefore, the peace referred to by the general public is to end this bloody war and build peace in a fractured society. Peace building is therefore a process of restoring normal relations between people. Peace building not only requires dealing with the past (reconciliation, apology and forgiveness, giving justice to the victims and survivors of the conflict, establishment of a cooperative relationship by replacing the adversarial or competitive relationship that used to exist in society) but also envisioning future and generating hope and dream. It can be achieve by getting process right (Baechler et al., 2008).

Once society falls into conflict, its effects remain longer even after several years of agreement between warring parties. Dealing with the issues in dispute (addressing concerns), reconciling discontents and normalising relations requires time, commitment, sincere efforts and the right process. Global experience of conflict transformation and peace building shows that the 'right process' helps to bring right outcomes.

Nepal is in a fragile transition from war to peace. This country has experienced a bloody armed conflict for a decade. This bloody conflict not only took the life of more than thirteen thousand people and caused damage to infrastructure worth billions of rupees but also paved the path for transformation of a feudal, centralized, monarchical unitary state into a modern, inclusive, federal republican state.

After reaching the 12-point understanding between the SPA and CPN (M), the people's revolution of April 2006 became successful and opened avenues for the political change that ultimately resulted in ending the armed conflict by signing the Comprehensive Peace Agreement. Invitation to the UNMIN,[3] , Agreement on Management of Arms and Armies, the promulgation of the Interim Constitution, formation of the Interim Legislative Parliament and the Interim Government, completion of the verification process of the PLA by a Joint Monitoring Coordinating Committee,[4] reaching agreements by the interim government with Madeshis, Janajaties and other concerned stakeholders, successful completion of the highly awaited and frequently postponed election of the Constituent Assembly (CA), declaration of Nepal as 'Democratic Republic' by the 1st meeting of the CA on 28 May 2008 and partly installing the power sharing arrangements (election of President, Prime

Minister and Chair of the Constituent Assembly) are the major building blocks for managing transition and making Nepal's peace process successful (Upreti, 2008b&c).

Nepal was a feudal, centralised, unitary and exclusionary monarchist nation for centuries with widespread discriminations based on sex, caste, ethnicity and religion. The ten years of armed conflict and 19 days of people's power in April 2006 had opened the avenues for a socially inclusive, economically prosperous and politically democratic nation. However, there is long way to go to fully realize these characteristics of Nepal. This can be achieved only when citizens of this country are engaged in democratic practices, state protects the human rights its citizens, ensures social justice and promotes harmony. Achieving economic development, experiencing political stability and peace and exercising democratic practices requires the right process at the right time with the right approach in addition to a clear vision of politicians, responsive state institutions and conducive contextual environment.

Violence and war leave behind much more damage than can be seen by the naked eye. The visible consequences – the dead and the wounded, raped and bereaved refugees and the displaced – and the material damage to buildings and infrastructure are social catastrophes to be addressed immediately. But the deep damage to our attitude is equally important to set them right for they leave scars on the human mind as trauma, guilt and hatred, a thirst for revenge. Reconciliation is much more than rebuilding, it is also rehabilitation of deeply wounded human beings, repair of social structure and of culture. If this is not addressed, wars and violence will be reproduced.

Achieving political stability and making the peace process successful requires an integrated approach, which is briefly discussed below:

11.2 MANAGING TRANSITION

It is crucially important to smoothly manage transition to achieve stability and democracy and materialise transformation. Managing transition requires appropriate dealing with the following important and complementary elements:

- Sincere execution of the power-sharing arrangements
- Constant monitoring of the peace process
- Sincere implementation of understandings and agreements
- Ensuring transitional justice and rule of law
- Guaranteeing transitional security
- Free and fair elections
- Facilitating disarming, demobilizing and reintegration process
- Security sector restructuring
- Implementation of reconciliation, rehabilitation, recovery and reconstruction

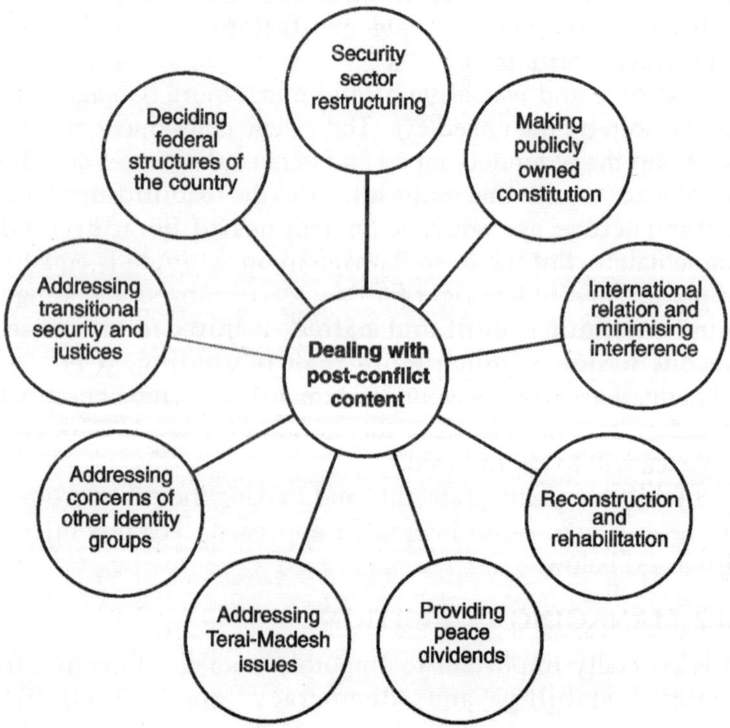

- Managing and or addressing public expectation and frustration
- Obtaining international support.

11.2.1 Power-sharing Arrangements

A power-sharing arrangement is fundamental in making the peace process successful. During the transition period, the interim arrangements are made between the previously warring parties. Hence, a coalition culture among the power-sharing parties is crucial in making the power-sharing arrangement functional. In Nepal, enough provisions for power-sharing arrangements are outlined in the CPA and Interim Constitution. Accordingly, SPA including CPN (M) leaders are in important power structures (e.g. interim government, interim legislature parliament, diplomacy) but the coalition culture is lacking. They perceive that the power exercised by them is the reward for them for their past activities. They do not feel the responsibility to smoothly manage the transition and achieve stability and democracy and peace. The action and behaviour of actors of the current power-sharing arrangement are creating enormous operational problems and making peace process shaky and fragile (Baechler et al., 2008). Those who are out of the circle of power-sharing arrangements are disgruntled and gradually organising to oppose the decisions and actions of SPA-CPN (M).

BOX 11.1: Uniqueness of Nepal's Peace Process

- Largely managed by internal actors unlike heavy direct involvement of external actors
- Fighting political forces (democratic political parties and CPN Maoists) coming together to fight against the then monarchy (as a greater enemy). Hence the triangular conflict (between the king, democratic parties and the Maoists) turned in to bipolar (the king v/s political parties) forcing the king to surrender, reaching to CPA and finally abolishing monarchy.
- Greater contribution of civil society
- People's power reflected in the *Janaandolon* II
- Greater international support to people and parties after the takeover of the king in 1st February 2008
- Solidarity for change from bureaucracy, judiciary, business sector

and other many sectors of society

- Rebellion force selected by people as largest political party from the election
- Cooperation by military (instead of attempting to go for military rule and respecting political change and CPA),
- Active engagement of domestic peace and conflict transformation researchers and practitioners in seeking solution
- Huge pressure from human rights community (nationally and internationally) to come to peaceful solution of the armed conflict.

Making the peace process successful requires including as many groups of actors as possible in the transition management process that develops ownership. However, this aspect is blatantly missing in the current transitional management of peace process. The expertise, knowledge, skills and competencies of independent, intellectuals, academics, professionals, specialists and analysts who are not members of any political parties are not brought into the peace process. This is an organic group with the tremendous capacity of opinion building and access to information.

11.2.2 Translating Agreements into Action

The success or failure of any peace agreements at transition largely depends upon the sincere implementation of the provisions outlined in the agreements and understanding. Global experiences of management of the peace process show that the parties signing the peace agreements have a tendency during the transition, of violating the provisions articulated in these agreements (by mis- or wrong interpretation, inaction, opposite action, etc.) and blaming the other side for non-compliance (Barnes, 20002; Aditya et al., 2006).

SPA and CPN (M) had made numerous agreements and understanding. Some of them are: 12-points understanding, 8 point-understanding, 25-point code of conduct, CPA, 5-point letter to UN, Interim Constitution, agreement on management of arms and armies, 23-point agreements. However, critical examination of the situation of their implementation reveals that most of them are either partly implemented or not implemented at all or interpreted differently or taking opposite actions. Most of the provisions implemented are related to power sharing (getting in power and position) and most of the provisions not implemented are related to the direct concerns of Nepalese people. This is a risky approach of dealing with the peace process at transition.

11.2.3 Monitoring of the Peace Process

It has been observed that more than 40 per cent of peace agreements had collapsed within 4 years of their signing. This is mainly because of lack of proper monitoring and sincere implementation of the agreed provisions. Hence, an effective monitoring is crucially important to make peace process successful and achieving stability, peace and democracy. The monitoring mechanism should be independent, powerful and impartial to work as a watchdog and make sure that the parties signing agreements follow the provisions contained in the agreement honestly and sincerely. This is also a technical issue and therefore requires technical competencies. In the past, politically loaded personalities with their biased orientation were picked up to balance power and therefore the committee not only fell into controversy but also largely failed to perform its highly demanded functions.

In the case of Nepal, monitoring of the peace process is extremely weak. The government and SPA-CPN (M) did not internalise the indispensability of the peace process monitoring mechanisms. In the past, the ceasefire monitoring team had resigned mainly because of non-cooperation of the government and later the proposed chairperson for the monitoring of peace process refused to take the responsibility because of the past bitter experiences of non-cooperation of the state and political parties. Making transition successful requires strong monitoring mechanisms with full mandate, resources and authority.

11.2.4 Ensuring Transitional Justice

The growth and support of transitional justice since the early 1990s has led to a myriad means and choices for post-conflict societies and the international community to address past human rights violations in an effort to curb reoccurrence, enhance reconciliation and to provide a measure of accountability. In the context of post-conflict peace building, the transitional justice mechanism established, from international tribunals to special courts, was heralded as bringing an end to human rights violations and war crimes and deterring future abuses. There was optimism that these judicial mechanisms would be the answer to the woes of crimes committed during conflict and be a means of redress for victims. Alongside this proliferation of judicial means of addressing past human rights violations in post-conflict societies grew a discourse on the virtues of non-retributive reconciliatory mechanisms of justice versus that of criminal accountability. Non-judicial means of accountability, particularly truth commissions, were increasingly promoted. Consequently, a wide range of different types of judicial and non-judicial mechanisms to address past crimes were developed, enhanced or promoted in a relatively short period.

Transitional justice is one of the fundamental elements in securing justice to conflict victims. According to the International Centre for transitional Justice, *"Transitional justice refers to a range of approaches that society undertake to recon with legacies of wide spread or systematic human rights abuse as they move from a period of violent conflict or oppression towards peace, democracy, the rule of law, and respect for individual and collective rights"*. Truth seeking, prosecution, reparation and reconciliation are some of the major focus of transitional justice (Upreti, and Bastola, 1997).

Transitional justice has become part of the post-conflict peace-building process, where it is viewed as essential to reconciliation and reintegration of civil society after conflict. The debate on transitional justice has frequently been posited as one of peace versus justice, or judicial versus non-judicial measures for redressing past wrongs, where criminal prosecutions have often been argued to promote destabilisation and resumption of conflict, whereas truth-seeking as a means of accountability has been purported to enhance peace and reconciliation (Kriz, 1995). On a broad level, the primary objectives of transitional justice are in essence twofold: first, to begin processes of reconciliation among the parties to the conflict and the affected populations by establishing a process of accountability and acknowledgement; and second to deter reoccurrence, ensuring sustainable peace (Bassiouni, 2000). Both judicial and non-judicial accountability can encourage reconciliation of post-conflict societies. However, reconciliation is a complex concept and not easily defined; it has been described in numerous ways from acknowledgement and repentance from the perpetrators and forgiveness from the victims (Avruch & Vejarano, 2002), non-lethal co-existence (Tepperman, 2002), as democratic decision-making and reintegration, and as four concepts namely truth, mercy, peace and justice (Odendaal, 997). Crucially, reconciliation is a process, which end-state can be reached by different means and lengths of time.[5]

Truth seeking, prosecution, reparation and reconciliation are some of the major focus of transitional justice (Upreti, 2007b). According to the Encyclopedia of Genocide and Crimes Against Humanity (2004), transitional justice refers to a field of activity and inquiry focused on how societies address legacies of past human rights abuses, mass atrocity, or other forms of severe social trauma, including genocide or civil war, in order to build a more democratic, just, or peaceful future.[6] Therefore, transitional justice should not be understood in a narrow sense of 'justice during transition'. The notion of transitional justice not only includes the concept of legal justice according to the international legal principles but also wider areas of reparations programmes and truth-seeking mechanisms, political transformation from conflict to peace and stability. Hence, it is a long and complicated process that requires firm commitment from the parties signing the peace agreement.

Transitional justice is a powerful concept to understand dynamics and a process of emergence of society from the armed conflict. While examining the translation of the concept of transitional justice into practice in war-ridden conflict like Nepal, it falls into legal, political, moral and operational dilemmas and practical complications. In the case of Nepal, it is highly contested and resisted. The tension between dealing with the past and moving forward for the future is prevalent phenomenon and ultimately 'political compromise and negotiation' determines the course of action of transitional justice. The bill on Truth and Reconciliation Commission prepared and brought for discussion by the Ministry of Peace and Reconstruction in August –September 2007 is an example of this complication.

The role of law in realising rule of law in transition is crucial but frequently questioned once the contributions of legal actors and institutions to war to peace transition are far below the public expectation. Often legal implementation operates on the framework of legal engineering of the society. In the situation of a country like Nepal which, having itself transited from war to peace, role of law is crucial but severely weak. Success of Nepal's transitional justice depends upon what extent it respects international laws that provide some legal obligations such as preventing human rights abuses, investigating past crimes, identifying and punishing human rights abusers, imposing sanctions against persons responsible for violence, facilitating reparations to victims, accepting international human rights and humanitarian provisions to prevent human rights abuses, and promoting reconciliation and reintegration. Therefore, ensuring transitional justice in Nepal depends upon the readiness of the government of Nepal to respect international human rights and humanitarian provisions (Upreti, 2007b).

International human rights provisions (four Geneva Conventions and additional protocols), international humanitarian laws and various UN Conventions (e.g. International Convention on the Elimination of All Form of Racial Discrimination; Convention on the Rights of the Child; Convention on the Elimination of All Form of Discrimination Against Women; International Convention on Economic, Social and Cultural Rights; etc.), Report of the Secretary General to the Security Council on 'the rule of law and transitional justice in conflict and post conflict societies'[7] and the report of the independent expert submitted to the 61 session of Commission of Human rights to up date the set of principles to combat impunity[8] are important arrangements that guide reconciliation and social and political reintegration.

Many conflict victims of Nepal have suffered from forced displacement, abduction, arbitrary detention, killing, destitution of property, physical assault and torture, extortion, rape and sexual abuses, amputation. Peaceful co-existence, trust, empathy and healing are possible only if justice is done to the victims and the crimes of the past are acknowledged and punished. The whole efforts of central and local levels have to ensure justice to victims to promote reconciliation and reintegration. The following actions in integrated way help to ensure justice:

a) Full functioning of TRC
b) Prosecution of perpetrators as per the law
c) Restoring victims and victimised communities, which is possible through mediation between the victims and perpetrators
d) Punishing police, military and wartime guilty officials committed aggression as disciplinary action
e) Providing compensation to conflict victims.

All these activities are proposed for long-term psychological rehabilitation of conflict victims. Urgent attention on dealing with women and girls suffered from specific sexualised violence (such as sexual abuses, rape, molestation, etc.) during the time of armed conflict is needed. They also need special legal assistance. Free legal services to conflict victims at district and local levels through district chapters of Bar Association or NGOs specializing in legal services is crucially essential.

11.2.5 Transitional Security

Success or failure of peace process at the time of transition depends upon ensuring security to its citizens and the former warring parties. The vested interest groups benefiting from weak security situation or those who do not want peace, stability and progressive change create insecurity, weaken transition and pose various challenges to the fragile peace process. Massive proliferation of small arms and associated crimes and violence in Nepal is one of the numerous examples of this intension (Upreti and Nepali, 2006). Hence, containing or controlling criminals and arms smugglers is extremely essential to make the peace process a success. Police and armed police forces alone cannot achieve transitional security if political forces and citizens of the country do not proactively engage in establishing transitional security.

It is urgently needed to fill-up the severe political vacuum existed at the village level. Starting and strengthening joint political activities by all political parties across the country, engaging citizens in political process, adopting integrated and non-conventional security approach (going beyond relying on security force for realising transitional security), coordinated action in the border areas with Indian security forces and administration and dialogue with the Indian politicians are some of the measures to be taken immediately to improve transitional security. War-to-peace transition in many war-ridden countries has demonstrated that border regulation/ management is crucially important to make the peace process successful (Barnes, 2002, Aditya et al., 2006).

The post-conflict situation is very much determined by security situation at local level, trust of people on government, assurance of justice and accountability, economic opportunity and social well being.[9] The information collected from the field reveals that local security is an absolute prerequisite for a successful post-conflict transformation. A concerted action of police, local people and political parties is needed for achieving community security.

11.2.6 Free and Fair Elections

Election is one of the fundamental components of the peace process and the successful management of the transition that provides the foundation for the stability and democracy. Fresh election provides mandate, laws and regulations and legitimacy required for the transformation of the old state and institutionalises the achievements made during the time of transition. However, ensuring free and fair election and higher participation of the eligible voters is a precondition. The Kenyan election and the subsequent violence in early 2008 indicate that holding election by any means is not the right solution. The important aspect of election is its legitimacy and ownership. Therefore, free, fair and the election process and outcomes owned by people should be the precondition for election. The Constituent Assembly formed by the elected representatives of people has provided a tremendous opportunity to institutionalise the achievements made so far and opened avenues for restructuring of the state as well as severe risks of being failure and source of ethnic and territorial conflict. Hence, political parties and decision makers have to accept certain constitutional principles and democratic ideals to minimise risks and maximise potential of the elected constituent assembly. Regrettably, the Constituent Assembly has so far been very tactically used for narrow vested political interests at the cost of national interests.

11.2.7 Disarming, Demobilizing and Reintegration of Ex-combatants

Disarming is a process of handing over of the arms used by individuals to the authorities who are responsible for the safe storage, redistribution or even the destruction of those arms (Gleichmann et al., 2004). Demobilization is a act of either disbanding arms unit, reducing the number of combatants or an interim stage before reassembling entire armed forces (ibid:15). Reintegration is a social and economic process by which ex-combatants acquire civilian status and gain access to civilian forms of work and income (ibid: 15).

Regarding the DDR of the Maoist PLA, clause 11.1.3 'Registration of Maoist Army Combatants at Cantonment Sites' of the agreement states: *"Only those Maoist army combatants who have been properly registered at cantonment sites will be eligible for possible integration into the security forces fulfilling the standard norms. Any discharged personnel will be ineligible for possible integration. Those who are eligible for integration into the security forces will be determined by a special committee as agreed in the Comprehensive Peace Accord.*[10] *This integration process will be determined in subsequent agreement with the parties. Upon registration Maoist army combatants, if found to be born after 25 May*

1988, will be honourably and automatically discharged... The Interim Council of Ministers will form a special committee to supervise, integrate and rehabilitate the Maoist army combatants". This section provides the important basis for DDR in Nepal.

From the verification process, UNMIN came up with two categories of PLA. The first category is qualified PLA and second category is unqualified PLA. The disqualified PLA from the UNMIN verification process should be reintegrated into society and it requires special knowledge, skills, procedures, resources and mechanism. Similarly, the qualified PLA, as per the provision of CPA, has to integrate into state security forces or adjust in any other appropriate structures. This is one of the main tasks for achieving durable peace in the country.

DDR is fundamentally important for sustaining peace and providing security to communities across the country, as inclusion of qualified PLA combatants into national security forces (police and army) and reintegration of ex-combatants from both sides into society is crucial. It is therefore not possible to transform machinery of conflict into one that supports sustainable peace and development without appropriate DDR. Security sector reform (Ball, 2002; Kumar and Sharma, 2005; OECD, 2004; Schnabel and Ehrhart, 2005) and relationships between citizens and security forces are crucial in promoting greater security sector governance; a prerequisite of any successful DDR programme (Aditya et al., 2006).

11.2.8 Security Sector Restructuring

Security Sector Restructuring (SSR) is a crucially important element in making the peace process successful. It is a process of transforming police, army, paramilitary, local security units, intelligence and other authorised security-related agencies by changing, redefining or expanding their mandate, procedures of operation, strengthening parliamentary supervision mechanisms and stronger civilian control according to democratic governing principles. This issue is discussed in depth in Chapter Ten. SSR in the context of Nepal is an approach to address shortcomings and weaknesses of security sector by establishing new vision and procedures that comply with the internally accepted security governance principles and practices (Upreti, 2007a).

11.2.9 Reconciliation, Reintegration, Rehabilitation and Reconstruction

The CPA is the fundamental basis of reconciliation and reintegration. There are several sections related to reconciliation and reintegration. Among them Section 5.2.4 is one of the important provisions. It states, "*Both parties agree to form a National Peace and Rehabilitation Commission to initiate process of rehabilitation and providing relief support to the persons victimized by the conflict and normalize the difficult situation created due to the armed conflict*". Similarly, Section 5.2.5 states, "*Both parties agree to form a high level Truth and Reconciliation Commission on mutual understanding to conduct investigation about those who were involved in gross violation of human rights at the time of the conflict and those who committed crime against humanity and to create the situation of reconciliation in the society*". TSection 5.2.8 states, "*Both parties express the commitment to allow without any political prejudice the people displaced due to the armed conflict to return back voluntarily to their respective ancestral or former residence, reconstruct the infrastructure destroyed during the conflict and rehabilitate and socialize the displaced people into the society*". Section eight of the CPA makes provisions of dispute settlement and implementation mechanism. It states:

1. Both parties agree to become responsible and accountable in an individual and collective manner and not repeat in future mistakes committed in the past and also correct these mistakes on a gradual basis (8.1);
2. The National Peace and Rehabilitation Commission shall be set up as per the need for making the campaign for peace successful. The composition and working procedures of the Commission shall be as determined by the interim Council of Ministers (8.2);
3. Both parties are committed to settle all kinds of present or possible future differences or problems through mutual talks, understanding, consensus and dialogue (8.3);

4. Both parties express commitment that the interim Council of Ministers shall constitute and determine the working procedures of the National Peace and Rehabilitation Commission, the Truth and Reconciliation Commission, the High-level State Restructuring Recommendation Commission and other mechanisms as per the need to implement this agreement, the Interim Constitution and all the decisions, agreements and understandings reached between the Seven-Party Alliance, the Government of Nepal and the CPN (M) (8.4).

The strongest point of the CPA for the purpose of reconciliation and social and political reintegration is the specific provisions of formation of National Peace and Rehabilitation Commission and Truth and Reconciliation Commission. Similarly, the provision of protection of political, social, economic, cultural and religious rights of people is another strong provision in the CPA. If these provisions were honestly translated into action, it would greatly contribute to realizing reconciliation and reintegration. The weakest aspect of CPA is the overload of sweeping statements, without clear articulation of how they are going to be translated into operation. The elaboration of implementation mechanism and clear time-bound responsibility would help to implement the CPA.

Success or failure of any agreement depends upon the willingness and accountability of the parties signing such agreement. In the case of CPA, both the government and the CPN (M) turned out to be weak in sincerely implementing their promises. For example, one of the paragraphs in the preamble states, '*By putting democracy, peace, prosperity, progressive social and economic transformation, independence, integrity, sovereignty and prestige of the state in the centre-stage, implement the commitments made by both the sides to hold the election to constituent assembly by mid June 2007 in a free and fair manner,*'. The reality is that the election has been postponed thrice. Such non commitment enhances public mistrust in them. Several provisions [for example, nationalization of property of late king and queen (3.3), End feudal land ownership (3.7), controlling corruption (3.11), establishment of different commissions (8.2 and 8.4), end all forms of feudalism (3.6), no collection of donation (5.2.1), making information about the disappeared people within 60 days (5.2.3), not to illegally seize or capture anyone's private property (7.5.5) etc.], to be sincerely implemented to make the peace process successful are not implemented by both sides simply because of lack of willingness and commitment. The work of Dina Esposito and Dina Crocker (2004) related to post-conflict strategy for Sudan concludes that signing of a historic peace agreement alone does not guarantee successful post-conflict reconciliation, reintegration and reconstruction and therefore sustained economic assistance and forward learning decisions must be essential.

Archbishop Emeritus of South Africa Desmond Tutu said, *'Examining the painful past, acknowledging it and understanding it, and above all transcending it together, is the best way to guarantee that it does not and cannot happen again"* (foreword in Bloomfield et .al., 2003). Reconciliation and reintegration reorients people from the adversarial and antagonistic relation of the time of conflict to more mutually respected and cooperative relations. Essentially, reconciliation develops healing relations between victims and offenders that are needed for durable peace and democracy. Establishing democratic processes and structures is the fundamental basis for addressing post-conflict challenges. However, democracy cannot travel and it has to build locally. Similarly, democracy functions in a situation of injustice and legacy of violence in any post conflict situation. Therefore, reconciliation is an integral part of developing and strengthening broader democratic process. The major concern in establishing the post-conflict societies is to ensure that the people engaged in violence will not resume their violent acts (Upreti, 2006a).

After the Constituent Assembly election on 10 April 2008, Nepal entered into a new phase of transition to achieve broader socio-economic and political transformation. However, transformation is successful only when citizens of this country reunite and work together in achieving social harmony; economic development and political stability. Reconciliation and reintegration (R&R) are some of the fundamental building blocks in making the transition successful and achieve lasting peace in the country. Hence, promotion and strengthening of reconciliation and reintegration is precondition for successful peace building in Nepal.

Reconciliation: Reconciliation is a process of searching for justice, healing, forgiveness, pattern of cooperation and coexistence as well as understanding needs, fears and aspirations of past antagonists, whereas reintegration is a process of acceptance of ex-combatants, IDPs and conflict victims in community. Reconciliation is a process of examining the past and addressing the legacy of the past violence and rebuilding the broken relationships (Bloomfield et al., 2003). Hence, it is process of developing a shared vision of an interdependent and fair society by acknowledging and dealing with the past and building positive relationships, through a significant cultural, attitudinal, social, economic and political change[11] (Hamber & Kelly, 2004).

Reconciliation and reintegration is dealing with victims including internally displaced persons (IDPs) and ex-combatants or former soldiers from both sides. According to the United Nations Declaration of Basic Principles of Justice for Victims of Crime and Abuse of Power, General Assembly Resolution 40/34, 29-11-1985, 'victims are persons, who individually or collectively, have suffered harm, including physical or mental injury, emotional suffering, economic losses and substantial impairment of their fundamental rights, through acts or omissions that do not yet constitute violation of national criminal laws but of internationally recognized norms relating to human rights'. As documented by INSEC in its yearly Human Rights Year Books since the beginning of the armed conflict, there are thousands of cases of killings, disappearance, torture, rape, and forced donations, threats of attack, arrest and violation of human rights. Victims are displaced, ex-combatants or ex-soldiers, physically and mentally injured, children, women, elderly and disabled, or other people who are directly and or indirectly affected by the armed conflict, etc.

Reconciliation is a process of continuous engagement in addressing the sufferings, pains and tragedies of the conflict victims, developing their confidence, bringing communities together to develop harmony by better understanding the motives and intensions of offenders and exploring the ways and means to provide justice. Developing confidence, re-establishing mutual trust and deepening understanding between former enemies is a tremendously huge challenge but extremely essential element of achieving a lasting peace in Nepal. During reconciliation, it is likely that there will have to be negotiated processes of adaptation, which permit the accommodation of disparate views between returnees and those communities in which they are being resettled. The goal should be to learn to live with differences, to understand and accommodate diversity. As harnessing relationships is so central, all efforts must be guided by the three-fold goals of hope, healing and reconciliation in seeking integration and the creation of a cohesive community.

Limiting reconciliation into a practice of keeping aside the sufferings of conflict victims and survivors and providing an excuse to offenders appears if the reconciliation is either conceptually misunderstood or used as only outcomes (forgive and forget). However, important aspect of the reconciliation is its process to address justice, healing and truth. As reconciliation is a voluntary process, no one can impose it on another the victims themselves acknowledge, remember and learn from the past and finding ways to live in future with rebuilding relations and expanding hope. Hence, it is a process of deep change of an individual with a reconciliatory 'forgive but not forget' (Tutu, 1999) framework. In essence, reconciliation is not an excuse for impunity.

Reconciliation is a continuous and long-term process and the quick-fix approach cannot achieve lasting peace (Tutu, 1999). Being a voluntary process of transformation of relations, it demands change in belief, attitude, aspiration, emotion and feeling of the protagonists, sufferers and even community members, which is quite difficult and even painful (Galtung, 2000; Bloomfield et. al., 2003). Breaking negative stereotypes and prejudices requires engaging individuals (one-time enemy) as well as communities and therefore it is a broad and inclusive process.

Any reconciliation and social and political reintegration strategy must be able to address entrenched hatred, mistrust and uncertainty, reducing rural-urban and centre-periphery asymmetries, keeping the R&SPR process undisturbed from the spoilers, creating security environment, preventing from manipulation and misuse of resources, etc. It is essential to use a conflict lens when identifying and prioritising R&SPR tasks and promoting people-to-people dialogue as well as reduce partisan perception. Numerous studies (Kreimer et al.,2000; UNIFEM; 2004; Hamber and Kelly 2004; Specht and Carlien 1998; Centro de Estudios Internacionales 1995; Department of Foreign Affairs and International Trade Canada, 1997; Mokalobe 1999; Barron 1996; de Watteville (ud), Fusato 2003; Honwana 2005, MacCormack, 2003; Palmer, 2002; Aditya *et al.*, 2006 and Skaar et al., 2005) have shown that reconciliation and reintegration is complicated, lengthy and requiring concerted efforts from government, society and local people and therefore requires clear strategy, appropriate institutional arrangements and commitment at political and societal levels (Upreti, 2006b, 2007d).

Reintegration: Reintegration is a complex psychological (a process of psychological accommodation of people to be reintegrated from their present lifestyle to a normal civilian life), social, political and economic process of mainstreaming demobilized soldiers or ex-combatants and their families and other conflict victims as active members of either their communities or new communities and becoming active producers in civilian life (Upreti, 2007d). However, this paper mainly deals with social and political reintegration. Reconciliation is a first step of reintegration. Achieving reintegration is extremely difficult without facilitating proper reconciliation. Hence efforts are made to formulate a strategic basis for reconciliation, which consequently leads to achieving reintegration.

Reintegration constitutes social, political and economic components. Social reintegration is a process of acceptance of former soldiers and their dependants, IDPs, and their conflict victims by local communities. Political reintegration is a process by which demobilized soldiers and other conflict-affected individuals, and communities participate in structures and processes of political organizations in their communities and societies. Economic integration is related to employment opportunities, and marketable skills. It is not dealt with in this paper because economic integration is dealt with separately.

In a post-conflict situation, the first issue that comes to the forefront once the dust of conflict starts settling is how to deal with the warring parties and reintegrate them to the mainstream of the society and create a national army inclusive of all stakeholders? This demands the transformation of the security system which includes all actors, their roles, responsibilities and actions working together to manage and operate the system in a manner that is more consistent with democratic norms and sound principles of good governance and thus contributes to a well-functioning security framework'.

On a conventional level, reintegration is a process of assimilation of disarmed[12] *and demobilized*[13] *armed forces of warring parties (the state and the rebels) and their families into the civilian socio-economic life. Reintegration is a process of acceptance of ex-combatants and former soldiers and their families by host communities and developing a situation of mutual co-existence.*[14] *Former adversaries and other conflict victims have to reconstruct their lifestyles, community relations and actively participate in civic life. The reintegration is inevitably a lengthy and difficult process.*[15] *Hence, reintegration is a complex and long-term economic, political, social and psychological process of transition of ex-soldiers from their military life to a civilian life of conflict victims from conflict-related stress to normal life (Aditya et al., 2006). Hence, political, social, economic and psychological reintegration is integral part of successful reconciliation (Tutu, 1999; Bloomfield et al., 2003). The political participation of conflict-affected people (IDPs, ex-combatants and other conflict victims) is accepted and acknowledged by society in all social and political structures and mechanisms and they could transform their relation to start normal civilian life.*

There is no shortcut and simple prescription or ready-made roadmap for reintegration. It entirely depends upon the local context, commitments of the parties involved in the armed conflict and willingness of international community to support the indigenous processes. Reintegration cannot and should not be imposed from outside and it has to evolve from local initiatives. The problem is even more compounded by the short-term nature of donor project funding modalities of rehabilitation programmes, which does not contribute to achieving sustainable rehabilitation effects. The way forward to solve the problem is to initiate a home-grown reconciliation programme, which is people-centred and owned by the population. Lessons of war-torn countries such as Guatemala and South Africa tell that every society and community has its own ways of reintegration and they can develop it (Aditya et al., 2006; Harvery, 2004; Tutu, 1999). Hence, reintegration process is context specific and particularly focused on building collective ownership for dealing with the violent legacy of the past, establishing and promoting working relations at present and building a shared vision, concerted efforts and collective and individual commitments for a better future.

Reintegration concepts are interdependent and intertwined in shaping a peaceful societal system, particularly in a war-torn society. Conflict scholars such as David Bloomfield, Tersea Barnes and Luc Huyse (2004) argue that 'while democratic compromise produces solutions regarding issues in conflict, reconciliation and reintegration addresses the relationships between those who will have to implement those solutions'. Hence, reconciliation and reintegration strengthen democracy by developing the working relations necessary for successful practice.

A successful reintegration requires a process that addresses the legacy of the past violence and rebuilding of the broken relationships, actors (cooperation from both perpetrators and victims-survivors; willingness and commitment from government and community) and effective instruments (laws, procedures and operational arrangements) to address the past and develop a common vision for the future. Reconciliation and reintegration have to permanently prevent the use of past as a source of renewed conflict, to break the ongoing cycle of violence, to consolidate peace and to strengthen newly established democratic institutions and political process.

In order to minimize misunderstanding and to iron out the differences arising during reintegration period, a platform has to be set up where these issues could be discussed openly. The problems faced by former combatants, former soldiers, IDPs and members of host communities must come out in the open, so that they can help in developing a common understanding of the origin of the conflict. Such a process might help in developing inclusiveness and tolerance within the society, which by itself is the sign of a healthy environment, which can promote reconciliation by breaking the barrier of misunderstanding.

Reintegration is an integral part of a lengthy and holistic post-conflict reconstruction and recovery process (security sector transformation, building state institutions, re-establishing rule of law, reforming social sectors, reviving economy and financial reconstruction, and reconstruction of infrastructures[16]) in building the fractured society and therefore it is not quick fix. It is a lengthy, continuous and complicated process and path to justice that requires patience, forgiveness and resources. Reconciliation starts with rebuilding trust, a sense of security and confidence for future. If people see the possibility of recurrence of past horrors, they do not feel secure and do not trust the reconciliation and reintegration process. Hence, a high-profile South African Truth and Reconciliation Commission (1995-2003) has focused on 'truth' and 'forgiveness'.

Certain elements exist in every society bind people together. Different aspects of social organization such as the networks, norms and trust that allow society to function are called social capital (Putman, 1993). Nat Colletta, Markus Kostner and Ingo Wiederhofer (1996) argue that 'social capital goes beyond the basic level of human association trust that welds a civil society together; it also encompasses organisations, networks, and unwritten mores and values (Colletta, Kostner and Wiederhofer, 1996:73) Social capital provides a binding capacity for the community to work together. Reconciliation and social and political reintegration require robust social organizations. People through formal or informal authorities develop rules to govern themselves and their local resources, ensure collaboration. Social capital often helps in coordination and cooperation among local people and between local groups and outsiders and assist in consensus building in accomplishing social actions and enhancing human capacity, overcoming jealousies, tensions and disputes. However, often war-torn societies encounter serious damage of social capital, which needs to revitalise to promote reconciliation and social and political reintegration.

Case studies of UNIFEM (2004) in Liberia and Papua New Guinea show that the process of reintegration of conflict victims and ex-combatants and their families to adapt economically, socially and politically in civilian life depends upon recognition and respect in addition to provision of package of compensation (in cash or kind or symbolic), training and engaging in economic activities. Collaboration with conflict victims promotes respect and reorganisation between conflict victims and the host community. A UNIFEM (2004) study in Liberia and Papua New Guinea found that it is difficult for female conflict victims to socially, economically and politically reintegrate compared to male victims.

Brandon Hamber and Grainne Kelly (2004) suggested the following reconciliation and reintegration process with five interwoven and inter-related strands that are important for R& R strategy of post-conflict situation:

1. Developing a shared vision of an interdependent and fair society
2. Acknowledging and dealing with the past
3. Building positive relationships
4. Significant cultural and attitudinal change
5. Substantial social, economic and political change.

Based on the above discussion, the following conceptual schema can be drawn, which provide an analytical roadmap for the facilitation of reconciliation and social and political reintegration in a fractured society like ours.

Experiences around the world as well as literature demonstrate that building confidence and trust for a peaceful coexistence; participation of victims and survivors in social and political organizations; revealing truth; ensuring justice, establishing mutual recognition and respect and providing compensation and relief and rebuilding the damaged social capital existed in the community are preconditions for a successful reconciliation and social and political reintegration process.

Rehabilitation: Rehabilitation is a process of settling conflict victims by providing physical and psychological means in a new setting. Recovery is a process of bringing conflict victims in normal situation that requires social, psychological and financial supports. Both rehabilitation and recovery are long processes and require special attention (Upreti, 2007d).

The local community is the primary resource for rehabilitation and end result for reintegration. It is crucial to work with the community and not for it. People need to be helped to help themselves. Programmes have to be geared to the 'real needs and priorities' of the community. This requires major changes in attitude and methods of working with the community. The community must have the sense of ownership and responsibility towards the reintegration projects, as the only way of ensuring true sustainability of peace. Often, success of social reintegration depends upon the attitudes of communities towards people to be reintegrated and willingness of the targeted people to be part of the integrated community. Further, the perceived historical role of the people to be reintegrated during the time of armed conflict determines the degree of willingness of reconciliation of community or society.

In the case of former soldiers, their lifestyles were shaped by a hierarchical system of command and control, and guided by rigidly defined formal rules and regulations. Hence, support and counselling for the people suffering from psychological stress and trauma during the time of armed conflict is needed for reintegration. The psychological reintegration strongly focuses on the psyche and willingness of ex-combatants or ex-soldiers, conflict victims as well as host community.

Reconstruction: Reconstruction in the strict sense is a process of rehabilitation and recovery of mainly physical infrastructures. However, in a broader sense, reconstruction also involves social, political, spiritual, physical and financial abilities of conflict victims to accomplish their normal life (Upreti, 2007d).

Communities during the time of the armed conflict were deeply divided. Social characteristics of the communities existed before the starting of armed conflict (such as common identity, cooperation, social networks and inter-personal relations, respect and trusts, etc.) has been drastically changed. Field study reveals that communities are struggling to promote reconciliation, maintain harmony and re-start collaboration. Hence, community rebuilding should be the priority of national as well as local government, NGOs and political parties.

One of the meaningful ways of reconciliation is creation of various symbols, platforms and mechanisms that unify divided members of community; promote healing and bring people together for concerted actions. Establishment of peace parks, gardens and community halls; building of schools, community halls, service centres, etc. in memory of the conflict victims, erection of statue/sculptures of people killed during the time of conflict; establishing memorials, scholarship, awards and prizes, declaring certain roads, public places in the name of conflict victims, etc. are some of the possible activities that promote reconciliation. Organising periodic activities in the community by bringing people together and helping to unify a divided community will also help in the healing process and emotional resilience. However, it requires special caution to minimise potential division and disputes. Resources should be allocated to train facilitators and conflict victims on how to help traumatized people. Similarly, people wounded or disabled from the armed conflict, chronically ill because of exposure to armed conflict need medical care, counselling and rehabilitation facilities and training. Sensitizing conflict victims to adjustment is crucial. Similarly, it is essential to connect reconciliation and social and political reintegration to the national strategy of post-conflict development and political transformation.

Several symbolic unifiers created in the past, such as naming of the roads and public places, erection of statues, rehabilitation of handicapped people, etc. have proved to be effective. A reconciliation and reintegration strategy has to integrate and learn from the successful experiences.

Target Groups for RRRR

For the purpose of reconciliation and reintegration, conflict-affected people can be grouped into: (a) families of people killed, (b) abducted people ands their families, (c) internally displaced people and their families, (d) missing people and their families, (e) injured or wounded people, and other generally affected people. Similarly, different age and gender groups of conflict victims such as children, adult, old, elderly people and women require specific reconciliation and reintegration focus. The primary actors of the reconciliation and reintegration are victims, offenders and protagonists (parties in conflict). Other key actors are community, government, support organizations (non-governmental, judicial, private or aid agencies). Reconciliation and reintegration requires understanding of how the armed conflict affects different social groups such as children, women, elderly people, disabled, students, internally displaced persons, etc. For example, often women suffer from sexual abuses (mass rape, forced pregnancy and marriage, prostitution, or molestation) during the period of armed conflict that promotes social stigmatization and marginalization. In reconciling women suffering from sexual offences, the offenders need to be identified and punished. However, often and in many societies women do not come forward and tell that they were raped or sexually abused because it is a taboo. Even if they do, they will be stigmatized and ostracized in society. In such a situation, special confidential arrangements of dealing with this issue by trained female investigators, psycho-social analysts are needed. Establishing trustful and respectful relations between male and female in society is important for the successful social reintegration. The recognition of victims and their empowerment as well as identifying the offenders is an important element in reconciliation and reintegration.

The Mozambique is often cited as a model for post-conflict reconstruction, reconciliation and reintegration (DFID, 2005), where disenfranchised groups were socially, politically and economically reintegrated into the mainstream and reduced partisan perception. The success Mozambique achieved was through the concerted efforts of the government, private sector and civil society.

11.2.10 Managing Public Expectations and Frustration

One of the major characteristics of the transition is higher expectation of people and possibility of turning it into deep frustration. When there is end of civil war, the people suffering for a long time want to get rid of all the problems and difficulties they faced in the past. They expect their demands to be fulfilled, their voices to be heard and their opinions to be respected. If political leaders or decision makers fail to hear them, address their concern or at least fail to constructively engage with them, people feel frustrated and go against the leadership or even against the peace process. Once the trust in political leadership is eroded, it is extremely difficult for leaders to manage the transition and make the peace process successful. Therefore, it is most essential for political leaders and decision makers to deal with the expectations of people and address frustration in time. One of the most established methods of addressing such expectations and frustration is to engage with them, openly discuss the potentials and limitations and make them part of the decision-making process. Nepalese politicians never applied this principle and therefore are facing serious difficulties with Medeshi people, Janajaties, women, minorities. Making every decision either for the vested political and personal interests or inaction for a long time (e.g. withholding decisions for appointing ambassadors and vice chancellors of universities) puts transition into crisis or obstruct smooth function of peace process.

11.2.11 Obtaining International Support

On one side, international support not only in terms of financial resources but also moral and symbolic aspects is crucially important to make the peace process successful. On the other, it is also equally tricky for political leaders to be entirely relying on the political decision of international forces. Hence, finding a balance between support and interference is crucially important. It is not uncommon for the international community (particularly the international powers) to directly engage in internal affairs of the countries facing civil war or armed conflict and political crisis. But maintaining good relations and keeping them away from internal interference is the task of political leaders. In the case of Nepal, political leaders are excessively relying upon the external political power. When politicians engage in obtaining small personal benefits (such as scholarships for their children, international visits or accepting other gifts and benefits) from international power centres, their credibility is finished.

11.2.12 Management of PLA

Agreement on Management of Arms and Army between the Government of Nepal and the CPN (M) and accepted by the UN contains provisions of reintegration of ex-combatants, child soldiers and other concerned people. Article 1.1 of the agreement "Principles" clearly states, "*Both parties fully agree to not include or use children who are 18 years old and under in the armed forces. Children thus affected would be immediately rescued and necessary and appropriate assistance will be provided for their rehabilitation*". Article 4.1.3 'Registration of Maoist army combatants at cantonment sites' of the agreement states, "*All Maoist army combatants will be registered at the main cantonment sites. ...Only those Maoist army combatants who have been properly registered at cantonment sites will be eligible for possible integration into the security forces fulfilling the standard norms. ... Those who are eligible for integration into the security forces will be determined by a special committee as agreed in the Comprehensive Peace Accord. This integration process will be determined in subsequent agreement with the parties. Upon registration Maoist army combatants, if found to be born after 25 May 1988, will be honourably and automatically discharged. Discharged Maoist army combatants must: release all weapons, uniforms and other military gear; and, agree not to return to cantonment sites unless mutually agreed by UN monitors in consultation with the parties. The assistance packages to be provided to voluntarily discharged personnel will be agreed by the parties in advance of cantonment. The Interim Council of Ministers will form a special committee to supervise, integrate and rehabilitate the Maoist army combatants".*

Successful management of arms and armies is the precondition for making the peace process successful in Nepal. However, this is one of the least understood, least realized and least acknowledged issues at the political level. No comprehensive strategy on dealing with the child fighters and disqualified members from the cantonment has been observed so far. What happens to them once they are released and go into community? How they will be integrated into the community? If communities are not sensitized enough to receive them, what implication will it have no the peace and reconciliation? are some of the crucial issues not getting enough attention. How long will PLA remain in cantonments and Nepal army in barracks? What happens to qualified PLA and excess number after new size of national army is defined? There is no comprehensive plan for security sector restructuring. So far, the concept of disarming, demobilization and reintegration as well as security sector reform is understood and interpreted very narrowly. Hence, the peace process will not be successful by signing agreements alone and full commitment from all concerned is a precondition that is largely a mission at present.

The 'Preamble' of the Interim Constitution provides a broader framework for the reconciliation and reintegration. Some of its clauses state, ...*"Expressing full commitment to democratic ideals and norms, including Competitive Multi Party Democratic System, Civil Liberty, Fundamental Rights, Human Rights, Adult Franchise, Periodical Elections, Full Press Freedom, Independent Judiciary and principles of the rule of law", "Guaranteeing the basic rights of the Nepali citizen to formulate their Constitution for themselves and to participate in free and fair elections of the Constituent Assembly in a free-from-fear environment", "Keeping Democracy, Peace, Prosperity, forward-looking Economic-Social changes and the Country's Sovereignty, Integrity, Independence and self-respect at the centre of everything",....* . Similarly, Part 4 of the Constitution outlines 'Duties, Directive Principles, and Policies of the State', which is one of the fundamental bases for reconciliation and reintegration. Among many relevant articles, Articles 33 (Duties of the State), 34 (Directive Principles of the State) and 35 (State Policies) are crucially important.

However, the Interim Constitution became a constant source of tension particularly in addressing some of the fundamental issues. Some of the main contentious issues were related to: electoral system (candidates elected on the basis of First Past the Post from each of the Election Constituents v/s on the basis of Proportional Electoral System for the political parties considering the whole country as one single constituent), representation of ethnic diversity and gender composition in the state structures, restructuring of the state, etc. These issues led to the Terai uprising, strong opposition from ethnic groups, women and minorities. Hence, the transition became more complicated after the promulgation of the Interim Constitution.

In an assessment report about the ongoing peace process in Nepal (July 2007), the UN Secretary-General Ban Ki-moon observes that though the peace process in on track, the national political scene is becoming more complex and challenging to deliver peace and stability. He further added, *"Renewed and expanded efforts will have to be made to sustain the successful trajectory of the peace process"*. Despite the frequent reiteration of political leaders for making a peace process successful, many agreed upon tasks in the CPA such as restructuring of the state, ensuring civil, political, economic, cultural rights of people, addressing issues related to IDPs and disappeared people, security sector restructuring, etc. are not getting proper attention. The security situation is deteriorating and several armed groups are adding complications in already fragile transition.

11.3 STRUCTURES REQUIRED FOR MANAGING TRANSITION AND MAKING THE PEACES PROCESS SUCCESSFUL

Getting the process right for achieving peace and stability requires conducive structures. Based on the experiences of more than 50 war-ridden countries, the following structures are important to make the peace process successful.

11.4.1 National Peace Commission

A powerful and resourceful constitutionally provisioned National Peace Commission (NPC) is needed to be managed by competent team selected through a parliamentary hearing-cum-competitive process. The commission should be an apex body dealing with entire peace process. It has to be equipped with competent professional experts on peace process. The commission has to bring necessary experiences, expertise, and resources. It has to convene a peace conference, or round table conference, or consultative conference to facilitate smooth implementation of provisions outlined in the CPA. It has also to orderly document issues of the concerned people, prioritize and make necessary arrangements for debating at national level. It has also to explore suitable structures to implement negotiated settlement provisions. NPC has to coordinate with government departments, ministries, civil society and international community regarding the issues related to peace. NPC has to find solutions to the problems, difficulties, disputes and unclear matters which may arise in the peace process and to implement the agreed upon points immediately. It has to closely work with government, political parties and civil society.

11.4.2 Peace Secretariat

A strong Peace Secretariat to serve for the National Peace Commission should be constituted. Its functions should be to provide secretarial service to NPC and to execute the provisions outlined in various agreements and understanding to make the peace process successful. The head of the Peace Secretariat should function as member secretary of NPC. The officials working at NPC should not be transferred for at least some years to ensure the knowledge and skills gained in the secretariat are used in the peace process. The peace secretariat has to have the executive responsibility. Ministry of Peace and Reconstruction (MoPR) can largely serve this purpose.

11.4.3 Research and Resource Centre

The armed conflict and peace process in Nepal is a relatively new phenomenon. But there are many countries in the world, which have already undergone the situation of armed conflict for decades and decades. They have very important, useful theoretical and practical experiences, knowledge and skills in conflict management and peace process. Nepal needs to utilise such experiences, knowledge and skills, which can be done through research, analysis and comparative study. Nepal lacks sufficient reference materials and document-based resources relating to the conflict transformation, peace negotiation, war, and security and so on. Therefore, it has become urgent to establish a research and resource centre that works as a specialised agency to assist NPC and other concerned actors.

11.4.4 Different Technical Committees and Task Forces

A successful peace process needs skills, knowledge, information, acquaintance, and methodological procedures that can come from technical expertise. Therefore, a strong team of technical experts in important areas such as 'managing process', 'negotiation', 'reconciliation', 'investigation', 'formation of federation', 'psycho-social counselling', etc. has to be arranged in the NPC to assist the peace process. Issue-specific task forces are equally important in making the peace process successful. Such task forces could work on land reform issues, economic restructuring, developing reparation package, etc. Such strictures are more temporary in nature but frequently needed at the time of transition from war to peace.

11.4.5 Peace Process Monitoring Committee

One of the major causes of the disruption or breaking of peace process is the lack of a proper autonomous, independent, competent 'Peace Process Monitoring Committee'. Making peace process successful requires not only parties signing the CPA abide by the agreed principles but also effective monitoring mechanism. This committee has to monitor 'Ceasefire Agreement', 'Ceasefire Code of Conduct' and all agreements and understanding reached between the parties. A specialised body at the highest level to monitor the implementation of CPA is essential that has to address any issues and obstacles arise while implementing CPA. Three main actors (civil society, government and political parties) have to represent this body and have to work closely with UNMIN, NHRC and local human rights and civil society groups.

Post-conflict stability largely depends upon proper monitoring and coordination. Hence, the government needs to develop human resource and allocate required financial resources to monitor and coordinate peace related activities. It is always essential to be aware of elite capture of resources allocated for the post-conflict peace dividends. Special attention on monitoring of post-conflict activities is needed for special groups such as youth, children, girls and women who have experienced abuses (sexual and others), and who are isolated families and/or communities due to conflict are addressed. Monitor whether the compensation package is addressing support needs of the disabled, wounded, and other people with special needs.

11.4.6 'Conflict Transformation and Peace Building Units' Within Political Parties

Now it has become urgent for the political parties to form conflict transformation and peace building units within their party structures and develop their capacity. Such units should study and monitor the conflict, consult and coordinate with the National Peace Commission, Peace Secretariat, Peace Process Monitoring Committee, Maoist, government, army, civil society, diplomatic missions and other concerned sides of the conflict.

11.4.7 Truth and Reconciliation Commission

Hundreds of thousands of Nepalese people are affected by the decale-long armed conflict. They are negatively affected by the destructive activities such as killings, intimidation, extortion, forceful eviction from their home, kidnapping, tortures, etc. They are impaired, internally displaced or migrated, raped, their personal properties are damaged. The victims and survivors are going through disappointment, frustration, humiliation, revenge and retaliation, and some of them are also involved in social crimes and violence. So, giving justice (through individual penal prosecution, international or internal tribunal, hybrid courts, wetness protection and trial monitoring, etc.), psychological remedy, reparation and reconciliatory activities are extremely necessary to arouse hope in them, return them to usual life and make them creative. A separate institution having specialised expertise is required for that and therefore Truth and Reconciliation Commission (TRC) is needed. Within the TRC, there should be the following committees to deal with the special issues:

Government of Nepal has prepared a draft bill of TRC but it was seriously criticism because of some of the provisions that could seriously undermine the very essence of truth and reconciliation. The government has to revise the bill with addressing concerns raised by human rights community and establish TRC. The main tasks of TRC are to reveal truth and psychological rehabilitation of conflict victims and ensure justice and reconciliation. Once TRC reveals the truth, punishment or amnesty are two ways ahead, depending upon the situation and context. Amnesty is part of the healing process. Healing is a process of recovering from emotional and psychological scars of the armed conflict. It depends upon the intensity, duration and scale of the violence (longer the violence, difficult to healing), level of the heart caused by the opposition, division in society, stability in society, past culture of community and commitment and willingness of the transitional and new governments. Healing of pain, guilt, emotion, hatred of those people whose families are killed, those people who are tortured, bereaved, maimed, assaulted and raped, injured, abducted, homeless, intimidated and humiliated is difficult and takes time.

The TRC has to focus on verification of the facts and disclosure of truth, recommending sanctions against perpetrators and assist in commemoration of and tribute to victims and facilitate apology and forgiveness where appropriate. Criminal prosecution mechanisms and national tribunals can be established to provide justice to victims of conflict. Hybrid mode of prosecution may be needed only if domestic judicial mechanism is unable or unwilling to facilitate the process of giving justice. If prosecution is used in providing justice to victims of armed conflict, primarily it has to be investigated and prosecuted domestically.

11.4.7.1 Disappearance Investigation Committee

More than a thousand people were displaced during the conflict. Their investigation is a precondition for making the peace process successful. It requires specialized knowledge, skills and commitment and therefore needs a specialized institution fully responsible for the investigation and brings the reality in public. It has to coordinate with NHRC, civil society-led human rights organizations, OHCHR, and NPC.

11.4.7.2 Reparation Committee

Reparation is one of the fundamental components of a successful peace process. It provides a physical and psychological basis for moving ahead. In the reparation package rehabilitation, compensation, restitution, creation of memorials, public apologies by wrongdoers and commemoration are some of the important elements.

The government has to make sure that compensation for the conflict victims is provided in a transparent and accessible way and distributed through a local inclusive mechanism. Compensation can be in the form of cash, kind and symbolic in nature. International human rights and humanitarian laws (e.g. Geneva Convention, ICC Rome Statute, etc) recognize reparation as one of the means of reconciliation and reintegration. Efforts at local level have to be concentrated on restoration of people's rights, returning of property captured during the time of the active armed conflict and facilitate rehabilitation. Restoration of physical and mental health and providing medial and psychological care and legal and social services are an integral part of the compensation package to be provided at the local level. A reparation and compensation package is effective only when a complete database of the conflict victims is available.

Reparation and compensation is one of the highly potential areas of misuse of resource or politicisation as it involves a huge amount of resources. Therefore, a clear legal and monitoring mechanism is required and that has to be established by representing conflict victims, civil society, political parties and government officials. The compensation package should be decided by this mechanism, not on ad hoc basis.

The reparation package has to concentrate on rapid restoration of essential services to assist conflict victims, ensuring their safety and security; and helping conflict victims in rehabilitate in their previous houses and communities.

Facilitate a special package of basic support s for reconciliation and social reintegration of especially tracing unaccompanied children and reunifying them with their families or relatives, arranging for food and proper shelter, education, healthcare, employment. The reparation package has to develop based on the categorisation of the conflict victims presented in Section 4.2.1.

The government should ensure that compensation to conflict victims of the armed conflict should go hand-in-hand with larger strategies of post-conflict social development and political and social transformation.

There is always the risk of perception of host community towards reconciliation and social and political reintegration of especially ex-combatant as a 'reward for committed atrocities' or local communities are excluded from the reparation packages. There can also be resentment from host communities. Hence, monitoring and coordination mechanism at local level is needed to take preventive measures by dialogue and awareness rising discussion in advance. Receiving communities must be informed in advanced about the purpose, intention and procedures, reintegration package, potential impacts and finally collect their feedback and suggestions. Local Peace Committee could be one of such mechanisms for coordination and monitoring. Local monitoring and coordination committee composed of journalists, lawyers, leaders of civil society and local units of political parties and the government representatives could ensure transparent and accountable reconciliation and reintegration.

11.4.7.3 Education and Awareness Committee for Elimination of Impunity and Assurance for Reoccurrence

Preparing society to move ahead requires a massive education and awareness campaign right from household level to national level. It demands special content, process and activities and therefore a specialized agency is required. It has to coordinate with media, academic and non-academic institutions and civil society to promote truth and reconciliation and healing in society.

11.4.7.4 Displacement Management Committee

Global experiences of armed conflict and its management show that internal displacement and forced migration is one of the major by-products and successful conflict resolution is not possible without addressing the displacement issues. In Nepal, displacement issue is highly politicized. Economic incentives are given only to those who are close to power centres and politically affiliated with the powerful politicians. The really needy displaced people have not getting benefit from the state. The existing approach of dealing with displacement issues cannot appropriately solve the problem and therefore cannot contribute to the peace process. Hence, a specialized agency is needed to deal with all aspects of conflict-induced displacement and forced-migration.

11.4.8 Donors Peace Support Group

As experienced around the world, international communities remain a highly influential external force in the conflict-torn host countries. They directly or indirectly involve in conflict transformation and peace process. However, because of their own approaches, strategic interests, commitment on specific issues or simply because of their personal characteristics, they do not cooperate or even compete. This proves to be counterproductive to the host countries (Aditya et al., 2006). International communities wishing to see durable peace and functional democracy in Nepal should form a 'Donors Peace Support Group'. This group should monitor their activities that are fuelling conflict, or doing harm (e.g. arms sale) and provoking parties in conflict. They have to coordinate their activities, avoid duplication, formulate their own code of conduct and implement it, assist the peace structures such as National Peace Commission, support only such development activities that ensure peace dividends to conflict affected people, poor, marginalised, socially excluded and lower class people. They have to engage with civil society in a more transparent and accountable way and stand against the violation of human rights. Such donors' helping group has done good work in Columbia.

11.4.9 Constitutional Court

A Constitutional Court is necessary for finding solutions of constitutional and legal complications that may arise in the process of forming a new constitution from the Constituent Assembly. It has to protect basic democratic principles, norms, values such as human rights, multiparty competition, periodical election system, etc. in the new constitution. Such a constitutional court had played very important roles in South Africa.

11.4.10 State Restructuring Committee

Nepal has decided to go in for a federal republic. But the debate in federal structures of the country is centred on emotion, biases, self-centric vested interests (to be leader of particular group or to get personal benefit), sensestionality and romanticism rather than scientific principles of federalism, realism and pragmaticism. If the existing level of debate is not shifted, it will lead to nowhere than the communal, ethic or territorial conflict and tension because none of the ethic groups is in majority and going for ethnic federalism or '*Samagra Medesh one Pradesh*' type of federalism ignoring the diversity and plurality of population, language, culture, speciality.

11.5 MITIGATING NEGATIVE IMPACTS OF ARMED CONFLICT ON NATURAL RESOURCES AND ENVIRONMENT

Conservation and natural resources could play an important role in environmental peace making if proper attention is given in this area (Buckles, 1999; Matthew *et al.*, 2001; WWF; 2000). Biodiversity and forests are a few of the highly affected sectors by the armed conflict within natural resources. In addition to the armed conflict, governance crisis: lack of transparency, accountability and stability were other contributing factors in deteriorating conservation and natural resources in Nepal.

Armed conflict has not only caused negative impacts, it has also positively contributed to altering the unequal social relations in society and opened avenues for addressing environmental concerns and problems faced by natural resource sector. Breakdown of community resource management and environmental systems is a common phenomenon in Nepal as an effect of the armed conflict. Citing empirical evidences and previous research findings, this paper concludes that acute insecurity and instability, governance problems, social and economic inequalities and environmental injustice have greatly contributed to escalation of the armed conflict. The degradation of natural resources and threat to biodiversity in Nepal is the combined outcome of armed conflict, civil disorder and poor governance.

Conservation awareness through conservation education, media mobilization (for example, collaboration with media in production and telecasting/airing conservation documentaries), and policy dialogues at the local level is crucially important. Immediate concerted action on preventing habitat destruction is needed if we want to conserve our pristine biodiversity and conservation of Nepal.

Proactive engagement of conservation organizations in essential to make sure that the new constitution made by the

Constituent Assembly adequately incorporates conservation concerns. Poor people residing in surroundings of the parks and protected areas lack means of livelihood. If conservation organization in specific and the government of Nepal in general are not able to create livelihood basis, cooperation from them in achieving conservation will be difficult. New vision, new policy, new strategy, new institutional arrangement, new methodological approaches and fresh perspective are essential to make sustainable use and management of natural resources and environmental services. The contribution of environmental sector in achieving sustainable peace, social harmony depends upon the willingness of policy makers and politicians to develop and implement appropriate strategies.

Intimate engagement with political parties on defining and refining their 'conservation policy' is crucial to conserve nature and protect biodiversity. Conservation organizations have not made enough efforts to closely work with related parliamentary committees and continuous engagement with political parties. One of the main challenges of less responsible behaviour of political parties towards conservation is because of lack of full understanding of important contribution and dynamic nature of conservation.

Establishing community-based (a) biodiversity monitoring mechanisms, and (b) anti-poaching units (including local communities of Buffer zones, park authority and local administration where appropriate) is crucially important at the time of transition.

Redefining the engagement and role of military in parks (there is intense debate on this issue and therefore it is essential to clarify the needs, relevance, level and scale of engagement of army from the DNPWC (in which level, where and how much strength is required, if needed). There are cases of latent conflict between the warden (head of the park) and the chief of the local army barrack like 'two lions in one den'.

It is found that linking tourism, ecotourism and nature conservation through public-private-partnership arrangement between government-conservation sector and corporate sectors is insufficient. Religion-based conservation and tourism in collaborating with the religious groups and inter-faith organizations is crucially important but yet to be realized in full potential.

Industrial wastes in the park areas by urban waste are negatively impacting conservation. No EIA provisions are applied to establish industries in the surroundings of parks. Urgent need of "River Authority' is highly realized to regulate and or control urban waste disposal in river.

Poaching is becoming a lucrative business and therefore expanded its roots from Tibet to India and internationally and has strong connections with power centres. Hence, controlling poaching requires a national focus and it is not possible alone by DNPWC or any other single department. Engagement of parliamentary committees in this issue is crucial.

The armed conflict and associated events have caused significant environmental damage, degradation of natural resources and deterioration of conservations efforts. In recovering from the damages it is important to recognise environmental rights in the forthcoming constituent assembly election and subsequent new constitution; environmental impact assessment (EIA) and conflict impact assessment (CIA) needs to be integrated into a post-conflict reconstruction and rehabilitation. Coordinated efforts on environmental monitoring, strengthening enforcement mechanisms, carrying routine EIA and CIA, promoting participatory processes, employing economic incentives for obeying environmental laws, sharing vital information, sincere implementation of international conventions and laws related to environment, developing capacity by providing basic infrastructures and training, inter-ministerial coordination, strengthening decentralised community based natural resources, environment and conservation approaches, preparation of emergency response and contingency plans are some of the important factors in achieving better environmental services and sustainable use and management of natural resources.

Concerns of landless, marginalized, indigenous and disadvantaged people residing around parks and conservation areas are essential. Inclusion from women, ethnic community, *dalit*, and poor in decision making and benefit sharing should be the priority of conservation organisations to reduce poverty and address structural causes of conflict.

Reconstruction and rehabilitation support of conservation organisations have to promote equity-based livelihood basis and well being of poor, marginalised and conflict-affected people around conservation areas. Restoration of basic infrastructures and social capital, public services and community-based services are obviously priority issues in a post-conflict situation. Employment and income generation, community water supply and sanitation, community development, institutional capacity building and empowerment of socially excluded, marginalised sections of society are some of the important activities that have to be incorporated in conservation goals.

Conflict risk assessment (CRA) is a concept, process, tool as well as strategy. It is a concept because it provides powerful understanding of conflict situation and level of associated risks. CRA is a process because it is not a one-time event and has to be continuously practised during the entire period of conflict, as a conflict situation is always dynamic and scale, intensity and patterns frequently change. It is also a tool of analysing the degree, intensity and effects of conflict as it offers specific instruments to assess conflict. CRA is also a strategy because it is intended to minimise potential conflict risks to development and devise appropriate response options. Hence conservation organisations have to incorporate CRA in their restoration plans.

11.6 ESTABLISHMENT OF CONFLICT VICTIMS' DATABASE

So far, there is no proper database of conflict victims. Developing a comprehensive database of conflict victims (age, sex, economic status, types, number, etc.), nature of abuses and damage, scale and intensity at local (community and hamlet level) is a precondition for successful reconciliation and reintegration. It is not possible to take appropriate reconciliation and reintegration action without detail information. The detailed victims' database with different categories will also help to make the compensation and reparation transparent and need-based. The database can be developed by mobilising local civil society organisations/VDCs, etc. In this database, categorisation of conflict victims is required. For practical purposes, the following categories are proposed:

- Most affected people and communities
- Affected people, and communities
- Less affected people and communities.

Similarly, different groups of people are within most affected and affected category and they need different methods of reconciliation and different approaches. Hence, the following grouping could help in implementing reconciliation:

- People killed and their families
- People abducted and their families
- People missing and their families
- Injured people
- Internally displaced people
- People with lost property.

The needs of different age and sex group of victims are different and therefore the following grouping can help for facilitating RR:

- Children (male and female)
- Youth (male and female)
- Elderly people (male and female)

11.7 INVOLVING CONFLICT VICTIMS IN SOCIO-ECONOMIC ACTIVITIES

It was observed in the field that once conflict victims are engaged in social and political spheres, they concentrate on the present and future than looking at the past. on the contrary, if people are isolated, alone, not mentally and physically active, they recall their horrible past memory and develop a mental response accordingly that ultimately leads to either revenge and retaliation or hopelessness and helplessness. Therefore, engaging conflict victims in social and political activities according to their capacity and ability has to be priority at the local level. They can be engaged in social and political activities by participating in community-based organizations, local users committees, and social and political activities. This type of participation revitalises local social capitals, gradually develops mutual trust and builds confidence and new social relations. Different social networks, common forums and platforms, and religious and philanthropic organizations exist in community and reconciliation and reintegration has to use these social capitals. Engaging conflict victims in social activities gradually develops their confidence and finally incorporates them in the political process (participate even in local committees of political parties, right based campaigns, development activities of VDC, etc.). Facilitate solidarity networks, meetings, gatherings and social events that reduce distress and trauma and promote healing and reconciliation of conflict victims. It is also equally essential to identify specific training needs for conflict victims that will develop confidence, ensure short- and medium-term relief to economic hardship and to ensure stable livelihoods.

Mobilisation of locally available resources (knowledge, skills, tools and techniques) is essential for post-conflict transition. In some societies, various traditional institutions, arrangements and associations are very active and popular. For example, Ghatu is a powerful and effective person in the Gurung community. Faith healers (*Dhami-Jhakri*), priests, local teachers, and elderly people are other important facilitators of community reconciliation. Hence, assessment of local capacity has to be started together with the developing of a comprehensive database of conflict victims.

One of the urgent areas of intervention is psychological counselling of conflict victims at local levels. They suffer profoundly from trauma, stress, fear and hopelessness. Reviving their hope for future requires psychological counselling. Improvement of psychological health and social well being of individuals exposed to ten years of violent conflict takes considerable time and efforts of psychological counselling. Developing a sense of belongingness and normalisation of daily life of people requires a feeling of security and constant efforts for a long time. Community mediation has proved to one of the effective approaches to deal with the contending issues.

Post-conflict reconstruction is a priority of the nation. Construction of physical infrastructure such as roads, schools, health posts and public buildings, drinking water and irrigation, electricity plants at community levels are important peace dividends and sources of local employment generation. Hence, engaging survivors of conflict in productive areas diverts their attention form recalling the past and employment is one the best ways of engaging them. Those survivors interested in participating in the reconstruction programme at their communities should be given priority. Engaginge conflict victims in productive work (employment) enhances and stabilises reconciliation and reintegration.

Post-conflict activities have to focus on reviving or reactivating and mobilising locally existing religious, cultural and social indigenous organisations in facilitating psychological recovery of people affected by armed conflicts. Schools, VDCs, CBOs, local units of political parties, civil society and philanthropic institutions need to engage in reconciliation and reintegration. Political integration can be done by ensuring participation of conflict victims in political processes through establishment of working groups on political issues relevant to them. Local units of political parties could play a facilitating role in enhancing political integration. Communities reconcile with shocks, tension and conflict by using specifically developed local practices. Locally existing indigenous or traditional institutions, organisations and individuals such as Ghatu (leader in Gurung community), faith healers, priests, local teachers, and elderly people in remote rural areas are important facilitators of community reconciliation. They help conflict victims to develop social networks that bolster feelings of empowerment and security and overcome feelings of helplessness and insecurity.

11.8 MANAGING CHANGE REQUIRES CHANGING BEHAVIOUR AND ACTION OF POLITICAL LEADERS

It is virtually impossible to transform the feudalistic,

centralised, unitary, monarchist and exclusionary country into a modern, equity oriented, federal Nepal without transforming perspective, thinking, action and behaviour of all people of Nepal. Transformation requires in:

a) Attitude, behaviour, perspective, thinking and action of major actors (political leadership, bureaucracy, judiciary, security forces, social elites and their organizational structures, procedure and mode of representation);
b) Rules (most of the existing laws, rules and provisions are the controlling and exclusionary and need change,
c) Issue (Nepali society is transforming from civil war to durable peace and hence all issues and agenda of the war-time must be changed and the role of government should be facilitating instead of controlling),
d) Structures (transformation is required in existing structure and power relations),

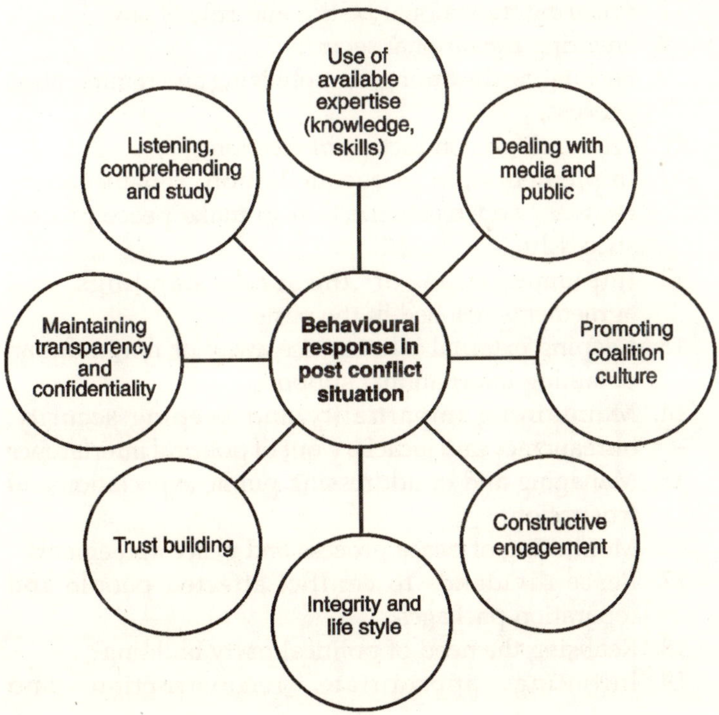

e) Context (transformation of exclusionary and controlling patterns of governance),
f) Value (e.g., social change through violent action to social change through peaceful action, non-violence, and co-existence).

11.9 CHALLENGES OF POST CONFLICT TRANSFORMATION

1. Agreeing on federal structures
2. Coping with unanticipated challenges emerging in the course of transition.
3. Agreeing on creation of structures as required by the peace agreements,
4. dealing with past and transitional justice,
5. Economic growth and stability
6. ensuring peace dividends to conflict victims and poor sections of society,
7. Ensuring transitional Justice and rule of law,
8. ensuring transitional security[17],
9. Facilitating disarming, demobilizing and reintegration process,
10. Free and fair conduction of elections,
11. Implementation of reconciliation, rehabilitation, recovery and reconstruction to make peace process successful,
12. Implementation of the understandings and agreements reached in the past,
13. Keeping external interference away or minimum an obtaining international support,
14. Maintaining impartiality and keeping security, bureaucracy and judiciary out of political interference
15. Managing and or addressing public expectation and frustration,
16. Monitoring of peace process and peace agreements,
17. Peace dividends to conflict affected people and reparation packages.
18. Realising the need of political party building[18]
19. Initiating appropriate reconstruction and

development[19]

20. Security system restructuring

11.10 CONCLUSIONS

While examining the management of the current transition in Nepal, some of the fundamental components of the peace process discussed in the preceding sections are missing or ignored from the beginning. Multiple political interests, opaque dealing and power-hungry action and behaviour of key political actors have shaped the entire peace process. One of the main weaknesses is the lack of honest implementation of the written or unwritten promises and agreements by the political parties.

The whole peace process is non-transparent, elite-centric and consequently exclusionary in nature. Neither the political parties nor the government seriously worked to ensure the above-mentioned elements of management of peace process. They did not sincerely implement the agreements and understandings made in the past but frequently made more understandings and agreements. The decision makers were reluctant to sincerely implement the agreements and understandings reached in different times as a part of peace process. They largely forgot the essence of the 2006 April people's movement. They were mainly reactive rather than proactive in dealing with the concerns of people (e.g. if some groups exert pressure through strikes, agitation and use of force, they reluctantly accept their demands but are still resistant to implement them). Political leaders in the decision-making position were avoiding the issues of restructuring the army, ending impunity, taken action to the proven human rights violators and sincere implementation of various components of transition management and elements of the peace process. The main political leaders and political parties are excessively guided by very narrow vested personal and party interests rather than broader national interests. The repetitive postponement of the constituent assembly election is a vivid example of this character.

The mindset of key political actors and their unwillingness to go for an inclusive state is a major challenge for successful management of transition and transformation of the unitary top-down exclusionary state into a federal inclusive and democratic nation. They have not yet been able to internalise the need of fundamental transformation of Nepal's feudal system, giving equal rights to all sections of society. They thought themselves alone only responsible for the nation and all other people are just trouble creators.

Managing people's expectations, bringing international power centres to support the peace process and successfully accomplishing fair election are some of the major challenges to Nepal's transition.

Nepal's peace process can be successful only when Nepali politicians set aside all their vested and narrow political interests and work collectively for the broader national interests and collectively respond to the genuine demand of different groups and stand together aginst the demands that poses threat to national security or question the souverginty of the country. It is crucial to review the past achievements and problems faced focusing on process, mechanisms, and outcomes, spirit of various agreements (avoiding blames and counter blames) and come forward with new commitments, necessary institutional arrangement and appropriate process and procedure that ensure smooth transition from war to peace and address all grievances of Nepalese people.

During the time of active armed conflict, local people have developed different strategies to cope with the adverse situation. The most common strategy was avoidance or passive acceptance of the prevalence of either party. The respondents explained that they avoid issues that bring potential confrontation or tensions or risk for them. Instead, they engage in such activities that bring collaboration and people supporting each others or working together for common purpose. In some instances, they also use religious or social events that bring people together to promote local harmony and encourage forgiveness. Regular assessment of the situation and responding accordingly (for example, going out of village for some weeks if they feel that situation is going to be tense in the village). Sharing and exchange of information among the close circle and mobilisation of existing networks (friends, relatives, etc.) in obtaining information were important activities of their risk assessment.

Despite their frustration, confusion, anger and feeling of uncertainties and insecurities; local people are still waiting for change and positive development. The respondents expressed hope in the young leadership of political parties and civil society. The respondents explained that they were not thinking of having CPN (M) in parliament and government, Nepal army in barracks and PLA in cantonment recalling the situation of 2004-5 where full-scale war spread across the country. This is a ray of hope for the peaceful and prosperous future of Nepal. They reiterate their wish for smooth implementation of CPA and fair constituent assembly election. When communities begin to examine the cause of war, why it has come to their village and start reflecting what can be done to minimize its impacts, the process of conscientisation allows communities to develop and utilize coping mechanisms which enables them to survive the conflict and which can then be transferred into the economic recovery process during the post-conflict era. In many ways, the conflict provides a unique opportunity to reassess community processes and practices. This is a hope for better future. Some of the key informants frequently referred to the empowerment brought about by the armed conflict. They argue that the ten years of armed conflict have not only created devastating effects on human rights abuses and damage of social and economic wealth but also laid a strong foundation for the transformation of feudal, hierarchical, centralised and exclusionary state and societal structures into a modern, inclusive, federal democratic state and equitable society. They refer to the participation of women in PLA, empowerment of dalit, indigenous communities and minority groups as some of the examples of empowerment.

In an interview,[20] Ms. Dilsara Nepali from Laxmipur VDC, Ward No. 5, Paluthan said, "*We lost ten years fighting among Nepalese people without achieving anything. Thousands of innocent people lost their life and many more wounded. Our village was full of fear, insecurity and horror. We were not able to go to our relatives.*

Since the CPA was signed, our village is peaceful and we are not observing serious insecurity and tension. We want to work in our farms in peaceful environment; we want to send our children safely to school. We want peace forever".

Case 11.1: Traditional institutions and practices useful for reconciliation

Many traditional reconciliation mechanisms and practices are existed in communities. Some of the examples of common mechanisms are religious occasions and festivals, marriage ceremonies and other celebration where local people gather, discuss issues and settle problems.

Some of the key persons engaged in local reconciliation are faith healers (*Dhami-Jhakri*), prist (*Purohit*)[21], local teachers, and elderly people. Certain ethnic groups have their own indigenous system of mediation, healing and solving conflict in their community.

Traditionally based reconciliation practices at local level are often guided by their values and customs (*riti-thiti*). One of several examples is *Sagun-garne* (reconciliation) existed since long time in ethnic communities of Gurung, Mangar, Tamang, Jirel, Surel. *Sagun garne* is a common reconciliation method based on cultural tradition. In this method, a gift (usually liquor, eggs, meat, etc.) is exchanged between the people/community to be reconciled, in the presence of villagers. The exchange of gift is performed after discussing the matter in the public gathering of villagers and conflicting parties. Once they reach a settlement, they start '*sagun garne*' (by accepting the gifts) and celebrating the reconciliation with drinking local liquor. Some religious and cultural festivals are particularly used for reconciliation such as *Dashain*[22] (used as an occasion to reconcile and strengthen relations by visiting each other's houses, exchanging gifts and good wishes), *Tihar* (establishing or strengthening sister-brother relation), Edh (Muslim festival where all gather and pray for good, social harmony and reconciliation), *Ghewa* (a Tamang death ritual where people from the community gather and settle conflict between their community members) (Upreti, 2002a, 2008a).

Dhikuri (a voluntary credit and saving rotating mechanism existed for the welfare of their members) of the Thakalis, Bheja (a multi-purpose voluntary welfare organisation created by members) of the Magar community, Rodhi (a type of informal entertainment club) and Gola (voluntary social organisation active in Western Hills) of the Gurung community, Guthi (a voluntary multi-purpose social organisation) of Newar commuity, Parma (a labour exchange arrangement) of Limbu community, Khyal (a voluntary social organisation active in Mid-west Nepal engage in multi-purpose activities) of Tharu are some of the common grassroots institutions (Bhattachan, 2007) which can be mobilised to promote reconciliation and harmony in society.[23] These institutions are not only practising grass roots democracies but also working to promote harmony, conciliation and building collective identity.

These indigenous mechanisms, forums and networks are existed and effective in several communities and geographical areas of the country and they are actively involved in settling community level disputes and welfare of their community.

Thousands of people have faced torture and abuse from both sides during the decade-long armed conflict. Reconciling such pain requires special measures and constant efforts at local level and appropriate compensation from the central level.

In summary, major sources of conflict that have to be address in the psot conflict transiton and beyond are:

a) intentions of accessing and controlling power and resources,
b) establishing and maintaining identity,
c) promoting, strengthening and expanding certain ideology and ideological differences,
d) mal-governance (greed and grievances) or operational failure of governance system (lack of transparency, accountability, rule of law, participation of people etc.).

If the causes of social conflicts are not addressed in time, the non-violent conflict transmits into violence or armed conflict. Therefore, the sole strategies of the post-conflict war to peace transition have to focus on addressing root causes of conflict.

While summarising the structures required to make the post conflict transiton successful the following structures seem impornat:

- Commission on Land Reform
- Security Commission and or National Security Council

- Security Sector Restructuring or other related committees,
- Committee on Disappeared Persons
- Local Peace Committee
- Administrative Restructuring Commission
- Thematic Committees (e.g., Peace Trust Fund)
- National Peace and Rehabilitation Commission
- High level State Restructuring Recommendation Commission
- Political party structures
- National Peace Commission Including Peace Secretariat (MoPR),
- Research and Resource Centre,
- Peace Trust Fund Management Committee
- Technical Committees and Special Task Forces (for thematic issues)

Similalry, the post-conflict transition must

a) address root causes of the conflict and structural inequalities;
b) build trust, cohesion and harmony at community;
c) develop community resilience to cope with the adverse impacts of conflict;
d) create space and opportunities for peace building,
e) ensure visible benefit form the project to socially excluded and marginalized people and making sue that they are included in the decision making process;
f) prevent possible widening of gap between rich and poor and enforces discriminations;
g) make sure that development interventions are not introducing new conflicts and tensions and ensure that resources are not captured and manipulated by elites or warring parties. This is possible through incorporating PCIA into development programme and project.

End Notes

1. Published in *Readings on Governance and Development,* (XI), pp.: 35-49. (July 2008).
2. *The Kathmandu Post,* 25 April 2006.
3. The 5622nd Meeting of Security Council had established United Nations Political Mission in Nepal (UNMIN) by unanimously adopting the resolution 1740 (23 January 2007) as per the request of the Government of Nepal and the CPN (M).
4. For details about the Joint Monitoring Committee, see the decision (SC/8942) of 5622nd Meeting (PM) of the Security Council of UN.
5. This paper distinguishes between national reconciliation and individual reconciliation. National reconciliation is achieved when societal and political processes function and develop without reverting to previous patterns or the framework of the conflict. Individual reconciliation is the ability of each human being to conduct his or her life in a similar manner as prior to the conflict, without fear or hate. This is an important distinction because each can come about independently of each other.
6. See The Encyclopedia of Genocide and Crimes against Humanity (2004), vol. 3, pp. 1045-1047 for details.
7. See S/2004/616 (23 August 2004) the report of the Secretary General to the Security Council entitled 'the rule of law and transitional justice in conflict and post conflict societies for detailed information.
8. See the report of the independent expert Ref.E/CONFLICT.4/ 2005/102/Add.1 (8 February 2005) submitted to the 61 session of Commission of Human Rights to update the set of principles to combat impunity for details.
9. Studies of Rebecca Linder (2005) in Afghanistan and Alcira Kreimer, Paul Collier, Colin Scott and Margaret Arnold (2000) in Uganda have also shown the similar results.
10. Section 4.4 of the Comprehensive Peace Agreement states, "The interim cabinet shall form a special committee to carry out monitoring, integration and rehabilitation of the Maoist combatants".
11. See A Brandon Hamber & Gráinne Kelly (2004) entitled 'Working Definition of Reconciliation' *Paper published by Democratic Dialogue,* Belfast, September 2004 for details.
12. *Disarmament* is a process of collection, control and disposal of weapons in the post-conflict peace process.
13. *Demobilization* is both a process and an outcome of releasing troops

from security service and therefore it is a political process. The determination of individuals to be demobilized and discharging from service is a political decision. A demobilization programme may include encampment of soldiers, relinquishing weapons and equipment; leave a unit; exchange their uniform for civilian clothing; receive identification papers; medical attention; compensation; short training courses; and other forms of assistance.

14. There is a widely held belief among politicians, intellectuals, activists and scholars that reintegration is only for insurgents. However, the fact of the matter is that reintegration applies to both: the state security forces and the insurgents once they lay down arms and agree to lead a civilian life.
15. See Iqbal Riza, Assistant Secretary General for UN Peacekeeping Operations, quoted in *Demobilized Soldiers Speak: Reintegration and Reconciliation in Nicaragua, El Salvador and Mozambique*, Managua, Nicaragua: Centro de Estudios Internacionales, 1995, page 4 for details.
16. See 'Post Conflict Development: Meeting New Challenges' edited by Gerd Junne and Willemijn Verkoren (2006). Delhi: Viva Books Private Limited, for details.
17. In any war-torn countries one of the major challenges after signing the peace agreements is maintaining security situation. Though the term, 'post conflict' is contested in Nepal particularly after the emergence of several small armed groups and their engagement in violence, the operational definition of post conflict is 'a situation after the formal signing of the CPA on 21 November 2006 by the government and the CPN (M) that ends armed conflict and parties earlier engaged in fights, violence and war start to implement the provisions of the agreements'. The transitional security of Nepal particularly in Terai17 is severely challenged by small armed groups such as Janatantrik Terai Mukti Morcha (Jwala Singh); Janatantrik Madesh Mukti Morcha (Goit), Janatantrik Terai Mukti Morcha (Bisphot Singh), Madeshi Mukti Tiger, Terai Cobra; Python, Terai Baggi, Terai Army, Madeshi Virus Killers Party, Royal Defence Army, Gorkha Line Mukti Morcha, Liberation Tigers of Terai Ilem (LTTE), Kirat Workers Party (mainly Udayapur and Khotang). In addition to these armed groups, there are other criminal groups active in Terai (Chhotelal Sahani; Sanju Baba, Raju Singh Rathor and Munna Singh Groups are few of many others mainly operating from India), rural areas and towns and creating severe insecurity and violence. This is serious

immediate security concern that state has to address (Upreti, 2008e). Nepalese people are seriously suffering from insecurity and violence. Phenomena of criminality led insecurity such as kidnapping of children, murder and attempted murder, rubbery, illegal trafficking of arms and ammunitions, human trafficking, drugs abuses and trafficking, atrocities, murders, killings, massacres, forced displacement became serious (Upreti and Nepali, 2006). This phenomenon, particularly from Terai is growing particularly after signing of the CPA. The transitional situation is getting further complicated after creation of the coercive nature of organisations such as Young Communist League17 (YCL), Youth Force (YF) and *Madesh Rakshya Bahini* by political parties. The official justification of need for creation of such forces by political parties does not match with the actions. The only legally defined institutions such as police, army and private security system approved by the government have coercive rights. However, these organisations are operating without any legal mandate that consequently weakens state security apparatus, creates parallel functioning and adds insecurity. Any one can easily understand that coercive forces created by political parties serve their vested interests. Once powerful political parties have created such coercive forces severely weakened police force (by politicisation or political protection) can not contain them. Hence, Nepal's security situation is facing dilemma.

18. Political parties are the leading force in nation building and democracy and their governing style determines destiny of this country. Support to democratise political parties, promoting internal democracy and development of younger leadership are crucially important to make transformation successful. The practices of exclusion and under recognition in political process are the outcome of feudal mindset and changing such attitude requires intimate engagement and dialogue-cum-practice.
19. Reconstruction and development is one of the most important elements in achieving peace and stability. New vision, new policy, new strategy, new institutional arrangement, new methodological approaches and fresh perspective on development are essential to make development sector responsive and contributing to make peace process successful. Adopting conflict sensitive development approaches is one of the main options for policy makers to maximise the contribution of development sector in achieving sustainable peace, social harmony and living standard of Nepalese

people. The newly created Ministry of Peace and Reconstruction has central role in developing conflict sensitive development vision, policies and strategies for the promotion of reconstruction and development.

20. Interviewed on 29 June 2007 at Meeting Hall of Paluthan Community Forestry Users Group, Dang district.
21. The *Purohit* is a culturally and socially recognised person to perform religious ceremonies and acts as a mediator or counsellor.
22. A major Hindu festival in Nepal where all community members gather in public places and resolve pending conflicts, unsettled issues and decide collective community works.
23. See Bhattachan, Y. K. (2007) for detail. Democracies in Indigenous

References

Ackerman, P. and Duvall, J. (2005), People Power Primed: Civilian Resistance and Democratization. *HarvardIinternational Review.* Summer, pp. 42-47.

Ackerman, P. and Kruegler, C. (1994), *Strategic Non-violent Conflict: The Dynamics of people's Power in the Twentieth Century.* Westport: Praeger.

Adhikari, R. (2005), Policy paper on Building Confidence in Tourism through Crisis Management. Kathmandu: Nepal Association of Tour Operators.

Adhikari, S. (2006), Internally Displaced Persons: An Assessment of Social Situation and Development Planning Implications. MA Thesis submitted to South Asian Institute of Technology, Purbanchal University.

Aditya A., Upreti, B. R. and Adhikari, P.K. (2006), *Countries in Conflict and Processing of Peace: Lessons for Nepal.* Kathmandu: Friends for Peace.

African Rights (2000), *Confessing to Genocide: Responses to Rwanda's Genocide Law.* Kigali: African Rights Working for Justice.

AI, (2005a), Nepal: *A Long Ignored Human Rights Crisis now on the Brink of Catastrophe.* 18 February 2005, ASA 31/022/2005. London: Amnesty International.

AI, (2005b*), Nepal: Killing with Impunity.* 20 January 2005, ASA31/001/2005. London: Amnesty International.

AI, (2002), *Nepal: Spiralling Human Rights Crisis.* AI-Index: ASA 31/016/200 04/04/2002. London: Amnesty International.

Aldrich, R. and Wotherspoon, G. (eds.) (2001), *Who's Who in Contemporary Gay & Lesbian History: From World War II to the Present Day.* New York: Routledge.

Ali, A.G. (2000), The Economics of Conflict in Africa: An Overview. *Journal of African Economies.*, Vol. 9.

Aliston, L.G, Mibecap, G. and Muller, B. (2000), Land Reform Policies, the Sources of Violent Conflict, and Implications for Deforestation in the Brazilian Amazon. *Journal of Environmental Economics and Management*. Vol. 39.

Anderson, M. B. (1999), *Do No Harm: How Aid Supports Peace—Or War*. Boulder and London: Lynne Rienner Publishers.

Andre, C. and Platteau, J. P. (1998), Land Relations under Unendurable Stress: Rwanda Caught in the Malthusian Trap. *Journal of Economic Behaviour and Organization*. Vol. 34.

Arcand, J-L and Chauvet, I. (2002), Foreign Aid, Rent-Seeking Behavior, and Civil War. CERDI-CNRS, Université d'Auvergne.

Arcand, J-L and Nicolas, Pons-Vignon, (2003), Land and Violent Conflict: Exploring Ways of Using Land Policy to Secure Sustained Peace. (Draft) prepared for the Informal Experts Meeting on "Land and Conflict: What Role for donors?" held in June 19-20, 2003 at the Paris: OECD, Paris.

Augustiana, T. & Pakpahan. M. (2004), Women and Peacebuilding: Central Sulawesi and Morth Maluku. Jakarta: UNDP and National Planning and Development Board (BAPPENAS).

Austin, J. E., and C. E. Bruch (2000), The Environmental Consequences of War. Cambridge, UK: Cambridge University Press.

Avruch, K. & Vejarano B. (2002), Truth and Reconciliation Commissions: A Review Essay and Annotated Bibliography. *The Online Journal of Peace and Conflict Resolution*. Issue 4.2, Spring, p. 4.

Badal Commission Report (1996), Badal Uchachastariya Bhumisudhar Sujhab Ayog 1994. Kathmandu: P.B. Publisher.

Baechler, G. (ed.) (2002), *Promoting Peace: The Role of Civilian Conflict Resolution*. Bern: Staempfli Publisher Limited.

Baechler, G., Acharya, N., Dammann, P., Rajbhandari, R. And Upreti, B. R. (2008), *Nepal Building New Road to Peace*. Kathmandu: SDC.

Baechlor, G. (2006), Conflict Transformation through State Reform. Berghof Research Centre for Constructive Conflict Management.

Baillat, A. (2004), Hydropolitices in Small Mountain States. Two Cases of Cross-Asymmetries: The Kingdom of Lesotho and the Republic of South Africa, the Kingdom of Nepal and the Republic of India. Geneva: Graduate Institute of International Studies.

Baldwin, D. (1997), The Concept of Security. *Review of International Studies*, Vol. 23.

Ball, N. (2002), Enhancing Security Sector Governance: A Conceptual Framework for UNDP. www. undp. org/bcpr/jssr/docs/ UNDP_ SSR_ Concept_Paper_9 October.

Banerjee, D. (2000) (ed.) South Asia at Gun Point: Small Arms and Light Weapons Proliferation. Colombo: Regional Centre for Strategic Studies.

Barnes, C. (ed.) (2002), Owning the Process. Public Participation in Peace Making. Featuring South Africa, Guatemala & Mali. Accord Issue 3/2002. London: Conciliation Resources.

Barron, M. (1996), When the Soldiers Come Home: A Gender Analysis of the Reintegration of Demobilized Soldiers Mozambique 1994-96. UK: School of Development Studies of the University of East Anglia,

Bassiouni, M.C. (ed.) (2000), *Post-Conflict Justice*. New York: Transnational Publishers.

Becker, H. (2003), Women, Politics and Peace in Northern Namibia. In: *Women and Peace in Africa* (pp. 47-73). Paris: UNESCO Workshop.

Begum, K. (1987), *Tension over the Farakka Barrage: A Techno-political Tangle in South-Asia*. Dhaka: University Press Limited.

Belbase, N. and Thapa, B. (2004), Legal Review of Protected Areas with Special Reference to KTWR (preliminary draft with provisional title). Kathmandu: IUCN Nepal.

Benda-Beckmann F., K. Benda-Beckmann, R. Pradhan, and H. L. Spiertz. (1997), Introduction. In: R. Pradhan, F. Benda-Beckmann, K. Benda-Beckmann, H.L. Spiertz, S. K. Khadka, and H. Azharul (Eds.). *Water Rights, Conflicts and Policy*. Kathmandu: FREEDEAL Pp. 1-11.

Benda-Beckmann, F. (1999). Between Free Riders and Free Raiders: Property Rights and Soil Degradation in Context. Paper presented in International Workshop on ' Economic Policy Reforms and Sustainable Land Use in LDCs: Recent Advances in Quantitative Analyses.' June 30 to July 2, 1999. Wageningen: WUR.

Bernstein, H. Crow, B. and Johnson, H. (eds.) (1992) *Rural Livelihoods: Crisis and Responses*. Oxford: Oxford University Press.

Bhandari, K. (2004), *Nepalese tourism: Crisis and beyond Nepal's endeavor for tourism recovery*. Kathmandu: Kalyan Bhandari.

Bhandari, R. K. (2007), Drinking Water Management: Call Privatization Solve all Problems? *The Himalayan Times* of 9 May 2007.

Bhandari, S. (2003). *Study on Farmers' Rights in Nepal*. Kathmandu: Action Aid Nepal.

Bhandari, S. and Karki, B. (ed.) (2005), *Future of the Nepalese Constitution*. Kathmadnu: Law Associates Nepal.

Bhattachan, Y. K. (2007), Democracies in the Indigenous Organisations of Nepal. In: Koirala, B.N., Khadka, A. and Khadka, R. (eds.) (2007), Democratic Indigenous Practices of NEPAL. Kathmandu: Nepal Centre for Creative Research. pp. 7-13.

Bhattarai, A.M. and Pokharel, M.R. (2004), Property and Land Relations in Nepal: Tenants, Land Reform and Land-use Planning (A Draft Report). Kathmandu: Action Aid Nepal.

Bhattarai, B.R. (2003), *The Nature of Underdevelopment and Regional Structure of Nepal: A Marxist Analysis*. Delhi: Adroit Publishers.

Bhattarai-Ghimire, and Upreti, B. R. (2007), Conflict Induced Displacement: An Emerging Phenomenon of Internal Migration in Nepal. In: Chapter on the forthcoming book 'Transformation, Inclusion and National Integration' (eds.) Pyakurel, K. N., Upreti, B. R. and Sharma, S. R. Kathmandu: Kathmandu University. Pp. 101-140.

Bigombe, B.; Collier, P. and Sambanis, N. (2000), Policies for Building Post-conflict Peace. *Journal of African Economies* Vol. 9. No. 3. Pp. 323-348.

Binswanger, H.; Deininger, K. and Feder, G. (1995), Power, Distortions, Revolt and Reform in Agricultural Land Relations. In: Behrman, J. and T. Srinivasan, (eds). *Handbook of Development Economics*. Vol.3. Amsterdam; New York and Oxford: Elsevier Science.

Bista, D.B. (1991), *Fatalism and Development: Nepal's Struggle for Modernisation*. Calcutta: Oreint Longman.

Bista, D.B.; Ijima I., Hiroshi, M.Y. and Nyshi, N. (1982), Anthropological and Linguistic Studies of the Gandaki Areas of Nepal. Initiative for the Study of Language and Culture of Asia and Pacific.

Blom, A., and J. Yamindou (2001), The History of Armed Conflict and its Impact on Biodiversity in the Central African Republic. Washington, DC, USA: Biodiversity Support Programme.

Blom, E., Bergmans, W., Dankelman I., Verweij P., Voeten M., and Wit P., (eds.) (2000), Nature in War: Biodiversity Conservation during Conflicts. Leiden: The Netherlands Commission for International Nature Protection.

Bloomfield, D. Barnes, T. and Huyse, L. (2003), Reconciliation after Violent Conflict: A Handbook. Stockholm: International IDEA.

Brabant, K. V. (2000), Operational Security Management in Violent Environment. ODI - HPN Good Practice Review. London: Overseas Development Institute.

Bramwell, B. and Bernard, L. (2006), Tourism Collaboration and Partnerships, Politics, Practice and Sustainability. London: Viva Books Private Limited

Brandt Commission (1980), North-South: A Programme for Survival. Cambridge: The MIT Press.

BRCCCM, (2003), Berghof Handbook for Conflict Transformation. Berghof Research Centre for Constructive Conflict Management: Budrich: Leske & Budrich.

Brockett, C. (1992), Measuring Political Violence in Central America. *American Political Science Review*. Vol. 86. No. 1.

Bromley, D.W. (1992), Making the Commons Work: Theory, Practice and Policy. California: Institute of Contemporary Studies.

Brun, C. (2003), Permanent Impermanence: Dilemmas of Long term Displacement in Sri Lanka, Conference Report 7-8 February 2003, Researching Internal Displacement: State of the Art Trondheim: Norway.

Brzoska, M. (2003), Development Donors and the Concept of Security Sector Reform. Occasional Paper.

Buckles D. (ed.) (1999), Cultivating Peace: Conflict and Collaboration in Natural Resource Management. Ottawa/Washington: IDRC/World Bank Institute.

Budathoki, P. (2003), A Category V protected Landscape Approach to Buffer Zone Management in Nepal. *Parks* 13(2), Pp 22-30.

Bush R.A. (1995), Dispute Resolution- the Domestic Arena: A Survey of Methods, Applications and Critical Issues. In: John A. Vasquez et. al., (eds.). Beyond Confrontation: Learning Conflict Resolution in the Post-Cold War Era. Michigan: The University of Michigan Press. Pp.9-37.

Bush, K.D. and Opp, R.J. (1999), Peace and Conflict Impact Assessment (Chapter 9) In: Daniel Buckles (eds.), Cultivating Peace: Conflict and Collaboration in Natural Resource Management. Ontario: IDRC/World Bank.

Byrne, D (1999), Social Exclusion. Open University Press.

Caplan, L. (1990), Tribes in the Ethnography of Nepal: Some Comments on Debate. *Contributions to Nepalese Studies*. Vol. 17. No. 2. Pp. 129-145.

Caplan, L. (2000), *Land and Social Change in East Nepal. A Study of Hindu Indigenous Relations*. Kathmandu: Himal Books.

CBS. (1961). Sample Census of Agriculture of Nepal. Kathmandu: CBS.

Centro de Estudios Internacionales (1995), Demobilized Soldiers Speak: Reintegration and Reconciliation in Nicaragua, El Salvador and Mozambique. Managua: Nicaragua.

Chalmers, M. (2000), Security Sector Reform in Developing Countries: an EUPperspective. Joint report published by Saferworld and the Conflict Prevention Network, http://www.saferworld.co.uk/pubsecu.htm.

Chapagain, D.P.; Pyakuryal, K.N. and Pokharel, B.K. (1998), Land Policy, Land Management and Land Degradation in the HKH Region. Nepal Country Paper. Kathmandu: ICIMOD.

Chapagain, D.P. (1999), Land Tenure in Nepal: Status and Main Issues. A paper prepared for GTZ/IMU Nepal.

Chapagain, D.P. (2001), Status Review and Dialogue: Land and Agriculture. Kathmandu: World Conservation Union (IUCN).

Chazee, L. (2003), Conflict, Lessons Leaned, Impacts and Implication in Development Project Design in Nepal. Manila: Asian Development Bank.

Clark, H. (2000), Civil Resistance in Kosov". London: Pluto.

Clastres, P. (1974), Society against the State. Washington.

Colletta, N.J. Kostner, M. and Wiederhofer, I. (1996), The Transition from War to Peace in Sub-Saharan Africa. Washington: The World Bank.

Collier, P. (2000), Doing Well out of War: An Economic Perspective. In: Berdal, M. and D.M. Malone (eds.). Greed and Grievance: Economic Agendas in Civil Wars. Boulder and London: IDRC/ Lynne Rienner.

Collier, P. and Hoeffler, A. (1998), On the Economic Causes of Civil War. *Oxford Economic Papers*. Vol. 50. Pp. 563-573.

Collier, P. and Hoeffler, A. (2001), Greed and Grievance in Civil War. Working Paper, Washington: World Bank.

Collier, P. and Hoeffler, A. (2002), Aid, Policy and Growth in Post-Conflict Societies. Washington: World Bank Policy Research Working Paper 2902 (October).

CPN (1999), Conflict Impact Assessment: A Practical Working Tool for Prioritising Development Assistance in Unstable Situation. Brussels: Conflict Prevention Network.

Conservation International (2001), From the Forest to the Sea: Biodiversity Connections from Guinea to Togo. Washington, DC, USA: Conservation International.

Cramer, C. and Weeks, J. (2000), Conflict and Agriculture in Developing Countries. In: State of Food and Agriculture 2000. Rome: FAO.

Crow, B. (1992), Rural Livelihoods: Action from Above. In: Bernstein, H. Crow, B and Johnson, H (1992) (eds.) *Rural Livelihoods: Crisis and Responses*. Oxford: Oxford University Press. Pp 251-273.

Crow, B. and Lindquest, A. (1990), Development of the Rivers Ganges and Brahmaputra: The Difficulty of Negotiating a New Line. Milton Keyes: Development Policy and Practice Research Group.

CSRC (2005), Land Rights: Bi-Annual Publication, December 2005. Kathmandu: Community Self Reliance Centre.

CSRC (2004), Advocacy for Land Rights. Kathmandu: Community Self Reliance Centre

CSRC (2003), A Study Report on Land Rights in Nepal: Present Reality and Strategies for Future. July 2003. Kathmandu: Community Self Reliance Centre.

Cuny, F.C., and Hill R.B. (1999), Famine, Conflict and Response: A Basic Guide. West Hartford, CT, USA: Kumarian Press.

Curle, A. (1971), *Making Peace*. London: Tavistock Publications.

Curtis, D. (2001), Politics and Humanitarian Aid: Debates, Dilemmas and Dissension, Report of a conference organized by ODI, POLIS at the University of Leeds and CAFOD, London, 1 February 2001 HPG Report 10 April 2001 Overseas Development Institute

Cutts, M., and Dingle A. (1998), Safety First: Protecting NGO Employees Who Work in Areas of Conflict. London, UK: Save the Children.

Dabelko, G., (ed.) (2001), Environmental Change and Security Project Report. Washington, DC: The Woodrow Wilson Centre.

Dabelko, G., (ed.) (2000), Environmental Change and Security Project Report. Washington, DC: The Woodrow Wilson Centre.

DCAF and IPU (2003), Parliament Oversight of the Security Sector: Principles, Mechanisms and practices. Geneva: Geneva Centre for the Democratic Centre of the Armed Forces (DCAF) and Inter-Parliamentary Union (IPU).

Deininger, K. (2003), Causes and Consequences of Civil Strife. Micro-Level Evidence from Uganda. Washington: World Bank.

Deng, F. M. (1999), Report of the Representative of the Secretary General, Addendum_Specific Groups and Individuals: Mass Exoduses and Displaced Persons Commission on Human Rights.

Deng, F. M. (2004), Specific Groups And Individuals Mass Exoduses and Displaced Persons, Commission On Human Rights, United Nations, Economic and Social Council.

Department of Foreign Affairs and International Trade Canada (1997), Practical Disarmament, Demobilization and Reintegration Measures for Peace-building. Ottawa: Department of Foreign Affairs and International Trade Canada.

DFID (2005), Provision of Infrastructure in Post Conflict Situation. London: Department for International Development.

DFID (2003), Security Sector Reform Policy Brief. January 2003. London: Department for International Development.

DFID (2002a), Post Conflict Reconstruction Task Framework. London: Department for International Development.

DFID, (2002b), Understanding and Supporting Security Sector Reform. London: Department for International Development.

Dhakal, D.R. (2004); Plight of Internally Displaced Persons (IDPs) In Nepal: A Call for an Urgent Intervention by the HMG/Nepal, United Nations, and International Community. Kathmandu: Community Study and Welfare Centre (CSWC).

Dixit, A. and Gyawali, D. (2003), A Cultural Theory Perspective on Environment and Scarcity in Nepal. In: Environment, Development and Human Security (ed.) Nijam, A. Boulevard: University Press of America.

Dixit, A., Adhikari, P. and Thapa, R.R. (2004), Ground Realities for Himalayan Water Management. In: Panos Institute South Asia (2004), Disputes Over the Ganges: A Look at Potential Water Related Conflicts in South Asia. Kathmandu: Panos Institute South Asia. Pp. 158-191.

Dowding, K. (1996), Power. Minnesota: University of Minnesota Press.

Duijn L.V. (2003), Nepal IDP Research Initiative Findings. Kathmandu: Netherlands Development Organization (SNV).

Ebo, A. (2005), The Challenges and Opportunities of Security Sector Reform in Post-Conflict Liberia. Geneva Centre for the Democratic Control of Armed Force. Occasional paper No. 9.

Elbadawi, I and Sambanis, N. (2000), Why Are There So Many Civil Wars in Africa? Understanding and Preventing Violent Conflict. *Journal of African Economies.* Vol. 9.

Esposito, D. and Crocker, B. (2004), To Guarantee the Peace: An Action Strategy for a Post-Conflict Sudan. A Report for the Secretary of State's Africa Policy Advisory Panel.

Fitzpatrick, D. (2002), Land policy in post-conflict circumstances: Some Lessons from East-Timor. Working Paper No. 58. 'New Issue in Refugee Research Series. UNHCR.

French, J.R.P. & Raven, B. (1959), The Bases of Social Power. In: D. Cartwright (ed.). Studies in Social Power. Ann Arbor, MI: University of Michigan Press.

Fusato, M. (2003), Disarmament, Demobilization, and Reintegration of Ex-Combatants. G. Burgess and H. Burgess (eds.) Beyond Intractability. Conflict Research Consortium, University of Colorado, Boulder.

Gaige, F.H. (1975), *Regionalism and Nationalism in Nepal.* Delhi: Vikas Publishing House.

Galtung, J. (2000a), *Peace by Peaceful Means: Peace and Conflict, Development and Civilization.* London: Sage Publications.

Galtung, J. (2000b), Conflict Transformation by Peaceful Means: Participants' Manual, Trainers' Manual. Geneva: UN Disaster Management Training Programme.

Gautam U., Agrawal N. and Subedi R. (eds.) (1992), Nepal Managing Large Surface Irrigation projects: A Participatory Review. Study document NEP/89/006. Kathmandu: Department of Irrigation, HMG/Nepal.

Gautam, S., Banskota, A. and Manchanda, R. (2003), Women in the Maoist Insurgency in Nepal. In: Thapa, D (ed.), Understanding the Maoist Movement in Nepal. Kathmandu: MartinChautari. Pp. 93-124.

Gersony, R. (2003), Sowing the Wind: History and Dynamics of the Maoist Revolt in Nepal's Rapti Hills. Kathmadnu: USAID/Mercy Corps International.

Ghale, Y. (2008) Women, Globalization and Land based Exclusion in Nepal (Chapter 7), In: Upreti, B.R. Sharma, S.R. and Basnet, J. (eds.) Land Politics and Conflict in Nepal: Realities and potentials for social transformation. Kathmandu: Community Self Reliance Centre (CSRC), South Asia Regional Coordination Office of NCCR

North South and Human and Natural Resources Studies Centre (HNRSC), Kathmandu University. Pp. 143-178.

Ghandi, M.K. (1938), *Hind Swaraj, or Indian Home Rule*. Ahmedabad: Navajivan Publishing House.

Ghandi, M.K. (1950), *Satyagraha in South Africa*. Ahmedabad: Navajivan Publishing House.

Ghimire, K. (1992), *Forest or Farm? The Politics of Poverty and Land Hunger in Nepal*. Delhi: Oxford University Press.

Gleichmann, C., Odenwald, M. Steenken, K. and Wilkinson, A. (2004), Disarmament, Demobilization and Reintegration: A Practical Field and Classroom Guide. Swedish National Defence College, Pearson Peace-keeling Centre, German Technical Cooperation and The Norwegian International Defense Centre.

Global IDP Project (2004); Internal Displacement: Global Overview of Trends and Developments, Norwegian Refugee Council.

Global Witness (2004), *Breaking the Links between the Natural Resource Conflict and Corruption*. London: Global Witness.

Global Witness. (2001), *The Role of Liberia's Logging Industry on National and Regional Insecurity*. London, UK: Global Witness.

Global Witness.(1999), A Crude Awakening. London, UK: Global Witness.

Global Witness (1998), A Rough Trade: The Role of Companies and Governments in the Angolan Conflict. London, UK: Global Witness.

Gomez, M. (2002); National Human Rights Commissions and Internally Displaced Persons; Illustrated by the Sri Lankan Experience An Occasional Paper July The Brookings – SAIS Project on Internal Displacement.

Goodhand, J. (2000), Nepal Conflict Assessment, DFID Nepal. Kathmandu: DFID-Nepal.

Gore, A. (1992), *Earth in balance: Forging a new common purpose*. London: Earthscan Publications.

Grandon, R. (2007), Nepalese Tourism The Challenges. Kathmandu: Nepal Association of Tour and Travel Agents.

Greene, O. (2003), Security Sector Reform, Conflict Prevention and Regional Perspectives. *Journal of Security Sector management*. Vol. 1, No. 1, pp. 1-15.

Grossman, H. (1991). A general Equilibrium Model of Insurrections. *American Economic Review*. Vol. 81, pp. 912-921.

Kievelitz, U. and Polzer T. (2002), Nepal Country Study on Conflict Transformation and Peace Building. Deutsche Gesellschaft fur Technische Zusammenarbeit (GTZ) GmbH..

Gurr, T.R., Marshall M.G., and Khosla D. (2000), Peace and Conflict: A Global Survey of Armed Conflicts, Self-Determination

Movements and Democracy. College Park, MD, USA: Centre for International Development and Conflict Management.

Gyawali, D. and Dixit, A. (2001), Water and Science: Hydrological Uncertainties, Developmental Inspirations and Uningrained Scientific Culture. *Future*, 33, pp. 689-708.

Gurung, H. (2005), Indigenous Peoples and Development Aspects. Statement made at International Conference of IAIA on Indigenous Peoples and Impact Assessment, Boston, 29 May 2005 organised by Eeyou Istchee Tebtebba Foundation, World Bank and Hydro Qubec.

Hachhethu, K. (2001). State, democracy and insurgency: a case study of the Maoist insurgency in Nepal. A paper presented in the conference 'The Maoist Movement in Nepal: Context, Causes and Implications'. School of Oriental and African Studies, London. 2-3 November 2001.

Hachhethu, K., (2003), The Question of Inclusion and Exclusion in Nepal: Interface between State and Ethnicity. Paper presented at 'The Agenda of Transformation: Inclusion in Nepali Democracy' organised by the Social Science Baha, Kathmandu, 24-26 April, 2003.

Hardin, G. (1968), The Tragedy of Commons. *Science*. 162: Pp.1243-1248.

Harris, P. and Reilly, B. (1998), Democracy and Deep Rooted Conflict: Options for Negotiation. Stockholm: International Institute for Democracy and Electoral Assistance (International IDEA)

Hart, T., and Mwinyihali R. (2001), Armed Conflict and Biodiversity in Sub-Saharan Africa: The Case of the Democratic Republic of Congo (DRC). Washington, DC, USA: Biodiversity Support Programme.

Harvey, R. (2004), Children and Armed Conflict: A Guide to International Humanitarian and Human Rights Law. Essex: Children and Armed Conflict Centre.

Hatton, J., Couto M., and Oglethorpe J. (2001), Biodiversity and War: A Case Study from Mozambique. Washington, DC, USA: Biodiversity Support Programme.

Herbst, J. (2000), Economic Incentives, Natural Resources, and Conflict in Africa. *Journal of African Economies*. Vol. 9., Pp.270-294.

Hillman Smith, A.K K., and Smith F. (1997), Conservation Crises and Potential Solutions: Example of Garamba National Park Democratic Republic of Congo. Paper presented to the II World Congress of the International Ranger Federation, San Jose, Costa Rica, September 25–29, 1997.

Hirschman, A.O. (1981), The Changing Tolerance for Income Inequality in the Course of Economic Development. In Essays in Trespassing: Economics to Politics and Beyond. Cambridge: CUP.

Hogger, R. (2001), Contributing to New Strength: an Analysis of Threats and Opportunities in the Development Co-operation between Nepal and Switzerland.

Holtzman, S.B. and Nezam, T. (2004), Conflict-Induced Displacement in Europe and Central Asia, living in limbo, The International Bank for Reconstruction and Development / The World Bank

Homer-Dixon, T. F. (1994), Environment, Scarcity, and Violence. Princeton, NJ, USA: Princeton University Press.

Honwana, A. (2005). Healing and Social Reintegration in Mozambique and Angola. Chapter in *Roads to Reconciliation*. Skaar, E., Gloppen, S. & Suhrke, A. (eds.) Oxford: Lexington Books.

Howel, J. Upreti, B.R. and Adhikari, J.N. (2005), Implementing the Rural Access Programme, Evaluation Summary Report no. 7, October 2005. Kathmandu: Rural Access Programme.

HRW (2002), Fast Track Land Reform in Zimbabwe. HRW Human Rights Watch Report. Vol. 14. No. 1. New York: Human Rights Watch.

Huntington, S.P. (1957), *The Soldier and the State: The Theory and Politics of Civil-Military Relations*. London: The Belknap Press of Harvard University Press.

Hussein, K.; Seddon, D. and Sumberg, J. (1999), Increasing Violent Conflict between Herders and Farmers in Africa: Claims and Evidence. *Development Policy Review*. Vol. 17.

Hutt, M. (2004), *Himalayan 'People's War': Nepal's Maoist Rebellion*. London: Hurst and Company.

IANSA (2003), Implementing the Programme of Action 2003: Action by State and Civil Society. London: International Action Network on Small Arms, International Alert and Saferworld.

IANSA (2004), Arm trade is out of control. Source; www.controlarms.org, London.

ICG (2006a), Beyond Victimhood: Women's Peace Building in Sudan, Congo, Brussels and Uganda. Africa Report No 112 (28 June 2006). Nairobi/Brussels: International Crisis Group.

ICG (2006b), Nepal: From People Power to Peace?, Asia Report No.115, 10 May 2006. Kathmandu and Brussels: International Crisis Group.

ICG (2005a), Nepal Dealing with Human Rights Crisis. Asia Report No 94, 24 March 2005. Kathmandu and Brussels: International Crisis Group.

ICG (2005b), Nepal's New Alliance: The Mainstream Parties and the Maoists, Asia Report No.106, 28 November 2005. Kathmandu and Brussels: International Crisis Group.

ICG (2005c), Towards a Lasting Peace in Nepal: The Constitutional Issues. Asia Report No. 99, 15 June. Brussels/Kathmandu: International Crisis Group.

ICG (2005d), Nepal Dealing with Human Rights Crisis. Asia Report No 94, 24 March 2005. Kathmandu and Brussels: International Crisis Group.

ICG (2004), Nepal: Dangerous Plans for Village Militias, Asia Briefing, 17 February 2004. Kathmandu and Brussels: International Crisis Group.

ICG (2003a), Nepal Obstacle to Peace. Brussels/Kathmandu: ICG. No 57. Kathmandu and Brussels: International Crisis Group.

ICG, (2003b). Nepal Backgrounder: Ceasefire-Soft Landing or Strategic Pause, Research No 50, 10th April 2003 Brussels/Kathmandu: International Crisis Group.

ICIMOD (2000), Land Policies, Land Management and Land Degradation in the Hindu Kush-Himalayas: Nepal Study Report. Mountain Farming Systems Case Study Series, No. 00/2. Kathmandu: Socioeconomic and Ethno-Political Research and Training Consultancy (P) Ltd. and ICIMOD.

ICRC (2005), The Situation of Internally Displaced Persons in Serbia and Montenegro. Issue paper, 1, May 2005. Geneva: ICRC.

IDD (2005), Report on the Inter-Agency Internal Displacement Division (IDD) Mission to Nepal (11-22 April 2005). Kathmandu: UNDP.

IIMI (1990), Assistance to Farmers-Managed Irrigation Systems. IIMI Country Paper-Nepal-No. 3. Kathmandu: International Irrigation Management Institute-Kathmandu Office.

IMC (1990), Water Use Conflicts and Their Resolution in Selected Irrigation Systems in Nepal. IMC Applied Study Report No 13. Pokhara: Irrigation Management Centre.

INSEC (2007), Human Rights Year Book 2007. Kathmandu: Informal Sector Service Centre.

INSEC, (2006), Human Rights Yearbook 2006. Kathmandu: Informal Sector Service Centre.

INSEC (2005), Human Rights Year Book 2005. Kathmandu: Informal Sector Service Centre.

INSEC (2002), Nepal Human Rights Year Book 2002. Kathmandu: Informal Sector Service Centre.

Islam, M.R. (1987), *Ganges Water Dispute: Its International Legal Aspects*. Dhaka: University Press Limited.

Jacobs, M. and Schloeder C. (2001), Impacts of Conflict on Biodiversity and Protected Areas in Ethiopia. Washington, DC, USA: Biodiversity Support Programme.

Jafari Jafar (2005), Bridging out, nesting a field: Powering a new platform. *The Journal of Tourism Studies*, Vol. 16, No.2, Dec. 2005, pp. 01-05.

Johnson, H. (1992), Rural Livelihoods: Action from Below. In: Bernstein, H. Crow, B and Johnson, H (1992) (eds.) *Rural Livelihoods: Crisis and Responses*. Oxford: Oxford University Press. Pp 274-3000.

Junne, G. and Verkoren, W. (eds.) (2006), *Post Conflict Development: Meeting New Challenges*. New Delhi: Viva Books Private Limited.

Jwala, P. (2002), *Baicharik Bhumari ma Maobadi Andolon*. Kathmandu: Sangin-Madan Prakashan.

Kalpers, J. (2001), Overview of Armed Conflict and Biodiversity in Sub-Saharan Africa: Impacts, Mechanisms, and Responses. Washington, DC, USA: Biodiversity Support Programme.

Karki, A. and Seddon D. (2003), (eds.) *The People's War in Nepal: Left Perspectives*. New Delhi: Adroit Publishers.

Kasperson, R.E., Golding D. and Kasperson J.X. (1999), Risk, Trust and Democratic Theory. In: Cvetkovish, G and Lofstedt, R. (Eds.) *Social Trust and the Management of Risk*. London: Earthscan Publications, Pp. 22-41.

Khanal, D.R. (2006) (BS 2063), *Sasastra Dundama Samudayik Ban* (Community Forestry in Armed Conflict), Kathmandu: Federation of Community Forestry Users of Nepal.

Khanal, K. (2003), Ethnicity and Autonomy: Some Issues for Consideration in Remaking the Constitution. Paper presented at 'The Agenda of Transformation: Inclusion in Nepali Democracy' organised by the Social Science Baha, Kathmandu, 24-26 April 2003.

Khatiwada P. (2004), Internally Displaced persons (IDPs) in Nepal; Problems and Challenges. *Nepal Journal of Contemporary Studies* Volume 4, No.2 Nepal Centre for Contemporary Studies, Kathmandu. Pp 45-63.

King, M. L. (1963), Why We Can't Wait. New York: New American Library.

Kreimer, A., Collier, P., Scott, C.S., and Arnold, M (2000), Uganda: Post Conflict Reconstruction. Washington: The World Bank.

Krippendorf, E. (1973), Peace Research and the Industrial Revolution. *Journal of Peace Research*, Vol. 10, 185-201.

Kritz, N. (ed.) (1995), Transitional Justice: How Emerging Democracies Reckon with Former Regimes, Vols. I–III. Washington, D.C.: U.S. Institute of Peace Press.

Kumar, D. (2004), Proximate causes of conflict of Nepal. A Paper presented at International Workshop on 'Causes of Internal Conflicts and Means to Resolve Them: Case Study of Nepal organised in 22-24 February 2004.

Kumar, D. and Sharma, H. (2005), Security Sector Reform in Nepal: Challenges and Opportunities. Kathmandu: Friends for Peace.

Kunwar, R.R. (2006), Tourists and Tourism Science and Industry Interface. Kathmandu: International School of Tourism and Hotel Management.

Lawati, M. (2003), Inclusive Democratic Political institutions for Nepal. Paper presented at 'The Agenda of Transformation: Inclusion in Nepali Democracy' organised by the Social Science Baha, Kathmandu, 24-26 April 2003.

Leonhardt, M. (2000), Conflict Impact Assessment of EU Development Co-operation with APC Countries: A Review of Literature and Practices. London: International Alert and Safeworld.

Leus, X., Wallace, J. and Loretti, A. (2000); Internally Displaced Persons; From the Emergency and Humanitarian Action Department of the World Health Organization, Geneva, Switzerland Paper was presented at the Humanitarian Affairs Segment of ECOSOC 2000, New York, 19–20 July.

Lihamba, A. (2003), Women's Peace Building and Conflict Resolution Skills, Morogoro Region, Tanzania. In UNESCO, *Women and Peace in Africa*. Paris: UNSCO Workshops. Pp.111-131.

Linder, R. (2005), Voices of a New Afghanistan. Washington: Post Conflict Reconstruction Project of Centre for Strategic and International Studies.

MacCormack, C. (2003), Promoting Psychosocial well being Among Children Affected by Armed Conflict and Displacement: Principles and Approaches Working Paper No. 1; Working Group on Children Affected by Armed Conflict and Displacement Save the Children/US Chair, Save the Children Alliance.

Mackinlay, J. and Upreti, B. R. (2003), The King and Mao. *The World Today*. London: Royal Institute of International Affairs. Pp. 26-27.

Mahat, R.S. (2005), *In Defence of Democracy: Dynamics and Fault Lines of Nepal's Political Economy*. New Delhi: Adroit Publishers.

Mainali M, 2003. Development vs the Maobadies. In: Thapa, D. (2003). (ed.), Understanding the Maoist Movement in Nepal. Kathmandu: MartinChautari. Pp. 125-127.

Mallik, B. and Bandyopadhyay J. (2004), West Bengal: Reductionist Engineering and Conflict. In: Panos Institute South Asia (2004), Disputes Over the Ganges: A Look at Potential Water Related Conflicts in South Asia. Kathmandu: Panos Institute South Asia. Pp.55-90.

Martinelli D. P. and Almeida A. P. (1998), Negotiation, Management, and Systems Thinking. *Systemic Practice and Action Research*. 11 (3): 319-334.

Mathew, R. and Upreti, B. (2005), Nepal: Environmental Stress, Demographic Changes and the Maoists. Environmental Change and Security Programme Report. Issue 11. Woodrow Wilson International Centre for Scholars. Pp-29-39.

Mathey, M.J., Dejan, T., Deballe, M., Sopio, R., Koulaninga, A., & Moga, J. (2003), The Role Played by Women of the Central African

Republic in the Prevention and Resolutions of Conflicts. In UNESCO, Women and Peace in Africa (pp. 35-46). Paris: UNESCO Workshop.

Matthew, R., Halle, M., and Switzer, J. (2001), Conserving the Peace: How Protecting the Environment Today Can Prevent Conflict and Disaster Tomorrow. IUCN/IISD Task Force on Environment & Security. Winnipeg, Canada: International Institute for Sustainable Development (IISD).

McCarthy, R.M. and Sharp G. (1997), Non-violent Action. A Research Guide. New York and London: Garland Publishing, Inc. 1997.

McCay, B.J. and Acheson, J.M. (eds.). (1987), The Questions of the Commons: The Culture and Ecology of Communal Resources. Tucson: University of Arizona Press.

McNeely, J.A. (2000), War and Biodiversity: An Assessment of Impacts. In: The Environmental Consequences of War. Austin, J., and C.E. Bruch, (eds.) Cambridge, UK: Cambridge University Press.

Ministry of Culture, Tourism and Civil Aviation (2007), Nepal Tourism Statistics (NTS) (2006). Kathmandu: MoCTCA.

Misra, C. (2004), Locating the 'Causes' of the Maoists Struggle. A Paper presented at International Workshop on 'Causes of Internal Conflicts and Means to Resolve Them: Case Study of Nepal organised in 22-24 February 2004.

Mitchell, C. R. (1981), The Structure of International Conflict. London, Macmillan. 1981.

Mohamed A.M. (2003), The Role of Somali Women in the Search for Peace. In UNESCO, War and Peace in Africa. Paris: UNESCO Workshops. Pp. 75-110.

Mokalobe, M. (1999), Demobilization and Re-Integration of Ex-Combatants in South Africa, Johannesburg: Group for Environmental Monitoring.

Moore, W. H. and Shellman, S. M. (2002), Refugee or Internally Displaced Person? To Where Should One Flee? Department of Political Science The Florida State University USA Web Sites http://garnet.acns.fsu.edu/~whmoore/; http://garnet.acns.fsu.edu/~sms6202/

Muller, E. and Seligson, M. (1987), Inequality and Insurgency. *American Political Science Review*. Vol. 82. Pp.425–451.

Murdoch, J. and Sandler, T. (2002), Economic Growth, Civil Wars, and Spatial Spillovers. *Journal of Conflict Resolution*. Vol. 46. Pp. 91–110.

Myers, N. (1996), *Ultimate Security: The Environmental Basis of Political Stability*. Washington, DC, USA: Island Press.

Nafziger, E.W. and Auvinen, J. (2002), Economic Development, Inequality, War, and State Violence. *World Development*. Vol. 30. No. 2.

Nagel, S. (2006), Conflict Sensitive Programming and Implementation Draft SARD Concept Paper. Manila: ADB, SARD/SANS.

Nayak, P. (1998), Economic Development and Social Exclusion in India. Delhi: School of Economics/University of Delhi.

Nepal Travel Media Association (2007), Report on Peace and Press Vital Forces for Tourism Development. Kathmandu: Nepal Travel Media Association.

Nepal Travel Trade Reporter (2006), Conflict & its impact on tourism. NTTR, June 12-18, 2006, pp. 30-31.

Neumayer, E. (2004), The Impact of Political Violence on Tourism. UK: Sage Publications.

New Era (1988), A Study of Legal System and Legal Situation in Rural Areas of the Kingdom of Nepal. Kathmandu: Friedirich Naumann Foundation.

Ngongo-Mbede, V. (2003), The Traditional Mediation of Conflicts by Women in Cameroon. In UNESCO, *Women and Peace in Africa*. Paris: UNESCO Workshops. Pp.27-34.

Nickson, R.A. (2003), Democratisation and Growth of Communism in Nepal. In: Thapa, D. (Ed.), Understanding the Maoist Movement in Nepal. Kathmandu: MartinChautari. Pp. 2-33.

ICMD (2006), Internal Displacement: Global Overview of Trends and Developments in 2005. Norwegian Refugee Council-Internal Displacement Monitoring Centre.

NPC (2003), The Tenth Five Year Plan. Kathmandu: National Planning Commission.

Ntahobari, J., & Ndayiziga, B. (2003), The Role of Burundian Women in the Peaceful Settlement of Conflicts. In UNESCO, *Women and Peace in Africa*. Paris: UNESCO Workshops. Pp.11-26.

Nyheim, D., Leonhardt, M. and Gaigals C. (2001), Development in Conflict: A Seven Step Tool for Planners. London: Forum for Early Warning and Early Response (FEWER), International Alert and Saferworld.

OCHA (2003), No Refuge: The challenge of internal displacement. Geneva: UN OCHA

Odendaal, A. (1997), 'For All Its Flaws. The TRC as a Peace building Tool', CCR, Vol. 6, No. 3/4, December 1997, p. 1.

OECD, (2004), Security System Reform and Governance: Policy and Good Practice, http://www. oecd.org/dac/conflict, 19 May.

OECD/DAC (2002), Review of Development Partnership in Nepal: Review Team's Main Findings and Recommendations. January 2002.

OECD (2001), The DAC Guidelines: Helping Prevent Violent Conflict. Paris: Organisation for Economic Co-operation and Development.

Ohlsson L. (ed.) (1995), *Hydropolitics: Conflict over Water as Development Constraints*. London and New Jersey: ZED Books.

Oli K. P. (1998), Conflict Resolution and Mediation in Natural Resource Management. Kathmandu: IUCN-Nepal.

Orner, R., Schnyder, U. (2003), *Early Psychosocial Interventions for War Affected Populations; Early Interventions in Emergencies*. Oxford University Press.

Ostrom, E. (1990), *Governing the Commons: The Evolution of Institutions for Collective Actions*. New York: Cambridge University Press.

Pahari, A. (2003), From Liberation to Insurgency: The Politics of Paradoxes in Nepal. Paper presented at 'The Agenda of Transformation: Inclusion in Nepali Democracy' organised by the Social Science Baha, Kathmandu, 24-26 April, 2003.

Palme, O. (1982), *Common Security: A Blue Print for Survival*. New York: Simon and Schuster.

Palmer, I. (2002); Psychosocial Costs of War in Rwanda. *Advances in Psychiatric Treatment*. Vol. 8, pp. 17–25.

Panday D.R. (1999), Nepal's Failed Development: Reflections on the Mission and the Melodies. Kathmandu: Nepal South Asia Centre.

Panday D.R. (2001), Corruption, Governance and International Co-operation: Essays and Impressions on Nepal and South Asia. Kathmandu: Transparency International Nepal.

Pandey, B. (1994), Small Rather than Big: Case of Decentralized Power Development in Nepal. *Water Nepal*. 4 (1), 181-190.

Panos Institute South Asia (2004); Disputes over the Ganges: A Look at Potential Water Related Conflicts in South Asia. Kathmandu: Panos Institute South Asia.

Philipson, L. (2002), Conflict in Nepal: Perspectives on the Maoist Movement. Kathmandu: DFID.

Phillips, D.J. H., M. Danoudy, J. Ojendal, A. Turton and S. McCaffrey (2006), Trans-boundary Water Cooperation as a Tool for Conflict Prevention and for Broader Benefit Sharing. Stockholm: Ministry for Foreign Affairs, Sweden.

Phuong, C. (2003); *The International Protection of Internally Displaced Persons*. Cambridge University Press.

Pizam A. and Mansfeld Y. (1996), *Tourism, Crime, and International Security Issues*. England: John Wiley and Sons Ltd.

Platteau, J-P. (1996), The Evolutionary Theory of Land Rights As Applied to Sub Saharan Africa: A Critical Assessment. *Development and Change*. Vol. 27,.pp. 29-86.

Plumptre, A., Masozera M., and Vedder A. (2001), The Impact of Civil War on the Conservation of Protected Areas in Rwanda. Washington, DC, USA: Biodiversity Support Program.

Pokharel, B. (2004), Cost of Conflict in Nepal. A Paper Presented at the Seminar of "Cost of Conflict in Nepal" organised by Nepal Foundation for Advanced Studies, June 9, 2004. Kathmandu.

Pokharel, D.M. (2005), Legal Aspects of Land Rights in Nepal. Land First. A Biannual Publication of CSRC. Kathmandu: CSRC. Pp. 8-10.

Porto, J.G. and Parsons, I. (2003), Sustaining the Peace in Angola: An Overview of Current Demobilization, Disarmament and Reintegration. Bonn: Bonn International Centre of Convention.

Pradhan R. and U. Pradhan (1996), Staking a Claim: Law Politics and Water Rights n Farmers Managed Irrigation Systems in Nepal. In: J. Spiertz, and M. Wiber (eds.), *The Role of Law in Natural Resource Management*. VEGA Publications. Pp. 61-76.

Pradhan R., F. Benda-Beckmann and K. Benda-Beckmann (eds.) (2000), Water Land and Laws: Changing Rights to Land and Water in Nepal. Kathmandu: FREEDEAL.

Pradhan R., F. Benda-Beckmann, K. Benda-Beckmann, H.L. Spiertz, S. K. Khadka, and H. Azharul, (eds.) (1997). Water Rights, Conflicts and Policy. Proceeding of Workshop held in Kathmandu, Nepal. Jan. 22-24, 1996. Kathmandu: International Irrigation Management Institute.

Putnam, R. D. (1993), *Making Democracy Work: Civic Tradition in Modern Italy*. Princeton, NJ: Princeton University Press.

Pyakuryal, K.N., Upreti, B. R, and Sharma, S.R. (eds) (2008). Nepal: Transition to Transformation. Kathmandu: HNRSC, NCCR North-South.

Rana, R.S. and Sharma, S. (2004), Development Cooperation and Conflict. Paper presented at the workshop Causes of Internal Conflicts and Means to resolve them: Case Study of Nepal, at Nagarkot, Feb 21-22, 2004.

Ranger, T. (1992), Afterworld: War, Violence and healing in Zimbabwe. *Journal of Southern African Studies*, Vol. 18 No. 3.

Regmi, M.C. (1978), *Land Tenure and Taxation in Nepal*. Kathmandu: Ratna Pustak Bhandar.

Regmi, M.C. (1976), *Land Ownership in Nepal*. Berkeley: University of California Press.

Regmi, M.C. (1972), *A Study of Nepali Economic History 1768-1846*. Delhi: Adroit Publihers.

Regmi, M.C. (1963), *Land Tenure and Taxation in Nepal*. Vol.1. The State as Landlord: Raikar Tenure. Berkeley: University of California Press.

Rehn, E. and Sirleaf, E.J. (2002), Women, War, Peace (Independent Experts' Assessment on the Impact of Armed Conflict on Women and Women's Role in Peace Building-Progress of the World's Women 2002, Vol.1). New York: United Nations Development fund for Women (UNIFEM).

Reychler, L. and Paffenholz, T. (2004), Peace and Conflict Impact Assessment Systems. Field Diplomacy Initiative.

Richards, M. (1997), The Tragedy of the Commons for Community Based Forest Management in Latin America. Natural Resource Perspective No. 22. London: Overseas Development Institute.

RMO, (2005), A Guidebook to Safe and Effective Development in Conflict: A Tool for Analysis. Kathmandu: Risk Management Office of GTZ and DFID.

Roy, A. (2008), *Prachanda: An Unknown Revolutionary*. Kathmandu: Mandala Book Point.

Russett, B.M. (1964), 'Inequality and Insurgency: The Relation of Land Tenure to Politics.' *World Politics*. Vol.16.

Sandy, L.R. and Perkinns, R. (2002), The Nature of peace and its Implications for Peace Education. *Online Journal of Peace and Conflict Resolution. 42:1-8*

Schell, J. 2003.The Unconquerable World: Why Peaceful Protest is Stronger than War.

Schlager, E. and E. Ostrom (1992), Property Right Regimes and Natural Resources. *Land Economics*. 68(8): 249-262.

Schmidt, H. (1997), Healing the Wounds of War: Memories of Violence and the Making of History in Zimbabwe's Most Recent Past. *Journal of Southern African Studies*, Vol. 21, No. 2, pp. 301-10.

Schnabel, A. and Ehrhart H-G. (eds.) (2005), Security Sector Reform and Post Conflict Peace Building. New York, Tokyo and Paris: United Nations University Press.

Schwartz, D. M., Deligiannis T., and Homer-Dixon T.F. (2000), Commentary: Debating environment, population, and conflict." In: Environmental Change and Security Project Report. G.D. Dabelko, (ed.) Washington, DC, USA: The Woodrow Wilson Centre.

Seddon, D. and Adhikari, J. (2005), Conflict and Food Security. A Preliminary Analysis. Kathmandu: RRN.

Seddon, D. and Hussein, K. (2002), The Consequence of Conflict: Livelihoods and Development in Nepal. London: ODI Working Paper 185.

SEF/KSI (2000), The precarious Transformation of War-Torn Societies. Human Security, Institutional Reform and Social Change: Experiences from Ethiopia, Guatemala and Georgia. A Background paper. Development and Peace Foundation/ Catholic Social Institute.

Setting priorities for preventive Action in Nepal: Final Report of the Web Conference 25 Jan-1st Feb 2001, (http://www.preventconflcit.organisation/nepal finalreport.html).

Shakya, M. M. and Chitrakar A. (2006), Cost of Conflict on Nepal's Conservation Efforts. Kathmandu: WWG.

Shambaugh, J., Oglethorpe J., and Ham R. (with contributions from Sylvia Tognetti). (2001), The Trampled Grass: Mitigating the impacts of armed conflict on the environment. Washington, DC, USA: Biodiversity Support Programme.

Sharma, S. (2003), The Maoist Movement: An Evolutionary perspective. In: Thapa, D (ed.), *Understanding the Maoist Movement in Nepal.* Kathmandu: MartinChautari. Pp. 362-380.

Sharp, G. (1973), The politics of non-violent action (3 vols.), Boston: Porter Sargent.

Shrestha, M. B. (2000), *Nepalese Aviation and Tourism.* Kathmandu: Pramila S. Shrestha.

Shrestha, N.R. (1997), *In the Name of Development: A Reflection in Nepal.* Kathmandu: Educational Enterprise.

Sinclair, M. (2002), Learning For A Future: Refugee Education In Developing Countries (http://www.alnap.org/AR2002/

Singer, J.D. and Small, M. (1994), Correlates of War Project: International and Civil War Data. (1816-1992). Inter-University Consortium for Political and Social Research. Ann Arbor, MI.

Skaar, E; Gloopen, S. & Suhrke, A. (eds.) (2005), *Roads to Reconciliation.* Oxford: Lexington Books.

Skaperdas, S. (1992), Cooperation, Conflict, and Power in the Absence of Property Rights. *American Economic Review.* Vol. 82, pp. 720-739.

Slim, H. and Eguren, L.E. (2004), Humanitarian Protection: A Guidance Booklet.

Slovic, P. (1999), Perceived Risk, Trust and Democracy. In: Cvetkovish, G and Lofstedt, R. (eds.) *Social Trust and the Management of Risk.* London: Earthscan Publications, pp. 22-52.

Specht, I. and Carlien v. E. (1998), Enlargement: A challenge for social and economic reintegration: Targeting ex-combatants or all war affected people? The Liberian Experience. Geneva: International Labour Organization.

Squire, C. (2001), Sierra Leone's Biodiversity and the Civil War. A Case Study Prepared for the Biodiversity Support Program. Washington: Biodiversity Support Programme.

Steins, N.A. (1999), All Hands on Deck: An Interactive Perspective on Complex Common Pool Resource Management Based on Case Studies in the Coastal Waters of the Isle of Wight (UK), Connemara

(Ireland) and the Dutch Wadden Sea. Published PhD Dissertation. Wageningen: Wageningen University.

Stephan, M. J and Mundy, J. (2006), A Battlefield Transformed: From Guerrilla Resistance to Mass Non-violent Struggle in the Western Sahara. Journal of Military and Strategic Studies, Spring, Vol. 8, Issue 3, pp. 1-32.

Stewart, F. (2000), Crisis Prevention: Tackling Horizontal Inequalities. *Oxford Development Studies*. Vol. 28. Pp. 245-262.

Story, A. (1999), Economics and Ethnic Conflict: Structural Adjustment in Rwanda. *Development Policy Review*. Vol. 17.

Swain, A. (1996), The Environmental Trap: The Ganges River Diversion, Bangladeshi Migration and Conflicts in India. Uppsala: Department of Peace and |conflict Research, University of Uppsala.

Tamang, A. and John, F. (2006), Asylum of Exploitation: Internally Displaced Children in the Worst form of Child labour Due to the Armed Conflict in Nepal, Kathmandu: Save the Children, KREHPA and Terre des Homes.

Tarasofsky, R.G. (2000), Protecting specially important areas during international armed conflict: a critique of the IUCN draft convention on the prohibition of hostile military activities in protected areas. In: *The Environmental Consequences of War: Legal, Economic, and Scientific Perspectives*. J. Austin and C.E. Bruch, (eds.) Cambridge, UK: Cambridge University Press.

Tarnow, E. (2000), A Quantitative Model of the Amplification of Power through Order and the Concept of Group Defence. http://cogprints.org/4275/ (23 January 2007)

Tepperman, J.D. (2002), 'Truth and Consequences', Foreign Affairs, March/April p. 7.

Terres des homes Nepal (2005), A Survey Report of IDP Children in Banke District: Nutritional Status of Conflict Children Victims of the Armed Conflict in Nepal. Kathmandu: Terres des Homes Nepal.

Thapa, D. (2001), Day of the Maoist (Essay). Himal South Asia. May 2001. Kathmandu: Himal Association, pp. 4-21.

Thapa, D. (ed.) (2003), Understanding the Maoist Movement in Nepal. Kathmandu: MartinChautari.

Thapa, D. and Sijapati, B. (2003), *A Kingdom under Siege: Nepal's Maoist Insurgency, 1996 to 2003*. Kathmandu: The Printhouse.

Thapa, H. B. (2002), *Anatomy of Corruption*. Kathmandu: Published by Sangita Thapa.

The Constitution of the Kingdom of Nepal 1990

Theotocatos, N. and Zetter, R. (2003), Land, Property and Peace

Building: The Role of Property Commissions in Post-Conflict Reconciliation and the Restitution of Property. Research Project. Unpublished.

Topperwin, N. (2008), Introducing Federalism: Power-sharing, local self-government and electoral systems. A Draft paper distributed in meetings.

Tourism for Rural Poverty Alleviation Programme (2003), *Rural Tourism.* Vol: 1 Issue: 4. Kathmandu: TRPAP.

Trefon, T. (2001), The social cost of conflict in the Democratic Republic of Congo. Paper presented at the Norwegian Committee for Africa. Oslo, Norway, March 28, 2001.

Tutu, D. (1999), *No Future without Forgiveness*. London: Rider.

UNDP (2004), Nepal Human Development Report: Empowerment and Poverty Reduction. Kathmandu: UNDP Nepal.

UNEP (2006), Environmental Considerations of Human Displacement in Liberia: A Guide for Decision Makers and Practitioners. Geneva: United Nations Environmental Programme.

UNEP (2003a), Desk Study on the Environment in Iraq. Geneva: United Nations Environment Programme.

UNEP (2003b), Afghanistan: Post Conflict Environment Assessment. Geneva: United Nations Environment Programme.

UNESCO (2003). Women and Peace in Africa: Case Studies on traditional conflict resolutions practices. Paris: UNESCO Workshops.

UNHCR (United Nations High Commission on Refugees) (1997), The State of the World's Refugees 1997-1998: A Humanitarian Agenda. New York: Oxford University Press, 1997.

UNHCR, (1996), Environmental Guidelines. Geneva, Switzerland: United Nations High Commissioner for Refugees

UNICEF, (1997), Report on Pilot Project for the Social Reintegration and Demobilisation of Child Soldiers in Eastern DRC. (Unpublished). http://www.ginie.org/ginie-criseslinks/childsoldiers.html

UNIFEM (2004), Getting it right, doing it right: Gender and Disarmament, Demobilization and Reintegration. New York; United Nations Development Fund for Women.

Union of Trekking, Travel and Rafting Labor Unions (2007), *UNITRAV*, Vol. 9. Kathmandu: UNITRAV

United Nations (2001), Report of the Panel of Experts on the Illegal Exploitation of Natural Resources and Other Forms of Wealth of the Democratic Republic of Congo. Report available on the Internet at http://www.un.org/News/dh/latest/drcongo.htm#_msocom_2

Upadhaya, U. (2006), Insurgency Affected People of Nepal: Rehabilitation. Kathmandu: Kaushila Foundation for Peace and Innovative Initiatives and Institute for Integrated development Studies (IIDS).

Upadhayaya, P.K. (2006), Contribution of International Organizations/ Agencies in the Development of Tourism in Nepal, Kathmandu: Pranil Upadhayaya.

Upadhayaya, P.K. (2008), Role of Tourism in Conflict Mitigation and Peace Building: A Case study of Nepal (PhD research proposal), Kathmandu: Pranil Upadhayaya.

Upreti, B.R. and Muller-Boeker, U. (eds.) (forthcoming), Livelihoods insecurity and Conflict in Nepal. Kathmandu/Bern: Swiss national Centre of Competence in Research North-South. Upreti,

Upreti, B.R. (2008a), Dispute Settlement at the Local Level: Observations and Lessons from Nepal (Chapter 7). In: David N. Gellner and Krishna Hachhethu (Eds.), Local Democracy in South Asia: Micro-processes of Democratization in Nepal and its Neighbours. Governance, Conflict, and Civic Action: Volume 1. New Delhi: The Micro politics of Democratization: European South Asian Exchange on Governance, Conflict and Civic Action. Pages, 150-174.

Upreti, B.R. (2008b), Moving ahead: From Transition to Transformation. *In:* Pyakuryal KN, Upreti BR, Sharma SR, editors. *Nepal: Transition to Transformation.* Kathmandu: HNRSC, NCCR North-South, pp. 201-222

Upreti, B.R. (2008c), Peace process in Nepal. *Swiss Peace Policy, Publication of the Swiss Federal Department of Foreign Affairs* 2008 (1): 4-13.

Upreti, B.R. (2008d), Managing War to Peace transition in Nepal. *Readings on Governance and Development*, (XI), Pp.: 35-49. (July 2008).

Upreti, B.R. (2007a), A study on effects of Maoist insurgency on environmental sanitation and health of internally displace persons of urban areas of Kathmandu city of Nepal. A paper submitted to the Internal Conference on Health and Environmental Research Challenges in Urban Poor Settlement going to be organised by Swiss Centre for Scientific Research in Cote de Ivorie from 3-5 September 2007.

Upreti, B. R. (2007b), Security Sector Transformation in the Changing Political Context: Special Reference to Nepalese Army, [A conflict transformation and peace building perspective]. A discussion paper presented at the Seminar on 'Democratic Transition and Nepalese Army Reforms' organized by Nepalese Army Command and Staff College, at Army Headquarters on 23-24 August 2007 at Kathmandu.

Upreti, B.R. (2007c), Armed Conflict and Development: Learning from Nepal. Synthesis of Good Practices from Livelihoods and Forestry Programme. Kathmandu: Livelihood and Forestry Programme

Upreti, B.R. (2007d), Reconciliation and Social and Political Reintegration in Nepal, A Background Paper prepared for National Human Development Report 2008 going to be published by UNDP in collaboration with the National Planning Commission.

Upreti B.R. (2007e), Changing political context, new power relations and hydro-conflict in Nepal. *In*: Rotberg F, Swain A, (eds). Natural Resources Security in South Asia: Nepal's Water. Stockholm: Institute for Security and Development Policy, pp. 15-65.

Upreti B.R. (2007f), Social exclusion and conflict. *In:* Aditya, A., editor. *Inclusive State: Reflection on Reinventing Nepal.* Kathmandu: South Asia Partnership Nepal. Pp. 46-57

Upreti B.R. (2007g), Addressing structural causes of conflict and promoting peace through conflict sensitive development: Some lessons from Nepal. *In:* Dhungana H, Logan M, (Eds). *Sustainable Development in Conflict Environments: Challenges and Opportunities.* Kathmandu: Canadian Centre for International Studies and Cooperation (CECI), pp 53-66.

Upreti, B.R. (2007h),*Quick Impact Assessment of the Armed Conflict on Environment and Biodiversity in Nepal.* Kathmandu: World Wildlife Fund.

Upreti, B.R. (2007i): Conflict transformation and peace building: Conceptual understanding and opportunities for implementation. In: Pyakuryal, K.N., March, K., and Acharya, B. (eds.) Nepal in Conflict: Theoretical Understanding, Conflict Resolution, Conflict transformation and Peace Building. Kathmandu: Sociological/ Anthropological Society of Nepal. , pp. 12-52.

Upreti, B.R. (2006a), *Armed Conflict and Peace Process in Nepal: The Maoist Insurgency, Past Negotiation and Opportunities for Conflict Transformation.* New Delhi: Adroit Publishers.

Upreti, B.R. (2006b), One State, Two Regimes: Policy and Institutional Challenges for Managing Natural Resources in Nepal. Paper presented in session No. 18 "Institutions for Sustainable Resource Management and Livelihood Security in Asia" organized by ESSP OSC in Beijing from 9-12 November 2006

Upreti, B.R. (2006c), Reconciliation at Post Conflict Situation in Nepal. A paper presented at the 'National Symposium on Constituent Assembly and Inclusive Democracy' organized by Kathmandu Law School, 7-9 June 2006 at Kathmandu

Upreti, B.R. (2006d), Nurturing Peace: Conflict Sensitive Approach to

Development in Nepal. Kathmandu: Peace Secretariat, Government of Nepal.

Upreti, B.R. (2005a) Changing Political Context and Conflict Dynamics in Nepal: A Quick Assessment. Kathmandu: CARE Nepal.

Upreti, B.R. (2005b), Working on Conflict: Peace and Conflict Impact Assessment of Commercial Agriculture Development Project in Eastern Nepal. Final Report. Manila: Asian Development Bank.

Upreti, B.R. (2004a), The Price of Neglect: From Resource Conflict to Maoist Insurgency in the Himalayan Kingdom. Kathmandu: Bhrikuti Academic Publications

Upreti, B.R. (2004b), Resource conflicts and their resolution practices in Nepal. *Mountain Research and Development Journal* Vol. 24, No.1, pp. 60-66.

Upreti, B.R. (2004c), Causes and Consequences of the armed conflict in Nepal. A paper presented at the seminar "Consequences of Maoist Movement: Role of HMG, United Nations and Stakeholders for the Protection and Assistance of Internally Displaced Persons" organized by CSWC Kathmandu, Nepal on 1st February 2004.

Upreti, B.R. (2004d), Land Conflict in Nepal: Peasants' Struggle to Change Unequal Agrarian Social Relations. *Journal of Community, Work and Family*, Vol. 7, No. 3, pp. 371-394.

Upreti, B.R. (2004e), Sustainable Livelihoods, Environmental Security, and Conflict Mitigation in Protected Areas of Nepal: Trend and Challenges. A Preliminary Draft report. Kathmandu: IUCN.

Upreti, B. R. (2004f), Neglected Reality: Resource Governance and Conflict in Nepal. In: *Readings on Governance and Development* (Vol. III) Mukti Rijal (Ed.). Kathmandu: Institute of Governance and Development. Pp. 95-111.

Upreti, B.R. (2004g), Understanding the Dynamics of Conflict in Nepal. A Background Paper prepared for the Human Development Report 2004 of UNDP Nepal.

Upreti, B.R. (2004h), Dynamics of Resource Governance, Resource Scarcity and Conflict in Nepal. *Journal of Forest and Livelihoods.* Vol. 4. No.1.

Upreti, B.R. (2003a), People's Participation in Peace Process in Nepal. *Participation*. 5(5), pp. 9-11.

Upreti, B.R. (2003b). Social exclusion, centralism and conflict: Challenges for conflict transformation in Nepal. A paper presented at the International Conference 'The Agenda of Transformation: Inclusion in Nepali Democracy' organised by Social Science Baha in Kathmandu from 24-26 April 2003.

Upreti, B.R. (2003c), Interactive Conflict Management: An Alternative Methodology to Address Social Conflict at Local level.

International Journal of Development Issues, No. 2, Vol. 2, pp.77-90.

Upreti, B.R. (2003d), Environmental Governance to Address Resource Scarcity and Conflict in Nepal. Paper presented on June 7th, 2003 at the Environmental Conflict Resolution: A Right Based Approach. Kathmandu: Environmental Law Committee of Nepal Bar Association.

Upreti, B.R. (2003c), Security Sector Reform: A Neglected Agenda. *The Kathmandu Post*, 9 May 2003.

Upreti, B.R. (2002a), *Management of Social and Natural Resource Conflict in Nepal: Realities and Alternatives*. New Delhi: Adroit Publishers.

Upreti, B.R. (2002b), Nepal: A Nation in Search of Peace and Development. A Country assessment Report. Berne: Swiss Agency for Development and Co-operation.

Upreti, B.R., (2002c), The Management of Natural Resource Conflict: Case Studies from Nepal. *European Bulletin of Himalayan Research*. Spring 2002 (22) pp. 37-60.

Upreti, B.R. (2002d), Conflict Analysis and Impact Assessment of Development Programmes and Projects. *Participation: A Participatory Development Journal* 4(4) Pp. 13-17.

Upreti, B.R. (2001), Conflict Management in Natural Resources: A Study of Land, Water and Forest Conflict in Nepal. Wagenignen: Wagenignen University, the Netherlands.

Upreti B.R. (2000a), Beyond Rhetorical Success: Advancing the Potential for the Nepalese Community Forestry Programme to Address Equity Concerns. In: Wollenberg E., D. Edmunds, L. Buck, J. Fox and S. Brodt (Eds.) Social Learning in Community Forest Management: Linking Concept and Practice. A Joint Publication of CIFOR and the East-West Centre.

Upreti B.R. (2000b), The Effects of Changing Land use Systems in Agricultural Biodiversity: Experiences and Lessons from Nepal. In: Xu Jianchu (Ed.) Links Between the Culture and Biodiversity. Proceedings of the Culture and Biodiversity Congress 20-30 July, Cunming, Yunnan, China, 21-30 July 2000. *Yunnan Science and Technology*. Pp. 327-337.

Upreti B.R. (1999), Managing local Conflicts over Water Resources: A Case Study from Nepal. *AGREN, ODI Network Paper* No. 95, July 1999.London: Overseas Development Institute.

Upreti, B.R. and Adhikari, J (2006), Reality Revisited: Marginalized Indigenous Communities' Access to Natural Resources in Nepal: National Laws, Policies and Practices. A Report prepared for the Action Aid Nepal and Food and Agriculture Organisation of United Nations. Kathmandu: AAN and FAO.

Upreti, B.R. and Dhungana, D.N. (2006), Peace Process and Negotiation in Nepal: Revisiting the Past and Envisioning the Future. In:

Simkhada, S.R. and Oliva F. (Eds.) The Maoist Insurgency in Nepal (Monograph), pp. 214-252.

Upreti, B.R. and Ghimire, A. (2008), The Policy Response to Internally Displaced Persons: Reconciliation, Rehabilitation, Resettlement and Reintegration, Repatriation. A paper presented at the national seminar organised by National Human Rights Commission on 'IDP National Policy, 2007: Implementation for Rehabilitation, Resettlement and Reintegration to Internally Displaced Persons in Nepal' at Kathmandu, 30 July 2008.

Upreti, B. R. and Upadhaya, P. K. (2008), Relationship between Armed conflict, Peace and Tourism in Nepal. Paper Presented at the International Conference on Research for Development organized by National Centre of Competence in Research North-South in Bern on 2-4 July 2008.

Upreti, B.R. and Karna, V.K. (2007), Reconciliation and Social and Political Reintegration in Nepal. A Background Paper prepared for National Human Development Report 2008 going to be published by UNDP in collaboration with the National Planning Commission. Kathmandu: UNDP and NPC.

Upreti, B.R., Timsina, N.P., Upreti, U, Shivakoti, I.C., Adhikari, K.P. and Upreti, S. (2005), Searching for New direction: Reorienting NARMSAP to Work on the Conflict Situation in Nepal (A report on conflict impact assessment of NARMSAP). Kathmandu: Royal Danish Embassy.

Upreti, B.R.and Nepali R.K. (eds.) (2006), Nepal at Barrel of Gun: Proliferation of Small Arms and Light Weapons and their Impacts. Kathmandu: South Asia Small Arms Network-Nepal.

Upreti, B.R. and Ghale, Y. (2002). Factors Leading to Agro-biodiversity Loss in Developing Countries: The Case of Nepal. *Biodiversity and Conservation*. 11 (9) Pp. 1607-1621.

Upreti, B.R., Sharma, S.R. and Basnet, J. (2008), Land Politics and Conflict in Nepal: Realities and potentials for social transformation. Kathmandu: Community Self Reliance Centre, NCCR North South and Human and Natural Resources Study Centre of Kathmandu University.

Upreti, T. and Bastola K. P. (1997), Transitional Justice and Human Rights. Kathmandu.

Uvin, P. (1998), Aiding Violence. West Hartford, CT, USA: Kumarian Press.

Wabbes C.S. (2000), The evolving role of an international conservation organisation in times of war: WWF in the Democratic Republic of Congo. In: Nature in War: Biodiversity Conservation During Conflicts. Blom *et al.,(*eds.). Leiden, The Netherlands: The Netherlands Commission for International Nature Protection.

Wade R. (1982), The Study of Administrative and Political Corruption: Canal Irrigation in South India. *Journal of Development Studies.* 18(3): 287-328.

Walt, S.M. (1991), The Renaissance of Security Studies. *International Studies Quarterly*, June.

Wehr, P., Burgess, H. and Burgess, G. (eds.) (1994). Justice without Violence, Boulder: Lynne Rienner. 1994.

Willy, L.A. (2003), Land Rights in Crisis: Restoring Tenure Security in Afghanistan. AREU/UN.

Winterbottom, R., and L. A. Neme (1997), Environmental Flashpoints in Sub-Saharan Africa. Washington, DC, USA: International Resources Group, Ltd.

Wolf, A.T. (2004), Regional Water Cooperation as Confidence Building: Water Management as a Strategy for Peace. Berlin: Adelphi Research.

Wolf, E. (1969), *Peasant Wars of the Twentieth Century*. New York: Harper and Row.

World Wildlife Fund (2000), Stakeholder Collaboration: Building Bridges for Conservation. Washington, DC, USA: World Wildlife Fund.

Yadav, R.P. (2005), Land Tenure and Taxation in Nepal: Winrock International Policy Outlook Series No. 7. Kathmandu: Winrock International.

Yonzon, P. (2004), Threats to Nepal's protected areas. Parks 14 (1): 35-39.

Zimmermann, W. and Hubner-Schmid, K. (2000), Land Tenure Issues in Post-Conflict Countries: The Case of Bosnia and Herzegovina. GTZ Project Report.